FOREST MENSURATION

FOREST MENSURATION

Fourth Edition

BERTRAM HUSCH
THOMAS W. BEERS
JOHN A. KERSHAW, JR.

JOHN WILEY & SONS, INC.

For general information on our other products and services or for technical support, please contact our Customer Care Department within the United States at (800) 762-2974, outside the United States at (317) 572-3993 or fax (317) 572-4002.

Wiley also publishes its books in a variety of electronic formats. Some content that appears in print may not be available in electronic books. For information about Wiley products, visit our website at www.wiley.com

Library of Congress Cataloging-in-Publication Data:

Husch, Bertram, 1923–
  Forest mensuration/Bertram Husch, Tom Beers, John Kershaw.—4th ed.
    p.cm.
  Includes bibliographical references (p.).
  ISBN 0-471-01850-3 (cloth)
  1. Forests and forestry—Mensuration. 2. Forest surveys. I. Beers, Thomas W. II. Kershaw, John, 1962– III. Title.
  SD555.H8 2003
  634.9'285–dc21

Printed in the United States of America   2002068995

10 9 8 7 6 5 4 3 2 1

This book is dedicated to
Charles I. Miller
1916–1997
(Professor of Forestry, Purdue University, 1946–1982)
Professor, Colleague, and Friend

CONTENTS

PREFACE

In the 20 years that have passed since the third edition of this book was published, our experience in teaching and applying the techniques of forest mensuration and in planning and executing forest inventories have led us to make changes that we believe will increase its value as a textbook for undergraduate students and as a reference for practicing foresters. The extensive bibliography should serve as a useful guide for specific references on advanced topics. The fourth edition has been prepared mainly by the first and new coauthors.

The structure of the book is similar to the third edition with several modifications. An important addition is a chapter on basic statistical concepts. The ideal situation would be that students have taken a course in statistical methods prior to studying forest mensuration. Since this may not be the case, we feel that as a minimum, our text should include a brief introduction to the fundamental concepts of statistical methods and present calculation procedures only for the most basic statistical parameters. Obviously, a complete treatment of statistical methods cannot be included in a text on forest mensuration. Consequently, we cite appropriate references for the statistical methods required to utilize the basic concepts mentioned. In addition, brief mention of the utility of global positioning systems and geographic information systems as tools in forest mensuration have been added. Here again, a detailed treatment of these advances is beyond the scope of this text. Knowledge of these systems is best obtained from courses and specialized texts and references on these topics.

Among the other changes in the text, treatment of the fundamental measurements has been consolidated in the chapter on the principles of measurement. A new chapter on stand parameters has been added. Recognizing that forest mensuration now must consider nontimber vegetation parameters, a new chapter on the topic has been included covering regeneration, lesser vegetation, woody detritus, and carbon. At the same time, the text does not attempt to cover the measurement of other resources associated with forestland. Rather than try to include a cursory and inadequate treatment of the measurement and analysis of such characteristics as wildlife, soils, water, and scenic and recreational values, we feel that these are better covered in texts on these specific topics. Wherever possible, we have utilized both the English and metric systems of measurement. Finally, the treatment of sampling with varying probability has been simplified but continues to cover the topic adequately.

The authors acknowledge the help of many friends and colleagues during preparation of this revision. Dr. David R. Larsen, University of Missouri, provided useful feedback on content and style during the early stages of development. Dr. Douglas A. Maguire, Oregon State University, and Dr. Peter Marshall, University of British Columbia, provided useful advice on topics to include in the chapter on nontimber forest vegetation. Dr. Edward Loewenstein and Dr. James Flewelling provided data used in Chapter 8. Special thanks are extended to BAP Forestry, Fredericton, New Brunswick, for the loan of equipment appearing in many of the figures. Additional photographs were provided by Dr. John Moser, Purdue University, The Ben Meadows Company, Forestry Suppliers, Inc., Grube KG Forstgerätestelle, Jenoptik Laser Optik Systeme GmbH, and Manifold Net Ltd. Marika Godwin and Elizabeth McGarrigle provided valuable assistance in organizing, locating, and checking references. Elizabeth McGarrigle and Tzeng-Yih Lam carefully read the page proofs and caught many errors that eluded the authors' eyes. Colleagues and students at the University of Brunswick, friends, and family are especially thanked for their encouragement, patience, and understanding during the final preparation of this book.

The authors note the passing of Charles I. Miller, a coauthor on previous editions of the book. Charlie dedicated almost 40 years to the teaching and development of forest mensuration at Purdue University. We recognize his contribution both to the book and to the field of forest mensuration.

B.H.
T.W.B.
J.A.K.

1

INTRODUCTION

In a few years, North America will mark the one hundredth anniversary of the publication of the first book on forest mensuration. In that book, Henry S. Graves (1906) wrote: "Forest mensuration deals with the determination of the volume of logs, trees, and stands, and with the study of increment and yield." The *Dictionary of Forestry* (Helms, 1998) states that "forest mensuration is the determination of dimensions, form, weight, growth, volume, and age of trees, individually or collectively, and of the dimensions of their products." This definition is essentially a paraphrase of the 1906 definition given by Henry S. Graves. Although some foresters feel that this definition is still adequate, in this book we consider that mensuration should embrace new measurement problems that have arisen or have been recognized as the horizons of forestry have expanded.

If we accept the challenge of a broader scope, we must ask: To what degree should mensuration be concerned with measurement problems of wildlife management, recreation, watershed management, and the other aspects of multiple-use forestry? Furthermore, one might argue that it is unrealistic to imagine that forest mensuration can take as its domain such a diverse group of subjects. The objection becomes irrelevant if we recognize forest mensuration as a subject that provides principles applicable to all measurement problems. Thus, we view the measurement and quantification of all aspects of forest vegetation within the domain of forest mensuration. In this book, in addition to a treatment of the traditional measurement problems of forestry, we also provide a foundation of principles for solving measurement problems in other aspects of forestry.

During the latter half of the twentieth century, the application of statistical theory and the use of computers, electronics, and lasers wrought a revolution in the solution of forest measurement problems. Consequently, mensurationists must have a degree of competence in their use as well as in basic mathematics and statistics. Knowledge of calculus is also desirable. In addition, familiarity with systems analysis and operational research, approaches to problem solving that depend on model building, and techniques that include simulation and mathematical programming is valuable, especially in advanced and more sophisticated treatments of forest mensurational problems.

1-1. ROLE OF FOREST MENSURATION IN FOREST MANAGEMENT

Forest mensuration is a keystone in the foundation of forestry. Forestry in the broadest sense is a management activity involving forestland, the plants and animals on the land, and humans as they use the land. Thus, the forester is faced with many decisions in the management of a forest. The following questions are examples of the problems that must be solved for a particular forest:

1. What silvicultural treatment will result in best regeneration and growth?
2. What species is most suitable for reforestation?
3. Is there sufficient timber to supply a forest industry and for an economical harvesting operation?
4. What is the value of the timber and land?
5. What is the recreational potential?
6. What is the wildlife potential?
7. What is the status of biodiversity on the area?
8. What is the status of the forest as a carbon sink?

A forester needs information to answer these and countless other questions and to make intelligent decisions. Whenever possible, this information should be in quantifiable terms. The axiom holds: you can't efficiently make, manage, or study anything you don't locate and measure. In this sense, forest mensuration is the application of measurement principles to obtain quantifiable information for forest management decision making.

To summarize, *forest mensuration* is concerned with the obtaining of information about forest resources. The ultimate objective of forest mensuration is to provide quantitative information regarding this resource that will allow making reasonable decisions on its destiny, use, and management.

1-2. FOREST MENSURATION AS A TOOL FOR MONITORING FORESTS

To many, a forest, if not affected by cutting, fire, or some other calamity, is a stable, unchanging entity. Actually, a forest is a dynamic system that is changing continuously, although this may not be evident over a short term such as a few years. However, changes are continuous: Some trees increase their dimensions, others die, and new trees germinate and enter the forest. Consequently, the information obtained about the status of a forest area at a given time is only valid for a length of time that depends on the vegetation itself and on environmental and external pressures affecting the forest. This means that the mensurational information regarding the forest must be updated periodically by monitoring procedures so that the appropriate management decisions may be taken.

Much of the forestland in North America and other parts of the world are under active forest management. In many jurisdictions, foresters are required to complete detailed long-term forest management plans. These plans require foresters to make detailed predictions about the growth and yield of forest resources and how harvesting and other forest management activities influence the flow of timber and other resources. Based on the outputs from these models, forest managers make decisions about where, when, how, and how much forestland should be treated. Good forest management decisions require good tools to analyze the impact of management activities on the quantities and flows of the various forest resources. These tools require good models, and ultimately, these models require good data. The acquisition of these data is the subject of this book.

Throughout the twentieth century, the demand on forest resources increased worldwide. In the foreseeable future, this increase is expected to continue. During the last 40 years, not only have the demands for timber increased, foresters also have been required to manage for other resources, including wildlife habitat, water quality, recreational opportunities, and biodiversity. An increase in the public awareness of the influence of human activities on the environment has resulted in the development of a number of forest certification procedures to ensure that forest management activities are sustainable both economically and environmentally. These procedures require forest managers to document and monitor the impact of forest management activities on all forest resources.

In North America, one of the longest-running forest monitoring programs is the Forest Inventory and Analysis (FIA) program of the U.S. Forest Service. This program began in 1930 as the U.S. Forest Survey and was originally designed as a periodic assessment (8- to 15-year intervals) of timber resources on a state-by-state basis. Recently, the FIA has expanded its scope to include an assessment of all forest vegetation and is moving toward an annual assessment rather than a periodic assessment (Gillespie, 1999). The Forest Health Monitoring program (USDA, 1998) has been merged with FIA for reasons of efficiency and data coordination. The new FIA program is scheduled for full implementation by 2003 and will provide objective and scientifically credible data on key forest ecosystem processes such as (1) forest area; (2) structure and composition; (3) changes in forested area; (4) changes in number of species; (5) tree growth rates, mortality, and harvest levels; and (6) changes in the forest ecosystem with respect to the soil and other vegetative community attributes. This information has many important uses (FIA Web site: *http://fia.fs.fed.us/about.htm*), including:

1. Helping policymakers at the federal and state level to formulate good forest policy, and to assess the sustainability of current and past policy
2. Enabling land managers to devise better management plans and to assess the effects of current and past management practices on the land
3. Serving as a starting point for scientific investigations in a variety of areas that involve changes in forest ecosystems over time
4. Formulating business plans that will be both economically and ecologically sustainable over time
5. Keeping the public informed about the health and sustainability of the nation's forests

FIA provides data for all forestlands (public and private) within the United States and its territories (Puerto Rico, the U.S. Virgin Islands, and U.S. Pacific territories). FIA also provides an online data retrieval system. Similar national inventory systems are in place in many other countries throughout the world.

As discussed above, monitoring must consider the changes in the composition, structure, size, and health of the forest (Max et al., 1996). To be effective, monitoring must be comprehensive. In these situations, foresters must increase the scope of their inventories to include information on all vegetation, not just the timber. To be cost-effective, forest managers will be required to design and implement new sampling strategies and measurement procedures to meet the demand for increased information. Efficient use of models in monitoring requires the development of forest growth and yield simulators and forest management tools that predict changes in all vegetation, not just the timber.

As North America moves into the second century of forest management, forest mensuration still has an active and exciting role in meeting the demands for information crucial to complex forest management decision making.

2

PRINCIPLES OF MEASUREMENT

Knowledge is to a large extent the result of acquisition and systematic accumulation of observations, or measurements, of concrete objects and natural phenomena. Thus, measurement is a basic requirement for the extension of knowledge. In its broadest sense, *measurement* consists of the assignment of numbers to measurable properties. Ellis (1966) gives this definition: "Measurement is the assignment of numerals to things according to any determinative, nondegenerate rule." (*Determinative* means that the same numerals, or range of numerals, are always assigned to the same things under the same conditions. *Nondegenerate* allows for the possibility of assigning different numerals to different things, or to the same things under different conditions.) This definition implies that we have a scale that allows us to use a rule, and that each scale inherently has a different rule that must be adhered to in representing a property by a numerical quantity.

The numbering system in general use throughout the world is the *decimal system*. This can probably be attributed to the fact that human beings have 10 fingers. But the decimal system is merely one of many possible numbering systems that could be utilized. In fact, there are examples of other numbering systems used by earlier civilizations (e.g., the vigesimal system based on 20, utilized by the Mayas, and the sexagesimal system of the Babylonians, based on 60). Our own system of measuring time and angles in minutes and seconds comes from the sexagesimal system. Systems to other bases, such as the duodecimal system, based on 12 (which seems to have lingered on in the use of dozen and gross) may also have been used. For a discussion of the history of number theory, the student is referred to Ore (1988). With the development of the electronic computer, interest has been revived in numbering systems using bases other than 10. Of primary interest is the binary system because electronic digital computers that use two basic states have been found most practical.

2-1. SCALES OF MEASUREMENT

Table 2-1 shows a classification of different kinds of scales and their applications according to Stevens (1946). The four scales of measurement are nominal, ordinal, interval, and ratio. A very important feature of this table is the column "permissible statistics." Measurements made on a *ratio scale* permit the use of all the types of statistics shown for all the scales. Those made on an *interval scale* can utilize the statistics in this scale as well as the preceding scales, but not those on a ratio scale. Similarly, measurements on an *ordinal scale* can utilize statistics permitted for this scale as well as those on a *nominal scale*. Finally, measurements made on a *nominal scale* can utilize only those statistics shown for this scale and not any of those on the following scales.

The *nominal scale* is used for numbering objects for identification (e.g., numbering of tree species or forest types in a stand map). Each member of the class is assigned the same numeral (e.g., the assignment of code numbers to species). The order in which classes are recorded has no importance. Indeed, the order could be changed without changing the meaning.

The *ordinal scale* is used to express degree, quality, or position in a series, such as first, second, and third. In a scale of this type, the successive intervals on the scale are not necessarily equal. Examples of ordinal scales used in forestry measurements are lumber grades, log grades, piece product grades, Christmas tree grades, nursery stock grades, and site quality classes. The order in which classes or grades are arranged on an ordinal scale has an intrinsic meaning. Classes are arranged in order of increasing or decreasing qualitative rank, so that the position on the scale affords an idea of comparative rank. The continuum of the variable consists of the range between the limits of the established ranks or grades. As many ranks or grades can be established as are deemed suitable. An attempt may be made to have each grade or rank occupy an equal interval of the continuum; however, this will rarely be achieved, since ranks are defined subjectively with no assurance of equal increments between ranks.

The *interval scale* includes a series of graduations marked off at uniform intervals from a reference point of fixed magnitude. There is no absolute reference point or true origin for this scale. The origin is chosen arbitrarily. The Celsius temperature scale is a good example of an interval scale. Noting equal volumes of expansion referenced to an arbitrary zero scales off equal intervals of temperature.

The *ratio scale* is similar to the interval scale in that there is equality of intervals between successive points on the scale; however, an absolute zero of origin is always present or implied. Ratio scales are the most commonly employed and the most versatile in that all types of statistical measures are

TABLE 2-1. Classification of Scales of Measurement

Scale	Basic Operation	Mathematical Group Structure	Permissible Statistics	Examples
Nominal	Determination of equality (numbering and counting)	Permutation group $X' = f(X)$, where $f(X)$ means any one-to-one substitution	Number of cases Mode Contingency correlation	Number of forest stand types Assignment of code numbers to species in studying stand composition
Ordinal	Determination of greater or less ranking	Isotonic group $X' = f(X)$, where $F(X)$ means any increasing monotonic function	Median Percentiles Order correlation	Lumber grading Tree and log grading Site class estimation
Interval	Determination of the equality of intervals or of differences (numerical magnitude of quantity, arbitrary origin)	Linear group $X' = aX + b$, where $a > 0$	Mean Standard deviation Correlation coefficient	Fahrenheit temperature Calendar time Available soil moisture Relative humidity
Ratio	Determination of the equality of ratios (numerical magnitude of quantity, absolute origin)	Similarity group $X' = cX$, where $c > 0$	Geometric mean Harmonic mean Coefficient of variation	Length of objects Frequency of items Time intervals Volumes Weights Absolute temperature Absolute humidity

The second through fifth columns are cumulative in that all characteristics listed opposite a particular scale are additive to those above it. In the column that records the group structure of each scale are listed the mathematical transformations that leave the scale invariant. Thus any numeral X can be replaced by another numeral X', where X' is the function of X, $f(X)$, listed in this column. The criterion for the appropriateness of a statistic is invariance under the transformations in the third column. Thus the case that stands at the median of a distribution maintains its position under all transformations that preserve order (isotonic group), but an item located at the mean remains at the mean only under transformations as restricted as those of the linear group. The ratio expressed by the coefficient of variation remains invariant only under the similarity transformation (multiplication by a constant). The rank-order correlation coefficient is usually considered appropriate to the ordinal scale, although the lack of a requirement for equal intervals between successive ranks really invalidates this statistic (Stevens, 1946).

7

applicable. It is convenient to consider ratio scales as either fundamental or derived.

- Such things as frequency, length, weight, and time intervals represent *fundamental scales*.
- Such things as stand volume per hectare, stand density, and stand growth per unit of time represent *derived scales*. (These are derived scales in that the values on the scale are functions of two or more fundamental values.)

2-2. UNITS OF MEASUREMENT

To describe a physical quantity, one must establish a unit of measure and determine the number of times the unit occurs in the quantity. Thus, if an object has a length of 3 meters, the meter has been taken as the unit of length, and the length dimension of the object contains three of these standard units.

The *fundamental units* in mechanics are measures of length, mass, and time. These are regarded as independent and fundamental variables of nature, although scientists have chosen them arbitrarily. Other fundamental units have been established for thermal, electrical, and illumination quantity measurement.

Derived units are expressed in terms of fundamental units or in units derived from fundamental units. Derived units include ones for the measurement of volume (cubic feet or meters), area (acres or hectares), velocity (miles per hour, meters per second), force (kilogram-force), and so on. Derived units are often expressed in formula form. For example, the area of a rectangle is defined by the function

$$\text{area} = W \cdot L$$

where W and L are fundamental units of length

Physical quantities such as length, mass, and time are called *scalar quantities* or *scalars*. Physical quantities that require an additional specification of direction for their complete definition are called *vector quantities* or *vectors*.

2-3. SYSTEMS OF MEASUREMENT

There are two methods of establishing measurement units. We may select an arbitrary unit for each type of quantity to be measured, or we may select fundamental units and formulate from them a consistent system of derived units. The first method was employed extensively in our early history. For example, units for measuring the length of cloth, the height of a horse, or land distances were all different. Reference units were objects such as the width of a barleycorn, the length of a man's foot, the length of a man's forearm (a cubit), and so on. However, these primitive units lacked uniformity. Vestiges of this system still exist, particularly in English-speaking countries (foot, yard, pound, etc.) although the units are now uniform.

The second method of establishing a system of units is illustrated by the metric system. In this system, an arbitrary set of units has been chosen that is uniformly applicable to the measurement of any object. Moreover, there is a logical, consistent, and uniform relationship between the basic units and their subdivisions.

2-3.1 Metric System

This system of weights and measures was formulated by the French Academy of Sciences in 1790. The system was adopted in France in 1799 and made compulsory in 1840. In 1875, the International Metric Convention, which was established by treaty, furnished physical standards of length and mass to the 17 member nations. The General Conference on Weights and Measures (referred to as CGPM, from the French "Conférence Générale des Poids et Mesures") is an international organization established under the convention. This organization meets periodically. The CGPM controls the International Bureau of Weights and Measures (BIPM), which is headquartered at Sèvres, near Paris, and maintains the physical standards of units. The U.S. Bureau of Standards represents the United States on the CGPM and maintains its standards of measure. For a concise description of the metric system and its use, see USMA (1999).

The metric system has been adopted by most of the technologically developed countries of the world. Although conversion in Great Britain and the United States has met with resistance, a gradual changeover is taking place. In 1866, the U.S. Congress enacted legislation authorizing, but not mandating the use of the metric system in the country. Then, in 1975, the Congress enacted the Metric Conversion Act and established the U.S. Metric Board to coordinate the voluntary conversion to the metric system. In 1982, the Office of Metric Programs replaced the Metric Board. To date, no states have enacted legislation mandating the adoption of metric units. Nevertheless, the globalization of the world economy has put pressure on the United States to convert to the metric system.

The 11th meeting of the CGPM in 1960 adopted the name *International System of Units* with the international abbreviation SI (from the French "Le Système International d'Unités"). This is now the accepted form of the metric system. The SI considers three classes of units: (1) base units, (2) derived units, and (3) supplementary units. There are seven *base units*, which by convention are considered dimensionally independent. These are the meter, kilogram, second, ampere, kelvin, mole, and candela. Combining base units according to algebraic statements that relate the corresponding quantities forms the derived units. The *supplementary units* are those that the CGPM established without stating whether they are base or derived units.

Here is a list of dimensions measured by these base units, along with definitions of the units. The conventional symbol for each unit is shown in parentheses.

1. *Length—meter* or *metre* (m). The meter is the length of the path traveled by light in a vacuum during a time interval of $1/299\,792\,458$ of a second.

2. *Mass**—*kilogram* (kg). The kilogram is equal to the mass of the international prototype standard, a cylinder of platinum–iridium alloy preserved in a vault in Sèvres, France.

3. *Time—second* (s). The second has been calculated by atomic standards to be $9\,192\,631\,770$ periods of vibration of the radiation emitted at a specific wavelength by an atom of cesium-133.

4. *Electric current—ampere* (A). The ampere is the current in a pair of equally long parallel straight wires (in a vacuum and 1 meter apart) that produces a force of 2×10^{-7} newton between the wires for each meter of their length.

5. *Temperature—kelvin* (K). The kelvin is $1/273.15$ of the thermodynamic temperature of the triple point of water. The temperature 0 K is called *absolute zero*. The kelvin degree is the same size as the Celsius degree (also called *centigrade*). The freezing point of water (0°C) and the boiling point of water (100°C) correspond to 273.15 K and 373.15 K, respectively. On the Fahrenheit scale, 1.8 degrees are equal to 1.0°C or 1.0 K. The freezing point of water on the Fahrenheit scale is 32°F.

6. *Amount of substance—mole* (mol). The mole is the base unit used to specify quantity of chemical elements or compounds. It is the amount of substance of a system that contains as many elementary entities as there are atoms in 0.012 kilogram of carbon-12. When the mole is used, the elementary entities must be qualified. They may be atoms, molecules, ions, electrons, or other particles or specified groups of such particles.

7. *Luminous intensity—candela* (cd). The candela is $1/600\,000$ of the intensity, in the perpendicular direction, of 1 square meter of a blackbody radiator at the temperature at which platinum solidifies (2045 K) under a pressure of 101 325 newton per square meter.

At present, there are two supplementary units, the radian and the steradian. They are defined as follows:

---

*The term *weight* is commonly used for mass, although this is, strictly speaking, incorrect. Weight of a body means the force caused by gravity, acting on a mass, which varies in time and space and which differs according to location on Earth. Since it is important to know whether mass or force is being measured, the SI has established two units: the kilogram for mass and the newton for force.

TABLE 2-2. Examples of Derived Units

Quantity	SI Unit	Symbol
Area	square meter	m^2
Volume	cubic meter (the liter, 0.001 cubic meter, is not an SI unit although commonly used to measure fluid volume)	m^3
Specific volume	cubic meter per kilogram	$m^3 \cdot kg^{-1}$
Force	newton ($1\,N = 1\,kg \cdot m \cdot s^{-2}$)	N
Pressure	pascal ($1\,Pa = 1\,N \cdot m^{-2}$)	Pa
Work	joule ($1\,J = 1\,N \cdot m$)	J
Power	watt ($1\,W = 1\,J \cdot s^{-1}$)	W
Speed	meter per second	$m \cdot s^{-1}$
Acceleration	(meter per second) per second	$m \cdot s^{-2}$
Voltage	volt ($1\,V = 1\,W \cdot A^{-1}$)	V
Electric resistance	ohm ($1 = 1\,V \cdot A$)	Ω
Concentration (amount of substance)	mole per cubic meter	$mol \cdot m^{-3}$

- The *radian* (rad) is the plane angle between two radii of a circle that cuts off on the circumference an arc equal to the radius. It is 57.295 78 degrees for every circle.

- The *steradian* (sr) is the solid angle at the center of a sphere subtending a section on the surface equal in area to the square of the radius of the sphere.

Derived units are expressed algebraically in terms of the base units by means of mathematical symbols of multiplication and division. Some examples of derived units are given in Table 2-2. There are a number of widely used units that are not part of SI. These units, which the International Committee on Weights and Measures (CIPM) recognized in 1969, are shown in Table 2-3.

TABLE 2-3. Supplementary Units

Unit	Symbol	Equivalence in SI Units
minute	min	$1\,min = 60\,s$
hour	h	$1\,h = 60\,min = 3600\,s$
day	d	$1\,d = 24\,h = 86\,400\,s$
degree (angular)	°	$1° = (\pi/180)\,rad$
minute (angular)	′	$1' = (1/60)° = (\pi/10\,800)\,rad$
second (angular)	″	$1'' = (1/60)' = (\pi/648\,000)\,rad$
liter	L	$1\,L = 1\,dm^3 = 10^{-3}\,m^3$
metric ton	t	$1\,t = 10^3\,kg$

TABLE 2-4. SI Prefixes and Abbreviations

Prefix	Symbol	Factor	
yotta	Y	10^{24}	1 000 000 000 000 000 000 000 000
zetta	Z	10^{21}	1 000 000 000 000 000 000 000
exa	E	10^{18}	1 000 000 000 000 000 000
peta	P	10^{15}	1 000 000 000 000 000
tera	T	10^{12}	1 000 000 000 000
giga	G	10^{9}	1 000 000 000
mega	M	10^{6}	1 000 000
kilo	k	10^{3}	1 000
hecto	h	10^{2}	100
deca	da	10^{1}	10
deci	d	10^{-1}	0.1
centi	c	10^{-2}	0.01
milli	m	10^{-3}	0.001
micro	μ	10^{-6}	0.000 001
nano	n	10^{-9}	0.000 000 001
pico	p	10^{-12}	0.000 000 000 001
femto	f	10^{-15}	0.000 000 000 000 001
atto	a	10^{-18}	0.000 000 000 000 000 001
zepto	z	10^{-21}	0.000 000 000 000 000 000 001
yocto	y	10^{-24}	0.000 000 000 000 000 000 000 001

To form decimal multiples of SI units, the prefixes or abbreviations listed in Table 2-4 are used.

2-3.2   English System

The English system of weights and measures is still widely used in the United States, but it is gradually being supplanted by the more logical and consistent metric system (SI). This may be a long procedure since resistance due to custom and tradition is strong, and the conversion is currently voluntary. Great Britain has taken a more vigorous stance and conversion to the metric system is proceeding more rapidly. The units of the English system still commonly used in the United States are practically the same as those employed in the American colonies prior to 1776. The names of these units are generally the same as those of the British Imperial System; however, their values differ slightly.

   In the English system, the fundamental length is the *yard*. The British yard is the distance between two lines on a bronze bar kept in the Standards Office, Westminster, London. Originally, the U.S. yard was based on a prototype bar, but in 1893 the United States yard was redefined as 3600/3937 meter = 0.914 401 8 meter. The British yard, on the other hand, was 3600/3937.0113 meter = 0.914 399 meter. The foot is defined as the third part of a yard, and the inch as a twelfth part of a foot. In 1959, it was agreed by Canada, United States, New Zealand, United Kingdom, South Africa, and Australia that they would adopt the value of 1 yard = 0.9144 meter. In the United Kingdom, these new values were used only in scientific work, the older, slightly different values being used for other measurements.

In the British system, the unit of mass, the avoirdupois *pound*, is the mass of a certain cylinder of platinum in the possession of the British government (1 pound = 0.453 592 43 kilogram). Thus, the U.S. pound and the British pound were not exactly equal. The 1959 agreement of English-speaking countries established a new value of the 1 pound = 0.453 592 37 kilogram. In the British system, the second is the base unit of time, as in the metric system.

Secondary units in the English system also have different values in the United States and the United Kingdom. For example, the U.S. gallon is defined as 231 cubic inches. The British gallon is defined as 277.42 cubic inches. There are other secondary units used in English-speaking countries that are as arbitrary as the gallon, but some are derived from the fundamental units. For example, the unit of work in English and American engineering practice has been the foot-pound.

Very commonly, conversions from one system of measurement to another are required. Appendix Table A-1 shows unit conversions for length, area, volume, and mass in the English and metric systems.

2-4. VARIABLES

A *variable* is a characteristic that may assume any given value or set of values. A *variate* is the value of a specific variable. Some variables are *continuous* in that they are capable of exhibiting every possible value within a given range. For example, height, weight, and volume are continuous variables. Other variables are *discontinuous* or *discrete* in that they only have values that jump from one number or position to the next. Counts of the number of employees in a company, of trees in a stand, or of deer per unit area are examples of discrete variables. Numbers of individuals observed in classes may be expressed as percentages of the total in all classes.

Data pertaining to continuous variables are obtained by measuring using interval and ratio scales. Data pertaining to discrete variables are obtained using nominal and ordinal scales. The process of measuring according to nominal and ordinal scales consists of counting frequencies of specified events. Discrete variables describe these events. The general term *event* can refer to a discrete physical standard, such as a tree that exists as a tangible object occupying space, or to an occurrence that cannot be thought of as spatial, such as a timber sale. In either case, the measurement consists of defining the variable and then counting the number of occurrences. There is no choice for the unit of measurement—frequency is the only permissible numerical value. A discrete variable can thus be characterized as a class or series of classes of defined characteristics with no possible intermediate classes or values.

A class established for convenience in continuous measurements should not be confused with a discrete variable. Classes for continuous variables (e.g., measurements of tree diameters) are often established to facilitate handling of data in computation. Frequencies may then be assigned to these classes. These frequencies represent the occurrence or recurrence of certain measurements of a continuous variable placed in a group or class of defined limits for convenience. It is frequently convenient to assign a code number or letter to each class of a discrete variable. It is important to be aware that the code numbers have no intrinsic meaning but are merely identifying labels. No meaningful mathematical operations can be performed on such code numbers.

At times, it may not be clear whether a discrete or continuous variable is being measured. For example, in counting the number of trees per acre or per hectare, the interval, one tree, is so small and the number of trees so large that analyses are made of the frequencies as though they described a continuous variable. This has become customary and may be considered permissible if the true nature of the variable is understood.

2-5. PRECISION, ACCURACY, AND BIAS

The terms *precision* and *accuracy* are frequently used interchangeably in nontechnical parlance and often with varying meaning in technical use. In this book they will have two distinct meanings. *Precision* as used here (and generally accepted in forest mensuration) means the degree of agreement in a series of measurements. The term is also used to describe the resolving power of a measuring instrument or the smallest unit in observing a measurement. In this sense, the more decimal places used in a measurement, the more precise the measurement. *Accuracy*, on the other hand, is the closeness of a measurement to the true value. Of course, the ultimate objective is to obtain accurate measurements. *Bias* refers to the systematic errors that may result from faulty measurement procedures, instrumental errors, flaws in the sampling procedure, errors in the computations, mistakes in recording, and so on.

In sampling, *accuracy* refers to the size of the deviation of a sample estimate from the true population value. Precision, expressed as a standard deviation, refers to the deviation of sample values about their mean, which, if biased, does not correspond to the true population value. It is possible to have a very precise estimate in that the deviations from the sample mean are very small; yet, at the same time, the estimate may not be accurate if it differs from the true value due to bias (Fig. 2-1). For example, one might carefully measure a tree diameter repeatedly to the nearest millimeter, with a caliper that reads about 5 mm low. The results of this series of measurements are precise because there is little variation between readings, but they are biased and inaccurate because of faulty adjustment of the instrument. The relation between accuracy A, bias

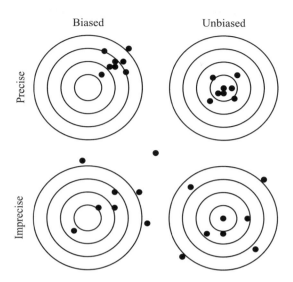

FIG. 2-1. Precision, bias, and accuracy of a target shooter. The target's bull's-eye is analogous to the unknown true population parameter, and the holes represent parameter estimates based on different samples. The goal is accuracy, which is the precise, unbiased target. (Adapted from Shiver and Borders, 1996.)

B, and precision P can be expressed as $A^2 = B^2 + P^2$. This indicates that if we reduce B^2 to zero, accuracy equals precision.

2-6. SIGNIFICANT DIGITS AND ROUNDING OFF

A *significant digit* is any digit denoting the true size of the unit at its specific location in the overall number. The term *significant* as used here should not be confused with its use in reference to statistical significance. The significant figures in a number are the digits reading from left to right beginning with the first nonzero digit and ending with the last digit written, which may be a zero. The numbers 25, 2.5, 0.25, and 0.025 all have two significant digits, the 2 and the 5. The numbers 25.0, 0.250, and 0.0250 all have three significant figures, the 2, 5, and 0. When one or more zeros occur immediately to the left of the decimal position and there is no digit to the right of the point, the number of significant digits may be in doubt. Thus the number 2500 may have two, three, or four significant digits, depending on whether one or both zeros denote an actual measurement or have been used to round off a number and indicate the position of the decimal point. Thus zero can be a significant figure if used to show the quantity in the position it occupies and not merely to denote a decimal place. A convention sometimes used to indicate the last significant

digit is to place a dot above it. Thus, 5,121,000 indicates four significant digits
and 5,121,000 indicates five significant digits. Another method is to divide a
number into two factors, one of them being a power of 10. A number such as
150,000,000 could be written as 1.5×10^8 or in some other form, such as
15×10^7. A convention frequently used is to show the significant figures in
the first factor and to use one nonzero digit to the left of the decimal point.
Thus the numbers 156,000,000 (with three significant figures), 31.53, and
0.005301 would be written as 1.56×10^8, 3.153×10, and 5.301×10^{-3}.

If a number has a significant zero to the right of the decimal place following a nonzero number, it should not be omitted. For example, 1.05010 indicates six significant digits, including the last zero to the right. To drop it
would reduce the precision of the number. When used to locate a decimal
place, zeros are not significant. In the number 0.00530, only the last three
digits, 5, 3, and 0 are significant; the first two to the right of the decimal place
are not.

When the units used for a measurement are changed, it may change the
number of decimal places but not the number of significant digits. Thus a
weight of 355.62 grams has five significant figures, as does the same weight
expressed as 0.35562 kilogram, although the number of decimal places has
increased. This emphasizes the importance of specifying the number of significant digits in a measurement rather than simply the number of decimal places.

2-6.1 Significant Digits in Measurements

The numbers used in mensuration can be considered as arising as pure numbers, from direct measurements, and from computations involving pure numbers and values from direct measurements. *Pure numbers* can be the result of a
count in which a number is exact, or they can be the result of some definition.
Examples of pure numbers are the number of sides on a square, the value of π,
or the number of meters in a kilometer.

Values of direct measurements are obtained by reading a measuring instrument (e.g., measuring a length with a ruler). The numerical values obtained in
this way are approximations in contrast to pure numbers. The number of
significant digits used indicates the precision of the approximation. For example, measurement of a length could be taken to the nearest one, tenth, or
hundredth of a foot, and recorded as 8, 7.6, or 7.60. Each of these measurements implies an increasing standard of precision. A length of 8 feet means a
length closer to 8 than to 7 or 9 feet. The value of 8 can be considered to lie
between 7.5 and 8.5. Similarly, a length of 7.6 means a measurement whose
value is closer to 7.6 feet than to 7.5 or 7.7. The value of 7.6 lies between
7.5500...01 and 7.6499...99 or, conventionally, 7.55 and 7.65. In the
measurement 7.60, the last digit is significant and the measurement implies a
greater precision. The value 7.60 means that the actual value lies anywhere
between 7.59500...01 and 7.60499...99, or, conventionally, 7.595 and 7.605.

Recording more significant digits than were observed is incorrect. Thus a length measurement of 8 feet taken to the nearest foot should not be recorded as 8.0 feet since this may mislead the reader into thinking that the measurement is more precise than it actually is. On the other hand, one should not omit significant zeros in decimals. For example, one should write 112.0 instead of 112 if the zero is significant.

Since the precision of the final results is limited by the precision of the original data, it is necessary to consider the number of significant digits to take and record in original measurements. Keep in mind that using greater precision than needed is a waste of time and money. A few suggestions follow:

1. Do not try to make measurements to a greater precision (more significant digits) than can reliably be indicated by the measuring process or instrument. For example, it would be illogical to try to measure the height of a standing tree to the nearest tenth of a foot with an Abney level.

2. The precision needed in original data may be influenced by how large a difference is important in comparing results. Thus if the results of a series of silvicultural treatments are to be compared in terms of volume growth response to the nearest tenth of a cubic meter, there would be no need to estimate volumes more exactly than the nearest tenth of a cubic meter.

3. The variation in a population sampled and the size of the sample influences the precision chosen for the original measurement. If the population varies greatly, or if there are few observations in the sample, high measurement precision is worthwhile.

2-6.2 Rounding Off

When dealing with the numerical value of a measurement in the usual decimal notation, it is often necessary to round off to fewer significant digits than originally shown. Rounding off can be done by deleting unwanted digits to the right of the decimal point (the fractional part of a number) and by substituting zeros for those to the left of the decimal place (the integer part). Three cases can arise:

1. If the deleted or replaced digits represent less than one-half unit in the last required place, no further change is required.

2. If the deleted or replaced digits represent more than one-half unit in the last required place, this significant figure is raised by one. (Note that if the significant figure in the last required place is 9, it changes to zero and the digit preceding it is increased by one.)

3. If the deleted or replaced digits represent exactly one-half unit in the last required place, a recommended convention is to raise the last digit by one if it is odd but let it stand if it is even. Thus 31.45 would be rounded to 31.4 but 31.55 would be 31.6.

Here are a few examples:

Number	Four Significant Figures	Three Significant Figures	Two Significant Figures
4.6495	4.650	4.65	4.6
93.65001	93.65	93.6	94
567,851	567,900	568,000	57,000
0.99687	0.9969	0.997	1.0

2-6.3 Significant Digits in Arithmetic Operations

In arithmetic operations involving measurements, where figures are only approximations, the question of how many significant digits there are in the result becomes important. In multiplication and division, the factor with the fewest significant figures limits the number of significant digits in the product or quotient. Thus, in multiplying a numerical measurement with five significant figures by another with three significant figures, only the first three figures of the product will be trustworthy, although there may be up to eight digits in the product. For example, if the measurements 895.67 and 35.9 are multiplied, the product is 32,154.553. Only the first three figures in the product—3, 2, and 1— are significant. The number 895.67 represents a measurement between 895.665 and 895.675. The number 35.9 represents a measurement between 35.85 and 35.95. The product of the four possible limiting combinations will differ in all except the first three digits:

$$895.665 \ (35.85) = 32,109.59025$$
$$895.665 \ (35.95) = 32,199.15675$$
$$896.675 \ (35.85) = 32,109.94875$$
$$895.675 \ (35.95) = 32,199.51625$$

Therefore, the first three figures are the only reliable ones in the product. Similarly, in dividing a measurement with eight significant digits by a measurement with three significant figures, the quotient will have only three significant figures.

If a measurement is to be multiplied or divided by an exact number or a factor that is known to any desired number of significant digits, a slightly different situation occurs. For example, a total weight could be estimated as the product of a mean weight having five significant digits times 55. The 55 is an exact number and could also be validly written as 55.000. The product would thus still have five significant digits. It may be helpful to remember that multiplication is merely repetitive addition, and the 55, in this case, means that a measurement is added exactly 55 times. Similarly, if the 55 objects had been weighed as a group, to five significant digits, dividing by 55 would give a mean weight to five significant figures. In these cases, the number in the measurement controls the significant digits. Another case occurs if a measurement is to be multiplied or divided by a factor such as π or e (base of Naperian logarithms) that are known to any number of significant figures. The number of significant digits in π or e should be made to agree with the number in the measurement before the operation of multiplication or division so that there is no loss in precision.

A good rule in multiplication or division is to keep one more digit in the product or quotient than occurs in the shorter of the two factors. This minimizes rounding-off errors in calculations involving a series of operations. At the end of the calculations, the final answer can be rounded off to the proper number of significant figures.

In addition and subtraction, the position of the decimal points will affect the number of significant digits in the result. It is necessary to align numbers according to their decimal places in order to carry out these operations. The statement that measurements can be added or subtracted when significant digits coincide at some place to the left or right of the decimal point can be used as a primary guide. Also, the number of significant digits in an answer can never be greater than those in the largest of the numbers, but may be fewer. As one example, measurements of 134.023 and 1.5 can be added or subtracted as shown below, since significant digits coincide at some place:

$$
\begin{array}{r}
134.023 \\
+ \quad 1.5 \\
\hline
135.523
\end{array}
$$

The sum has only four significant digits and should be expressed as 135.5. The last two significant figures of 134.023 cannot be used, since there is no information in the smaller measurement for coinciding positions. Measurements should be taken to uniform standards of significant figures or decimal places to avoid discarding a portion of a measurement, as we did in the case of the last two digits of 134.023.

Another example to consider is the addition of a series of measurements, where the final total may have more figures than any of the individual measurements. The number of significant digits in the total will not exceed the number in the largest measurement. Consider the 11 measurements shown here:

Measurement	Range	
845.6	845.55	845.65
805.8	805.75	805.85
999.6	999.55	999.65
963.4	963.35	963.45
897.6	897.55	897.65
903.1	903.05	903.15
986.9	986.85	986.95
876.3	876.25	876.35
863.2	863.15	863.25
931.2	931.15	931.25
998.1	998.05	998.15
10,070.8	10,070.25	10,071.35

The total, 10,070.8, contains six digits, but only the first four are significant. Each measurement can be thought of as an estimate within a range, as shown in the two right-hand columns. The sum of the lesser values is 10,070.25 and that of the larger is 10,071.35. The total value of the sum of the 11 measurements can fall anywhere within these limits. The significant figures are 1, 0, 0, and 7. Beyond this, the digits are unreliable.

2-7. DATA SUMMARY AND PRESENTATION

When recording, summarizing, and presenting numerical information the following general precepts should be observed. If text or tables are presented as computer files, the name of the program and the file name should be mentioned. Specifying the version of the program is important since a file prepared with a new version of a program may not be readable by an older version of the program.

The use of points and commas in the recording and presentation of numbers varies in different countries. In the United States and English Canada, a decimal is indicated by a point and groups of figures for hundreds, commas separate thousands, and so on. For example, a figure such as five hundred and fifty thousand, three hundred and twenty-five and fifteen hundredths would be written as: 550,325.15. In some other countries the use of points and commas is exactly reversed. Under this system the number would be recorded as 550.325,15. In international dealings and reports the system of numerical presentation should be specified.

Similarly, in the United States and Canada the term *billion* is used, but not in some other countries. For example, in the United States a number could be specified as five billion, three hundred and thirty million, two hundred and thirty-four thousand, one hundred, fifteen and written as 5,330,234,115. In some other countries this number would be described as five thousand three hundred and thirty million, two hundred and thirty-four thousand, one hundred and fifteen.

2-7.1 Tables

Tables are useful for the recording and presentation of data. The following points should be observed in their use.

1. All tables should have a brief but descriptive title. In general, the title should state what is being shown, where it came from, and when it was measured.
2. If several tables are presented, they should be given numbers. If information from the table is presented in the text, the table number should be mentioned.
3. The type or types of units in the table should be shown as headings in the columns or rows.
4. The headings of columns or rows should be brief. Notes at the bottom of tables can be used to clarify the meaning of concise headings.
5. If classes are used for summarization of numerical information, the midpoints should be shown. Class limits should be explained in the text or as a footnote to the table.

2-7.2 Graphic Presentation

Charts and *graphs* are pictorial or diagrammatic representations of relationships between two or more variables. They are used for three purposes: illustration or communication, analysis of relationships between variables, and as a graphical means of carrying out arithmetical operations or computations. For a detailed discussion of graphic techniques in forest mensuration, see Husch (1963), and for a more general overview of graphical techniques, see Cleveland (1994) or Tufte (1990).

A *graph* is a diagram on a plane surface illustrating the relationship between variables. Since paper presents a plane surface with two usable dimensions, length and width, it is convenient to depict a two-variable relationship by assigning a variable to each of the two dimensions. It is possible to depict a third variable with a more complex form, but to illustrate or solve functions of more than three variables is impossible for practical purposes.

Many types of graph paper are available, including numerous highly specialized designs. The three most important kinds used in forest mensuration are rectilinear or rectangular coordinate, logarithmic, and semilogarithmic graph papers. On *rectilinear paper*, both the abscissa and ordinate axes are divided using uniform scales and a series of equidistant points. *Semilogarithmic paper* has one of its axes divided using a uniform scale, but a logarithmic scale divides the other axis. *Logarithmic paper* has both axes divided with logarithmic scales.

The relationship between a dependent and independent variable of the type $Y = f(X)$ can be represented graphically on rectilinear or logarithmic papers by a line. Conventionally, the *abscissa* or X-*axis* is assigned to the independent variable and the *ordinate* or Y-*axis* to the dependent variable. The line representing the relationship, whether straight or curved, is given the general name *curve*. A relationship involving one dependent and two independent variables requires three dimensions and is represented by a *surface*.

A curve may be plotted from a given mathematical function where the relationship between two variables has been defined by a specific equation. Common mathematical functions used in forest mensuration are the straight line, parabola, and exponential.

Empirical curves are developed by plotting paired observations of two variables on graph paper and placing a line that best shows the general relationship. The relationship and curve can be determined by regression analysis or by fitting a freehand curve.

The following points should be observed when constructing figures:

1. All figures should have a brief but descriptive title. As with tables, the title should state what is being measured, where it came from, and when the data were collected.
2. If several figures are presented, each figure should be given a number. If the figure is referred to in the text, the figure number should be mentioned.
3. Each axis should include an appropriate range of values for the data being shown. The range should be inclusive of all data and not too broad to distort the relationship being shown. It has been customary to include the origin (0,0) with broken lines on the axis, but this has fallen out of common use in the past few years.
4. Each axis should be labeled clearly, stating what values are being shown and including their units.
5. If multiple sources of data are being shown on the figure, appropriate symbols should be used to distinguish between the data, and a legend included identifying each symbol.
6. If multiple curves are presented, different line types should be used and a legend included identifying each line.

For a complete discussion on the visual presentation of data, see Cleveland (1994) or Tufte (1990).

2-7.3 Class Limits

Measurements of a variable can be recorded as falling within limits of size classes. This may be done for assignment to a frequency table and subsequent statistical calculations, or for recording and presentation of a large number of measurements and results in tabular form. The use of size classes for indicating tree diameters and heights, quantities of timber, and so on, is a commonplace requirement in forest mensuration. The following, taken from Husch (1963), indicates the main points to keep in mind when using size classes.

In establishing classes, the total range of size is divided into suitable intervals. Classes for measurements of continuous variables must be of equal size if analysis methods applicable to continuous data are to be used. If unequal size classes are established, analysis methods for discrete variables are required. Considering continuous-type data, no universal rules are possible to indicate the number and size of classes to employ. It is important to bear in mind that the series of measurements will probably be analyzed by statistical procedures, and the requirements for these procedures and the interpretation of their results will influence the chosen class interval. There are a number of guides to keep in mind when using classes:

1. The chosen class size should result in a sufficient number of classes to exhibit the frequency pattern associated with the type of data. For example, if tree diameters were measured to the nearest 0.1 inch, and diameter classes of 0.1 inch were then chosen, there would be an excessive number of classes with small frequencies in each. The frequency pattern would not be clear, and the advantages of establishing classes would not be realized. If, on the other hand, 5-inch classes were used, there would be only a few classes with large frequencies in each, again not very revealing. The use of 1-inch classes would be more appropriate.

2. The value of any item in a class must be assumed to be at the midpoint of the class; therefore, classes must not be so large as to cause appreciable differences between actual measurements and assumed midpoint values. The limits of an interval, of course, are equidistant from the midpoint.

3. The precision of the defined class limits will depend on the precision to which the measurements are taken. The actual limits are the limits of implied accuracy when recording a measurement. For example, tree height measurements may have been taken to the nearest foot and then classified by using a 10-ft class interval, as shown below. The actual class limits are presented together with their approximations and midpoints. (The approximate class limits and midpoints, as shown, are used to simplify presentation and allow computational work.)

Actual Height Class Limits (ft)	Approximate Height Class Limits (ft)	Approximate Midpoint (ft)
55.500...01–65.499...9	55–65	60
65.500...01–75.499...9	65–75	70
75.500...01–85.499...9	75–85	80

4. Measurements that fall exactly at a class boundary, such as 65, must be assigned to either the upper or lower class on a random basis, since it is just as likely that the true value is above as below the boundary value; however, it is generally acceptable to assign boundary values consistently to one of the classes (e.g., 65.0 could always be assigned to the 70 class and 75.0 to the 80 class).

5. It is acceptable to establish any desired class interval if these principles are maintained and if there is proper recognition of midpoints.

2-8. FUNDAMENTAL MEASUREMENTS

In this section we describe the most important fundamental and derived measurements used in forest mensuration: linear, time, weight, area, and volume. Other measurements, such as for thermal, electrical, and illumination quantities for velocity, force, and so on, may be required at times, and reference should be made to texts on these specific topics.

2-8.1   Linear Measurements

Linear, or length, *measurement* consists of determining the length of a line from one point to another. Since the configuration of objects varies, a length might be the straight-line distance between two points on an object or the curved or irregular line distance between two points on an object. An example of the latter is the periphery of the cross section of a tree stem.

Length measurements can be made directly or indirectly. *Direct length measurement* is accomplished by placing a prototype standard of a defined unit beside the object to be measured. The number of units between terminals is the length. The application of a foot or meter rule is an example of a direct measurement. *Indirect linear measurement* is accomplished by employing geometry or trigonometry, or by using knowledge of the speed of sound or light.

The varied tasks of length measurement in forest mensuration include determination of the diameter or height of a tree, the length of a log, the width of a tree crown's image on an aerial photograph, the length of the boundary of a tract of land, and so on. These length measurements are covered in Chapters 4 and 5.

2-8.2   Time Measurements

Time is utilized in forestry (1) to denote position in a continuum of time at which some event took place, (2) to measure duration of a given event, and (3) to determine speed or rate at which an event or physical change occurred. An important time measurement in forest mensuration is the determination of tree and stand age (Sections 4-1 and 8-1).

Accurate measurement of time by establishing time standards poses difficult technological problems. Any measure of time is ultimately based on counting cycles of some regularly recurring phenomenon and accurately measuring fractions of a cycle. The ultimate standard for time is provided by the natural frequencies of vibration in atoms and molecules. Therefore, the fundamental time unit that has been accepted internationally is the atomic second (Section 2-3.1).

Several types of studies in forestry involve the relation of time with forest measurements. These include time series, and motion and time studies. In studying a time series, the primary object is to measure and analyze the chronological variation in the value of a variable. For example, one may study variation in air temperature over a period of time or fluctuations in the quantity of pulpwood produced. Motion and time studies consist of studying a complete process and dividing it into its fundamental steps. The length of time necessary to carry out the individual steps is observed. Attempts are then made to eliminate superfluous steps or motions and to minimize the work and time of the essential steps by improving the human contribution, by changing machines, or by rearranging the sequence of the steps. For a detailed overview of these types of studies, see Nievel (1993), and for applications related to forest mensuration, see Köpf (1976), Miyata et al. (1981), and Husch et al. (1982).

2-8.3   Weight Measurements

The force of attraction that Earth exerts on a body—that is, the pull of gravity on it—is called the *weight* of a body. Weight is often used as a measure of mass; however, the two are not the same. *Mass* is the measure of the amount of matter present in a body and thus has the same value at different locations (including zero gravity). *Weight* varies depending on location of the body in Earth's gravitational field (or the gravitational field of some other astronomical body). Since the gravitational effect varies from place to place on Earth, the weight of a given mass also varies. The distinction between weight and mass is confused by the use of the same units of measure: the gram, the kilogram, and the pound.

A decision to use weight as a measure of quantity depends on these factors:

1. *Physical characteristics of the substance.* The volume of material that occurs as irregular pieces, such as pulpwood, wood chips, coal, soil, seed fertilizer, and other solids, can be measured by filling a space or container of known volume; however, the ratio of air space to solid material will vary with the shape, arrangement, and compaction of pieces. This can seriously affect the accuracy and reliability of volume measurement.

2. *Logicalness of weight as an expression of quantity.* Weight may be the most useful and logical expression of quantity. For example, the weight measurement of pulpwood is advantageous because it can be done rapidly and accurately, and because the product derived, pulp, is expressed in weight. Indeed, when weight is the ultimate expression of quantity, it is logical to apply it consistently from the beginning. (Since transportation charges for forest products are based primarily on weight, weight becomes an even more logical expression of quantity.) Furthermore, a material may be composed of several components. For example, a tree consists of roots, stem, and crown; each part is composed of additional units. The ratio of any component to the whole, such as bark to wood in the merchantable stem, can best be expressed in terms of weight. When the entire tree is of interest (roots, branches, etc.), weight is the most logical measure of quantity.

3. *Feasibility of weighing.* The substance in question must be physically separable from material not relevant to the measurement, or weighing is not feasible. In addition, a weighing device must be available. For example, it might be desirable to determine the weight of the merchantable stem of a standing tree. But unless one felled the tree, separated the merchantable stem, and had a weighing machine available, it would be impossible to determine weight directly.

4. *Relative cost of weighing.* Weight might be a better expression of quantity than volume, but costs of weighing might be greater than costs of volume estimates, and vice versa. The final decision is influenced by the value of the material to be measured. When the value of material is high, the costlier procedure may be better if it is more accurate.

2-8.4 Area Measurements

Area is the measure of the size of a surface region, usually expressed in units that are the square of linear units: for example, square feet or square meters. In elementary geometry, formulas for the areas of simple plane figures and the surface area of simple solids are derived from the linear dimensions of these figures. Examples are given in Appendix Tables A-2 and A-3. The area of irregular figures, plane or solid, can be computed by the use of coordinates and integral calculus (Section 4-4). Also, the areas of simple plane figures can be obtained, or closely approximated, by the use of dot grids, line transects, or planimeters.

The most common area determinations in forest mensuration are the basal and surface area of trees (Section 5-2) and land areas (Chapter 4). Common conversion factors for different units of area are given in Appendix Table A-1B.

2-8.5   Volume Measurements

Volume is the measure of the solid content or capacity, usually expressed in units that are cubes of linear units, such as cubic meters and cubic feet, or in units of dry and liquid measure, such as bushels, gallons, and liters. Conversion factors for volume units in the English and metric systems are given in Appendix Table A-1C.

3

BASIC STATISTICAL CONCEPTS

The range of statistical applications in forest mensuration is immense. It is impossible to treat all aspects of statistics in a single chapter. The aim of this chapter is simply to provide an overview of statistical concepts utilized in forest mensuration and data analysis and to provide a brief summary of and calculation procedures for the fundamental statistical parameters. The main purpose of a chapter on statistics in this book is to explain basic concepts and not to present calculation methods. The practice of forest mensuration requires a much more complete understanding of statistics than can be presented in a textbook on mensuration. The application of statistical methods in forest mensuration requires an understanding of statistics that must be covered in specialized texts and in courses on statistics. For a more detailed review of statistics with applications in forestry, the reader is referred to Prodan (1968a), Freese (1974), and Zar (1998).

3-1. DESCRIPTIVE STATISTICS

As defined in Chapter 2, measurement is the assignment of numbers to measurable properties. Collections of numbers are referred to as *data*. Raw, unordered data are generally not very useful to the forester for making management decisions. The raw data can be organized, for example, in a frequency table (see Section 2-7.1) for better understanding of what they show. However, to be truly useful, most data need to be summarized into a set of concise, descriptive statistics. The two primary objectives of statistical methods are (Freese, 1974) (1) the estimation of population parameters, and (2) the testing of hypotheses about these parameters.

3-1.1   Population

A *population* in a statistical sense is a collection of elements that belong to a defined group. The elements may be individuals or a collection of individuals that may differ in their individual characteristics, but they all belong to the same category. The population elements should be defined at the same scale at which the information is desired. For example, if we desire to know the average diameter of trees in a given area, our population elements are the individual trees within this area. However, if we want to know the average volume per unit area, our population elements are typically collections of individual trees, usually on a plot of some predetermined size within the area of interest. A *census* is a complete enumeration of the information desired about every element in the population. If the information is collected without error, the population parameters can be computed exactly.

A population in which there are a limited number of physical elements or occurrences, such as the number of trees in a stand, is called *finite*. An *infinite* population has an unlimited number of elements. An infinite population is present when there are unlimited physical objects or occurrences or when samples are drawn from a population and are replaced before the next drawing.

3-1.2   Sample

In many situations, the population is infinite or so large that for all practical purposes, it is not feasible to enumerate or measure every element in the population. In this situation, a subset of individuals is observed and this subset is used to *estimate* the population parameters. This subset is commonly referred to as a *sample*. The individual items in a sample are termed *sampling units*. It is not information about the sample that is of primary interest, but rather, information about the population. The assumption is made that the information about the sample also holds for the population from which it was drawn. Thus inferences about the population are made from the sample information.

Consider the following example. It is desired to know the volume in cubic meters (m^3) of wood on a 1-ha (2.47-acre) forested area. The area is divided into sixteen 25 m × 25 m (82 ft × 82 ft) plots. The volume in cubic meters for each plot is shown in Fig. 3-1. In this case, the population is composed of the sixteen 25 m × 25 m plots. Both the selection of units from the population for inclusion in the sample and projection of sample estimates for the entire population are facilitated by defining the population in the same units as those selected in the sample (Shiver and Borders, 1996). The *sampling frame* is a list of all the sampling units in the population. In the example illustrated in Fig. 3-1, the sampling frame is the 16 row–column pairs that define the 25 m × 25 m plots: {1, 1}, {1, 2}, {1, 3}, . . . , {4, 2}, {4, 3}, and {4, 4}.

Column Row	1	2	3	4
1	8	16	27	3
2	13	5	29	4
3	7	24	27	10
4	13	12	2	8

FIG. 3-1. A 1-ha example forest divided into sixteen 25 m × 25 m plots. The numbers in each plot represent the number of cubic meters for that plot.

Every sample has a sampling frame. In the example of Fig. 3-1, the sampling frame is easy to define since the population is composed of only 16 sampling units. However, in many situations, the sampling frame may be unknown or difficult to list prior to completion of the sample. For example, if the average stem diameter for a forested area is desired, the sampling units are the individual trees. For even a small, forested area, the sampling frame might consist of several hundred individual trees. It would be impractical to attempt to list all of these individual trees. However, it is important to be aware that the sampling frame does exist despite the lack of an actual list (Shiver and Borders, 1996).

Sampling unit selection can be made with or without replacement. When sampling units are *selected with replacement*, each sampling unit may be selected more than once. For example, the 16 plots represented in Fig. 3-1 could be identified on small pieces of paper and placed in a hat. A sampling unit would be selected by choosing one of the slips of paper from the hat. The plot number would be noted and the paper returned to the hat for potential reselection. When sampling units are *selected without replacement*, each sampling unit may only be selected once. In this case, once a slip of paper is removed from the hat, it is not placed back in the hat for possible reselection.

Sample size refers to the number of sampling units selected from the population and *sample intensity* refers to the proportion of the population sampled (Zar, 1998). For any given sample size, there may exist many different possible combinations of sampling units that could be selected from the population. If sampling with replacement, the number of possible sampling unit combinations is (Shiryayev, 1984)

$$C = \frac{(N + n - 1)!}{n! \, (N - 1)!} \tag{3-1}$$

where n = sample size (i.e., number of sampling units included in sample)
          N = population size (i.e., total number of sampling units)

and ! denotes factorial expansion $[r! = r \cdot (r - 1) \cdot (r - 2) \cdots 3 \cdot 2 \cdot 1]$. In sampling without replacement, the number of sampling unit combinations is

$$C = \frac{N!}{n! \, (N - n)!} \tag{3-2}$$

where n and N are as above. For example, consider a sample of size 4 selected from the population shown in Fig. 3-1. When sampling with replacement, the number of potential combinations of sampling units from this population would be

$$
\begin{aligned}
C &= \frac{(16 + 4 - 1)!}{4! \, (16 - 1)!} \\
&= \frac{19!}{4! \cdot 15!} \\
&= \frac{19 \cdot 18 \cdot 17 \cdots 3 \cdot 2 \cdot 1}{(4 \cdot 3 \cdot 2 \cdot 1)(15 \cdot 14 \cdot 13 \cdots 3 \cdot 2 \cdot 1)} \\
&= \frac{19 \cdot 18 \cdot 17 \cdot 16}{4 \cdot 3 \cdot 2 \cdot 1} \\
&= \frac{93,024}{24} \\
&= 3876
\end{aligned}
$$

and when sampling without replacement, the number of possible combinations of sampling units would be

$$
\begin{aligned}
C &= \frac{16!}{4! \, (16 - 4)!} \\
&= \frac{16!}{4! \cdot 12!} \\
&= \frac{16 \cdot 15 \cdot 14 \cdots 3 \cdot 2 \cdot 1}{(4 \cdot 3 \cdot 2 \cdot 1)(12 \cdot 11 \cdot 10 \cdots 3 \cdot 2 \cdot 1)} \\
&= \frac{16 \cdot 15 \cdot 14 \cdot 13}{4 \cdot 3 \cdot 2 \cdot 1} \\
&= \frac{43,680}{24} \\
&= 1820
\end{aligned}
$$

So even relatively small populations can have many possible sampling unit combinations, and each of these combinations may result in different parameter estimates. The methods of drawing samples from a population are discussed in Chapter 13.* The variation in parameter estimates that arise because of sampling, referred to as *sampling error*, is discussed in detail below.

3-1.3 Statistics

Almost every population can be described or characterized by a set of parameters. Because these parameters describe certain qualities of the population, they are frequently referred to as *descriptive statistics*. In statistics, Greek letters are used to symbolize population parameters. A *population parameter* is a quantitative characteristic describing the population, such as an arithmetic mean or variance. A *population mean* is symbolized by μ, and the *population variance* by σ^2. A quantitative characteristic describing a sample is called *a statistic* and is written in the Roman alphabet. Thus the mean of a sample is $\bar{x}$, and its variance is s^2. In summary, statistics based on samples are used to estimate population parameters.

3-2. FREQUENCY DISTRIBUTIONS

A series of measurements can be consolidated into more manageable form by grouping measurements into classes (as described in Section 2-7.3) in a *frequency table*. The total list of measurements can then be assigned one by one to the appropriate classes, resulting in an ordered table showing the number of measurements falling into individual classes. The frequency data can then be shown graphically in a *histogram, frequency polygon*, or *frequency curve*. A histogram is a bar chart prepared by plotting frequency, either in number or percent, over size class (Fig. 3-2 is an example of a histogram). A series of rectangles of equal width is formed. Connecting the plotted points representing frequencies over size classes with straight lines forms a frequency polygon. If, instead of connecting each point, a smooth line is fitted to represent the general trend, a frequency curve is formed. A cumulative frequency curve is prepared by plotting the cumulative frequency numbers or percentages over size.

There are a number of typical frequency distributions that have been discovered and used in statistical work. Mathematicians have devised numerous theoretical distributions, some of which are of great practical value in applied work because actually observed measurements have been found to fit or approximate them. The properties of the theoretical distributions can then

---

*In Chapter 13 we present sampling designs used in forest inventory for estimating forest vegetation parameters, but the reader should understand that the designs described may be applied for sampling any kind of population.

be used in explaining relationships in the observed data. Three useful distributions most frequently used in forest mensuration are the *normal*, *binomial*, and the *Poisson*.*

Normal Distribution. The normal or Gaussian distribution is a theoretical distribution of great practical value. When summarized in a frequency table and then plotted in a graph of frequency over size, many types of measurements will approach a symmetrical pattern approaching the shape of a bell. This distribution has found wide application not only in the physical sciences but in the biological and social sciences as well. It is useful whenever there is a distribution of measured values that assume a symmetrical scattering about an arithmetic mean, with decreasing frequency of occurrence as the magnitudes of the individual values increase in their departure from the mean. The normal distribution has been found useful to data generated in two ways: (1) data resulting from repeated measurements of a fixed quantity (e.g., repeated measurements of the linear distance between two points), and (2) data resulting from the measurement of a specified variable on many individuals (e.g., heights of trees in an even-aged stand).

Binomial Distribution. This distribution occurs when only two alternatives are present for the variable. For example, beans in a jar may be either white or black. As sample beans are drawn from the jar with replacement, they are noted as either of the two colors and the numbers recorded. If sampling is carried out without replacement, a *hypergeometric distribution* occurs. For a population of size N, where A is the number of individuals having a given attribute, the proportion of items in the population having the attribute is $P = A/N$. The proportion not having the attribute is $1 - P = Q$.

Poisson Distribution. Like the binomial, the Poisson is a distribution of a discrete or discontinuous variable arising from enumeration. Measurement consists of noting the frequency of events or individuals of a certain class in a continuum of time or physical magnitude, such as length, area, or volume. The Poisson is the distribution that describes the pattern of frequencies for these classes.

   In this book only the properties of the normal distribution will be used. For use of the other distributions, the reader is referred to the references cited.

3-3. MEASURES OF CENTRAL TENDENCY

Frequency tables and graphs reveal an overall picture of the range and pattern of a series of measurements, but they lack the conciseness and explicitness that

---

*In Section 8-5 we describe another distribution frequently used in forest mensuration: the Weibull.

is conveyed by an average. An *average* is a numerical quantity that can be used to represent a group of individual values. The individual values tend to cluster about an average, which, consequently, is often referred to as a *measure of central tendency*. There are several measures of central tendency: arithmetic mean, harmonic mean, geometric mean, quadratic mean, median, and mode. The one to use should be appropriate for the data and for what it is supposed to show.

3.3.1 Arithmetic Mean

The most common measure of central tendency is the *arithmetic mean* or *arithmetic average*. The *population mean*, commonly designated μ, is the arithmetic average of all possible sampling units in the population:

$$\mu = \frac{\sum_{i=1}^{N} X_i}{N} \tag{3-3}$$

where μ = population mean
X_i = ith observation in population
N = total number of items in population

Calculation of μ requires that every individual within the population be measured without error. Most populations of interest in forest mensuration are very large and essentially can be considered infinite. It is a rare situation when μ is actually known.

The arithmetic mean of a sample of measurements drawn from a population is

$$\bar{x} = \frac{\sum_{i=1}^{n} X_i}{n} \tag{3-4}$$

where $\bar{x}$ = sample mean
X_i = ith observation in sample
n = sample size

The statistic $\bar{x}$ is an unbiased estimator of the population parameter μ. For any given sample of size n, $\bar{x}$ is the sample estimate of μ. Using the example forest shown in Fig. 3-1, the population mean is calculated as

$$\mu = \frac{\sum_{i=1}^{16} X_i}{16}$$

$$= \frac{8 + 16 + 2 + 13 + 5 + 29 + 4 + 3 + 7 + 24 + 27 + 104 + 13 + 12 + 2 + 8}{16}$$

$$= \frac{208}{16} = 13 \, \text{m}^3$$

A sample of size 4 is generated by randomly selecting row and column numbers: {1,2}, {3,4}, {2,1}, {3,1}. The corresponding volumes for these plots are: 16, 10, 7, and 13. From eq. (3-4), the sample mean associated with this sample is

$$\bar{x} = \frac{\sum_{i=1}^{4} X_i}{4}$$
$$= \frac{16 + 10 + 13 + 7}{4}$$
$$= \frac{46}{4} = 11.5\,\mathrm{m}^3$$

This sample of four plots yields an estimate of the population mean. Other samples of size 4 would yield other estimates of the population mean.

3-3.2 Quadratic Mean

The *quadratic mean* $\bar{x}_Q$ is the square root of the average squared value:

$$\bar{x}_Q = \sqrt{\frac{\sum_{i=1}^{n} X_i^2}{n}} \tag{3-5}$$

It finds its greatest use in computation of the standard deviation (Section 3-4.1). It is also useful in determining the diameter of a tree of average basal area (Section 8-2).

3-3.3 Harmonic and Geometric Means

The *harmonic mean* is the reciprocal of the arithmetic average of the reciprocals of a series of measurements. This is the appropriate average to use when dealing with rates. An estimate of this population parameter is given by the statistic $\bar{x}_H$:

$$\bar{x}_H = \frac{n}{(1/X_1) + (1/X_2) + \cdots + (1/X_n)} = \frac{n}{\sum_{i=1}^{n}(1/X_i)} \tag{3-6}$$

The *geometric mean* is used when averaging quantities drawn from a series of measurements that follow a geometric progression or the exponential law. The geometric mean is the nth root of the product of n values. The logarithm of the geometric mean is equal to the arithmetic mean of the logarithms of the individual values. An estimate of the population geometric mean is given by $\bar{x}_G$:

$$\overline{x}_G = \sqrt[n]{(X_1)(X_2)(X_3)\cdots(X_n)} = \sqrt[n]{\prod_{i=1}^{n} X_i}$$

$$\log\overline{x}_G = \frac{\log X_1 + \log X_2 + \log X_3 + \cdots + \log X_n}{n} = \frac{\sum_{i=1}^{n}(\log X_i)}{n} \quad (3\text{-}7)$$

In forest mensuration, the geometric mean is used to estimate average diameter when tree cross sections are elliptical and the major and minor axes (diameters) of the cross section are measured (Section 5-2).

3-3.4   Median and Mode

The *median* is the middle value when data are ordered from smallest to largest. It is the value that divides a frequency distribution into an equal number of items above and below. It differs from the arithmetic mean in being an average of position rather than of the magnitude of the values. The *mode* is the most frequent value observed in the data. It is the most commonly occurring value in a frequency distribution. For a detailed description of the median and mode and their associated statistical properties, refer to Zar (1998).

3-4.   MEASURES OF DISPERSION

An average gives a single value that characterizes a distribution of measurements. However, it reveals nothing regarding the spread or range of the values on which it is based. Such information is provided by *a measure of dispersion*. Because individuals within a population are not all identical in terms of size or value, the population is said to have *variation*. Measures of dispersion define the amount by which individuals in a set of measurements vary from the central tendency. The commonly used measures of dispersion are the range, mean deviation, and the variance or standard deviation. The range is the interval between the largest and smallest values in a series. It is a measure of minor significance since it only indicates the difference between extreme values at the ends of a distribution. The *mean deviation* is the average amount by which the individual values in a series of measurements will deviate from the arithmetic mean. To calculate this measure, the arithmetic mean is first obtained. Then the absolute difference (regardless of sign) between each item and the mean is found. These differences are summed and divided by the total number to obtain the mean deviation.

3-4.1   Variance and Standard Deviation

The most important measure of dispersion is the variance. *Variance* is the average squared deviation of individuals from the mean. The *population variance* is calculated from

$$\sigma^2 = \frac{\sum_{i=1}^{N}(X_i - \mu)^2}{N} \tag{3-8}$$

where σ^2 = population variance
μ = population mean
X_i = ith observation in population
N = total population size

As with μ, the calculation σ^2 requires that every individual within the population be measured. The variance of a sample drawn from the population is calculated using

$$s^2 = \frac{\sum_{i=1}^{n}(X_i - \bar{x})^2}{n - 1} \tag{3-9}$$

where s^2 = sample variance
$\bar{x}$ = sample mean (sample estimator of μ)
X_i = ith observation in sample
n = sample size

Like the sample mean, $\bar{x}$, s^2 is an estimator of σ^2. However, unlike the sample estimator for the mean [eq. (3-4)], the formula for the sample estimator of variance is not identical to the formula for the population. The denominator in the sample estimator is $n - 1$ rather than n. The $n - 1$ is referred to as *degrees of freedom* (d.f.) and reflects the fact that the sample mean, $\bar{x}$, is estimated from the data. Use of $n - 1$ makes the estimator an unbiased estimator of σ^2. An alternative formula for s^2, which is algebraically equivalent but computationally simpler, is

$$s^2 = \frac{\sum_{i=1}^{n} X_i^2 - \left(\sum_{i=1}^{n} X_i\right)^2 / n}{n - 1} \tag{3-10}$$

Variance can also be calculated as the difference between the squared value of the quadratic mean [eq. (3-5)] and the squared value of the arithmetic mean [eq. (3-4)]: $s^2 = \bar{x}_Q^2 - \bar{x}^2$ (Curtis and Marshall, 2000).

Variation is often expressed as the *standard deviation* rather than the variance. The standard deviation is the square root of the variance. Thus the *population standard deviation* is

$$\sigma = \sqrt{\sigma^2} = \sqrt{\frac{\sum_{i=1}^{N}(X_i - \mu)^2}{N}} \tag{3-11}$$

and the *sample standard deviation* is

$$s = \sqrt{s^2} = \sqrt{\frac{\sum_{i=1}^{n} X_i^2 - \left(\sum_{i=1}^{n} X_i\right)^2 / n}{n - 1}} \qquad (3\text{-}12)$$

Continuing with the example from Fig. 3-1, the population variance is calculated to be

$$\sigma^2 = \frac{\sum_{i=1}^{16} (X_i - 13)^2}{16}$$

$$= \frac{(8 - 13)^2 + (16 - 13)^2 + \cdots + (8 - 13)^2}{16}$$

$$= \frac{25 + 9 + 196 + 100 + 0 + 64 + 256 + 81 + 36 + 121 + 196 + 9 + 0 + 1 + 121 + 25}{16}$$

$$= \frac{1240}{16} = 77.5$$

and the population standard deviation is

$$\sigma^2 = \sqrt{\sigma^2} = \sqrt{7.5} = 8.8$$

For the sample of size 4, the sample variance is

$$s^2 = \frac{\sum_{i=1}^{4} X_i^2 - \left(\sum_{i=1}^{4} X_i\right)^2 / 4}{4 - 1}$$

$$= \frac{(16^2 + 10^2 + 7^2 + 13^2) - (16 + 10 + 7 + 13)^2 / 4}{3}$$

$$= \frac{574 - 46^2 / 4}{3} = \frac{574 - 529}{3} = 15$$

and the sample standard deviation becomes

$$s = \sqrt{s^2} = \sqrt{15} = 3.87$$

3-4.2 Coefficient of Variation

The standard deviation can be expressed on a relative or percentage basis as the *coefficient of variation*. The coefficient of variation is the standard deviation expressed as a percentage of the arithmetic mean. For the population,

$$CV = 100 \frac{\sigma}{\mu} \qquad (3\text{-}13)$$

For a sample,

$$CV = 100\frac{s}{\bar{x}}$$

The coefficient of variation for the example is $CV = 100(3.87/11.5) = 34\%$. The coefficient of variation is useful for expressing relative variability when comparing samples from populations where the means differ substantially. For a description of additional measures of dispersion and their associated statistical properties, see Zar (1998).

3-4.3   Covariance

When two variables are measured on sampling units, the way they vary in relation to each other is measured by their *covariance*. The two variables may be Y and X. Freese (1974) described the possible covariability as follows: "If the larger values of Y tend to be associated with the larger values of X, the covariance will be positive. If the larger values of Y are associated with the smaller values of X, the covariance will be negative. When there is no particular association of Y and X values, the covariance approaches zero." For simple random samples, the covariance, s_{XY}, of X and Y is

$$s_{XY} = \frac{\sum_{i=1}^{n}(X_i - \bar{x})(Y_i - \bar{y})}{n - 1} \tag{3-14}$$

3-5. SAMPLING ERROR

If a population is not entirely uniform, single sampling units or samples are unlikely to represent exactly the parameters of the entire population. Thus, estimates of population parameters based on samples are always subject to sampling errors resulting from the chances of drawing different individuals or samples. It is important to recognize the existence of these errors since they influence the interpretation of sample statistics.

By examining Fig. 3–1 it is easy to see that not only are there many different samples of size 4 possible from this population, but also that each sample can have a different estimate of the mean. Thus, for any given sample, the estimated sample mean is subject to *sampling error*, which is simply the difference between the true value of the population mean and the sample estimate.

As the sample increases in number, the average sampling error becomes smaller and the reliability of the population estimate becomes larger. A useful sampling method should provide some estimate of the average sampling error. This sampling error has nothing to do with the mechanical precision with which measurements are executed or recorded. The errors referred to here are due to variations in the population and to chance selection. We consider errors in more detail in Chapter 13.

3-5.1 Standard Error of the Mean

The sampling error for any one particular sample is not generally of interest and is almost always unknown since the population mean is unknown. What is of interest is the distribution of this error. Figure 3-2 shows the distribution of the means based on a sample of size 4 from the population shown in Fig. 3-1. From eq. (3-2) it was determined that there are 1820 possible combinations of samples of size 4 for this population. Using all of these sample estimates it is possible to calculate a variance and standard deviation for the estimated means. The standard deviation of the means is commonly called the *standard error of the mean* and represents the variability expected if the population was sampled repeatedly. Because the standard error represents the dispersion in estimates, it is a useful estimate of the sampling error.

The amount of sampling error present in any given sample is dependent on the underlying population variability and the sample size as shown in Fig. 3-3. By examining the example population shown in Fig. 3-1, it is easy to understand how sample size influences sampling error. For this example, the range of sample mean estimates for any sample of size n can quickly be determined by calculating the mean for the smallest n values and largest n values. For exam-

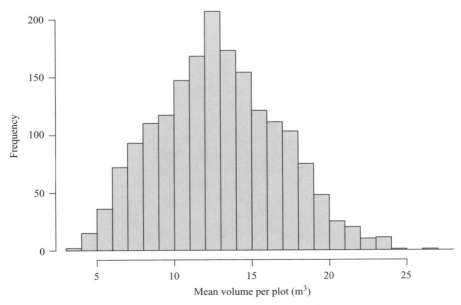

FIG. 3-2. Distribution of sample means based on a sample of size 4 from the sample forest shown in Fig. 3-1.

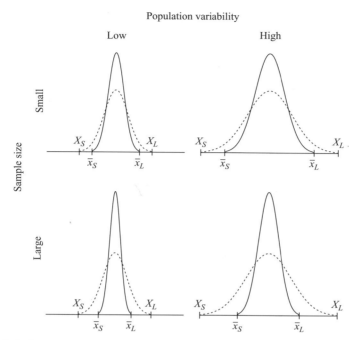

FIG. 3-3. Influence of population variability and sample size on distribution of individual sampling units and estimated means. X_S denotes the smallest individual sampling unit, X_L the largest individual sampling unit, $\bar{x}_S$ the smallest sample mean, $\bar{x}_L$ the largest estimated mean, the dotted line the population distribution, and the solid line the sample mean distribution.

ple, the four smallest values are {2, 3, 4, 5} for a minimum mean of 3.5, and the four largest values are {24, 27, 27, 29} for a maximum mean of 26.75; therefore, the range in sample means for a sample of size 4 is 3.5 to 26.75. The range for a sample of size eight is 6.0 to 20.0, and the range for a sample of size 12 is 8.0 to 16.0. As more individual sampling units are included in the sample, fewer units are excluded and less variability is possible.

Similarly, the influence of population variability on sampling error can be understood. If all 16 plots had the exact same value, there would be no population variability and even a sample of size 1 would produce no sampling error. If only one plot had a different value, the population variance would be very low. As the number of different values increases, the population variance increases; similarly, the number of different combinations increases and the sampling error increases. If the population range was twice as large as that observed in Fig. 3-1, the sampling error would also increase (Fig. 3-3).

The concept of sampling error, or standard error, makes sense only in repeated sampling since it is a standard deviation of different sample estimates. Strictly speaking, a standard error can be calculated only if there are two or more sample means. In most forestry situations, only one sample is taken. Fortunately, the standard error can be estimated from only one sample using the *central limit theorem* (CLT), one of the most important theorems in statistics (Shiryayev, 1984). The CLT states that for any population with a finite mean μ and variance σ^2, the sample estimates of the means will follow approximately a normal distribution (as sample size increases) with mean μ and standard deviation of the means, $\sigma/\sqrt{n}$. The *normal distribution* is the typical bell-shaped distribution that most people commonly associate with statistics (Fig. 3-4).

The bell shape can be observed for the distribution of means shown in Fig. 3-2. It is important to note that the underlying population distribution does not have to be normal for the CLT to hold. In fact, population distributions can have any shape. With a reasonably large sample size, σ^2 can be estimated using s^2 [eq. (3-9)], and the standard error of the mean can be estimated using

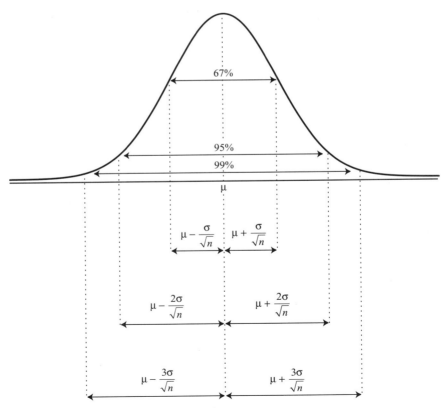

FIG. 3-4. Normal distribution for sample means. (After Shiver and Borders, 1996.)

$$s_{\bar{x}} = \frac{s}{\sqrt{n}}$$ (3-15)

where $s_{\bar{x}}$ = standard error of mean
         s = standard deviation
         n = sample size

The standard error for the example sample of size 4 would be estimated as

$$s_{\bar{x}} = \frac{3.87}{\sqrt{4}} = \frac{3.87}{2} = 1.94$$

When the entire population is measured, the sampling error is zero since the population mean can be calculated rather than estimated [eq. (3-3)]. When sampling finite populations without replacement, as the sample intensity increases, eq. (3-15) tends to overestimate the sampling error. For example, if eq. (3-15) were applied to the entire example population in Fig. 3-1, the standard error would be estimated as $s_{\bar{x}} = 8.8/\sqrt{16} = 2.2$. However, since the entire population has been observed, the sampling error should be zero. When finite populations are sampled without replacement, the *finite population correction factor* should be applied to the estimate of standard error of the mean:

$$s_{\bar{x}} = \frac{s}{\sqrt{n}} \sqrt{\frac{N - n}{N}}$$ (3-16)

where $s_{\bar{x}}$ = standard error of mean
         s = standard deviation
         n = sample size
         N = population size

Using the finite population correction factor, the estimate for standard error for the example sample of size 4 becomes

$$s_{\bar{x}} = \frac{3.87}{\sqrt{4}} \sqrt{\frac{16 - 4}{16}} = 1.94 \sqrt{\frac{12}{16}} = 1.94 \, (0.866) = 1.68$$

3-5.2 Confidence Interval

In brief, samples drawn in an unbiased manner from a population are assumed representative of the parent population. From these samples, statistics are calculated that are estimates of the population parameters. The degree of confidence placed in these estimates depends on the standard error of the parameter in question. Thus an estimate of a population parameter such as the arithmetic mean should properly be described not as a single figure, but rather, as a range within which we are confident that the true value or population parameter lies. The question immediately arises: How confident? The answer must be in terms of probability. An estimate of a population parameter must be in terms of a range with an associated probability. This range is called a *confidence interval*. The values that define the bounds of a confidence interval are called the *confidence limits*. Since the population parameter μ is a fixed value, it is the confidence limits and not μ that will vary for repeated samplings and will have a probability distribution. The confidence interval, then, is a statement used to describe an interval in which the true mean, μ, is expected to occur some percentage of the time. An interpretation of the meaning of the confidence interval is the conclusion that μ lies in the interval and will result on the average, in making so many correct statements out of 100, such as 95 out of 100 for a 0.95 probability level. It may also be interpreted as meaning that the probability is 0.95 that the interval obtained from sampling will contain the population parameter μ.

The limits to a confidence interval based on a sample are

$$\text{C.I.} = \bar{x} \pm t \cdot s_{\bar{x}} \qquad (3\text{-}17)$$

The value of t depends on the probability level chosen and the size of the sample n from which the mean was determined. The value of t can be obtained from Appendix Table A-4. Since the distribution of t depends on n, it is important to enter the table on the correct line using the appropriate *degrees of freedom*. The number of degrees of freedom to use in entering the table is the number of items in the sample less 1 (i.e., $n - 1$). For a chosen probability level such as 0.95, the t value is read under the column 0.05 $(1 - 0.95)$ in the table. The 0.05 indicates the probability that a larger value of t will occur 5 times out of 100. Conversely, this indicates that the probability of the given or smaller t value will be 0.95, the desired confidence level.

Considering the previous example of a sample of $n = 4$, the t value for a 95% confidence interval is found by locating the row corresponding to $4 - 1 = 3$ degrees of freedom and the column for 0.05 which indicates a value of $t = 3.182$. The 95% confidence interval for the example would be

$$\text{C.I.} = 11.5 \pm t \, (1.94)$$

$$= 11.5 \pm 3.182 \, (1.94)$$

$$= 11.5 \pm 6.16$$

The limits in which the population mean μ is expected to occur with a probability of 0.95 is then

$$5.3 \leq \mu \leq 17.7$$

This confidence interval gives the range of values that a sample mean will have some percentage of the time if the same population is repeatedly sampled with the same sample size. In the example above, it is expected that a sample of size 4 from the population shown in Fig. 3-1 would produce a sample mean between 5.3 and 17.7, 95% of the time. For calculation of confidence limits for forest inventory estimates, see Section 13-1.2.

3-6. SAMPLE SIZE DETERMINATION

The precision of the estimate of a population mean as measured by the confidence interval depends on the variation in the population, estimated by its variance, the number of sampling units measured, and the associated probability. This fact enables the necessary number of samples to be estimated if specifications are set up regarding the precision and probability required to state the estimate of the mean. The quantity to the right of the $\pm$ sign in the confidence interval [eq. (3-17)] can be thought of as the allowable error: $E = t \cdot s_{\bar{X}}$. Since $s_{\bar{x}} = s/\sqrt{n}$, allowable error can be expressed as: $E = ts/\sqrt{n}$. For the simplest case of random sampling from an infinite population, the sample size can be found by rearranging this formula, solving for n, yielding

$$n = \frac{t^2 s^2}{E^2} \tag{3-18}$$

where $n =$ minimum number of samples required to estimate μ to within $\pm E$ for a specified probability.

$t = t$ value associated with the specified probability from Appendix Table A-4. The use of t requires the probability and degrees of freedom, $n - 1$, where n refers to the sample size. Of course, to be correct, n should really be the number of samples that is being sought.

$s =$ standard deviation. Some prior knowledge or estimation of the variability of the population to be sampled must be available. This can be obtained by calculating the standard deviation of a small preliminary sample or from prior experience in similar populations. It is impossible to determine sample size without having some kind of prior knowledge of the population.

$E =$ allowable error. Some decision must be made regarding the allowable error. This is often stated in terms of a percentage of the mean.

For a finite population the formula is

$$n = \frac{t^2 s^2 N}{(NE^2 + t^2 s^2)} \tag{3-19}$$

where n, t, s, and E are as above and N is the total population size. For large finite populations the importance of this value decreases and for infinite populations has no meaning and the formula without N can be used.

Instead of using the standard deviation as an expression of population variability, the coefficient of variation may be utilized and the allowable standard error of the mean expressed as a percentage of the mean. In this case the formulas for sample size may be modified as follows: For an infinite population,

$$n = \frac{t^2 \cdot CV^2}{(E\%)^2} \tag{3-20}$$

For a finite population,

$$n = \frac{t^2 \cdot CV^2 \cdot N}{N(E\%)^2 + t^2 \cdot CV^2} \tag{3-21}$$

For example, to estimate the mean for the population shown in Fig. 3-1 to within 20% of the true mean with 95% confidence, the minimum sample size required would be computed as follows:

1. Make a reasonable guess for the value of n and determine t:

$$n_0 = 10$$

$$t = 2.262 \text{ (for 9 d.f. and 0.95 probability)}$$

2. Calculate the first estimate of sample size using $CV = 34$ and $E = 20$:

$$n_1 = \frac{(2.262)^2(34)^2}{20^2} = \frac{5915}{400} = 14.7 = 15$$

3. Compare n_0 with n_1; if equal, n_1 is the minimum sample size; if not, calculate a new estimate of n, using n_1 to determine t:

$$n_1 = 15$$

$$t = 2.145 \text{ (for 14 d.f. and 0.95 probability)}$$

and n_2 becomes

$$n_2 = \frac{(2.145)^2(34)^2}{20^2} + \frac{5319}{400} 13.3 = 14$$

4. The process is repeated until the estimates for n are the same:

$$n_2 = 14$$

$$t = 2.160 \text{ (for 13 d.f. and 0.95 probability)}$$

and n_3 becomes

$$n_3 = \frac{(2160)^2(34)^2}{20^2} = \frac{5393}{400} = 13.5 = 14$$

5. Since $n_3 = n_2$, the iteration terminates.

Thus 14 plots would be required to achieve the desired level of precision. In most situations, only a rough estimate of the minimum sample size is required. Here a single iteration can be utilized provided that the initial guess is close to the estimated sample size. Determination of sample size for different sampling designs is covered in Chapter 13.

3-7. ESTIMATION OF TOTALS

Foresters often use small plots as the basis for sampling forest vegetation. In the example above, $\frac{1}{16}$-ha plots were utilized. Traditionally, forest measurements are expressed on a per unit area basis: per acre in the English system and per hectare in the metric system. Scaling measurements from a per plot basis to a per unit area basis is straightforward because plot size is usually known. The scalar for converting per plot measurements to per unit area measurements is $m = 1/\text{plot size}$, where plot size is expressed as a fraction of the unit area. The scalar transformations for each parameter estimate described above are summarized in Table 3-1. The estimation of totals from forest inventory sample estimates is covered in Section 13-1.2.

TABLE 3-1. Effects of Scalar Transformations of the Form $Y = mX$ on Parameter Estimates

Parameter	Original Estimate	Transformed Estimate
Mean	$\bar{x} = \dfrac{\sum X}{n}$	$\bar{y} = m\bar{x}$
Variance	$s^2(X) = \dfrac{\sum X^2 - (\sum X)^2/n}{n-1}$	$s^2(Y) = m^2 s^2(X)$
Standard deviation	$s(X) = \sqrt{s^2(X)}$	$s(Y) = ms(X)$
Standard error	$s_{\bar{x}} = \dfrac{s(X)}{\sqrt{n}}$	$s_{\bar{y}} = ms_{\bar{x}}$
Confidence interval	$\begin{cases} \bar{x}_L = \bar{x} - ts_{\bar{x}} \\ \bar{x}_U = \bar{x} + ts_{\bar{x}} \\ \bar{x}_L \leq \mu_X \leq x_U \end{cases}$	$m\bar{x}_L \leq \mu_Y \leq m\bar{x}_U$

3-8. REGRESSION AND CORRELATION

Regression and correlation analyses are useful in evaluating the association between two or more variables and expressing the nature of the relationship. The two kinds of analyses have much in common, especially in computational procedures, but there is an important difference in their objectives.

Correlation analysis measures the degree of association between two or more variables. The objective of regression analysis is to quantify the relationship between a dependent variable and one or more independent variables. *Correlation* expresses the joint property or relationship between two or more variables to see how closely they are associated. *Regression*, on the other hand, implies a cause-and-effect relationship in which a change in the value of an independent variable will result in an expected average change in the dependent variable. The quantitative relationship is expressed by an equation and its graphic representation.

Regression Analysis. The first problem in regression analysis is to find the mathematical expression that will best fit the observations and its graphic form. The simplest form is a linear relationship between two variables, $Y = a + bX$. Some curvilinear relationships can be transformed into linear form by a logarithmic transformation. For example, $Y = aX^b$ can be transformed into $\log Y = \log a + b \log X$. The technique of linear regression analysis fits a straight line of the type $Y = a + bX$ in its best possible position by determining the values of the constants a and b. The best fit of the line is that position which will make the sum of the squared deviations of the observed Y values from the regression line a minimum. For this reason, the procedure of fitting a regression line is called the *method of least squares.* The method of least squares will give the best possible fit for the type of relationship chosen. However, the shape of the line and its equation may not originally have been the best choice. Some other line and its form equation may better express the relationship. The method of least squares fits any line chosen in its best possible position. The fitted line is called the *regression line.* Its mathematical expression is the *regression equation*, and its slope, b, is called the *regression coefficient.* In addition to simple linear regression between two variables, the relationship between a dependent variable and more than one independent variable is treated by multiple regression. For methods of regression analysis, see Freese (1974) and textbooks on statistical analysis.

Correlation Analysis. Correlation is a measure of the association between two or more random variables, both of which have a normal frequency distribution. When correlation exists, the sizes of the measurements of one variable are related to the sizes of the measurements of another variable. The brief discussion of correlation here is limited to the relationship between the measurements of two variables. The correlation between more than two variables requires multiple correlation analysis.

The measure of the degree of association between two variables, X and Y, in a correlation analysis is called the *correlation coefficient*. The population correlation coefficient ρ can have a numerical value varying between the limits of -1 to $+1$. When $\rho = 0$ there is no correlation. When $\rho = \pm 1$, there is a perfect relationship or association. An increase in the value of one variable would result in an unvarying increase for the other variable if $\rho = +1$, or an unvarying decrease if $\rho = -1$. Values between 0 and ± 1 indicate something between none and perfect correlation, with increasing intensity of association as the correlation coefficient approaches 1. The population correlation coefficient ρ is estimated by the statistic r, which can be obtained from sample observations. If repeated samplings were carried out, r would have a statistical distribution. Consequently, the likelihood of obtaining an observed value of r can be evaluated by a test of significance. The squared value of the correlation coefficient, r^2, is called the *coefficient of determination*. The coefficient of determination can be interpreted as indicating the percentage of the variation in one variable that is associated with the other variable.

3-9. HYPOTHESIS TESTING

In statistical work, a question continuously arises as to whether or not some event or sequence of events has happened as an unusual occurrence. To answer these and similar questions, *tests of significance* are used. There are numerous tests of significance, all having the common principle of evaluating the operation of chance versus some assumed cause. The fundamental idea of a significance test is to provide objective means for deciding whether or not apparent differences in measurements are likely to have occurred under some hypothesis.

3-9.1   Null Hypothesis

In tests of significance, a hypothesis is stated concerning the results that are expected. The hypothesis is then tested to see if there is evidence to support or refute it. The hypothesis used in all tests of significance is the *null hypothesis*. The null hypothesis is an assumption that there should be no difference between an observed and an expected result. The anticipated results may be based on past experience or prior knowledge, or they can be established arbitrarily for the test of significance. The *test of significance* evaluates the probability of occurrence of the observed difference, or a larger one, from the expected results, according to the null hypothesis. The null hypothesis is supported if the significance test shows the likelihood of any given or larger difference to be an unusual event. If the probability of this or a larger difference is low, or an unusual occurrence, the null hypothesis may be rejected, and the difference is termed *statistically significant*. A statistically significant result means that the probability of its occurrence is small. The corollary is that the probability of an unusual occurrence under the null hypothesis is large.

In other words, rejection of the null hypothesis implies that some other alternative hypothesis is true. The *alternative hypothesis* is usually that some suspected cause, which may have stimulated the investigation, is responsible for the difference observed.

3-9.2 Statistical Significance

All decisions regarding the null hypothesis are based on probability, not absolute certainty. Consequently, it is necessary to indicate the probability level on which the decision to reject the null hypothesis is based. This probability is called the *level of significance*. Statements of level of significance have conventionally been given in the terms *not significant, significant,* and *highly significant*. The numerical probabilities associated with these terms are shown in Table 3-2.

If P is greater than 0.05, the difference is not considered significant and the null hypothesis is retained. If the result of a test is significant, the null hypothesis is no longer tenable and some alternative hypothesis is accepted as true. If the null hypothesis is not rejected by a test of significance, it is not equivalent to a verdict of "proven." In this case there is no evidence for rejecting the null hypothesis, so it must be retained, at least for the present. There always exists the possibility that in the future it may be rejected on additional evidence.

Types of Significance Test. The kind of significance test to use depends on the nature of the problem and the kinds of measurements taken. For tests of the differences between two means involving continuous-type variables that follow a normal distribution, the t test is used. This test may also be used as an approximation for other distributions, such as the binomial and the Poisson. The chi-square test is used in evaluating the differences, observed under a null hypothesis, between sets of frequency measurements, which are taken for discrete-type variables in the binomial and Poisson distributions. Chi-square tests may also be utilized for frequency data from other distributions.

TABLE 3-2. Probabilities of Different Significance Levels

Significance Level	Probability of Occurrence	
	P	1 Out of n Chances
Not significant	Greater than 0.05	Greater than 1 out of 20
Significant	Less than 0.05 but not less than 0.01	Less than 1 out of 20 but not less than 1 out of 100
Highly significant	Less than 0.01	Less than 1 out of 100

3-9.3 t Test

The frequently used t test consists of evaluating the probability of occurrence of the difference between two means from data that follow a normal distribution. A null hypothesis is invariably implied in the test, even if not always stated explicitly. The null hypothesis is always that the two means come from the same population and that no difference is expected. If a difference is observed and the t test shows that it is unusual at a chosen significance level, the null hypothesis is rejected and an alternative hypothesis must be accepted.

The t test assumes that the difference between two means, and any successive differences for repeated trials, will have a normal distribution about a difference of zero. The probability of any observed difference can be estimated by expressing the observed difference and the standard deviation of this distribution of differences as a ratio. The observed difference in the two means is then in terms of t values. The probabilities associated with different-sized t values can then be ascertained from Student's t distribution, as shown in Appendix Table A-4.

The t test always involves two means. The two means may come from two sets of observed measurements, or the mean of a single set of measurements may be compared to a predetermined or hypothetical mean. In any case, the test is carried out and interpreted identically. The formula for t is

$$t = \frac{\bar{x}_1 - \bar{x}_2}{s_d} \qquad (3\text{-}22)$$

where $\bar{x}_1 - \bar{x}_2 =$ difference between two means

$s_d =$ sample estimate of standard deviation of population difference

If $\bar{x}_2$ is a predetermined or hypothetical mean, $s_d = s_{\bar{x}}$ and the degrees of freedom are $n - 1$. If $\bar{x}_2$ is another sample mean, then assuming that the two samples come from populations with equal variance $(\sigma_1^2 = \sigma_2^2)$, the s_d is estimated from

$$s_d = \sqrt{\left(\frac{1}{n_1} + \frac{1}{n_2}\right) \frac{(n_1 - 1)s_1^2 + (n_2 - 1)s_2^2}{n_1 + n_2 - 2}} \qquad (3\text{-}23)$$

where $s_1^2 =$ sample variance associated with $\bar{x}_1$

$s_2^2 =$ sample variance associated with $\bar{x}_2$

$n_1 =$ sample size associated with $\bar{x}_1$

$n_2 =$ sample size associated with $\bar{x}_2$

The degrees of freedom in this case are $n_1 + n_2 - 2$. For situations where the two population variances cannot be assumed equal or if the two samples are paired or otherwise correlated, refer to either Freese (1974) or Zar (1998). The probability associated with the calculated t can be found in Appendix Table A-4, observing the appropriate degrees of freedom.

If t is used to test the null hypothesis that two population means are the same versus an alternative hypothesis that they differ, regardless of how, it makes no difference whether $\bar{x}_1 - \bar{x}_2$ or $\bar{x}_2 - \bar{x}_1$ is used in the numerator of eq. (3-22). The null hypothesis would then be rejected for any value of t numerically greater than that shown for the probability level chosen. This is called a *two-tailed test*. The t values for a chosen probability level can be read directly from Appendix Table A-4. On the other hand, if the alternative hypothesis was that $\bar{x}_1$ was greater than $\bar{x}_2$ or $\bar{x}_2$ greater than $\bar{x}_1$, *a one-tailed test* is used. In this case, the t values are read from Appendix Table A-4 under the columns that are twice the desired level. Thus, for a 0.05 level of significance, t values are read in the column "0.10."

4

LAND AREA DETERMINATION

Generally speaking, foresters do not conduct many original property surveys. However, they often retrace old lines, locate boundaries, run cruise lines and transects, and so on. In fact, much forest mensurational work requires the location, delineation, preparation of maps, and determination of the magnitude of land areas and information on their characteristics and the organisms found thereon. Of prime importance are forestlands and their characteristics: topography, soils, water, forest and other vegetation, and wildlife. The methods and equipment to acquire and use this information go well beyond the field of forest mensuration and involve many other disciplines that cannot be covered here: They demand specialized training and references. Nevertheless, their existence and usefulness require brief mention.

For many years foresters have employed simple land surveying methods in fieldwork and have employed remote sensing from aerial photographs and from satellite imagery. Added to these techniques are the more recent developments of geographic information systems (GISs) and global positioning systems (GPSs).

In this book only a brief treatment of simple distance measurement and direction determination by magnetic compass is covered since, despite being approximate procedures, they are still of great use in fieldwork, especially in forest inventories. Although a text on forest mensuration cannot go into detail on aerial photographic interpretation, geographic information systems, or global positioning systems, mention must be made of their fundamentals and usefulness.

4-1. LAND DISTANCE AND AREA UNITS

Measurement of land distances and areas is a commonplace requirement in forest mensuration. Under the metric system the most important units are the meter and kilometer. Under the older English system, lengths are usually expressed in feet, yards, chains, or miles. However, older linear units are still often used or encountered in documents and deeds. The linear unit of a *chain* (often called *Gunter's chain*) is still used in much forest mensuration work and in land surveying. A chain is 66 ft long and is divided into 100 links, each 0.66 ft or 7.92 in. long.

Older length units that have fallen into disuse in land surveying (but may be found in older deeds) are poles, rods, and perches: 1 pole = 1 rod = 1 perch = 25 links = 16.5 ft. Four rods equal 1 chain. A length of 10 chains is a furlong.

Of primary importance in forest mensuration is the expression of land area. In the older English system, the most used expression of land area is the acre or fractions of it. An acre consists of 43,560 ft^2. This seemingly odd dimension is based on the older linear unit of a chain used in land surveying. One acre equals 10 square chains (10 ch × 1 ch or 660 ft × 66 ft = 43,560 ft^2). A mile is 5280 ft or 80 chains (80 × 66 = 5280). One square mile equals 640 acres (5280^2/43,560 = 640).

In the metric system the most commonly used expression of land area is the hectare. The hectare is an area of 10,000 m^2 or 0.01 km^2. Thus a land area of 100 m × 100 m or 0.1 km × 0.1 km is 1 hectare, approximately equivalent to 2.47 acres. Conversion factors for area between the English and metric systems are given in Appendix Table A-1.

4-2. MEASURING DISTANCES

In land surveying, the distance between two points is commonly meant to be the horizontal distance. Although slope distances are sometimes measured in the field, these distances are subsequently reduced to their horizontal equivalents, since horizontal distances are the ones used in the preparation of maps and in the computation of areas. The method used in obtaining the distance between two points is determined largely by the accuracy required. Traditional methods include pacing and chaining. Optical rangefinders and electronic distance measurement devices have been in use since the 1960s, but recent improvements in technology and reductions in costs have made these instruments more common. The accessibility of GPSs is revolutionizing the measurement of distances and areas in forest inventory work. GPS is described in Section 4-8; the other methods of distance measurement are described below.

4-2.1   Pacing

Where approximate results are sufficient, as in making tree-height measurements with certain hypsometers, in reconnaissance work, and in some types of cruising, distance can be obtained by *pacing*. Although many people think of a pace as a single step, the forester and others who work in natural resources often define a pace as a double step. Thus, as used here, a *pace* is two steps.

To graduate the pace, a recommended procedure is to establish a measured line of a convenient length such as 20 chains, 1320 ft or 400 m in terrain of the type encountered in fieldwork. Stakes should be set on the line at given distances: for example, in chains, at 0, 5, 10, 15, and 20 chains: in meters, at 0, 100, 200, 300, and 400 m. One should walk as naturally as possible, a minimum of four times over the line, record the number of paces between each pair of stakes, and compute the average number of paces between each pair of stakes and for each trip. From this, one can get a good picture of the consistency of the pacing and can determine the number of paces for the terrain. The pace should be graduated to meet the varying conditions encountered: wooded slopes of 0 to 10 percent, wooded slopes of 10 to 20 percent, open level woods, and so on. On slopes over 30 percent, in swamps, and in logged areas with slash on the ground, it is very difficult to pace accurately.

On steep slopes the method of *staff pacing* can be used. To staff pace one uses a 4.125-ft or 1.24-m staff. This gives 16 staffs to a chain, or 16 staffs to 20 m. The staff is used as follows for traveling uphill: While holding the staff horizontal, the ground position of the rear end of the staff is located by plumbing by eye and the forward end of the staff by contact with the ground. For traveling downhill: While holding the staff horizontal, the ground position of the rear end of the staff is in contact with the ground and the forward end is located by plumbing by eye.

With foot or staff pacing, an experienced pacer should consistently attain an accuracy of $\frac{1}{100}$ or better. Pacing skills need to be practiced regularly and checked periodically. Recent developments in affordable electronic distance measuring devices and GPS have resulted in pacing falling into disuse; however, these devices are subject to operational error, and pacing can be used as an important field check to identify and correct these errors.

4-2.2   Distances with Chains and Polytapes

The types of tapes commonly used by natural resource managers in North America to measure horizontal distances are the 100-ft *steel tape* and the steel *topographic trailer tape*. For measuring distances in meters, 30- and 50-m tapes are convenient to use. Tapes are usually constructed from steel, nylon-clad steel, fiberglass cloth, or plastic.

The basic procedure for measuring distance with either chains or tapes requires two people, traditionally referred to as the *head chainman* and the *rear chainman*. On level terrain, the chain (or tape) can be stretched directly on the ground. The starting point is marked with a pin and the head chainman pulls the zero end of the tape forward following the desired compass bearing. The rear chainman checks direction and warns the head chainman when the end of the tape is approaching by shouting "Chain". The head chainman pulls the tape taut until the rear chainman shouts "Stick". The head chainman then marks the zero position with another pin and shouts "Stuck." The rear chainman picks up the pin and follows the chain to the next pin and the head chainman pulls the chain forward to the next point. The procedure is repeated until the desired distance has been measured.

In rough terrain, the tape is held off the ground and plumb bobs are used to determine accurate pin placement. On very steep terrain, horizontal distances are obtained by either *breaking chain* or using a topographic trailer tape. Breaking chain is simply using shorter segments of the chain to hold a level line.

The topographic trailer tape is graduated in chains and links (Section 4-1). There are three tabs on a trailer tape: one at 0 links, one at 100 links (1 chain), and one at 200 links (2 chains). Beyond the 2-chain tab there is about $\frac{1}{2}$ chain of tape that trails the body of the tape. The trailer is used to convert slope distance to horizontal distance. The topographic trailer tape is used with a clinometer, such as an Abney level that has a *topographic (topo) arc*. The topographic arc is graduated in an angular unit that represents 1 unit vertically to 66 units horizontally. For example, a topo reading of +17 indicates a vertical rise of 17 ft per 66 ft, or 17 ft per chain.

Since a slope distance is greater than its horizontal equivalent, if one measures 2 chains along a slope, a correction must be added to obtain 2 chains of horizontal distance (Fig. 4-1). The trailer on the topographic trailer tape carries corrections for converting a slope distance of 2 chains to 2 chains of horizontal distance. These corrections are on the top of the tape. Corrections for converting a slope distance of 1 chain to 1 chain of horizontal distance are on the underside of the tape beyond the 1-chain tab. The corrections are applied as follows. For example, if a topo reading of 15 is obtained for a slope distance of

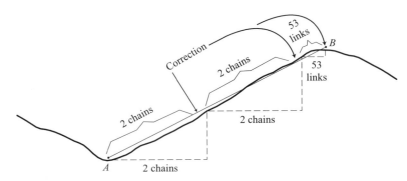

FIG. 4-1. Applying slope corrections.

2 chains, and the trailer is let out to the 15 graduation, the slope distance becomes the hypotenuse of a right triangle whose horizontal leg is 2 chains. If a topo reading of 20 is obtained for a slope distance of 1 chain, the proper correction is applied when the tape is let out to the 20-graduation mark on the underside of the tape beyond the 1-chain tab.

When it is necessary to measure slope distances of less than 1 chain or between 1 and 2 chains, tables are used to obtain the necessary corrections. For example, Table 4-1 shows the amount that must be added per chain of slope distance on different grades to obtain 1 chain of horizontal distance. Table values are obtained from

$$\text{correction per chain} = \sqrt{1.0 + \left(\frac{\text{topo reading}}{66}\right)^2} - 1 \qquad (4\text{-}1)$$

Thus, for a topo reading of 33, the correction per chain of slope distance is 0.118 chain (11.8 links). For other slope distances on the same grade, the correction equals the slope distance times 0.118 chain. For a slope distance of 0.73 chain, the correction will be 0.118 times 0.73, or 0.086 chain (8.6 links). When $0.73 + 0.086 = 0.816$ chain (81.6 links) is measured along the slope, a horizontal distance of 0.73 chain will be obtained. For a distance of 1.50 chains, the correction would be 0.118 times 1.50, or 0.177 chain (17.7 links).

Despite technological developments, the topographic trailer tape continues to be an important tool in land measurement. In rough, wooded, wild lands where great accuracy in distance measurement is not required, it permits fast, cheap measurement of boundary lines, cruise lines, and traverse legs as well as inexpensive method of obtaining elevations. Careful chaining on horizontal distances by experienced foresters should result in accuracies of $\frac{1}{1000}$ to $\frac{1}{2500}$.

4-2.3 Optical Rangefinders

Optical rangefinders work on the same principle as focusing a single-lens reflex (SLR) camera. A split image or double image is created in the viewfinder using mirrors or prisms. A focusing knob is used to make the two images coincident. Distance is either read from a vernier scale on the focusing knob or is calculated electronically. There are two types of optical rangefinders: fixed base and fixed angle. In a *fixed-base rangefinder*, the distance between the mirrors is fixed and the angle is manipulated to bring the images coincident. In a *fixed-angle rangefinder*, the angle is fixed and the distance is manipulated to bring the two images coincident.

Optical rangefinders are compact, lightweight, and inexpensive. Models with a range of about 10 to 75 m (30 to 200 ft) are available for less than US$50. Models with a range of 50 to 1000 m (150 to 3000 ft) cost around US$300. Optical rangefinders must be calibrated periodically and offer an accuracy of $\frac{1}{100}$.

TABLE 4-1. Correction Factors to Add to a 1-Chain Slope Distance on Different Grades to Obtain a 1-Chain Horizontal Distance[a]

Topo Reading	Correction (chains per chain)	Topo Reading	Correction (chains per chain)	Topo Reading	Correction (chains per chain)	Topo Reading	Correction (chains per chain)
1	0.000	31	0.105	61	0.362	91	0.703
2	0.000	32	0.111	62	0.372	92	0.716
3	0.001	33	0.118	63	0.382	93	0.728
4	0.002	34	0.125	64	0.393	94	0.740
5	0.003	35	0.132	65	0.404	95	0.753
6	0.004	36	0.139	66	0.414	96	0.765
7	0.006	37	0.146	67	0.425	97	0.778
8	0.007	38	0.154	68	0.436	98	0.790
9	0.009	39	0.162	69	0.447	99	0.803
10	0.011	40	0.169	70	0.458	100	0.815
11	0.014	41	0.177	71	0.469	101	0.828
12	0.016	42	0.185	72	0.480	102	0.841
13	0.019	43	0.194	73	0.491	103	0.854
14	0.022	44	0.202	74	0.502	104	0.866
15	0.026	45	0.210	75	0.514	105	0.879
16	0.029	46	0.219	76	0.525	106	0.892
17	0.033	47	0.228	77	0.537	107	0.905
18	0.037	48	0.236	78	0.548	108	0.918
19	0.041	49	0.245	79	0.560	109	0.931
20	0.045	50	0.255	80	0.571	110	0.944
21	0.049	51	0.264	81	0.583		
22	0.054	52	0.273	82	0.595		
23	0.059	53	0.283	83	0.607		
24	0.064	54	0.292	84	0.619		
25	0.069	55	0.302	85	0.631		
26	0.075	56	0.311	86	0.643		
27	0.080	57	0.321	87	0.655		
28	0.086	58	0.331	88	0.667		
29	0.092	59	0.341	89	0.679		
30	0.098	60	0.351	90	0.691		

[a]Correction factors for other than 1-chain distances are obtained by multiplying the correction factor by the slope distance in chains.

4-2.4   Electronic Distance Measurement Devices

The past decade has seen major improvements in laser technology. A number of laser-based rangefinders and distance measurement devices are currently available. These devices measure distance by measuring the flight time of short pulses of infrared light. Using the speed of light, the distance to an object is estimated by measuring the time it takes a laser pulse to travel to the target and back to the receiver.

Most laser rangefinders operate with or without reflectors. Without reflectors, the effective distance of most devices in forest conditions is about 20 m (Peet et al., 1997). Understory vegetation limits the effective range of most reflectorless lasers. With a reflector, most devices have an effective range of 50 to 100 m, depending on understory vegetation and weather conditions.

Accuracy of handheld laser-based rangefinders varies from about $\frac{1}{250}$ to $\frac{1}{2000}$ depending on laser strength, mode (reflectorless versus reflector), weather conditions, understory vegetation, and the surface roughness of the object being sighted. Accuracy of most devices is improved by using reflectors and/or tripods. Laser-based rangefinders vary in cost from about US\$300 to US\$3000.

Ultrasonic rangefinders are also used in forestry applications. These devices emit a narrow beam of sound waves that bounce off solid targets and return to the receiver. Using the speed of sound and elapsed time, the distance to the object is estimated. Effective use of most ultrasonic rangefinders in forestry conditions requires the use of a transponder. In this case, the receiver emits a sonic pulse, and when the transponder detects the pulse, the transponder emits a pulse back to the receiver. Most handheld sonic devices have a maximum range of about 20 to 30 m (60 to 100 ft). Sonic devices need to be calibrated frequently, especially if temperatures are fluctuating. Ultrasonic rangefinders vary in cost from about US\$150 to US\$1000.

4-2.5   Maps and Photos

Field distances can be determined using maps and aerial photographs of known scale. Distances along edges of cuts or other identifiable boundaries or between two points are measured on the map or photograph in inches or centimeters. These "map" distances are converted to ground distances using the map scale.

Map scales are generally given as representative fractions. A *representative fraction* (RF) specifies the number of ground units of distance represented by 1 unit of map distance. For example, an RF of 1:15000 means that 1 in. of map distance represents 15,000 in. on the ground. Generally, ground distances are specified in feet or meters rather than in inches or centimeters; therefore, representative fractions are often converted to dimensional equivalents by dividing the right-hand side of the RF by 12 to obtain ground feet per map inch, or by 100 to obtain ground meters per map centimeter. Map scales may also be shown graphically in the form of a *bar scale*. The bar scale depicts the map distances for standard ground distances such as 100 ft or 100 m using alternating strips of black and white rectangular bars. Bar scales are extremely useful when maps are reduced or enlarged from their original scales since the change in bar scale will be the same as the change in map scale.

The following example illustrates the conversion of map distance to ground distance. The distance between two points on a 1:15,000 scale photo was determined to be 6.8 in. (17.3 cm). With an RF of 1:15,000, 1 in. = 15,000/12 = 1250 ft; therefore, 6.8 in. on the photo = 6.8(1250) = 8500 ft on the ground. In metric units, with an RF of 1:15,000, 1 cm = 15,000/100 = 150 m; therefore, 17.3 cm = 17.3(150) = 2595 m on the ground.

4-3. MEASURING AREA IN THE FIELD

In situations where recent maps or photographs are not available, it may be necessary to determine the area of cuts or other management blocks using simple closed traverses made with a hand or staff compass and chain or other measuring tape. Starting at the most reliable corner available, the distances and bearings to each point, typically called a *station*, are measured and recorded. Backsights and frontsights are generally recorded and stakes driven into the ground at each station. The block boundary is traversed back to the origin. After the traverse is completed, the interior angles at each station are computed. If the bearings have been read and recorded properly, the sum of the interior angles should be equal to $180°(n-2)$, where n is the number of sides in the traverse. All basic surveying textbooks describe methods for adjusting the interior angles for errors. Once the interior angles are checked and adjusted, the traverse is plotted at a convenient scale. If the horizontal distances have been measured and recorded correctly, the traverse should *close* (i.e., form a complete loop). The tract area can be determined using one of the methods described below or calculated using the double meridian distance method. An introductory surveying textbook such as Wilson (1989) or McCormac (1999) should be consulted for detailed descriptions of field and analysis methods for closed traversing. GPS technology can also be used to determine areas in the field (Section 4-8.5).

4-4. MEASURING AREA USING MAPS AND PHOTOS

Areas of polygons on maps or aerial photographs can be digitized and determined using techniques provided by GISs (see Section 4-9). Alternatively, areas may be determined using older, manual methods such as calculation by coordinates, line transects, dot grids, or planimeters.

4-4.1 Area by Coordinates

Data from a closed traverse (Section 4-3) are often plotted as part of the process of checking the closure error. The points representing the stations can be converted to X–Y coordinates and the area calculated using the *continuous product method*. Given the direction and distance between two points A and B (Fig. 4-2) of each line forming the boundary of an area, the X and Y coordinates at the ends of each line can be calculated. The north–south vector is Y and the east–west vector is X. The coordinates of all vertices are obtained by addition or subtraction of successive vectors (Fig. 4-2), and the area of the figure, which must be closed, can be calculated by the continuous product method. If the X coordinates are designated as $X_1, X_2, X_3, \ldots, X_n$ and the Y coordinates as $Y_1, Y_2, Y_3, \ldots, Y_n$ the area of the polygon whose vertices are $(X_1, Y_1), (X_2, Y_2), (X_3, Y_3), \ldots, (X_n, Y_n)$ is

$$\text{area} = \tfrac{1}{2}[(X_1 Y_2 + X_2 Y_3 + \cdots + X_n Y_1) - (X_2 Y_1 + X_3 Y_2 + \cdots + X_1 Y_n)] \quad (4\text{-}2)$$

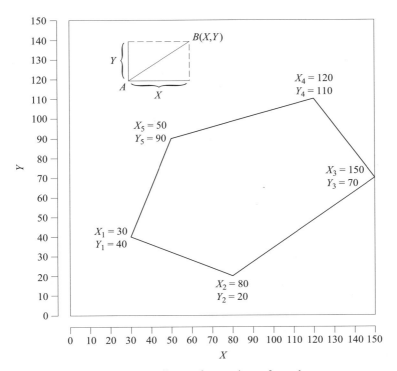

FIG. 4-2. Coordinates for vertices of a polygon.

Using the coordinate values given in Fig. 4-2, the area of the polygon is

$$\text{area} = \tfrac{1}{2}\{[30(20) + 89(70) + 150(110) + 120(90) + 50(40)]$$
$$- [80(40) + 150(20) + 120(70) + 50(110) + 30(90)]\}$$
$$= \tfrac{1}{2}(35,500 - 22,800)$$
$$= 6350 \text{ square units}$$

4-4.2   Area by Dot Grids and Line Transects

If a plane figure is drawn on rectangular coordinate paper consisting of uniform squares of known area (e.g., $0.01\,\text{in}^2$), the area of the figure can be estimated by counting the number of squares that fall within the boundaries of the figure. Where boundary lines include only portions of squares, one must estimate these portions and add their total to the total number of whole squares within the boundaries. If the figure represents an area drawn to a scale (e.g., a timber type), the area of the figure can be converted to the area represented by computing, for the known scale, the appropriate scale conversion (e.g., acres per square inch or hectares per square centimeter).

If a dot is placed in the center of each square on the rectangular coordinate paper and the lines are removed, a *dot grid* is formed. (Of course, the lines may be retained, if desired.) Each dot now represents an area equal to that of the square. The area of a plane figure can then be estimated by counting the number of dots that fall within the boundaries of the figure and can be converted to the area represented by computing the appropriate scale conversion. Dot grids, generally on transparent sheets, can be prepared or purchased with varying numbers of dots per unit area.

For example, in Fig. 4-3, a dot grid has been placed over a photo. There are 64 dots per square inch, so each dot represents $0.016\,\text{in}^2$. In the area outlined, 375 dots are counted. The area on the map is then $0.016 \times 375 = 5.86\,\text{in}^2$. The photo scale is 1:7920; therefore, $1\,\text{in.} = 7920/12 = 660\,\text{ft}$ and $1\,\text{in}^2 = 660^2 = 435,600\,\text{ft}^2 = 10\,\text{acres}$. The ground area is then found to be $5.86 \times 10 = 58.6\,\text{acres}$. For a more accurate estimate of area, the procedure should be repeated several times. Each time, the dot grid is randomly placed over the photo and the number of dots counted. The average number of dots is then determined and the areas calculated.

In addition to being used to obtain the area of individual figures, dot grids may be used to obtain area ratios. For example, a dot grid can be placed over a map or aerial photograph on which numerous forest types are outlined, and the number of dots within each type counted. Then the ratio of the number of dots in each type to the total number of dots on the map or photograph can be computed. The total area of the map or photograph can then be multiplied by the ratios to obtain the type areas.

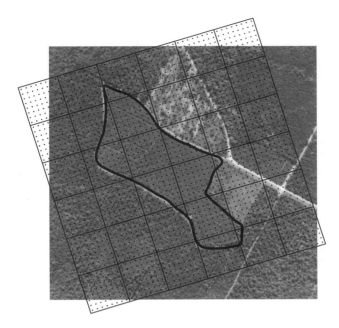

FIG. 4-3. Area by dot grid.

An analogous procedure for determining the area of plane figures is the *line-transect method*, which is used to determine area ratios. For example, equally spaced lines are drawn on a map or an aerial photograph on which numerous forest types are outlined, and the lengths of lines within each type are measured. Then the ratios of the lengths in each type to total line length on the map or aerial photograph can be computed. These ratios can be used in the same manner as ratios computed by the use of dot grids.

4-4.3 Area by Planimeters

The *planimeter*, invented in 1854 by Jacob Amsler, is a mechanical device for measuring the area of plane figures. With this instrument, areas can be obtained on maps, photographs, drawings, and diagrams. Over the years, Amsler's polar planimeter has been greatly improved, and other forms, such as the rolling disk planimeter, have been developed. In addition, computing planimeters with built-in calculators that can be programmed for any scale ratio are available.

The traditional polar planimeter consists of a *pole arm*, a *tracing arm*, and a *carriage*. The carriage furnishes bearings for a vertical measuring wheel that revolves on a horizontal axis. When set in position, the instrument rests on three points: a fixed point at the end of the pole arm, the measuring wheel, and the tracing point. As the tracing point is moved about, the instrument pivots about the fixed point and the wheel revolves. To determine an area, one simply moves the tracing point once around the boundary of a figure and reads the resulting movement of the measuring wheel, which is graduated for this purpose. In effect,

$$\text{area} = 2\pi r \cdot \text{TB} \cdot n \tag{4-3}$$

where r = radius of measuring wheel
       TB = length of planimeter tracing arm
        n = algebraic sum of rotations of measuring wheel

[Note that $2\pi r \cdot \text{TB}$ is a constant for a given planimeter. Thus the measuring wheel is graduated in terms of n times this constant.]

Modern digital planimeters work on a similar concept. The planimeter shown in Fig. 4-4 consists of a roller arm, tracing arm, integrating wheel, and encoder. The tracing point is moved once around the boundary to obtain area. The planimeter pivots on the roller arm as the tracing point is moved around the boundary.

4-5. DETERMINATION OF PHOTO SCALE

Photographs may be taken from the air or the ground. If an aerial photograph is exposed with the camera axis vertical, or nearly vertical, it is called a *vertical photograph*. If an aerial photograph is exposed with the camera axis intentionally tilted, it is called an *oblique photograph*. An oblique photograph in which the apparent horizon is shown is a *high oblique*; one in which the apparent horizon is not shown is a *low oblique*. If a photograph is taken from a fixed position on the ground, it is called a *terrestrial photograph*. Foresters deal primarily with vertical aerial photographs. However, one should understand that both oblique and terrestrial photographs have important mensurational applications.

Aerial photographs play an important role in forest mensuration. Most forest stand maps are prepared based on aerial photographs. Variables used to delineate stands vary from organization to organization, but in general include species composition, crown cover, density, and height. The resulting stand maps often form the basis of many forest inventory designs (Chapter 13). In addition to mapping, many aspects of forest mensuration, such as height measurement, can be made using stereoscopic photographs. The treatment of these subjects is beyond the scope of this book. For a detailed treatment of the interpretation and mensuration of aerial photographs, see Paine (1981).

Scale of an aerial photograph can be determined easily using a few simple formulas. The *scale*, or *representative fraction*, of a vertical photograph is the ratio of a distance on the photograph to the corresponding distance on the

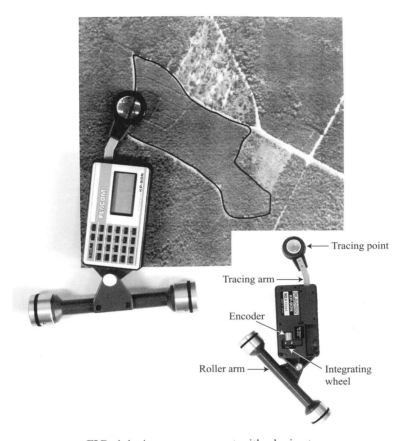

FIG. 4-4. Area measurement with planimeter.

ground when the object and image planes are parallel. From Fig. 4-5, the scale S is

$$S = \frac{\text{photo distance}}{\text{ground distance}} = \frac{ab}{AB} \qquad (4\text{-}4)$$

Scale can also be determined as the ratio of focal length f and altitude $(H - h)$:

$$S = \frac{f}{H - h} \qquad (4\text{-}5)$$

It should be noted that scale is expressed as a fraction with 1 as the numerator. Thus a photograph that has a scale of 1:12,000 has 1 unit on the photograph equal to 12,000 units on the ground.

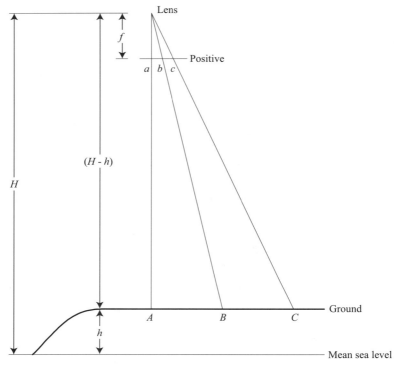

FIG. 4-5. How ground objects are imaged in the positive plane for vertical photographs. a, b, and c are photo images of ground points A, B, and C. Thus ab is photo distance, AB is ground distance, H is the height of the lens above mean sea level, h is the height of the terrain above mean sea level, and $H - h$ is the height of the lens above the ground (i.e., flying height above the ground).

To facilitate calculations, it is desirable to use the photo scale reciprocal (PSR = $1/S$) instead of scale. Then

$$\text{PSR} = \frac{AB}{ab} \qquad (4\text{-}6)$$

and

$$\text{PSR} = \frac{H - h}{f} \qquad (4\text{-}7)$$

Note that in all of the formulas above, distances must be in the same units.

From eqs. (4-6) and (4-7), the following relationship is obtained, from which other photo mensurational formulas can be derived:

$$\frac{AB}{ab} = \frac{H-h}{f} \tag{4-8}$$

Another useful relationship utilizes PSR and MSR (map scale reciprocal):

$$\frac{\text{PSR}}{\text{MSR}} = \frac{\text{map distance}}{\text{photo distance}} \tag{4-9}$$

A few examples will illustrate the use of the equations above and some scale conversions that are best computed from the PSR.

Example 1. The distance between two road intersections is 3350 ft on the ground and 4.22 in. on a photo. What is the PSR of the photo? Using eq. (4-6) gives us

$$\text{PSR} = \frac{AB}{ab} = \frac{12(3350)}{4.22} = 9526$$

Example 2. Find the PSR of a photograph taken with a 152.36-mm focal-length camera at an elevation of 1981 m above mean sea level over terrain that is 300 m above mean sea level. Using eq. (4-7), we have

$$\text{PSR} = \frac{H-h}{f} = \frac{1000(1981 - 300)}{152.36} = 11,033$$

Example 3. A photographic crew has a camera with an 8.25-in. focal-length lens. At what altitude (in feet) above the ground must they fly to produce prints with a scale of 1:20,000 (i.e., PSR = 20,000)? Using eq. (4-7) and solving for $H - h$ yields

$$H - h = \frac{f \cdot \text{PSR}}{12} = \frac{8.25(20,000)}{12} = 13,750 \text{ ft}$$

Example 4. Suppose that the smallest image that can be distinguished consistently on aerial photographs has a diameter of 0.002 in. If you fly some photographs with an 8.25-in. focal-length camera at an altitude of 11,000 ft above ground, what would be the ground distance of the smallest tree crown you could distinguish? Using eq. (4-8) and solving for AB, we obtain

$$AB = ab\frac{H-h}{f} = 0.002\frac{11,000(12)}{8.25} = 32 \text{ in.}$$

Example 5. Assume that you desire the PSR of a photograph depicting some of the same area covered by a quadrangle map. You measure the distance between two road intersections across the center of the photo and find it to be 6.35 in. The corresponding distance on the map is 4.36 in. If the MSR is 24,000, what is the PSR? Using eq. (4-9) and solving for PSR gives us

$$ \text{PSR} = \text{MSR}\,\frac{\text{map distance}}{\text{photo distance}} = 24{,}000\left(\frac{4.36}{6.25}\right) = 16{,}742 $$

Example 6. Compute the following scale conversions for a 9 in. × 9 in. vertical photograph with a scale of 1:20,000 (i.e., PSR = 20,000): feet per inch, chains per inch, miles per inch, and acres per square inch.

$$ \text{feet per inch} = \frac{\text{PSR}}{12} = \frac{20{,}000}{12} = 1666.67 $$

$$ \text{chains per inch} = \frac{\text{PSR}}{12(66)} = \frac{20{,}000}{792} = 25.25 $$

$$ \text{miles per inch} = \frac{\text{PSR}}{12(5280)} = \frac{20{,}000}{63{,}360} = 0.3157 $$

$$ \text{acres per square inch} = \left(\frac{\text{PSR}}{12}\right)^{2}\frac{1}{43{,}560} = \frac{400{,}000{,}000}{144}\left(\frac{1}{43{,}560}\right) = 63.77 $$

When one desires the reverse of any of these equations (e.g., inches per mile instead of miles per inch), one computes the reciprocal of the appropriate value. For example, if miles per inch = 0.3157, inches per mile = 1/0.3157 = 3.17.

4-6. DETERMINATION OF DIRECTION USING A COMPASS

The compass was one of the most important surveying instruments in the early centuries of the modern era for determining the direction of a line. It is not, however, an instrument of precision; results of great accuracy are not to be expected in compass surveys. On the other hand, it has the advantage of speed, economy, and simplicity. It is useful in retracing lines of old surveys established by compass, in running all types of boundary lines, in maintaining the direction of cruise lines, and so on. Many cases also arise in which the forester must depend on the compass for direction.

The direction of a line is generally indicated by the angle between the line and some line of reference (i.e., by an azimuth or a bearing). The line of reference is generally a true meridian or a magnetic meridian. The axis on which Earth rotates is an imaginary line cutting Earth's surface at two points: the north geographic pole and the south geographic pole. The *true meridian* at any location is the great circle drawn on Earth's surface passing through both poles and the location.

A compass consists of a magnetic needle on a pivot point, enclosed in a circular housing that is graduated in degrees. Most compasses have a sighting base attached so that it is possible to measure the angle between the line of sight and the position of the needle. An angle measured relative to the magnetic needle is referred to as a *magnetic azimuth* or *magnetic bearing*. Azimuths are horizontal angles measured clockwise from due north, whereas bearings are measured relative to a quadrant of the compass (i.e., NE, SE, SW, NW). Azimuths range from 0 to 360°, while bearings range from 0 to 90° referenced within a quadrant. For example, a bearing of N30°E corresponds to an azimuth of 30°, and a bearing of S30°E corresponds to an azimuth of 150°.

4-6.1 Magnetic Declination

The magnetic azimuth or bearing of a line can be determined by direct reading of a compass. Converting magnetic readings to true readings by applying the magnetic declination for the location can approximate the true azimuth or bearing in question. Many compasses used by foresters have the capability of being adjusted for declination. The *magnetic declination* is the angle between the true meridian and the magnetic meridian; it is considered east if the magnetic north is east of true north and west if magnetic north is west of true north (Fig. 4-6). Declination is often called *variation of the compass* or simply *varia-*

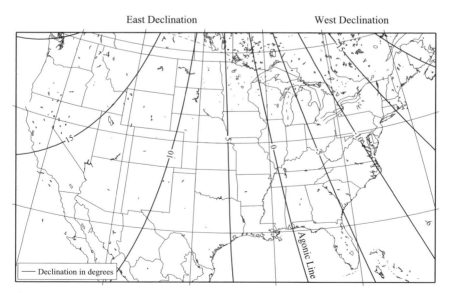

FIG. 4-6. Magnetic declination map of the United States. (From USGS National Geomagnetic Information Center.)

tion. When it is desired to attach a sign to declination east declination is considered positive, and west negative. The declination at any point can be measured with the compass when the true direction of a line can be obtained from isogonic charts such as those available from the U.S. Geological Survey. On these charts, *isogonic lines* are drawn through points where the magnetic declination is the same; the *agonic line* passes through points where the declination is zero.

At any specific point, Earth's declination is continually changing. These changes are daily variation, irregular, secular, and annual variation. *Daily variation* is a fairly systematic departure of the declination from the daily mean value. This repeats itself with fair regularity day after day. The amount of departure, however, depends on the time of day, the season, and other factors not entirely understood.

Usually, superimposed on the regular daily variation are *irregular* changes. When they become large, we say that there is a magnetic storm. These are associated with sunspots and are characterized by auroral displays and pronounced disturbances in radio-wave transmission. Since the amplitude of daily variation and irregular changes is not predictable for any one day, these changes are not considered in compass surveys.

In general, the average value of declination changes from one year to the next, and the change usually continues in one direction for many years. This is *secular* change. The amount of change in one year is called the *annual variation*. Unfortunately, there is sometimes an abrupt, unpredictable change in the rate of secular change. Thus secular change can be determined only by observations at magnetic observatories. Information from such observations are available in the United States for each state from the earliest date of valid observations to the present, at 10-year intervals up to 1900 and at 5-year intervals thereafter. This information, which is often needed for rerunning old survey lines and reestablishing corner markers in the United States, may be obtained from the National Geophysical and Solar Terrestrial Data Center at Boulder, Colorado by specifying latitude and longitude of the point in question.

In most regions the changes above are gradual enough so that one can use the same declination throughout an area for an entire season. But in some regions *local disturbances* cause large differences within small areas, sometimes several degrees within a short distance. These disturbances may be artificial, caused by human interference due to apparel worn by the observer, such as buckles, zippers, or glasses. Deposits of magnetite usually cause natural, local disturbances of several degrees. Other ores and geological formations cause smaller irregularities. However, even in undisturbed regions, minor irregularities are common. Almost anywhere, the declination at two points a short distance apart, such as 100 ft, may differ by a few minutes. Such disturbances are responsible for many of the shortcomings of the compass as a surveying instrument.

A compass survey should be made with the instrument in good condition, observing the instructions in the manual for the instrument. Although a compass may be in good operating condition, it may have an appreciable *index correction*; that is, there may be an angle between the real magnetic north and the direction shown by the compass. This correction for a specific compass may be determined by observation at a magnetic station (i.e., a marked point on the ground where the magnetic and true meridians have been determined accurately). In the United States, the National Geophysical and Solar Terrestrial Data Center at Boulder, Colorado can provide the description of the nearest magnetic station if one specifies the location of interest.

4-7. U.S. PUBLIC LAND SURVEYS

The U.S. rectangular surveying system was devised to establish legal subdivisions for describing and disposing of the public domain under the general land laws of the United States. The system uses chain units for length measurements and acres for area measurements, as described in Section 4-1. The system has been used in most of the United States with the exception of the older states along the Atlantic seaboard and in a few states where lands were in private hands before the federal government was founded. Many of the land holdings in states that do not use the U.S. rectangular surveying system are described by *metes and bounds* (*metes* means to measure or to assign by measure; *bounds* refers to a boundary); the length and direction of each side of the boundary are determined and the corners marked with survey monuments. The description of old surveys of this type are often vague and the corners difficult or impossible to relocate.

The Ordinance of 1785 established the rectangular surveying system. The system provides for townships 6 miles square, containing 36 sections 1 mile square. In any given region, the survey begins from an *initial point*. Through this point is run a meridian, called the *principal meridian*, and a parallel of latitude, called the *baseline* (Fig. 4-7a). With the establishment of an initial point, the latitude and longitude of the point are determined by accurate astronomical methods. Monuments are placed on the principal meridian and on the baseline at intervals of 40 chains.

Standard parallels or *correction lines* are then run for the district being surveyed. These lines, which are parallels of latitude, are established in the same manner as the baseline. They are located at intervals of 24 miles north and south of the baseline and extend to the limits of the district being surveyed. Standard parallels are numbered as First, Second, Third, and so on, Standard Parallel North, or South (Fig. 4-7a).

The survey district is next divided into tracts approximately 24 miles square by means of guide meridians. These lines are true meridians that start at points on the baseline, or standard parallels, at intervals of 24 miles east and west of the principal meridian, and extend north to their intersection with the next standard parallel. Because of the convergence of meridians, the distance between these lines is 24 miles only at the starting points. At all other points,

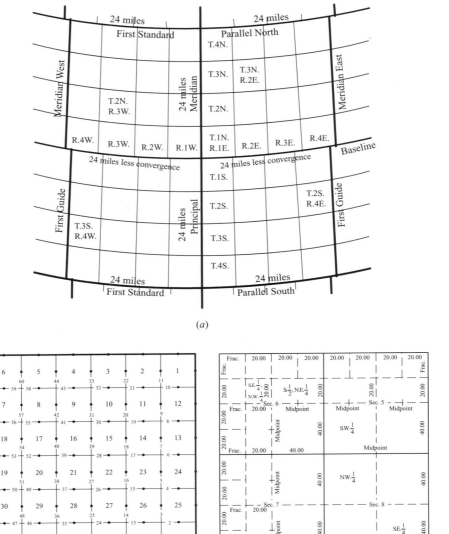

FIG. 4-7. U.S. Public Land Survey: (*a*) standard parallels and guide meridians; (*b*) subdivision of township; (*c*) subdivision of sections.

the distance between them is less than 24 miles. Guide meridians are numbered as First, Second, Third, and so on, Guide Meridian East, or West. Note that two sets of monuments are found on the standard parallels. The monuments that were set when the parallel was first located are called *standard corners* and govern the area north of the parallel. The second set, found at the intersection of the parallel with the meridians from the south, is referred to as the *closing corners* and govern the area south of the parallel.

The townships of a survey district are numbered meridionally (east–west) into ranges and latitudinally (north–south) into tiers from the principal meridian and the baseline of the district. As illustrated in Fig. 4-7a, the third township south of the baseline is in tier 3 south. Since the word *township* is frequently used instead of *tier*, any township in this tier is often designated as township 3 south. The fourth township west of the principal meridian is in range 4 west. By this method of numbering, any township is located if its tier, range, and principal meridian are given as Township 3 South, Range 4 West, of the Fourth Principal Meridian, abbreviated as T.3S., R.4W., 4th P.M.

In subdividing a township into 36 *sections*, the aim is to secure as many sections as possible that will be 1 mile on a side. To accomplish this, the error due to convergence of meridians is thrown as far to the west as possible by running lines parallel to the east boundary of the township, rather than running them as true meridians. Errors in linear measurements are thrown as far to the north as possible by locating monuments at intervals of 40 chains along the lines parallel to the east boundary of the township, all the accumulated error falling in the most northerly half-mile, which may be more or less than 40 chains in length.

The system used in numbering the sections of a township was established in 1796. This numbering system and the most recent order in which the lines are run to subdivide the township into sections (indicated by the numbers on the lines) are shown in Fig. 4-7b. This system of subdividing a township throws the errors due to survey and losses from convergence into the extreme north and west sections. Other sections, however, may contain more or less than 640 acres, due to survey errors. Nevertheless, the established boundaries are final, regardless of errors made in the original survey.

If any of the monuments of an original survey are missing, surveyors must know and observe the methods used in the original survey as well as the principles that have been adopted by the courts, in order to restore the missing corners correctly. Procedures for relocating original survey lines and corners are described in the U.S. Department of the Interior's (1973) *Manual of Instructions for the Survey of Public Lands in the United States.*

After all the original monuments have been found or any missing ones have been replaced, the first step in the subdivision is the location of the center of the section. Regardless of the location of the section within the township, this point is always at the intersection of the line joining the east and west quarter-section corners with the line joining the north and south quarter-section corners. By locating these lines on the ground, the section is divided into quarter sections containing approximately 160 acres each (Fig. 4-7c).

The method of dividing these quarter sections into 40-acre parcels depends on the position of the section within the township. For any section except those along the north and west sides of the township, subdivision is accomplished by bisecting each side of the quarter section and connecting the opposite points by straight lines (e.g., Sec. 8 in Fig. 4-7c). The intersection of these lines is the center of the quarter section. The method of subdividing the sections along the north and west sides of the township is shown in Fig. 4-7c. The corners on the north–south section lines are set at intervals of 20.00 chains, measured from the south, the discrepancy being thrown into the most northerly quarter-mile. Similarly, the monuments on the east–west lines are set at intervals of 20.00 chains, measured from the east, the discrepancy being thrown into the most westerly quarter-mile.

The rectangular system of subdivision provides a convenient method of describing a piece of land that is to be conveyed by deed from one person to another. If the description is for a 40-acre parcel, the particular quarter of the quarter section is first given, then the quarter section in which the parcel is located, then the section number, followed by the township, range, and principal meridian. Thus the 40-acre parcel labeled in Sec. 6 of Fig. 4-7c can be described as the S.E.$\frac{1}{4}$, N.W.$\frac{1}{4}$, Sec. 6, T.3S., R.4W., 4th P.M. The legal descriptions of other parcels appear in the figure.

4-8. GLOBAL POSITIONING SYSTEMS

Global positioning systems (GPSs) are used to determine accurately locations on Earth's surface. The technology has revolutionized surveying and fieldwork in almost all natural resource professions. Although the traditional methods described above are still widely used in forestry, GPS technology is being used to determine block boundaries, locate field plots, delineate special features such as wetlands, unique vegetation pockets, stream buffers and other protected areas, and laying out roads and trails. The components of the GPS system, how GPS works, and applications of GPS to forest mensuration are discussed here briefly. For a more complete treatment of GPS theory and applications, see Leick (1995) and Oderwald and Boucher (1997).

4-8.1   Components of GPS

The global positioning system consists of three components: a satellite segment, a control segment, and a user segment (Fig. 4-8a). The *satellite segment* consists of a network of 24 satellites in orbit around Earth at an altitude of 10,900 nautical miles. Each satellite completes an orbit around Earth every 12 hours. The network is configured so that the entire surface of Earth has complete satellite coverage 24 hours a day. The satellite system is called the NAVSTAR system and is operated by the U.S. Department of Defense.

The *control segment* is a series of six ground stations located around the world. The master control station (MCS) is located at Schriever Air Force Base near Colorado Springs, Colorado. The MCS receives data from the monitoring stations in real time 24 hours a day and uses that information to determine if

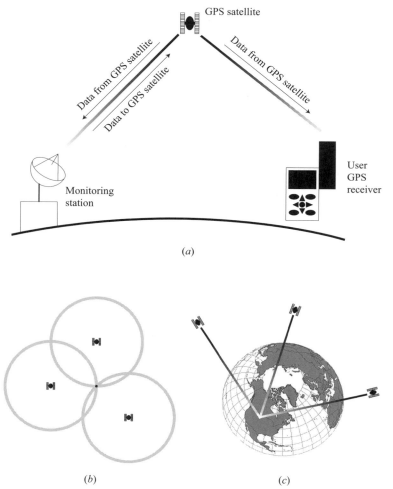

FIG. 4-8. GPS basics: (*a*) components of the system; (*b*) triangulation; (*c*) triangulation via satellite signal.

the satellites are experiencing clock or ephemeris changes, and to detect equipment malfunctions. New navigation and ephemeris information is calculated from the monitored signals and uploaded to the satellites once or twice per day. There are five passive monitoring stations, located at Colorado Springs, Hawaii, Ascencion Island, Diego Garcia, and Kwajalein. The monitor stations send the raw data back to the MCS for processing.

The *user segment* is the user and a GPS receiver. A GPS receiver is a specialized radio receiver, designed to listen to the radio signals being transmitted from satellites and to calculate a position based on that information.

GPS receivers come in many different sizes, shapes, and price ranges. GPS receivers used for forestry applications are described in Section 4-8.4.

4-8.2   How GPS Works

GPS works using triangulation (Fig. 4-8*b*). The GPS satellites emit a radio signal in the L-band region of the microwave spectrum. These signals travel at the speed of light (186,000 miles per second). Distances between satellites and a receiver are determined by measuring the time required for the signal to reach the receiver. Each satellite's signal contains an *ephemeris* (its own location), an *almanac* (the locations of other satellites), and clock information. Four satellites are required to establish the X, Y, Z (latitude, longitude, and elevation) coordinates for a location: one satellite to establish the time and three satellites for triangulation. The radio signals propagate from the satellite as a sphere; intersection of the three spheres determines the location of the receiver (Fig. 4-8*c*).

4-8.3   Accuracy of GPS

Accurate triangulation requires that distances between the receiver and satellites be determined precisely. Distance is determined in a number of ways using the various signals broadcast from the satellites. Two signals, the coarse acquisition code and the carrier phase code, are used in civilian applications. The precise code, a third type of signal is used primarily by military and other authorized personnel.

The *coarse acquisition code* (C/A) is the most widely used GPS signal. GPS satellites have very precise clocks that are monitored and updated from the master control station. A GPS receiver generates codes that match the codes generated by the satellites at the same time. Distance is estimated using the time between a signal being emitted from the satellite and the time the signal is received. Because the clock on the receiver never has exactly the same time as the clock on the satellite, the distances are really estimates and are referred to as *pseudoranges*. A signal takes only $\frac{1}{20}$ of a second to travel from the satellite to the receiver, so even very small differences in clock times can result in large errors in distance. Because of the error in distance estimation, satellite triangulation establishes a region in which the location is likely to be located (Fig. 4-8*b*).

The *carrier phase code* is a continuous signal, and distance is determined by counting the number of complete and fractional wavelengths between two locations. Carrier phase location is much more accurate than C/A location, but acquisition of carrier phase data is time consuming and requires expensive receivers.

Prior to May 2000, the U.S. government deliberately introduced error in the satellite signals. This error was called *selective availability* (SA). With SA, location accuracies in the range of ±100 m or more were common. Since

May 2000, the SA has been eliminated, except on a regional basis during periods of military conflict or other crises. Even inexpensive receivers now have accuracies of ±10 to 20 m. There are also a number of correction methods that can be applied to raw GPS location data to improve accuracies.

There are a number of factors that influence GPS accuracies:

- *Ephemeris data errors.* A satellite, at any given time, is never in its precisely assigned orbit. Satellite location errors generally result in location errors of about 1 m.
- *Satellite clock errors.* The satellite clocks are very precise and are frequently updated from the MCS. Each satellite signal carries the clock error so that satellite time can be corrected. Uncorrected clock errors generally result in location errors of about 1 m.
- *Atmospheric errors.* The ionosphere and troposphere cause signal interference. The amount of interference is dependent on weather conditions and the location of the satellite. Satellites directly overhead have smaller amounts of interference than do satellites near the horizon. Atmospheric errors generally create location errors in the range 3 to 5 m.
- *Multipath errors.* Multipath errors result from delays in signal reception caused by the signal bouncing off objects between the satellite and the receiver. Large buildings, mountains, and hills cause the greatest amount of multipath error; however, trees can also result in multipath error. Location error due to multipaths generally is in the range 2 to 3 m.
- *Receiver Noise.* Noise errors are the combined effect of code noise (around 1 m) and noise within the receiver (around 1 m).

Other errors, such as receiver malfunction and user mistakes, can result in blunders of unknown size.

4-8.4 GPS Receivers

Many different types of GPS receivers are available. Handheld receivers are used primarily in field applications. Handheld GPS units consist of an antenna, the GPS engine, a microprocessor to calculate and store locations, and a battery. The main difference between most receivers is the number of channels available to track satellites.

Receivers are categorized as either navigating receivers or mapping receivers. *Navigating receivers* are intended primarily for recreation uses, such as navigating to large features such as lakes or cabins. Most navigation receivers allow only single-point readings and dynamic lines. Navigation receivers are the least accurate of GPS receivers but are adequate for the applications intended. Costs, portability, and extended battery life are important considerations when selecting a navigating receiver. Navigation receivers cost between US$150 and about US$400.

Mapping receivers typically have many more options than navigating receivers, including the number of channels available, multiple point readings, static and dynamic lines, increased storage capacity, and the ability to interface with geographic information systems. For a comparison of the performance of different mapping receivers under forestry conditions, see Courteau and Darche (1997). High-quality mapping receivers cost between US$3000 and US$12,000.

4-8.5   Using GPS Data in Forest Mensuration

GPS data has a variety of applications in forest mensuration. Plot locations can be marked and cruise lines mapped. Block boundaries can be traversed and areas determined. Property boundaries, roads, and streams can be mapped. Data can be downloaded to geographic information systems and analyzed further or used to produce maps. Plot locations and cruise lines can also be located on geographic information systems and these data uploaded to the GPS receiver. The GPS receiver can then be used as a navigation tool for traversing cruise lines and locating plots.

To utilize GPS data effectively, one must understand how the GPS data are collected and analyzed. GPS data are typically represented as either points or lines. Points are estimates of location at a particular instant in time. Points may be based on single readings or multiple readings. A *single-reading point* is an estimate of location based on all available satellites at a single point in time. A *multiple-reading point* is the average of several single-reading estimates of the same location. Multiple-reading points are generally more accurate than single-reading points, however, more field time is required to obtain multiple readings.

Lines are connected points. In most GPS receivers, lines are created by collecting single-reading points at a specified time interval. These lines are typically called *dynamic lines* because they are created as the GPS receiver is moving. Lines can be created by connecting a series of multiple-reading points. These lines are called *static lines* because the GPS receiver must be held stationary at each point during the multiple-reading phase. Static lines are more accurate than dynamic lines; however, dynamic lines are generally quite accurate because the line is based on several connecting single-reading points.

Most GPS receivers are capable of calculating areas based on line data collected in the same manner as a closed traverse. Starting at a fixed location, the boundary of the block is traversed, with the GPS receiver collecting dynamic line data. The boundary is followed around to the starting point. The GPS receiver will ensure closure and calculate area. Area may also be calculated by connecting a series of multiple-reading points that close.

4-9. GEOGRAPHIC INFORMATION SYSTEMS

Geographic information systems (GISs) are powerful computer database programs that have the capability to input, store, manipulate and analyze, and output spatially referenced information (Longley, 1999). The organization and presentation of spatial information is crucial to many aspects of modern forest management (Reed and Mroz, 1997).

Different types of data within a GIS are stored as *layers* (Fig. 4-9). The GIS provides the capability of overlaying different layers or combining different layers through data manipulation and analyses to produce sophisticated maps. The ability to combine and manipulate different types of data rapidly makes GIS an ideal tool for foresters. For example, a forester might combine a soils layer with a forest cover layer and a roads layer to develop a map to identify which types of machinery to use for harvesting different blocks of timber. A layer identifying the location of unique or protected areas could be added to ensure that adequate buffers are provided to protect these features.

GIS data can be stored as either vector data or raster data. *Vector-based systems* use points, lines, or polygon areas stored as series of $X-Y$ coordinates. Various attributes, such as soil type, elevation, and forest cover type, are associated with the vector elements. In *raster-based systems*, the area is divided into a matrix of cells. Data attributes for a given layer are assigned on a cell-by-cell basis. Raster-based systems are generally faster than vector-based systems and perform overlays more efficiently. Vector-based systems have more compact data structures, tend to have higher spatial accuracy, and perform calculations related to the distribution of features more efficiently. Systems that can handle both types of data are available.

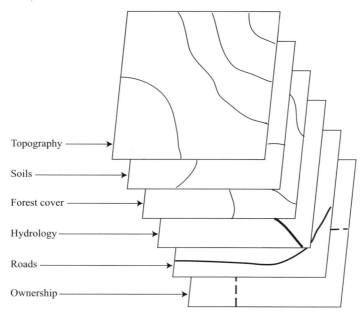

Topography

Soils

Forest cover

Hydrology

Roads

Ownership

FIG. 4-9. Data layers in GIS. (Adapted from Reed and Mroz, 1997.)

The applications of GIS to forestry are immense. Applications of GIS of particular interest to forest mensuration are discussed below. Descriptions of the technology involved, data sources and structures, and the manipulation and analysis of data are beyond the scope of a forest mensuration textbook. For more information the reader is referred to one of the numerous books dedicated to GIS theory and practice (e.g., Aronoff, 1989, Longley, 1999; Longley et al., 2001). A brief but complete description of GIS is given in Landres et al. (2001).

4-9.1 Applications of GIS to Forest Mensuration

The ability to locate points, draw lines, and measure areas makes GIS an ideal tool for inventory design. The sample designs discussed in Chapter 13 can generally be developed using a GIS. For example, if random sampling is being used, most GIS systems can generate random X–Y coordinates to use as plot centers. These coordinates can be combined with other desired layers to produce maps useful for locating the plots in the field. The data can be uploaded to GPS receivers and the receivers used to navigate to the plot locations. Some GIS packages even have the capability of determining distances and bearings between plots and can design optimal routes.

By combining desired layers, forests can be stratified in a number of ways. The areas associated with different strata can be determined and stratified sampling designs developed.

Results of inventories can be added to a GIS database as another layer. Volume per unit area or other stand parameters (Chapter 8) can be combined with other layers to produce useful maps for harvesting and other forest management activities. Data from previous inventories may be used in the design of new inventories. By comparing multiple inventories, changes such as growth, regeneration, and harvesting can be tracked.

5

INDIVIDUAL TREE PARAMETERS

In this chapter we discuss a variety of tree parameters: age, diameter and area, and height, as well as several parameters related to the crown. Instruments used for measurements and methods of calculation are also described.

5-1. AGE

The age of a tree is the length of time elapsed since germination of the seed or budding of the sprout. Information on age is important in relation to growth and yield and as a variable in evaluating site quality. In certain species, branch whorls can be used to determine age. Each season's height growth starts with the bursting of the bud at the tip of the tree; this lengthens to form the leader. The circle of branchlets that grows at the base of the leader marks the height of the tree at the very start of the season's growth. This process is repeated the following year, and a new whorl appears to mark the beginning of that season's growth. A count of these branch whorls thus gives the age of the tree (Fig. 5-1a). It is only in certain coniferous species, however, that whorls are well defined, and even in old trees of these species, the evidence of the former whorls can seldom be distinguished.

In some hardwood species, such as maples (*Acer* sp.) and beeches (*Fagus* sp.), the terminal bud scale leaves a distinct scar in the bark around the stem. The remains of these scars can often be seen for several years. By counting the number of scars from the terminal, the age of a tree at that point may be determined (Büsgen and Munch, 1929). As with counting whorls, this technique is limited to younger trees and branches and requires access to the upper stem to locate bud scale scars.

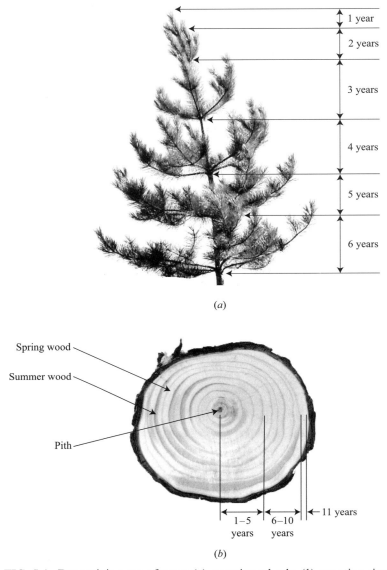

(a)

(b)

FIG. 5-1. Determining age of trees: (*a*) counting whorls; (*b*) counting rings.

Annual rings afford the best method of determining tree age in temperate regions. Here most trees grow in diameter by adding a new layer of wood each year between the old wood and bark. Formation of this layer begins at the start of the growing season and continues throughout. Woody tissue formed in the spring (*springwood* or *earlywood*) is more porous and lighter in color than woody tissue formed in the summer (*summerwood* or *latewood*). Thus annual growths of the tree appear on a cross section of the stem as a series of concentric rings (Fig. 5-1*b*). A count of the number of rings on a given cross section gives the age of the tree above the cross section.

Consequently, if the count is made on a cross section at ground level, the count gives total tree age. If the count is made on a cross section above ground level, the number of years for the tree to grow to the height of the cross section must be added to the ring count to obtain the total tree age. (The number of years for a young tree to reach stump height varies from 1 year for sprouts of broadleaved species to 20 years for coniferous seedlings growing on dry sites.)

In tropical and subtropical regions that have alternating wet and dry seasons, growth rings similar to those that occur in temperate regions are produced. These rings may be useful for determining tree age; however, in tropical regions that do not have a regular alternation in growing conditions, any rings that may be produced are useless for determining age. Several techniques have been proposed to estimate the age of tropical trees without rings, including radiocarbon dating and the use of periodic increment models (Martínez-Ramos and Alvarez-Buylla, 1999). Radiocarbon dating is limited to very long lived individuals (generally greater than 500 years), while the periodic increment models are limited to species with reliable long-term growth data and result in predictions of mean ages for a cohort of trees rather than individual tree ages (Chambers and Trumbore, 1999).

Difficulties may be encountered in making ring counts. In slow-growing trees, rings may be so close together that they are hard to count. In some species, the difference in appearance between springwood and summerwood is not marked, and rings are indistinct. In addition, abnormal weather during the growing season may lead, in certain species, to the formation of false growth rings—a dry spell may interrupt annual growth, and then growth may resume when rains come. Then, too, defoliation by insects may cause a tree to produce a second set of leaves and an additional growth ring for a given year. False rings, however, are not as clear as true growth rings and often do not extend around the entire circumference of a tree's cross section.

Ring counts are often made on a sawed surface such as a stump, although such surfaces are generally too rough to permit rings to be counted accurately. Consequently, rings on a smoothed strip extending from the bark to the center of a section should be cut with a sharp knife or plane and viewed with a hand lens to facilitate counting. On standing trees, an increment borer may be used (Fig. 5-2*a*). This consists of a hollow cutting bit that is screwed into the tree. The core of wood forced into the hollow center of the bit is removed with the extractor. The rings on this core are then counted (Fig. 5-2*d*). Unfortunately, the total age of large trees is difficult to obtain with an increment borer because the maximum practical length of a borer is between 16 and 20 in. and because of the difficulty of finding the pith.

Average radial growth may be determined from several increment cores (cores for this purpose are normally taken at breast height), but usually only

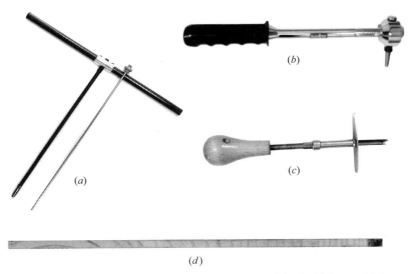

FIG. 5-2. Instruments to measure diameter increment and bark thickness: (*a*) increment borer; (*b*) increment hammer; (*c*) bark gauge; (*d*) increment core.

one core is taken. When a single core is taken, it should be extracted halfway between the long and short diameters of the tree. The length of the core depends on the past period for which the growth measurement is desired. If growth for the life of the tree is needed, the boring must reach the pith. If growth for a past period is needed as a basis of growth predictions, the boring should include the number of rings in the period, usually 5 or 10 years. If the width of the growth period is small (less than 2 in.), an increment hammer (Fig. 5-2*b*) may be used. The increment hammer is swung against the tree, and the hollow tip plunges into the wood. A small core, similar to the core from an increment borer, is extracted from the hollow tip.

Annual rings of trees have been used in dendrochronology for dating archaeological and geological events as far back as 3000 years and arranging them in order of occurrence. Basically, it is the study of annual rings in living trees and aged woods to establish a time sequence in the dating of past events. Dendrochronology has been used primarily for the analysis of annual rings from trees on sites where precipitation is the most limiting climatic factor affecting tree growth. Tree response is indicated by the width of annual rings—narrow rings when precipitation is low, wide rings when precipitation is high. Since climatic variations tend to occur over rather large regions, char- acteristically narrow rings in two or more trees can be matched, provided that the trees grew at the same time. Recognition of this fact led to cross dating, the foundation of dendrochronology (Fritts, 1976). Dendrochronology techniques have been applied to several wide-scale environmental problems, including climate change and air pollution studies. A comprehensive review of the techniques and applications of dendrochronology can be found in Cook and Kairiukstis (1990).

5-2. TREE DIAMETERS AND AREAS

A *diameter* is a straight line passing through the center of a circle or sphere and meeting at each end of the circumference or surface. The most common diameter measurements taken in forestry are of the main stem of standing trees, cut portions of trees, and branches. Diameter measurement is important because it is one of the directly measurable dimensions from which tree cross-sectional area, surface area, and volume can be computed.

Use of the word *diameter* implies that trees are circular in cross section. In many cases, however, the section is somewhat wider in one direction than another, or it may be eccentric in other ways. Since for computational purposes tree cross sections are assumed to be circular, the objective of any tree diameter measurement is to obtain the diameter of a circle with the same cross-sectional area as the tree.

The point at which diameters are measured will vary with circumstances. In the case of standing trees, a standard position has been established. In the United States, the diameter of standing trees is taken at 4.5 ft above ground level. This is referred to as *diameter at breast height* and is abbreviated to d.b.h. or dbh (Fig. 5-3a). In countries that use the metric system, the diameter of standing trees is taken at 1.3 m above ground level and was traditionally given the symbol d (IUFRO, 1959). However, it is currently common, especially in North America, to find the symbol dbh used to refer both to diameters measured at 4.5 ft above ground and to diameters measured at 1.3 m above ground level. Diameters at other points along the stem of a tree are often indicated by subscripts: $d_{0.5h}$ = diameter at half total height; $d_{0.1h}$ = diameter at 0.1 total height; d_6 = diameter at 6 m above ground level.

Diameters should be qualified as d.o.b. or dob (outside bark) or d.i.b. or dib (inside bark); however, when this designation is omitted from breast height measurement (dbh or d), as it often is, the measurement is assumed to be outside bark. Whether outside or inside bark diameter measurements are taken depends on the purpose for which the measurements are made. When a rule, or scale stick, is used on a cut section, it is simple to measure diameter inside or outside bark. One simply measures an appropriate line, or lines, on the section along which the bark is intact. If both d.i.b. and d.o.b. are measured, bark thickness is one-half the difference between them. If one measures d.o.b. and bark thickness, d.i.b. equals d.o.b. minus twice the bark thickness.

Bark thickness on standing trees can be determined with a bark gauge (Fig. 5-2c). The instrument consists of a steel shaft, half-cylindrical in shape, which is pushed through the bark. The cutting edge of this instrument is a half circle that is dull on one side so that the instrument can be driven through the softer

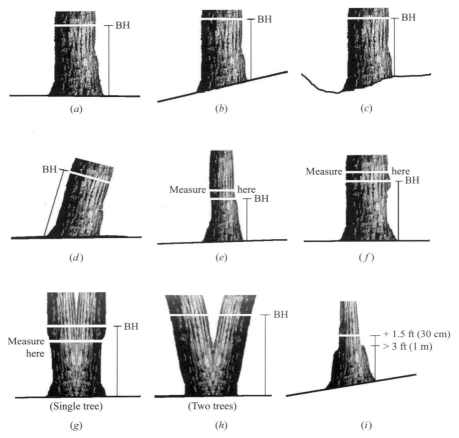

FIG. 5-3. Standard points for measurement of dbh: (a) level ground; (b) sloping ground; (c) uneven ground; (d) leaning tree; (e) crook at breast height; (f) defect at breast height; (g) forks at breast height; (h) forks below breast height; (i) buttressed tree. BH, breast height (4.5 ft in the English system, 1.3 m in the metric system).

bark but not through the wood. When the instrument's sliding cross arm is pressed against the bark, its thickness can be read on a scale without removing the instrument. When the bark is thick and tough, its thickness may be obtained by boring to the wood surface with an increment borer or a brace and bit and measuring from the bark surface to the wood with a small ruler.

In the United States, tree diameters have generally been measured and recorded in inches. (However, there is a growing use of metric system measurements, especially in research activities.) In countries where the metric system is used, diameters are measured in centimeters (occasionally, in millimeters).

In measuring at breast height in the field (dbh or d), the following standard procedures are recommended:

- When trees are on slopes or uneven ground, measure 4.5 ft (for dbh) or 1.3 m (for d) above the ground on the uphill side of the tree (Fig. 5-3b and c).
- When a tree is leaning, breast height is measured parallel to the lean on the high side of the tree. The diameter is measured perpendicular to the longitudinal axis of the stem (Fig. 5-3d).
- When a tree has a limb, bulge, or some other abnormality, such as a crook, at breast height, measure diameter above the abnormality; strive to obtain the diameter the tree would have had if the abnormality had not been present (Fig. 5-3e and f).
- When a tree consists of two or more stems forking below breast height, measure each stem separately (Fig. 5-3h). When a tree forks at or above breast height, measure it as one tree. If the fork occurs at breast height, or slightly above, measure the diameter below the enlargement caused by the fork (Fig. 5-3g).
- When a tree has a buttress that extends higher than 3 ft or 1 m, it is common to measure the stem at a fixed distance above the top of the buttress, usually at 1.5 ft or 30 cm (Fig. 5-3i).
- When a tree has a paint mark to designate the breast height point, assume that the point of measurement is at the top of the paint mark.

5-2.1 Instruments for Measuring Diameter

The most commonly used instruments for measuring dbh and d are calipers and diameter tape. Less precise measurements can be made with a Biltmore stick and Bitterlich's sector fork. Multipurpose laser-based instruments can also be used to measure tree diameters.

Calipers. Calipers are often used to measure tree dbh or d when diameters are less than about 24 in. or 60 cm. Calipers of sufficient size to measure large trees, or those with high buttresses (commonly found in tropical regions), are awkward to carry and handle, particularly in dense undergrowth. A beam caliper (Fig. 5-4a) may be constructed of metal, plastic, or wood, and consists of a graduated beam with two perpendicular arms. One arm is fixed at the origin of the scale and the other arm slides. When the beam is pressed against the tree and the arms closed, the tree diameter can be read on the scale. For an accurate reading, the beam of the caliper must be pressed firmly against the tree with the beam perpendicular to the axis of the tree stem and the arms parallel and perpendicular to the beam.

A more advanced and precise form of calipers is the Mantax computer caliper (Fig. 5-4b), developed by the Swedish firm Haglöf. With this instrument the diameter is measured in either the English or metric system and stored in the instrument, eliminating the need for recording the measurement on a field sheet or entering it in a field computer. The stored data can be read from the instrument or downloaded to a computer or to a printer.

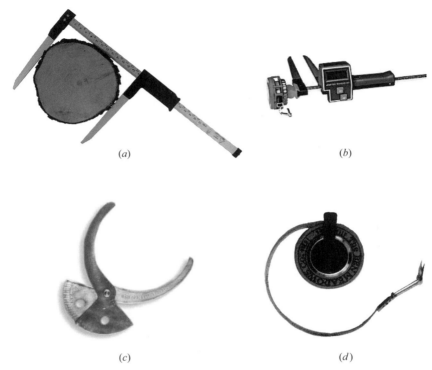

(a)

(b)

(c)   (d)

FIG. 5-4. Diameter measuring instruments: (a) beam calipers; (b) Mantax computer caliper; (c) tree calipers; (d) diameter tape.

Other forms of calipers have been devised. The fork caliper consists of a set of fixed arms with graduations calibrated so that when the fork is placed on the tree, the points of tangency indicate the tree diameter. Tree calipers, used for measuring small trees (< 8 in.) consist of a pair of curved arms that scissor on a vertex (Fig. 5-4c). When the arms are pressed against the tree, the fan-shaped scale at the vertex gives the diameter reading. The Finnish parabolic calipers is another form. It is, of course, important that all types of calipers be held perpendicular to the axis of the tree stem at the point of measurement.

When a tree cross section is elliptical, one might measure the major and minor diameters, d_1 and d_2, and obtain the average diameter from the arithmetic mean of d_1 and d_2. This would, however, overestimate the "true" diameter of the cross section. If the periphery of the elliptical cross section was measured with a tape, and the periphery divided by π (this assumes that the periphery is a circle), the "true" diameters of the cross section would also be overestimated. The best practice would be to use the geometric mean (Section 3-3.3) of the two measurements: $\sqrt{d_1 \cdot d_2}$. Table 5-1 illustrates the effect of eccentricity on the cross-sectional area.

TABLE 5-1. Effects of Eccentricity on Cross-Sectional Area Estimation

Ratio of Major:Minor Axes	Relative Axis Length		Diameter from Perimeter	Area Estimated Using:						
	Major	Minor		True Area	Major Axis	Minor Axis	Arithmetic Mean	Quadratic Mean	Geometric Mean	Perimeter
1:1	1.13	1.13	1.13	1.00	1.00	1.00	1.00	1.00	1.00	1.00
5:4	1.26	1.01	1.14	1.00	1.25	0.80	1.01	1.03	1.00	1.02
4:3	1.30	0.98	1.15	1.00	1.33	0.75	1.02	1.04	1.00	1.03
3:2	1.38	0.92	1.16	1.00	1.50	0.67	1.04	1.08	1.00	1.06
5:3	1.46	0.87	1.18	1.00	1.67	0.60	1.07	1.13	1.00	1.10
2:1	1.60	0.80	1.23	1.00	2.00	0.50	1.13	1.25	1.00	1.19
5:2	1.78	0.71	1.31	1.00	2.50	0.40	1.23	1.45	1.00	1.34
3:1	1.95	0.65	1.39	1.00	3.00	0.33	1.33	1.67	1.00	1.51
4:1	2.26	0.56	1.54	1.00	4.00	0.25	1.56	2.13	1.00	1.87
5:1	2.52	0.50	1.68	1.00	5.00	0.20	1.80	2.60	1.00	2.23

Unfortunately, tree cross sections often depart from elliptical form as well as from circular form. Consequently, for practical purposes when using calipers, the arithmetic average of the long and short "diameters," or axes, is utilized. If it is not feasible to secure the long and short diameters, the arithmetic average of two diameters perpendicular to each other is often used.

Diameter Tape. The diameter of a tree cross section may be obtained with a flexible tape by measuring the circumference of the tree and dividing by π ($D = C/\pi$). The diameter tapes used by foresters, however, are graduated at intervals of π units (inches or centimeters), thus permitting a direct reading of diameter (Fig. 5-4d). These tapes are accurate only for trees that are circular in cross section. In all other cases, the tape readings will be slightly too large, because the circumference of a circle is the shortest line that can encompass any given area (Table 5-1).

The diameter tape is convenient to carry, allows measurement of large trees, and in the case of eccentric trees, requires only one measurement. Although it is slower to use than other diameter-measuring instruments, the time element is generally not important. Care must be taken that the tape is positioned correctly at the point of measurement, that it is kept in a plane perpendicular to the axis of the stem, and that it is set firmly around the tree trunk.

Biltmore Stick. The Biltmore stick (Fig. 5-5), which can hardly be classed as a measuring instrument, is an aid in estimating diameter at breast height. It consists of a straight stick, normally 24 to 36 in. (61 to 91 cm) long that is held perpendicular to the axis of the tree stem. By holding the stick so that the 0-point of the graduation at one end of the stick lies on the line *EA*

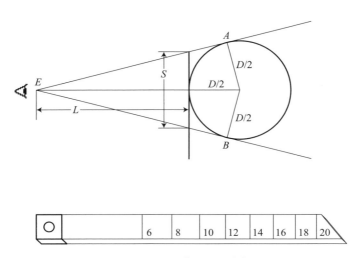

FIG. 5-5. Biltmore stick.

which is tangent to the tree cross section at A, the diameter of the tree can be read at the intersection at the other end of the stick on the line EB, which is tangent to the tree cross section at B. The distance L from the eye E to the tree is usually 25 in. (63.5 cm); however, it may be some other value. The graduations S of the stick for different values of D and L are obtained from the following formula:

$$S = \sqrt{\frac{D^2 L}{L + D}} \qquad\qquad (5\text{-}1)$$

Inaccuracies in estimating diameters with the Biltmore stick are due to (1) difficulty of holding the stick exactly the distance L from the eye, (2) the failure to keep the eye at breast height level, (3) the failure to hold the stick at breast height level, and (4) the eccentricity of tree cross sections (the Biltmore stick is correct only for circular cross sections). The advantage of the Biltmore stick is its ease of use and speed.

Sector Fork. Bitterlich's sector fork (Visiermesswinkel or Sektorluppe) (Fig. 5-6) is similar in principle to the Biltmore stick (Bitterlich, 1959). The instrument determines diameter from a sector of a circular cross section. One side of the sector is a fixed arm; one side is a line of sight. The line of sight intersects a curved scale on which diameters or cross-sectional areas are printed. It is not necessary to hold the instrument at a fixed distance from the eye because a sighting pin fixes the line of sight for any distance. The instrument is especially suited for measuring trees with diameters of less than 50 cm (about 20 in.), as in young plantations. An attachment (called a *double fork*) is available which permits measurement of diameters up to 200 cm.

Because many trees are eccentric in cross section, all instruments for measuring tree diameter will in the long run give results that average too large (Table 5-1). However, when an accurate determination of cross-sectional area is of prime importance, the calipers will give the best results. When different people caliper the same irregular tree, there will always be some variation in the measurements. A good part of this variation results because the tree is not always calipered in exactly the same place and direction. Since the element of varying direction does not affect measurements with the diameter tape, tape measurements are more consistent. Such consistency is important in growth studies, when the same trees are remeasured at intervals. Then the actual diameters of the trees are less important than the changes in diameter during the period between measurements. The diameter tape will accurately determine these changes. Errors due to eccentricity will appear in both measurements and will not significantly affect the difference between them. In any case, whenever repetitive diameter measurements are made to determine growth, it is desirable to mark the position of measurement with a scribe or paint mark. For a detailed study on the geometry of stem measurement and cross-sectional

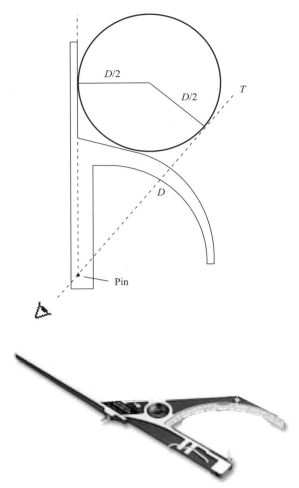

FIG. 5-6. Bitterlich's sector fork (Visiermesswinkel or Sektorluppe). T is the tangential line of sight, D is the diameter read from the scale.

area estimation, refer to Matérn (1990). A comprehensive review of various diameter measurement tools and their associated accuracies can be found in the recent review conducted by Clark et al. (2000).

When the average of a number of diameter measurements, d, is required, one might use the arithmetic mean. However, if the primary interest is to obtain an average for the calculation of cross-sectional area and volume, the quadratic mean (Section 3-3.2), is more appropriate:

$$\overline{d}_Q = \sqrt{\frac{\sum_{i=1}^{n} d_i^2}{n}} \qquad (5\text{-}2)$$

5-2.2 Measurement of Upper Stem Diameters

Tree stem diameters above breast height are often required to estimate form or taper and to compute the volume of sample trees from the measurement of diameters at several points along the stem. Of course, the tree can be felled and diameter measurements made at the desired points on the stem. To avoid felling trees, measurements can be made on standing trees.

Climbing a tree and using the instruments described in Section 5-2.1 can obtain upper stem diameters. In the past, diameters at the top of the first log (about 17 ft above ground) were sometimes taken by mounting calipers or a diameter tape on a pole (Ferree, 1946; Godman, 1949). These diameters were needed to determine Girard Form Class (Section 5-4).

Instruments for measuring upper stem diameters of standing trees allow diameters to be determined from the ground at some distance from a tree. Over the years, optical forks, optical calipers, fixed-base rangefinders, and fixed-angle rangefinders have been used for measuring upper stem diameters. These include the Barr and Stroud dendrometer, the Wheeler pentaprism, engineer's transit, the Speigel relaskop, the Tele-relaskop, and the Breithaupt Todis dendrometer. A summary of these instruments can be found in Grosenbaugh (1963a), Smith (1970), Husch et al. (1982), and Clark et al. (2000). Many of these instruments and methods are mainly of historical interest since most measurements of upper stem diameters of standing trees are made, at present, using the relaskop.

The relaskop (Fig. 5-7a) is an instrument of the optical fork type. An optical fork employs a fork angle on which the lines are tangent to the cross section at

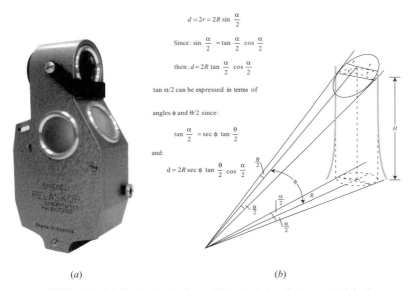

$$d = 2r = 2R \sin \frac{\alpha}{2}$$

Since: $\sin \frac{\alpha}{2} = \tan \frac{\alpha}{2} \cos \frac{\alpha}{2}$

then: $d = 2R \tan \frac{\alpha}{2} \cos \frac{\alpha}{2}$

$\tan \alpha/2$ can be expressed in terms of

angles ϕ and $\theta/2$ since:

$$\tan \frac{\alpha}{2} = \sec \phi \tan \frac{\theta}{2}$$

and:

$$d = 2R \sec \phi \tan \frac{\theta}{2} \cos \frac{\alpha}{2}$$

(a)					(b)

FIG. 5-7. (a) Speigel relaskop; (b) principle of the optical fork.

the level of the diameter measurement and on which the vertex is at the observer's eye. The basic geometry is shown in Fig. 5-7b. Note that $\cos(\alpha/2)$ can be approximated by using $\cos(\theta/2)$. The relaskop has the advantage of adjusting the diameter measurement automatically for the angle of inclination of the line of sight. Other models and attachments are available that improve the precision of upper stem diameters.

A laser-based instrument requiring a reflective target, the Criterion, was developed for the U.S. Forest Service, which can measure upper stem diameters as well as distances and heights (Carr, 1992). The instrument is no longer manufactured. The German firm Jenoptik (Jena, Germany) manufactures a laser-based dendrometer, the LEDHA-Geo (Fig. 5-8). This instrument utilizes a reflector-less laser for distance and height measurement and a fixed-base rangefinder to measure diameters at any point along the stem from distances up to 100 m. The accuracy of these devices is comparable to other optical dendrometers (Clark et al., 2000) but is not as accurate as traditional calipers and diameter tapes. Accuracy can be improved significantly if the devices are mounted on a tripod; however, significant overestimation of diameter, especially in larger trees, occurs (Skovsgaard et al., 1998).

5-2.3   Cross-Sectional Area

The cross-sectional areas of planes cutting the stem of a tree normal to the longitudinal axis of the stem are often desired. If the cross section of a tree is taken at breast height, it is called the *basal area*. The total basal area of all trees, or of specified classes of trees, per unit area (e.g., per acre or per hectare) is a useful characteristic of a forest stand. For example, basal area is directly related to stand volume and is a good measure of stand density (Chapter 8).

FIG. 5-8. Jenoptic LEDHA-Geo laser dendrometer.

When a tree cross section (for either a standing tree or a cut section) is circular, as it is often assumed to be, its area can be computed from its diameter or circumference:

$$g = \frac{\pi d^2}{4}$$

and since $d = c/\pi$,

$$g = \frac{c^2}{4\pi}$$

where g = tree cross-sectional area
d = diameter of cross section
c = circumference of cross section

In the United States diameter d is commonly expressed in inches and cross-sectional area g in square feet. Consequently, it is convenient to express g in square feet as a function of diameter d in inches:

$$g(\text{ft}^2) = \frac{\pi d^2}{4(144)} = 0.005454d^2 \qquad (5\text{-}3)$$

Using the metric system, diameter d is commonly expressed in centimeters, and cross-sectional area g in square meters. In this case,

$$g(\text{m}^2) = \frac{\pi d^2}{4(10,000)} = 0.00007854d^2 \qquad (5\text{-}4)$$

Unfortunately, cross sections of tree stems are often not circular. Thus, when they are assumed to be circular, errors in determining cross-sectional area may result (Table 5-1). For most purposes, the geometric mean of the long and short diameters, d_1 and d_2, of a section will give the most accurate results, although for practical purposes, a satisfactory practice is to take the arithmetic average of the long and short "diameters," or axes; or if it is not feasible to secure the long and short diameters, to take the arithmetic average of two diameters perpendicular to each other.

5-2.4   Surface Areas

Tree Bole. The exterior surface area of the stem of a tree approximates the cambial surface (i.e., the area under bark). This area represents the surface on which the wood substance accumulates and is therefore useful in the estimation of tree and stand growth. For tree stems that assume the shape of a geometric solid, the surface area can be computed by calculus or by the appropriate formula (Appendix Table A-3). For example, assume that the form of a tree approximates the paraboloid generating by revolving the equation

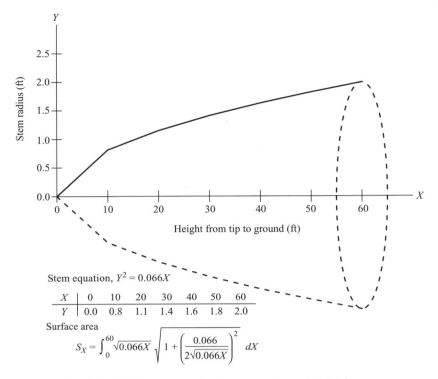

FIG. 5-9. Surface area of a tree stem of paraboloid form.

$Y^2 = 0.066X$ about the X-axis (Fig. 5-9). In this equation Y is the radius of the stem at a given point (e.g., at the stump), and X is the distance from the tree tip to the given point. The surface of the tree between $Y = 2$ ft (i.e., $X = 60$) and the tip of the tree (i.e., $X = 0$) can be determined by using the equation

$$S_x = 2\pi \int_a^b Y\sqrt{1 + \left(\frac{dY}{dX}\right)^2}\, dX$$

$$= 2\pi \int_0^{60} \sqrt{0.066X}\sqrt{1 + \left(\frac{0.066}{2\sqrt{0.066X}}\right)^2}\, dX$$

$$= 2\pi \int_0^{60} \sqrt{0.066X + 0.001089}\, dX$$

$$= 2\pi \left[\frac{2(0.066X + 0.001089)^{3/2}}{3(0.066)}\right]_0^{60}$$

$$= 2\pi \left[10.10(0.066X + 0.001089)^{3/2}\right]_0^{60}$$

$$= 159.25\pi \text{ square feet}$$
$$= 500.3 \text{ ft}^2$$

In this example, the same value would have been obtained if the formula for the surface area of a paraboloid (Appendix Table A-3) had been used. For more complex stem equations, the analytical procedure used above is appropriate.

Lexen (1943) has shown that using Huber's formula or Smalian's formula and substituting circumferences for cross-sectional areas and summing the surface areas for all sections in a tree can approximate bole surface area. Bole surface area can also be obtained by plotting on rectangular coordinate paper the circumference for several points along the stem and measuring the area below the curve drawn through these points using a planimeter. Swank and Schreuder (1974) tested sampling methods to estimate foliage, branch, and stem surface areas. Hann and McKinney (1975) developed prediction equations for the surface area of four species in the southwestern United States by using formulas for the surface areas of a cylinder, cone, and paraboloid.

Leaf Area. The surface area of the foliage of forest trees is a useful measure for the study of precipitation interception, light transmission through forest canopies, forest litter accumulation, soil moisture loss, and transpiration rates. Leaf surface area has also become an important component in many growth and yield studies and the models resulting from these studies. Leaf area may be expressed as a quantity (e.g., m^2 or ft^2) or as a ratio of leaf area to crown projection area (Section 5-5.1) or stand area, commonly referred to as *leaf area index.*

Measurement of the surface area of detached leaves, even on a small sample of foliage, is extremely time consuming. A variety of methods have been employed to measure leaf surface area; a description of the more commonly utilized methods can be found in the review by Larsen and Kershaw (1990). Because weighing foliage is generally easier than measuring surface areas, the typical approach to determining leaf surface area is to measure the surface area directly on a small sample of fresh foliage. This sample is then dried in an oven and the dried foliage weighed. The ratio of fresh surface area to dried weight is then used to estimate surface area on larger samples of dried foliage.

Because of the difficulty in measuring leaf surface areas directly, a number of techniques for estimating individual tree and stand-level leaf areas have been developed. These techniques fall into two broad classes: (1) subsampling techniques and (2) canopy estimation methods (Larsen and Kershaw, 1990). *Subsampling techniques* require destructive sampling of all or a proportion of the canopy of interest. The simplest method is the percentage sample where a fixed proportion of foliage is sampled for direct measurement. The sample units may be individual leaves or branches. Sample units may be selected by random, systematic, or stratified selection (see Chapter 13 for a description of these sample designs). Total foliage is estimated by scaling the sample values by the percentage sampled (Larsen and Kershaw, 1990). Another subsampling technique, the stratified clip method, uses a small plot projected vertically as a column through the canopy. All of the foliage within this space is carefully clipped, usually divided into preset height strata. The surface area of the foliage is measured directly or obtained by applying ratios of surface area to dry weight to the oven-dried samples. Total leaf surface area is obtained by scaling these measures to the whole tree or to the per unit area level (MacArthur and Horn, 1969). Valentine et al. (1984) developed a subsampling scheme for hardwood trees based on ratios of stem cross-sectional areas. This approach assumes that stems of a given size support similar amounts of foliage, and the ratio of stem cross-sectional area to branch cross-sectional area is used then to determine a sampling probability.

Litter traps are an alternative, nondestructive subsampling technique. Fine-meshed nets or screens are placed under the canopy and the surface area of foliage litter falling into the traps is used to estimate total foliage. Several years of sampling may be required to obtain accurate estimates of foliage in species that retain their leaves for more than one growing season (Trofymow et al., 1991).

Several indirect methods have been developed to estimate the amount of foliage in crowns and canopies. The most widely developed technique is the use of allometric relationships where the amount of foliage in a crown or canopy is estimated from easily measured tree and stand characteristics using regression models. Many allometric models utilize sapwood area as a predictor of leaf area (Turner et al., 2000). The *sapwood* is the living portion of the tree bole and is the zone where active transport of water and nutrients occurs. A functional relationship between sapwood area and foliage area, called the *pipe model theory*, was formulated by Shinozaki et al. (1964). The basic premise of this theory is that a unit of foliage requires a corresponding unit of sapwood for support. For many species, a linear relationship between sapwood area at breast height and total foliage area has been observed, and a number of equations predicting leaf area from sapwood area at breast height have been developed (e.g., Waring et al., 1982; Marshall and Waring, 1986; O'Hara and Vallappil, 1995). However, several researchers have observed significant biases in the predictions of leaf area from sapwood area at breast height (e.g., Dean et al., 1988). To address these biases, the basic relationship between sapwood area and foliage area has been modified to incorporate measures of stand density, height to crown base, total tree height, crown width, and other tree dimensions (e.g., Dean and Long, 1986; Long and Smith, 1988; Maguire and Batista, 1996; Turner et al., 2000).

Other indirect methods include light interception models (Ross, 1981; Pierce and Running, 1988; Campbell, 1986), point drop quadrats (Wilson, 1960, 1965), and photographic methods (MacArthur and Horn, 1969; Ondok, 1984; Wang and Miller, 1987). Recent improvements in both satellite and airborne remote sensing have resulted in several attempts to predict foliage area from reflectance data (Running et al., 1986; Peterson et al., 1987; Chen et al., 1997).

5-3. HEIGHT

Height is the linear distance of an object normal to the surface of Earth or some other horizontal datum plane. Aside from land elevation, tree height is the principal vertical distance measured in forest mensuration. *Tree height* is an ambiguous term unless it is clearly defined. For this purpose, a logical classification of height measurements that can be applied to standing trees of either excurrent or deliquescent form is shown in Fig. 5-10.

Total height is the distance along the axis of the tree stem between the ground and the tip of the tree. [In determining this height, the terminals (i.e., the base and tip of the tree) can be more objectively determined than other points on the stem. It is often difficult, however, to see the tip of a tree in closed stands and to determine the uppermost limit of a large-crowned tree.]

Bole height is the distance along the axis of the tree stem between the ground and the crown point. (As shown in Fig. 5-10, the crown point is the position of the first crown-forming branch. Therefore, bole height is the height of the clear, main stem of a tree.)

Merchantable height is the distance along the axis of the tree stem between the ground and the terminal position of the last usable portion of the tree stem. [The position of the upper terminal is somewhat subjective. It is taken at a minimum top diameter or at a point where branching, irregular form, or defect limit utilization. The minimum top diameter will vary with the intended use of the timber and with market conditions, for example, it might be 4 in. (10 cm) for pulpwood and 8 in. (20 cm) for sawtimber.]

Stump height is the distance between the ground and the basal position on the main stem where a tree is cut. (A standard stump height, generally about 1 ft, is established for volume table construction and timber volume estimation.)

Merchantable length is the distance along the axis of the tree stem between the top of the stump and the terminal position of the last usable portion of the tree stem.

Defective length is the sum of the portions of the merchantable length that cannot be utilized because of defect.

Sound merchantable length equals the merchantable length minus the defective length.

Crown length is the distance on the axis of the tree stem between the crown point and the tip of the tree. A tree characteristic used in tree and forest health monitoring is the *live crown ratio*. It is determined by dividing the live crown length by total tree live height (Alexander and Barnard, 1994).

Generally speaking, the techniques and instruments devised for general height measurement may be applied to tree-height measurement. However, instruments must be economical, light, portable, and usable in closed stands.

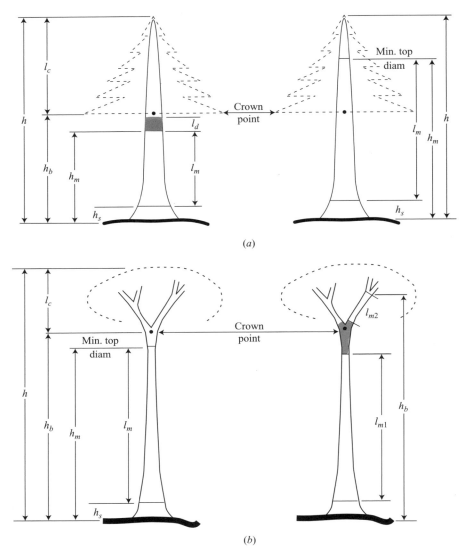

FIG. 5-10. Tree height and stem length classification: (*a*) excurrent form; (*b*) deliques-cent form. h, total height; h_b, bole height; h_m, merchantable height; h_s, stump height; l_c, crown length; l_m, merchantable length; l_d, defective length. Shading denotes defective portion.

Total tree heights may also be estimated from measurements made on aerial photographs, as described in Paine (1981).

The heights of short trees can be measured directly with an engineer's self-reading level rod, a graduated pole, or similar devices. The heights of many taller trees can be measured directly, with the aid of sectional or sliding poles made of wood, fiberglass, plastic, or lightweight metal. Although measurement with poles is slow, they are often used to measure height on continuous forest inventory plots where high accuracy is desired and merchantable length is less than 70 ft (±21 m).

Most height measurements of tall trees are taken indirectly with hypsometers. Hypsometers are based on the relation of the legs of similar triangles (geometric) or on the tangents of angles (trigonometric). (Note that terms such as altimeter and clinometer are also applied to instruments that are used to measure height.)

5-3.1 Hypsometers Based on Similar Triangles

A number of older instruments based on similar triangles were developed and have been used extensively over the years. These include the Christen, Merritt, Chapman, and JAL hypsometers. These instruments are less precise than the ones that utilize trigonometric relationships. The geometric-based hypsometers have the advantage of being simple and easily and cheaply constructed. The Christen and Merritt hypsometers developed in North America exemplify hypsometers based on the geometric relationships of similar triangles. In their original forms, both instruments used English system units. However, if desired, they can be constructed to show metric units.

The *Christen hypsometer* consists of a scale about 10 inches long (Fig. 5-11). To use the Christen hypsometer, a pole (usually 5 or 10 ft long) is held upright against the base of the tree, or a mark is placed on the tree at a height of 5 or 10 ft above the ground. The hypsometer is then held vertically at a distance from the eye such that the two inside edges of the flanges are in line with the top and base of the tree. It may be necessary for the observer to move closer to or farther from the tree to accomplish this, but except for this, the distance from the tree is immaterial. The graduation on the scale that is in line with the top of the pole, or the mark, gives the height of the tree. The following proportion gives the formula for graduating the instrument:

$$\frac{A'C'}{AC} = \frac{A'B'}{AB} \tag{5-5}$$

For a given length of instrument $A'B'$ and a given pole length or mark height AC, the graduations $A'C'$ can be obtained by substituting different values of height AB in the equation.

The *Merritt hypsometer* is a simple instrument, which is often combined with the Biltmore stick. It is a convenient aid in estimating the number of logs in a tree rather than height in feet. The hypsometer consists of a graduated stick that is held vertically at a predetermined distance, usually 25 in., from the eye (Fig. 5-12). If the stick is held 25 in. from the eye along a

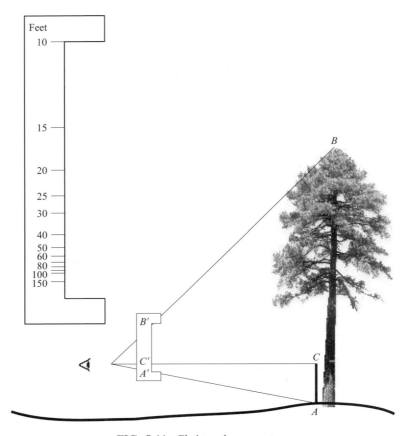

FIG. 5-11. Christen hypsometer.

horizontal line, the distance to the tree should be measured on the horizontal; if the stick is held 25 in. from the eye along a line to the lower end of the stick, as shown in Fig. 5-12, the distance to the tree should be measured on the slope. The observer must stand at a predetermined distance, such as 50 ft, from the tree. Then the height of the tree may be read on the stick at the point where the line of sight to the top terminal on the tree intersects the scale. In Fig. 5-12,

$$\frac{A'B'}{AB} = \frac{EA'}{EA} \tag{5-6}$$

If EA' is 25 in. and EA is 50 ft, for each 16 ft (the standard length of a log) of height in AB the length of $A'B'$ will be 8.0 in. The stick may thus be graduated in 8-in. intervals with the successive graduations marked 1, 2, and 3 indicating

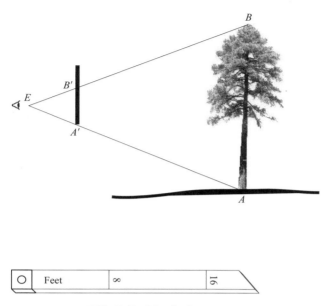

FIG. 5-12. Merritt hypsometer.

the number of logs. The stick may also be graduated using metric units, substituting centimeters and meters for inches and feet. When merchantable length is measured, as it often is with the Merritt hypsometer, one should remember that the line of sight *EA* must be to the top of the stump.

Although the Christen hypsometer may be used to measure any type of height, it is practical only for total height measurements. Furthermore, an examination of Fig. 5-11 shows a crowding of graduations at the bottom of the scale. This makes the instruments unreliable for the determination of the height of tall trees.

In using the Merritt hypsometer, it is difficult to hold the stick in a vertical position exactly 25 in. from the eye. Small deviations in orientation result in considerable errors in height readings. Therefore, the instrument should be used only to make rough checks on ocular height estimates.

5-3.2 Hypsometers Based on Tangents of Angles

Although numerous hypsometers of this type have been developed, the basic principle is the same for all of them. One first sights to the upper terminal of the height desired and takes a reading; one sights to the base of the tree, or the top of the stump, depending on the height desired, and takes a second reading. Figure 5-13*a* illustrates the situation, with the distance D and the angles α_1 and

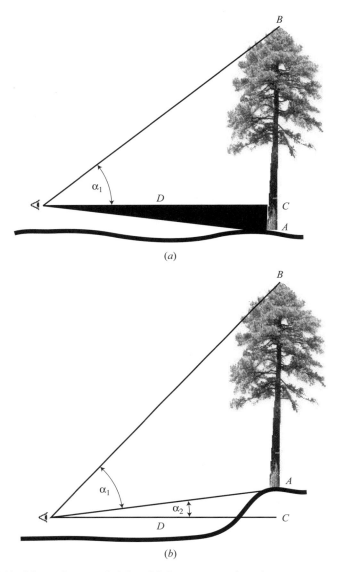

FIG. 5-13. Measuring tree height with hypsometers based on tangents of angles.

α_2 known. Then, if the vertical arc of the instrument is graduated in degrees, the total height of the tree may be calculated as follows:

$$\tan \alpha_1 = \frac{BC}{D}$$

from which we obtain

$$BC = D \tan \alpha_1$$

Similarly,

$$CA = D \tan \alpha_2$$

Since the height of the tree AB is $BC + CA$,

$$AB = D(\tan \alpha_1 + \tan \alpha_2) \tag{5-7}$$

On steep ground a situation as shown in Fig. 5-13b might occur. In this case, the height of the tree AB is $BC - CA$, and

$$AB = D(\tan \alpha_1 - \tan \alpha_2) \tag{5-8}$$

Hypsometers are often provided with arcs that are scaled rather than angular arcs. Scaled arcs, α_S, are based on angular units represented by the ratio of 1 unit vertically to D_S units horizontally. For any vertical angle α,

$$\tan \alpha = \frac{\alpha_S}{D_S} \tag{5-9}$$

where α = vertical angle
     α_S = scaled arc
     D_S = scale distance

The height of a tree is obtained using

$$AB = \frac{D}{D_S}\left(\alpha_{S,1} + \alpha_{S,2}\right) \tag{5-10}$$

where D = horizontal distance from tree
     D_S = scale distance
     $\alpha_{S,1}$ = upper scaled arc
     $\alpha_{S,2}$ = lower scaled arc

In the United States the percentage scale ($D_S = 100$ ft) and the topographic scale ($D_S = 66$ ft) have traditionally been used. Hypsometers with scales of 15, 20, 25, 30 and 45 are readily available. One should note that scales of this type (and this includes percentage and topographic scales) could be used with any units: feet, yards, meters, and so on. One has only to read the scale in the same unit as one measures the baseline. However, since scale numbers usually represent convenient base distances for tree measurement with a particular unit, the unit to use is generally indicated.

The most commonly used hypsometers in North America have been the Abney level, the Haga altimeter, the Blume–Leiss altimeter, and the Suunto clinometer (Fig. 5-14). The *Abney level* in its original form (Calkins and Yule, 1935) and modernized designs have been used for many years for measuring tree heights as well as land elevations. The instrument consists of a graduated arc mounted on a sighting tube about 6 in. long (Fig. 5-14*a*). The arc may have a degree, percentage, or topographic scale. When the level bubble, which is attached to the instrument, is rotated while a sight is taken, a small mirror inside the tube makes it possible to observe when the bubble is horizontal. Then the angle between the bubble tube and the sighting tube may be read on the arc.

The *Suunto clinometer* is a handheld device housed in a corrosion-resistant aluminum body (Fig. 5-14*b*). A jewel-bearing assembly supports the scale, and all moving parts are immersed in a damping liquid inside a hermetically sealed plastic capsule. The liquid dampens undue scale vibrations. The instrument is held to one eye and raised or lowered until the hairline is seen at the point of measurement. At the same time, the position of the hairline on the scale gives the reading. Due to an optical illusion, the hairline seems to continue outside the frame and can be observed at the point of measurement. The instrument is

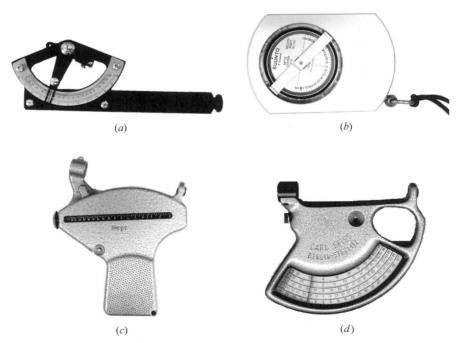

(*a*)   (*b*)

(*c*)   (*d*)

FIG. 5-14. Examples of hypsometers based on trigonometric principles: (*a*) Abney level; (*b*) Suunto clinometer; (*c*) Haga altimeter; (*d*) Blume–Leiss altimeter.

available with a rangefinder and several scale combinations: percent and degrees, percent and topographic, degrees and topographic, and feet and metric.

The *Haga altimeter* (Wesley, 1956) consists of a gravity-controlled, damped, pivoted pointer, and a series of scales on a rotatable, hexagonal bar in a metal, pistol-shaped case (Fig. 5-14c). The six regular American scales are 15, 20, 25, 30, percentage, and topographic scale. Sights are taken through a gun-type peep sight; squeezing a trigger locks the indicator needle, and the observed reading is taken on the scale. A rangefinder is available with this instrument.

The *Blume–Leiss altimeter* (Pardé, 1955) is similar in construction and operation to the Haga altimeter, although its appearance is somewhat different (Fig. 5-14d). The five regular metric scales are 15, 20, 30, and 40. A degree scale is also provided. All scales can be seen at the same time. The instrument is available with a rangefinder.

Hypsometers based on the tangents of angles are more accurate than those based on similar triangles. The Abney level, the Haga altimeter, the Blume–Leiss altimeter, and the Suunto clinometer are similar in accuracy. The Abney level, however, is slower to use, and large vertical angles are difficult to measure because of the effect of refraction on observations of the bubble through the tube from beneath. This makes the Abney level difficult to use in tall timber that is so dense that the tops cannot be seen from a considerable distance. A choice among the other three instruments is largely a matter of personal preference.

The *Spiegel relaskop* (Fig. 5-7a), originally designed for use in polyareal sampling (see Section 11-3), can be used as a clinometer with readings in degrees or percent that permit the calculation of tree height.

Recently, a variety of advanced electronic hypsometers have become commercially available. Some examples of these hypsometers are shown in Fig. 5-15. The Forest-Meter FL 8/2 (Fig. 5-15a) is a digital version of the Blume–Leiss hypsometer manufactured by the German firm Höhen- und Neigungsmesser. This instrument uses an optical rangefinder to measure horizontal distances and calculates height based on angular measurements. The Impulse Forest Pro laser hypsometer (Fig. 5-15b), manufactured by the U.S. firm Laser Technology (Denver, Colorado) and the Opti-logic 100LH (Fig. 5-15c) and 400LH, manufactured by the U.S. firm Opti-Logic (Tullahoma, Tennessee) are other examples of laser-based hypsometers. Both instruments can operate in reflector-less modes or reflector modes. When operated in reflector mode, a special laser reflector has to be placed on the tree being measured. The reflector improves accuracy in heavy undergrowth. Like the Forest-Meter, these instruments measure horizontal distances and calculate tree height based on angular measurements. The Haglöf Vertex III hypsometer (Fig. 5-15d) uses ultrasonic pulses together with a transponder fixed to the tree. The instrument measures distance, angle, and horizontal distance to the transponder and displays tree height. The Jenoptic LEDHA-Geo (Fig. 5-8) is also capable of laser-based distance and height measurement.

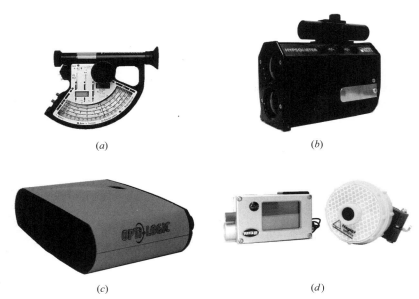

FIG. 5-15. Examples of electronic hypsometers: (*a*) Forest-Meter FL 8/2; (*b*) Impulse laser hypsometer; (*c*) 100LH; (*d*) Vertex III hypsometer.

Because these instruments are very advanced and display results at a fine resolution (centimeters for most devices), there is a tendency to mistake precision for accuracy (Skovsgaard et al., 1998). These instruments should be initially calibrated and the calibration checked frequently, especially after out-of-service periods and when temperatures fluctuate. When using reflector-less lasers, care must be exercised to ensure that the laser beam is reflected from the target tree and not from objects between the observer and the target tree. These instruments are also prone to the same measurement errors as the mechanical hypsometers (Section 5-3.3).

The major advantage of these devices is that horizontal distances are measured very precisely and potential calculation errors are eliminated. A major disadvantage of many of these instruments is their bulkiness. The Vertex III, which is similar in size to the Suunto clinometer, represents a major breakthrough in size for electronic hypsometers. The cost of these instruments (US$800 to US$3000) is also high relative to the mechanical instruments (US$100 to US$400). However, the increased speed of measurement makes these instruments economical over the long run.

5-3.3   Special Considerations in Measuring Tree Heights

It is difficult to measure accurately the height of large flat-crowned trees. There is a tendency to overestimate their heights (Fig. 5-16*a*). Care must be exercised

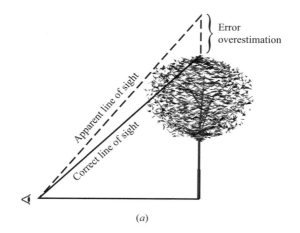

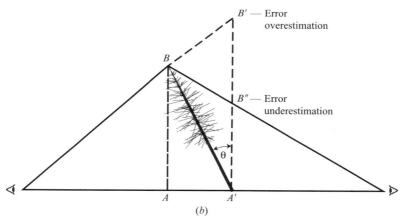

FIG. 5-16. Errors in tree height measurement: (*a*) correctly identify top of tree; (*b*) estimate error of leaning trees.

to focus the hypsometer on the tip of the tree; otherwise, total height determination for such trees are of little value. In general, the optimum viewing distance for any hypsometer is the distance along the slope equal to the height to be measured. This rule of thumb, which is adapted from Beers (1974), should be used with discretion. For example, if one were using a Suunto clinometer with a percentage scale to determine the merchantable height of a tree estimated to be about 56 ft, it would be logical to use a viewing distance of about 50 ft.

Since all hypsometers assume that trees are vertical, trees leaning away from an observer will be underestimated and trees leaning toward an observer will be overestimated (Fig. 5-16*b*). This error will be minimized if measurements are taken such that the lean is to the left or right of the observer. If leaning trees are to be measured, one should determine the point on the ground where a plumb bob would fall if suspended from the tip of the tree (point A on Fig. 5-16b). Then height should be measured from this point to the tip (point B on Fig. 5-16b). If stem length (distance $A'B$ on Fig. 5-16b) is desired, the measured height (AB) is multiplied by the secant of the angle of lean (θ). The difference will be small except for abnormally leaning trees.

The measurement of tree height with an accurate hypsometer is slow and expensive. Consequently, it is customary to make ocular estimates whenever precision is not essential, such as for commercial timber inventories where none of the required values are determined precisely, and where the large number of trees measured makes precision of individual measurements unimportant. An experienced person can obtain reliable ocular estimates. Ocular estimates are, however, subject to serious errors because of sudden changes in the timber type or the weather. Furthermore, most people do not make reliable estimates at the start of the day or after a rest. Consequently, estimates should be checked frequently by instrumental measurements.

5-4. FORM

The form of the main stem of a tree has been the subject of many studies and methods of expression in forest mensuration. The stimulus for studying form is its relation to the cubic volume of the tree. The form of the main stem of trees varies due to differences in the rates of diminution in diameter from the base to the tip. The diminution in diameter, known as *taper*, which varies with species, dbh, and age of trees and with sites, is the fundamental reason for variation in volume.

In a definitive study, Larson (1963) discussed the biological concept of stem form by a comprehensive review of the literature. Prodan (1965) presented a detailed summary of European approaches to the description of stem form, which was updated in Prodan et al. (1997). Form factors, form quotients, form point, and taper tables, curves, and formulas can express stem form. In all cases the ultimate objective is to utilize the expressions in the estimation of tree cubic volume.

5-4.1 Form Factors

A *form factor* is the ratio of tree volume to the volume of a geometrical solid, such as a cylinder, a cone, or a cone frustum, that has the same diameter and height as the tree. (The diameter of the geometrical solid is taken at its base; the diameter of the tree is taken at breast height.) A form factor is different from other measures of form in that it can be calculated only after the volume of the tree is known. In formula form, the form factor f is

$$f = \frac{V}{V_{gs}} \tag{5-11}$$

where $V =$ volume of tree
$V_{gs} =$ volume of geometrical solid of same diameter and height

Early in the nineteenth century it was recognized in Europe that the form of tree stems approached that of the solids discussed in Chapter 6. It was also recognized that there were many variations in form and that a tree rarely was of the exact form of one of these solids. Thus the form factor was conceived as a method of coordinating form and volume. The main objective of this early work was to derive factors that would be independent of diameter and height and by which the volume of standard geometrical solids could be multiplied to obtain the tree volume. For example, the ratio of the volumes of a paraboloid to a cylinder is 0.5 when the base diameter and the height of the two solids are equal: The volume of the paraboloid is obtained by multiplying the volume of the cylinder by 0.5.

The *cylindrical form factor* f_c, which has been the most commonly used, may be expressed by the equation

$$f_c = \frac{V}{gh} \tag{5-12}$$

where $V =$ volume of tree (cubic units)
$g =$ cross-sectional area of cylinder whose diameter equals tree dbh
$h =$ height of cylinder whose height equals tree height

This form factor has also been called the *false form factor*. The form factor based on cross-sectional area determined from the tree diameter at one-tenth of total height ($H/10$) has been termed the *real* or *true form factor* (Prodan et al., 1997). The usefulness of form factors to estimate the volume of trees of variable form is limited. However, there are some uses for the rapid approximation of volume as well as the volume of trees of little form variation.

5-4.2 Form Quotients

A *form quotient* is the ratio of a diameter measured at some height above breast height, such as one-half tree height, to diameter at breast height. In formula form the form quotient q is

$$q = \frac{d_h}{d} \tag{5-13}$$

where $d_h =$ diameter at height h above breast height
$d =$ dbh

Next to diameter at breast height and height, form quotient is the most important variable that can be used to predict volume of a tree stem. Thus it may be used as the third independent variable in the construction of volume tables (Chapter 6).

The original form quotient (Schiffel, 1899) took diameter at one-half total tree height $d_{0.5h}$ as the numerator and diameter at breast height d as the denominator. This was termed the *normal form quotient* $q_{0.5}$:

$$q_{0.5} = \frac{d_{0.5h}}{d}$$ (5-14)

For this form quotient, as tree height decreases, the position of the upper diameter comes closer to the breast height point until, for a tree whose height is double breast height, they coincide. To eliminate this anomaly, Jonson (1912) changed the position of the upper diameter to a point halfway between the tip of the tree and breast height $d_{1/2(h-4.5)}$ and called the ratio the *absolute form quotient* q_a:

$$q_a = \frac{d_{1/2(h-4.5)}}{d}$$ (5-15)

The absolute form quotient is a better measure of stem form than the normal form quotient. However, it is not a pure expression of stem form. It is not independent of diameter and height and it varies within a diameter–height class for a given species. For most species absolute form quotients diminish with increasing diameters and heights, varying between 0.60 and 0.80. The absolute form quotient is 0.707 for a paraboloid, 0.500 for a cone, and 0.354 for a neiloid when the diameter is taken at the base. These values hold irrespective of the diameter and height of the solid.

In determining the normal or absolute form quotient, the two diameters may be taken either outside or inside bark. Although it is difficult to obtain an accurate upper-stem-diameter inside bark, the ratio of the inside bark measurements is a better index of form than the outside bark measurements, because variable bark thicknesses do not then distort the ratio.

Originally the term *form class* was applied to classes of absolute form quotients, as in a frequency table. For example, form classes with intervals of 0.05 have been laid out as follows: 0.575–0.625, 0.625–0.675, 0.675–0.725, and 0.725–0.775. The midpoints of these classes, 0.60, 0.65, 0.70, and 0.75, were used to name the classes, and a tree falling into a particular class was said to have the form quotient of the midpoint of the class. Tree volume computations were classified by absolute form class as well as by diameter and height. Form class may be related to the density of the stand (Jonson, 1912) or to the form point.[*]

---

[*]*Form point* is the percentage ratio of the height to the center of wind resistance on the tree, approximately at the center of gravity of the crown, to the total tree height (Jonson, 1912). The greater the form point, the more nearly cylindrical will be the form of the tree. Fogelberg (1953) reported a study where form points were estimated for the various diameter classes of a standard. At present the form point is rarely used in forest mensuration.

In North America the term *form class* has been used in a different sense. In the course of work with the U.S. Forest Service, Girard (1933) developed a form quotient for use as an independent variable in volume table construction. This measure, termed *Girard form class*, q_g, is the percentage ratio of diameter inside bark at the top of the first standard log d_u to diameter at breast height, outside bark. When 16-ft logs are taken as the standard, the upper diameter $d_{u17.3}$ is taken at the height of a standard 1-ft stump plus 16.3 ft. Thus

$$q_g = 100\left(\frac{d_{u17.3}}{d}\right) \tag{5-16}$$

Girard form class is a useful form quotient that has been widely employed in U.S. forestry practice.

Efforts to develop form quotients that can be computed from more accessible diameters have led to a number of form quotients of the type advocated by Maass (1939). *Maass's form quotient* is the ratio of the diameter at 2.3 m above the ground to diameter at 1.3 m above the ground. However, unpublished studies by Miller (1959) of similar form quotients indicated that this quotient, whether measurements are inside or outside bark, is too variable for trees of the same species, diameter, and height to be of practical use.

5-4.3 Taper Tables, Curves, and Formulas

If sufficient measurements of diameters are taken at successive points along the stem of a tree, one can prepare average taper tables that give a good picture of stem form. Flewelling et al. (2000) describe a method for predicting upper stem diameters based on three measurements: dbh, total height, and one or more upper-stem-diameter measurements. Their multipoint profile system allows for upper stem measurements at any height and constructs a smooth profile prediction that passes through all the measurement points.

The ultimate purpose of all taper tables is to show upper stem diameters, which can then be used to calculate the volume of the sections of a tree and the entire tree as described in Section 6-1. Taper tables can assume several forms. Table 5-2 is an example of a taper table showing upper-log taper rates inside bark for standard log lengths according to diameter at breast height and merchantable height of standard logs. Table 5-3 is an example of another form of taper table. It shows the diameters of the stem at increasing heights as percentages of dbh. Separate tables are prepared for species and total height classes. Within each height class, table percentages are shown for different dbh classes.

5-5. CROWN PARAMETERS

Research over the past 20 years has begun to focus on understanding the mechanisms involved in forest growth and dynamics. Since foliage is the

TABLE 5-2. Average Upper-Log Taper Inside Bark (in.) in 16-ft Logs

dbh (in.)	Two-Log Tree 2nd Log	Three-Log Tree 2nd Log	3rd Log	Four-Log Tree 2nd Log	3rd Log	4th Log
10	1.4	1.2	1.4			
12	1.6	1.3	1.5	1.1	1.4	1.9
14	1.7	1.4	1.6	1.2	1.5	2.0
16	1.9	1.5	1.7	1.2	1.6	2.1
18	2.0	1.6	1.8	1.3	1.7	2.2
20	2.1	1.7	1.9	1.4	1.8	2.4
22	2.2	1.8	2.0	1.4	2.0	2.5
24	2.3	1.8	2.2	1.5	2.2	2.6
26	2.4	1.9	2.3	1.5	2.3	2.7
28	2.5	1.9	2.5	1.6	2.4	2.8
30	2.6	2.0	2.6	1.7	2.5	3.0

Source: Adapted from Mesavage and Girard (1946).

primary source of photosynthates in most forest vegetation, the use of crown dimensions, as a surrogate for foliage, has become an integral part of many forest growth and yield studies. Crown dimensions are also useful for predicting wildlife habitat value and monitoring forest health.

5-5.1 Crown Diameter and Area

Crown diameter measurements can be used to estimate diameter at breast height and therefore tree volume (Francis, 1986). This parameter is also utilized in tree and forest health monitoring (Tallent-Halsell, 1994). Estimates of crown

TABLE 5-3. Taper Percentages (Percent of dbh at Height on Tree) (Species × Total Height Class 30 m)

Height Location on Tree (m)	dbh Class (cm) 20–25	25–30	⋯	45–50
1	102.9	103.0		103.5
3	92.6	92.0		88.4
5	86.8	86.5		81.4
⋮	⋮	⋮		⋮
27	18.8	17.8		14.7
30	0.0	0.0		0.0

Source: Adapted from Prodan et al. (1997).

diameter are also used to determine the ratio of crown diameter to dbh and for estimating the crown competition factor (Chapter 8). Measurements can be made on vertical aerial photographs, if available, or by field measurements. Field determination is difficult because of the irregularity of a tree crown's outline. The field technique is to project the perimeter of the crown vertically to the ground and to make diameter measurements on this projection (Fig. 5-17a). The usual procedure is to take the average of the diameter of the crown's widest point and a second measurement at right angles. Most instruments used to achieve the vertical projection incorporate a mirror, a right-angle prism, or a pentaprism (Fig. 5-17b); they may be handheld or staff-mounted. Instruments that employ the pentaprism are recommended because they do not invert or revert images, and because slight movement of the prism will not affect the true right angle of reflection. Instruments and methods for determining vertical crown projection have been described by Husch (1947), Nash (1948), Raspopov (1955), Shepperd (1973), Cailliez (1980), and Tallent-Halsell (1994).

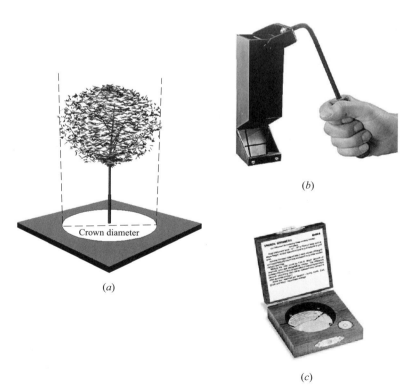

Crown diameter

(a)

(b)

(c)

FIG. 5-17. Crown projection measurement: (a) crown projection area; (b) right-angle prism densiometer; (c) spherical crown densiometer.

Crown diameters measured on vertical aerial photographs are more clearly defined than those measured on the ground, although crown diameters measured on aerial photographs are smaller than those measured on the ground, because parts of the crown are not resolved on photographs. However, the photo measurement is probably a better measure of the functional growing space of a tree and is better correlated with tree and stand volume.

Crown cross-sectional area is calculated from the formula for the area of a circle using one of the following: the average of the maximum and minimum crown diameters, two diameters at right angles, or from the maximum diameter and another at right angles to it.

5-5.2 Other Crown Characteristics

Crown surface area and volume can be estimated from crown diameter and length. Hamilton (1975) gives formulas for several assumed geometrical shapes. Schreuder et al. (1993) indicate that the crown surface area and volume for conifers and young hardwoods can be estimated as cones from the following:

$$S = \pi d_b \left(\frac{L}{2}\right) \tag{5-17}$$

and

$$V = \pi d_b \left(\frac{l}{12}\right) \tag{5-18}$$

where S = crown surface area (m^2 or ft^2)
  V = crown volume (m^3 or ft^2)
  d_b = diameter at crown base (m or ft)
  L = sloping length (m or ft) from apex of crown to base
  l = crown length (m or ft)

Sheng et al. (2001) describe a method of determining the crown surface area of conifers using digital photogrammetry.

Other crown characteristics used in tree and forest health monitoring are crown density, live crown ratio, crown dieback, and foliage transparency. Techniques for their measurement are presented in Tallent-Halsell (1994) and USDA (1998). Measurements for each variable are made for each tree. The measurements are estimated into 5 percent rating classes ranging from 0 to 100 percent. The ratings are based on the estimated percentage of the tree's crown that meets the definition of the variable.

Crown density is the amount of crown branches, foliage, and reproductive structures that blocks light visibility through the crown. A crown density–transparency card is used for making this estimate. The higher the rating, the denser and, presumably, healthier the tree. A spherical crown densiometer (Fig. 5-17c) is also used for estimating crown density and canopy coverage.

Live crown ratio is the percentage of total height supporting live foliage that is effectively contributing to tree growth. It is the ratio of live crown length to total tree height.

Crown dieback is recent mortality of branches with fine twigs, which begins at the terminal portion of a branch and proceeds toward the trunk and/or base of the live crown. The lower the rating, the lower the mortality and presumably the healthier the tree.

Foliage transparency is the amount of background (skylight, foliage of other trees) visible through the live normally foliated portion of the crown or branch. The lower the rating, the thicker the foliage and presumably the healthier the tree.

6

DETERMINATION OF TREE VOLUME

Although the most important portion of a tree, in terms of usable wood, is the stem, a tree can be considered as consisting of four parts: *roots, stump, stem,* and *crown.* The *roots* are the underground part of the tree that supplies it with nourishment. The *stump* is the lower end of the tree that is left above the ground after the tree has been felled. The *stem* is the main ascending axis of the tree above the stump. (Trees that have the axis prolonged to form an undivided main stem, as exemplified by many conifers, are termed *excurrent*; trees that have the axis interrupted in the upper portion due to branching, as exemplified by many broadleaved species, are termed *deliquescent.*) The *crown* consists of the primary and secondary branches growing out of the main stem, together with twigs and foliage.

In the past, since the roots and stumps of trees were less often utilized, little attention was given to the determination of their volume. Now, with increased interest in complete tree utilization and quantification of total biomass, estimation of the volume (and weight) of the roots and stump, as well as the crown of trees, is often important.

There has been, and continues to be, a need to determine the volume of crowns because crown-volume data may be used to describe fuel hazards, to estimate volume of material left from line-clearing operations, and to determine the volume of pulpwood and fuel wood in crowns. It is interesting to note that the cubic volume of the merchantable stem (to a 4-in. or 10-cm top diameter) of the average tree is about 55 to 65 percent of the cubic volume of the complete tree, excluding foliage, and that the cubic volume of the crown of the average tree, excluding foliage, is about 15 to 20 percent of the cubic volume of the complete tree, excluding foliage, for softwoods and 20 to 25 percent for hardwoods.

Since the stump, stem, and branches are all covered with bark, they are, when utilized, peeled in the woods or hauled, bark and all, to the mill where the bark is removed before the manufacturing process begins. Thus it is necessary to determine, at one time or another, unpeeled volume and bark volume. Volume has been, and will continue to be, the most widely used measure of wood quantity in forest mensuration, although weight as a measure of quantity has been increasing in importance. In the United States, the volume of trees is commonly expressed in *board feet* and *cubic feet*, although there is growing application of metric units. In countries that use the metric system, the volume of trees is generally expressed in *cubic meters* or some unit based on metric volume. Another unit, which was used frequently in Canada until the adoption of the metric system, was the *cunit*, or 100 cubic feet of solid wood.

6-1. DETERMINATION OF CUBIC VOLUME

Direct volume determinations of parts of trees are usually made on sample trees to obtain basic data for the development of relationships between the various dimensions of a tree and its volume (Sections 6-2 and 6-3). Relationships of this type are used to estimate the volumes of other standing trees. In the past, sample-tree measurements were often taken on trees cut in harvesting operations. Volume relationships developed from such measurements may lead to bias because they may not be representative of all trees in a stand. Preferably, measurements should be taken on a representative sample of all standing trees.

The direct determination of volume of any part of a tree involves clearly defining the part of the tree for which volume is to be determined and carefully taking measurements in accordance with the constraints imposed by the definition. For example, for purposes of measurement, we might include the portion of the stem above a fixed-height stump to a minimum upper-stem-diameter outside bark, or on stems that do not have a central tendency, to the point where the last merchantable cut can be made. For roots, we might include roots larger than some minimum diameter, and, for tops, we might include the branches and the tip of the stem to some minimum diameter outside the bark.

Generally speaking, a tree must be felled and the limbs cut into sections before one can obtain measurements to determine crown volume directly. To obtain measurements to determine root volume directly, roots must be lifted from the ground and the soil removed. For stem and stump volumes, however, the necessary measurements may be obtained from either standing or felled trees.

6-1.1 Determination of Cubic Volume by Formulas

Solid objects may assume the form of polyhedrons, solids of revolution, and solids of irregular shape. The standard formulas shown in Appendix Table A-3 can be used to compute the volumes of polyhedrons, such as cubes, prisms, and pyramids, and the volumes of solids of revolution, such as cones, cylinders, spheres, paraboloids, and neiloids.

The stems of excurrent trees are often assumed to resemble neiloids, cones, or paraboloids—solids that are obtained by rotating a curve of the general form $Y = K\sqrt{X^r}$ around the X-axis (Fig. 6-1). As the form exponent r in this equation changes, different solids are produced. When $r = 1$, a paraboloid is obtained; when $r = 2$, a cone; when $r = 3$, a neiloid; and when $r = 0$, a cylinder. However, the stems of excurrent trees are seldom exactly cones, paraboloids, or neiloids. In general, the form of most excurrent stems falls between the cone and the paraboloid. The merchantable portions of stems of deliquescent trees also resemble frustums of neiloids, cones or, paraboloids (occasionally cylinders). In general, they fall between the frustum of a cone and the frustum of a paraboloid.

It is more realistic, however, to consider the stem of any tree to be a composite of geometrical solids (Fig. 6-2). For example, when the stem is cut into logs or bolts, the tip approaches a cone or a paraboloid in form, the central sections approach frustums of paraboloids, or in a few cases, frustums of cones or cylinders, and the butt log approaches the frustum of a neiloid. Although the stump approaches the frustum of a neiloid in form, for practical purposes it is considered to be a cylinder.

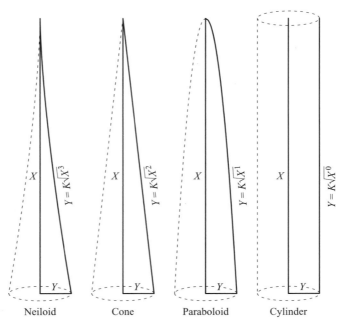

Neiloid   Cone   Paraboloid   Cylinder

FIG. 6-1. Solids of revolution descriptive of tree form.

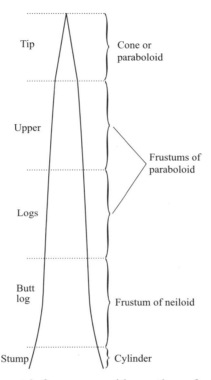

FIG. 6-2. Geometric forms assumed by portions of a tree stem.

Formulas to compute the cubic volume of the solids that have been of particular interest to mensurationists are given in Table 6-1. Newton's formula is exact for all the frustums we have considered. Smalian's and Huber's formulas are exact only when the solid is the frustum of a paraboloid.* For example, if the surface lines of a tree section are more convex than the paraboloid frustum, Huber's formula will overestimate the volume, whereas Smalian's formula will underestimate the volume. But if the surface lines of a tree section are less convex than the paraboloid frustum, as they often are, Smalian's formula will overestimate the volume, and Huber's formula will underestimate the volume. Assuming that Newton's formula gives correct volume values, it can be shown by subtracting Newton's formula first from Smalian's formula and then from Huber's formula that the error incurred by Smalian's formula is twice that incurred by Huber's formula and opposite in sign.

---

*Newton's formula is attributed to Sir Isaac Newton. Prodan (1965) claims that Huber's formula came into use in 1785 and Smalian's formula in 1894.

TABLE 6-1. Equations to Compute Cubic Volume of Important Solids

Geometric Solid	Equation for Volume V (cubic units)[a]	Equation Number
Cylinder	$V = A_b h$	(6-1)
Paraboloid	$V = \dfrac{1}{2}(A_b h)$	(6-2)
Cone	$V = \dfrac{1}{3}(A_b h)$	(6-3)
Neiloid	$V = \dfrac{1}{4}(A_b h)$	(6-4)
Paraboloid frustum	$V = \dfrac{h}{2}(A_b + A_u)$ (Smalian's formula)	(6-5)
	$V = A_m h$ (Huber's formula)	(6-6)
Cone frustum	$V = \dfrac{h}{3}\left(A_b + \sqrt{A_b A_u} + A_u\right)$	(6-7)
Neiloid frustum	$V = \dfrac{h}{4}\left(A_b + \sqrt[3]{A_b^2 A_u} + \sqrt[3]{A_b A_u^2} + A_u\right)$	(6-8)
Neiloid, cone, or paraboloid frustum	$V = \dfrac{h}{6}(A_b + 4A_m + A_u)$ (Newton's formula)	(6-9)

[a] A_b, cross-sectional area at base; A_m, cross-sectional area at middle; A_u, cross-sectional area at upper end; h, height or length.

In a study by Young et al. (1967) on 8- and 16-ft softwood logs of 4- to 12-in. diameters, volumes calculated by Newton's, Smalian's, and Huber's formulas were compared with volumes determined by displacement. Average percent errors of about 0 percent were obtained for Newton's formula, +9 percent for Smalian's formula, and −3.5 percent for Huber's formula. They also found that there were no significant errors for any of the three formulas on 4-ft bolts. In a study by Miller (1959) on 16-ft hardwood logs of 8- to 22-in. diameters, volumes calculated by the three formulas were compared with volumes determined by graphical techniques. Average errors of about +2 percent were obtained for Newton's formula, +12 percent for Smalian's formula, and −5 percent for Huber's formula.

It should now be apparent that in calculating cubic volume of trees and logs, mensurationists should select their methods carefully. Unless one is willing to accept a rather large error, Smalian's formula should not be used unless it is possible to measure sections of the tree in short lengths (4 ft or about 1 m). For longer lengths, such as logs of 8 or 16 ft (about 3 to 6 m), Newton's or Huber's formulas will give more accurate results.[*]

[*]A number of other formulas for calculating the cubic volume of logs or section were developed in European forestry, such as formulas of Hossfeld, Simony, Gauss and Simony, and Gieruszinski that are described in Prodan (1965) and Prodan et al. (1997). Japan has developed the following formulas which are used in international commerce with this country.

Newton's formula will give accurate results for all sections of a tree except for butt logs with excessive butt swell. For such butt logs, Huber's formula will generally give better results. Either the paraboloidal formula [eq. (6-2), Table 6-1] or the conic formula [eq. (6-3), Table 6-1] is appropriate to determine the volume of the tip. The cylindrical formula [eq. (6-1), Table 6-1] is normally used to compute the volume of the stump, although the stump actually approaches the neiloid frustum in form. Newton's and Huber's formulas cannot, of course, be applied to stacked logs, because it is not possible to measure the middle diameters.

Newton's formula may be used to compute the volume of the merchantable stem or of the total stem. If the sections are of the same length, the procedure can be summarized in a single formula. To illustrate, consider a stem with diameters from the top of the stump to a point where the last merchantable cut will be made, $d_0, d_1, d_2, d_3, d_4, d_5,$ and d_6, located at intervals of h units of length (Fig. 6-3a). To give each section three diameters, the volume is computed by sections of $2h$ length (Fig. 6-3b). With Newton's formula the volume in cubic feet V is then

$$V = \frac{2h}{6}c\left(d_0^2 + 4d_1^2 + d_2^2\right) + \frac{2h}{6}c\left(d_2^2 + 4d_3^2 + d_4^2\right) + \frac{2h}{6}c\left(d_4^2 + 4d_5^2 + d_6^2\right)$$

$$= \frac{2h}{6}c\left(d_0^2 + 4d_1^2 + 2d_2^2 + 4d_3^2 + 2d_4^2 + 4d_5^2 + d_6^2\right)$$

$$= \frac{2h}{3}c\left(\frac{d_0^2}{2} + 2d_1^2 + d_2^2 + 2d_3^2 + d_4^2 + 2d_5^2 + \frac{d_6^2}{2}\right)$$

where d_i = diameter (in. or cm) at ith measurement point
$\quad\quad\quad h$ = distance (ft or m) between measurement points
$\quad\quad\quad c$ = diameter to cross-sectional area conversion factor (0.005 454 for English system and 0.000 078 54 for metric system)

(*footnote continued*)

logs of less than 6 m length: $V = \dfrac{d^2 l}{10,000}$

logs of 6 m or more length: $V = \left(d + \dfrac{l' - 4}{2}\right)^2 \left(\dfrac{l}{10,000}\right)$

where V = volume (m^3)
$\quad\quad\quad d$ = smaller diameter rounded to lower even number (cm)
$\quad\quad\quad l$ = approximate length (m), rounded to lower 20 cm (e.g., 4.36 m rounded to 4.20 m)
$\quad\quad\quad l'$ = approximate length (m), rounded to lower whole meter (e.g., 4.36 m rounded to 4 m)

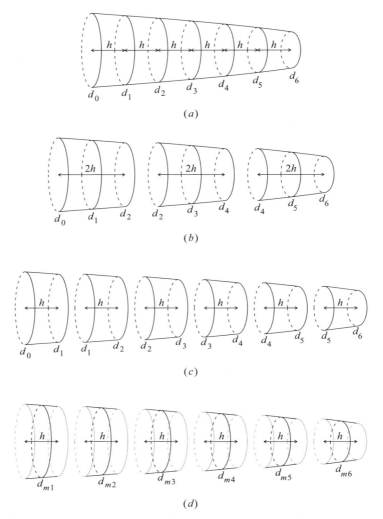

FIG. 6-3. Stem volume calculations: (*a*) log measurements; (*b*) Newton's method; (*c*) Smalian's method; (*d*) Huber's method.

This formula may be extended for as many sections as desired, provided that there are an odd number of diameters (i.e., an even number of sections of h length).

If the number of diameters measured is even, the last interval of h cannot be computed by Newton's formula, because it will have only two end diameters. Thus its volume must be found by Smalian's formula and added to the previous formula. For eight diameters, or seven intervals of h length, this yields

$$V = \frac{2h}{3}c\left(\frac{d_0^2}{2} + 2d_1^2 + d_2^2 + 2d_3^2 + d_4^2 + 2d_5^2 + \frac{5d_6^2}{4} + \frac{3d_7^2}{4}\right)$$

Grosenbaugh (1948) described a systematic procedure using this method.

The volume of the merchantable stem can also be calculated with good accuracy using Smalian's formula if the stem is divided into short sections. To illustrate, consider a stem with diameters measured from the top of the stump to a point where the last merchantable cut will be made, $d_0, d_1, d_2, \ldots, d_n$, located at intervals of h units of length along the stem (Fig. 6-3c). Then, according to Smalian's formula,

$$V = \frac{h}{2}c(d_0^2 + d_1^2) + \frac{h}{2}c(d_1^2 + d_2^2) + \cdots + \frac{h}{2}c(d_{n-1}^2 + d_n^2)$$

$$= \frac{h}{2}c(d_0^2 + 2d_1^2 + 2d_2^2 + \cdots + 2d_{n-1}^2 + d_n^2)$$

$$= hc\left(\frac{d_0^2}{2} + d_1^2 + d_2^2 + \cdots + d_{n-1}^2 + \frac{d_n^2}{2}\right)$$

To adapt Huber's formula to the computation of merchantable stem volumes, the diameter measurements are taken at the midpoints of the sections (Fig. 6-3d). When diameter measurements $d_{m1}, d_{m2}, \ldots, d_{mn}$ are taken at the midpoints of sections of h length, Huber's formula yields

$$V = hcd_{m1}^2 + hcd_{m2}^2 + \cdots + hcd_{mn}^2$$

$$= hc(d_{m1}^2 + d_{m2}^2 + \cdots + d_{mn}^2)$$

An example illustrating the calculations for each method is shown in Table 6-2 for a sample stem section.

6-1.2 Determination of Cubic Volume by Other Methods

Displacement. The most accurate method of measuring volume of an irregularly shaped solid is by measuring the volume of water that it will displace. For example, the cubic volume of any part of a tree may be found by submerging it in a tank in which the water displacement can be read accurately. To use such a tank, which is termed a *xylometer*, to measure the volume of a tree, it is necessary to fell the tree and cut it into sections that are small enough to fit into the tank. An example of the use of a xylometer to determine tree volume is found in Young et al. (1967).

TABLE 6-2. Sample Stem Measurements for Determination of Volume Using Newton's, Smalian's, and Huber's Methods

Measurement Number	Diameter (cm)	Length (m)	d^2 (cm^2)	Volume (m^3)			Huber's		
				Newton's	Smalian's	Midpoint d (cm)	d_m^2 (cm^2)	Volume (m^3)
0	24.6		605.16					
1	23.4	1.0	545.36	0.0855	0.0452	23.9	569.62	0.0447
2	21.9	1.0	479.14		0.0402	22.5	505.75	0.0397
3	20.1	1.0	403.95	0.0641	0.0347	21.2	447.89	0.0352
4	18.8	1.0	355.13		0.0298	19.5	378.76	0.0297
5	17.0	1.0	287.70	0.0459	0.0252	17.9	319.32	0.0251
6	15.8	1.0	248.10		0.0210	16.3	266.05	0.0209
Total				0.1956	0.1962			0.1954

Integration. The volume of a solid with known cross sections can also be obtained by summation of the volumes of cross-sectional slices of the solid. As shown in Section 6-1.1, a sum of such volumes approximates the volume of the solid. We take the integral that is suggested by this sum to be the volume

$$V = \int_a^b A(X)\, dX$$

in which the volume of a slice is expressed as a function $A(X)$ of X, times thickness dX, where thickness approaches zero. This procedure can be used for solids of any shape for which cross-sectional area can be expressed as a function.

Whenever the profile of a tree or section can be expressed by an equation, the formula for the stem volume obtained by rotating the graph of the equation $Y = f(X)$ about the X-axis (between $x = a$ and $X = b$) may be written as

$$V = \pi \int_a^b Y^2\, dX$$

In the integral, the radius Y of the solid of revolution must be expressed as a function of X. A cylinder is formed by rotating a rectangle around one side, a cone by rotating a right triangle around the vertical leg, a sphere by rotating a semicircle around the diameter, and a paraboloid by rotating a second-degree polynomial around its axis. The generalized formulas for the volumes of the solids shown in Appendix Table A-3 can be derived from the integral shown above by substituting the appropriate $f(X)$ for Y. For solids of revolution formed by curves of other shapes, simple formulas such as these are not available; integration is required to obtain volume.

To illustrate the procedure by a simple example, we will use Fig. 5-9 and compute the volume of the stem shown in the figure between a 1-ft stump and an upper limit that is 10 ft from the top (in Fig. 5-9, length is measured from the tip of the tree, therefore, the integral is over the range 10 to 59). The volume would then be

$$V = \pi \int_{10}^{59} 0.066X\, dX$$

Integrating and evaluating yields

$$V = \left(\frac{\pi \cdot 0.066X^2}{2}\right)_{10}^{59} = \left(0.104X^2\right)_{10}^{59}$$

$$= 0.104(59^2) - 0.104(10^2)$$

$$= 351.6\, \text{ft}^3$$

Since this solid is the frustum of a paraboloid, eq. (6-5) in Table 6-1 will yield the same result.

Graphical Method. A graphical method can be used for measuring the volume of solids that have circular cross section but that vary in diameter along an axis normal to the cross sections. To obtain the volume of a tree or section, one must have diameter measurements along the stem or section, preferably both inside and outside bark. It is most convenient to have measurements that were made at regular intervals; however, if sufficient diameter measurements are made so that the taper of the tree is depicted accurately, the measurements may be made at any chosen interval.

With suitable taper measurements for a given tree or section, the cross-sectional area or diameter squared, inside and outside bark, should be plotted over height on cross-sectional paper for each cross section measured. Then the points should be connected by smooth lines to give a profile that is analogous to that of one side of a longitudinal section taken through the center of the tree or section. A separate graph is prepared for each tree stem or section.

For the graph of a tree stem, it is useful to label diameters at important points, such as top of stump, breast height, log ends, and merchantable limit of the stem, and to record pertinent information on species, locality, observers, date, and so on. Measuring the required area on the graph and applying the appropriate conversion factor, one can obtain volume for the entire stem, or for any section, either inside or outside bark. For example, in Fig. 6-4, diameter squared is plotted over length for a section of a tree. The area under the curve can be obtained by using a planimeter or a dot grid, and converted to cubic

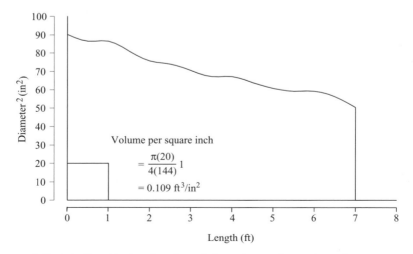

FIG. 6-4. Graphical estimation of the volume of a section of a tree.

volume by multiplying by cubic feet per square inch (or cubic meters per square centimeter) represented by the graph. Specifically,

$$C_f = AL$$

where C_f = conversion factor for ft^3/in^2 of graph (or m^3/cm^2 of graph)
$\quad\quad$ A = cross-sectional area per inch or centimeter of Y-axis
$\quad\quad$ L = length per inch or centimeter of X-axis

In the example, the conversion factor for ft^3/in^2 of graph is

$$C_f = \frac{\pi d^2}{4(144)} L$$

$$= 0.005454(20)(1)$$

$$= 0.109 \, \text{ft}^3/\text{in}^2$$

Since the area under the curve of the section is 24.75 in^2, the volume of the section is 24.75(0.109) = 2.70 ft^3.

6-1.3   Determination of Volume by Height Accumulation

The height accumulation concept was conceived and developed by Grosenbaugh (1948, 1954), who stated that the system can be applied by selecting tree diameters above breast height in diminishing arithmetic progression, say 1- or 2-in taper intervals, and estimating, recording, and accumulating tree height to each successive diameter. The system uses diameter as the independent variable instead of height, is well adapted to use with electronic computers, and permits segregation of volume by classes of material, log size, or grade. However, since optimum log lengths for top log grades depend on factors other than diameter, the best grades may not be secured.

To apply the system one must know the following information: L, the number of unit height sections between taper steps; H, the total number of L values below a given diameter; and H', the cumulative total of H values below a given diameter. If volume inside bark is desired, the mean bark factor k (see Section 6-1.4) is also required. Figure 6-5 illustrates the method for estimating cubic feet. In Fig. 6-5, diameter has been measured at stump height (0.5 ft) and at 4-ft intervals up the stem. In this example, 2-in taper steps and 4-ft unit height lengths are utilized. The stem measurements are used to determine the heights at which each taper step occurs. The first taper step ($d = 8$ in.) occurs at the top of the first unit length, thus $L_1 = 1$, $H_1 = 1$ and $H_1' = 1$. The second taper step ($d = 6$ in.) occurs at the top of the fourth height segment and $L_2 = 3$, $H_2 = 4$, and $H_2' = 5$. The complete height accumulation data for this tree would be

Diameter	L	H	H'
8	1	1	1
6	3	4	5
4	2	6	11
2	1	7	18
Total	7	18	35

Volume for this tree is then obtained from the equation

$$V = A\left(\sum H'\right) + B\left(\sum H\right) + C\left(\sum L\right) \tag{6-10}$$

where $A, B,$ and C = height accumulation coefficients
$L, H,$ and H' = are as above

The height accumulation coefficients for 2-in. taper steps and 4-ft unit heights are shown in Table 6-3 for various dib:dob ratios. Using a dib:dob ratio of 1 (i.e., volume outside bark), the example tree's volume would be estimated to be

$$V = 0.175(35) + 0(18) + 0.0291(7)$$
$$= 6.125 + 0 + 0.204$$
$$= 6.329 \, \text{ft}^3$$

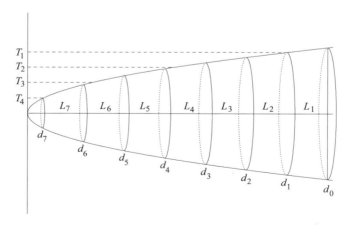

FIG. 6-5. Measurements for determination of volume by height accumulation.

TABLE 6-3. Height-Accumulation Coefficients *A*, *B*, and *C* Used to Compute Cubic-Foot Volume by 2-in. Taper Steps, 4-ft Unit Heights, and Various Mean dib:dob Ratios

Mean Ratio (dib:dob)	Volume Coefficients for Cubic Feet		
	A	*B*	*C*
1.00[a]	0.175	0	0.0291
0.95	0.158	0	0.0263
0.90	0.141	0	0.0236
0.85	0.126	0	0.0210

Source: Adapted from Grosenbaugh (1954).

[a]When computing volume outside bark, use coefficients for a ratio of 1.00.

The height accumulation method has no advantage for the simple volume estimation shown in Fig. 6-5. The technique has real utility in more complicated timber cruising applications. For example, Table 6-4 gives sample tree data needed to compute the volume V in cubic feet for a number of trees. Volume can be calculated for individual trees or for all trees combined using eq. (6-10) and the coefficients in Table 6-3. For the trees given in Table 6-4, the total cubic foot volume, inside bark, for a mean dib:dob ratio of 0.90 is

$$V = 0.141(210) + 0(94) + 0.0236(29) = 30.3 \, \text{ft}^3$$

TABLE 6-4. Sample Tree Data for Computation of Volume by Height Accumulation by 2-in. Taper Steps and 4-ft Unit Heights

Dbh	Dob Taper Steps					
	10	8	6	4	2	Sum
9.5	1	3	4	2	0	10
7.7		1	5	2	0	8
10.5	1	5	3	2	0	11
$L =$	2	9	12	6	0	29
$H =$	2	11	23	29	29	94
$H' =$	2	13	36	65	94	210

Similarly, individual-tree cubic-foot volume is

$$V_{9.5} = 0.141(75) + 0(33) + 0.0236(10) = 10.8\,\text{ft}^3$$
$$V_{7.7} = 0.141(46) + 0(23) + 0.0236(8) \quad= \;\; 6.7\;\text{ft}^3$$
$$V_{10.5} = 0.141(89) + 0(38) + 0.0236(11) = 12.8\,\text{ft}^3$$
$$\overline{30.3\,\text{ft}^3}$$

Grosenbaugh (1954) also gives coefficients for 1-in. taper steps and 1-ft unit heights, coefficients for determination of board-foot volume and surface area, formulas to calculate coefficients for other cases, and the theory of height accumulation. The potential utility of this unique system has generally been overlooked.

6-1.4   Bark Volume

Bark volume will average between 10 to 20 percent of unpeeled volume for most species. Often, one needs to know bark volume more accurately than this to determine peeled stem or log volume from unpeeled stem or log volume, the quantity of bark residue that will be left after the manufacturing process has been completed, and, in some cases, where the bark has value, the quantity of bark available. Of course, unpeeled stem or log volume can be computed from outside bark diameter and peeled stem or log volume from inside bark diameter. The difference between the two volumes is a good estimate of bark volume. However, the bark-factor method, which deserves more consideration than most foresters give it, is easier to apply and gives sufficiently accurate results for most purposes.

Bark thickness, which must be determined accurately to obtain reliable bark factors, may be determined as described in Section 5-2. The accuracy of bark measurements is increased if single-bark thickness is measured at two or more different points on a given cross section of the stem and if the average single-bark thickness b is computed. Then diameter inside bark d_{ib} may be computed from diameter outside bark d using $d_{ib} = d - 2b$. When d_{ib} is plotted as a function of d, the relationship will be linear, or close to linear, with a Y intercept approximately zero. Figure 6-6 shows this relationship for white oak for the cross section at breast height.

It is reasonable to assume that the prediction equation for this relationship may be written in the general form $d_{ib} = kd$. Because the regression coefficient k is normally determined at stump or breast height, it can be called the *lower-stem bark factor*. Such bark factors range from 0.87 to 0.93, varying with species, age, and site. However, since the major portion of the variation can be accounted for by species, it is reasonable and convenient to assume that this bark factor will remain the same, for a given species, at all heights on the stem.

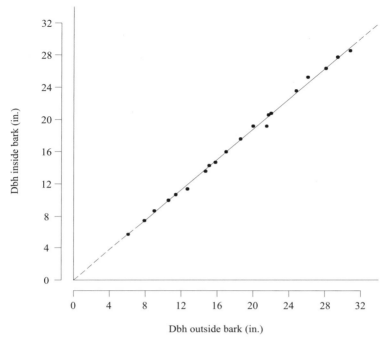

FIG. 6-6. Relationship between corresponding diameters inside and outside bark of white oak (see Table 6-5).

For many species, upper-stem bark factors often are not the same as lower-stem bark factors. To account for this, one might develop multiple regression equations to predict upper-stem bark factors from such variables as tree age, tree dbh, height above ground, and diameter outside bark at cross sections for which bark factor is desired. Examples of these equations can be found in Cao and Pepper (1986), Maguire and Hann (1990), and Muhairwe (2000).

The development of such equations requires much time spent on obtaining measurements in the field. Consequently, the common practice is to assume that the bark factor is the same at all heights on the stem. Whether we assume that the bark factor is the same at all heights on the stem or that the bark factor will be different at different heights on the stem, once the bark factor has been obtained, the method of using it to obtain bark volume is the same. In the following explanation it is assumed that k is the same at all heights on the stem.

An average value of k, to be reliable, should be based on 20 to 50 bark-thickness measurements and corresponding diameter–outside bark measurements. By the method of least squares, k is determined so that the sum of the squared deviation of the individual d_{ib} values (Y values) about the fitted regression line is a minimum. In this case, where we assume that when $d = 0$, then $d_{ib} = 0$, it is appropriate to use the following equation to determine k:

**TABLE 6-5. Diameter and Bark Measurements of
20 White Oak Trees**[a]

Dbh Outside Bark, d (in.)	Double Bark Thickness, $2b$ (in.)	Dbh Inside Bark, d_{ib} (in.)
30.8	2.2	28.6
14.7	1.1	13.6
24.8	1.2	23.6
20.0	0.8	19.2
21.7	1.1	20.6
7.9	0.4	7.5
15.8	1.1	14.7
12.7	1.3	11.4
18.6	1.0	17.6
17.0	1.0	16.0
26.1	0.8	25.3
28.1	1.7	26.4
10.6	0.6	10.0
6.1	0.4	5.7
29.4	1.6	27.8
15.1	0.8	14.3
21.5	2.3	19.2
22.0	1.2	20.8
11.4	0.7	10.7
9.0	0.3	8.7
Sum 363.3	21.6	341.7

[a]$\sum(dd_{ib}) = 7179.62$; $\sum d^2 = 7628.93$.

$$k = \frac{\sum(dd_{ib})}{\sum d^2}$$

When the variation of the dependent variable is proportional to the independent variable, as it generally is when d_{ib} is plotted over d, Meyer (1953) has shown that the following formula will give the same results:

$$k = \frac{\sum d_{ib}}{\sum d}$$

For the trees listed in Table 6-5 and plotted in Fig. 6-6, the first formula gives

$$k = \frac{7179.62}{7628.93} = 0.941$$

The second formula gives

$$k = \frac{341.7}{363.3} = 0.941$$

Agreement of these two formulas will not always be this good. In general, the second formula will, for practical uses, always give satisfactory results.

The bark thickness b, corresponding to an average value of k, can be determined as follows for any diameter d:

$$b = \frac{1}{2}(d - d_{ib})$$

and since $d_{ib} = kd$, then

$$b = \frac{1}{2}(d - kd) = \frac{d}{2}(1 - k) \tag{6-11}$$

Thus, for a white oak cross section 14.0 in. in diameter, the bark thickness is estimated to be

$$b = \frac{14.0}{2}(1 - 0.941)$$

$$= 0.413 \text{ in.}$$

The average value of k can also be used to obtain cubic bark volume V_B from cubic volume outside bark V for a given stem section. If diameter outside bark at the middle of the section d_m, diameter inside bark at the middle of the section $d_{m,ib}$, and section length L are all in the same units, we have

$$V = \frac{\pi d_m^2}{4}L \quad \text{and} \quad V_{ib} = \frac{\pi d_{m,ib}^2}{4}L$$

Because $d_{m,ib} = kd_m$, V_{ib} is then

$$V_{ib} = \frac{\pi}{4}(kd_m)^2 L = k^2 V \tag{6-12}$$

Finally

$$V_b = V - V_{ib} = V(1 - k^2) \tag{6-13}$$

and percent bark volume can be expressed as

$$V_b(\%) = (1 - k^2)(100) \tag{6-14}$$

When V_{ib} is determined by eq. (6-12), it will be theoretically correct. However, V_b determined by eq. (6-13) will be greater than the actual value. This is because V_b includes air spaces between the ridges of the bark. A study by Chamberlain and Meyer (1950) shows that the difference in volume between stacked-peeled and stacked-unpeeled cordwood is, on the average, 80 percent of the volume given by eq. (6-12). One might not expect this result. However, it comes about because in a stack of wood the ridges of the bark of one log will mesh with the ridges of another log, and because the weight of the logs will compress the bark. Thus, for practical purposes, eq. (6-13) can be rewritten to give the bark volume of cordwood in stacks V_{bs},

$$V_{bs} = 0.8V(1 - k^2) \qquad (6\text{-}15)$$

6-2. VOLUME TABLES

6-2.1 Estimation of Tree Volumes

A *volume table* is a tabulated statement of the average volumes of trees by one or more tree dimensions. In the United States, a majority of volume tables give volumes in board feet of lumber, although tables that give volumes in cubic units are available. In nations where the metric system is used, expression of volume in board feet is still common, although many volume tables give volume in cubic meters.

Tree volumes can be estimated from previously established relationships between certain tree dimensions and tree volume. Diameter, height, and form are the independent variables that are commonly used to determine the values of the dependent variable—tree volume. The final result is presented in formula or table form. The volume formula or volume table, then, gives the average content of individual trees (in board feet, cubic feet, cubic meters, cords or other units) in terms of one or more of the previously mentioned tree dimensions.

Local Volume Tables. Local volume tables give tree volumes in terms of diameter at breast height only. The term *local* is used because such tables are generally restricted to the local area for which the height–diameter relationship hidden in the table is relevant. Although local volume tables may be prepared from raw field data (i.e., from volume and diameter measurements for a sample of trees), they are normally derived from standard volume tables. Table 6-6 shows a typical local volume table.

Standard Volume Tables. Standard volume tables give volume in terms of diameter at breast height and merchantable or total height. Tables of this type may be prepared for individual species, or groups of species, and speci-

TABLE 6-6. Example of a Local Volume Table for Yellow Poplar (*Liriodendron tulipifera*) in Stark County, Ohio[a]

Dbh Outside Bark (in.)	Volume Per Tree (board feet)	Merchantable Length (ft)	Basis in Trees (number)
10	30	19.5	4
11	50	23	5
12	70	26.5	13
13	95	30	9
14	125	33	9
15	155	36.5	1
16	190	40	5
17	235	43	7
18	285	45.5	6
19	345	48	4
20	405	51	2
21	480	53.5	1
22	555	56	2
23	635	58	3
24	720	60	1
25	800	62	—
26	885	64	1
27	975	65.5	2
28	1065	67	1
29	1155	69	5
30	1245	70	9
31	1340	71.5	7
32	1435	72.5	7
33	1535	73.5	1
34	1630	74.5	1
35	1725	75	—
36	1825	76	—

Source: Adapted from Diller and Kellog (1940).

[a]Trees climbed and measured by personnel of Work Projects Administration Official Project 65-1-42-166, the Ohio Woodland Survey, using international rule ($\frac{1}{4}$-in. kerf)—merchantable stem to a variable top diameter. Measurements taken at 16-ft log lengths above a 2.0-ft stump height. Scaled as 16-ft logs and additional shorter top logs; top sections less than 8 ft in length scaled as fractions of an 8-ft log. Basis, 107 trees. Table prepared in 1939 by curving volume of merchantable length over dbh. Aggregate difference: Table is 0.8% low. Average percentage deviation of basic data from table, 19.4%.

fic localities. The applicability of a standard volume table, however, depends on the form of the trees to which it is applied rather than on species or locality; for each diameter–height class, the form of the trees to which the table is applied should agree with the form of the trees from which the table was prepared. Table 6-7 shows a typical standard volume table.

TABLE 6-7. Example of a Standard Volume Table, Using Board-Foot Volume, International $\frac{1}{4}$-in. Rule, for Red Oak (*Quercus rubra*) in Pennsylvania[a]

Dbh (in.)	Merchantable Height—Number of 16-ft Logs											
	$\frac{1}{2}$	1	$1\frac{1}{2}$	2	$2\frac{1}{2}$	3	$3\frac{1}{2}$	4	$4\frac{1}{2}$	5	$5\frac{1}{2}$	6
8	8	18	28	37	47	57						
9	11	23	35	48	60	73						
10	13	29	44	59	75	90	105	121				
11	17	35	54	72	91	109	128	146				
12	20	42	64	86	108	130	153	175	197			
13	24	50	76	102	128	153	179	205	231			
14	28	58	88	118	148	178	208	238	268	298	328	
15	33	67	102	136	170	205	239	274	308	343	377	
16	37	77	116	155	194	233	273	312	351	390	429	469
17		87	131	175	219	264	308	352	396	441	485	529
18		97	147	197	246	296	345	395	445	494	544	593
19		109	164	219	275	330	385	440	496	551	606	661
20		121	182	243	304	366	427	488	549	611	672	733
21			201	268	336	403	471	538	606	673	741	808
22			220	295	369	443	517	591	665	739	813	887
23			241	322	403	484	565	646	727	808	889	970
24			263	351	439	527	616	704	792	880	968	1057
25			285	381	477	572	668	764	859	955	1051	1147
26			309	412	516	619	723	826	930	1033	1137	1240
27				445	556	668	780	891	1003	1114	1226	1338
28				478	598	718	838	959	1079	1199	1319	1439
29				513	642	771	900	1028	1157	1286	1415	1543
30				549	687	825	963	1101	1238	1376	1514	1652
31					734	881	1028	1175	1322	1470	1617	1764
32					782	939	1096	1253	1409	1566	1723	1880
33					832	999	1165	1332	1499	1666	1832	1999
34					883	1060	1237	1414	1591	1768	1945	2122
35					936	1124	1311	1499	1686	1874	2061	2249
36					990	1189	1387	1586	1784	1983	2181	2379

Source: Adapted from Bartoo and Hutnik (1962).

[a]Stump height, 1 ft. Top diameter 8.0 in., inside bark. Block indicates extent of basic data. Basis, 210 trees. Sample trees scaled as 16-ft logs; top section measured to nearest foot. Standard error of regression coefficient = 0.00261. Proportion of variation accounted for by the regression = 0.974. Tabular values derived from regression $V = -1.84 + 0.01914D^2H$.

Form Class Volume Tables. Form class volume tables give volumes in terms of diameter at breast height, merchantable or total height, and some measure of form, such as the Girard form class or absolute form quotient. Such tables come in sets, with one table for each form class. The format of each table is similar to that of a standard volume table. Note that if a single form class table is chosen as representative of a stand, volume determinations may be in error because it is unlikely that all trees will be of the same form class. Furthermore, since form class varies with each tree size, species, and site, it is unlikely that variation in form class will be random. Thus it is difficult to obtain an accurate average form class for a stand, and it is therefore undesirable to use a single form class table for any extensive area.

6-2.2   Descriptive Information to Accompany Volume Tables

A volume table should include descriptive information that will enable one to apply it correctly. This information includes:

1. Species, or species group, to which the table is applicable, or the locality in which the table is applicable
2. Definition of dependent variable, volume, including units in which volume is expressed
3. Definition of independent variable, including stump height and top diameter limit, if merchantable height is used
4. Author
5. Date of preparation
6. Number of trees on which table is based
7. Extent of basic data
8. Method of determining volumes of individual trees (in basic data)
9. Method of construction
10. Appropriate measures of accuracy

Tables 6-6 and 6-7 include these items.

The first three items in the list should always be given. The remaining items are of less interest and are sometimes omitted. When measures of accuracy are given, they should be understood to be measures of accuracy of the table when it is applied to the data used in its construction. Such measures give no assurance that a volume table will apply to other trees. Thus, when an accurate estimate is required, a table should be checked against the measured volumes of a representative sample of trees obtained from the stands to be estimated.

6-2.3   Checking Applicability of Volume Tables

In an applicability check, one should compare the volume of sample trees with the estimated volume from the volume table to be checked. Three conditions should be observed in selecting sample trees:

1. Sample trees for a given species, or species group, should be distributed through the timber to which the volume table will be applied.
2. No sizes, types, or growing conditions should be unduly represented in the sample.
3. If a sample of cut trees is used, this sample, if not representative of the timber, should be supplemented by a sample of standing trees.

Definite rules for measuring sample trees should be established. As an example, the following rules are satisfactory for the eastern United States:

1. Diameters along the tree stem, inside and outside bark, should be measured at 8-ft intervals above a 1-ft stump, and at stump height, breast height, and merchantable height.
2. Diameter should be measured to nearest $\frac{1}{10}$ in. and bark thickness to nearest $\frac{1}{20}$ in.
3. Knots, swellings, and other abnormalities should be avoided at points of measurement by taking measurements above or below them.
4. Total or merchantable heights should be measured to the nearest foot. (Utilization standards for the timber in question should be considered in determining the upper limit of merchantable height.)

Table 6-8 illustrates how the comparison of measured and estimated volumes of sample trees should be made. For practical purposes, the aggregate difference of a test sample should not exceed $2 \cdot CV/\sqrt{n}$, where CV is the coefficient of variation of the volume table being tested and n is the number of trees used in the test. Since the coefficient of variation for the table tested in Table 6-8 is 15 percent, the table is applicable without correction.

$$\frac{2(15)}{\sqrt{62}} = 3.8\% > 1.0\%$$

If desired, checks may be made by diameter classes. Of course, more complicated statistical tests, such as the chi-square goodness-of-fit test, might be used. The procedure above is, however, generally satisfactory.

When a table is judged to be inapplicable, one should adjust the table or obtain a better table. Practical methods of making adjustments are described by Gevorkiantz and Olsen (1955).

TABLE 6-8. Comparison of Measured and Estimated Volumes of Sample of Red Oak

Dbh Class (in.)	Sample Trees (number)	Measured Volume (board feet)	Estimated Volume[a] (board feet)	Aggregate Difference (%)
13.0–15.9	14	2,010	2,045	−1.7
16.0–18.9	10	2,003	1,943	+3.1
19.0–21.9	9	3,041	3,106	−2.1
22.0–24.9	21	9,257	8,895	+4.1
25.0–27.9	4	2,084	2,223	−6.3
28.0–30.9	3	2,130	2,110	+0.9
31.0–33.9	0	—	—	—
34.0–36.9	1	870	860	+1.2
All classes	62	21,396	21,182	+1.0

Source: Adapted from Gevorkiantz and Olsen (1955).

[a]From volume table.

6-3. CONSTRUCTION OF VOLUME TABLES

The following principles of volume table construction given by Cotta early in the nineteenth century are still valid: "Tree volume is dependent upon diameter, height, and form. When the correct volume of a tree has been determined, it is valid for all other trees of the same diameter, height, and form." Since the time of Cotta, hundreds of volume tables have been constructed and used. Numerous methods have been used to construct the tables. However, since the middle of the twentieth century, there has been a trend, particularly for broadleaved species, to reduce the number of volume tables used by adopting composite volume tables, tables applicable to average timber, regardless of species. Where the same standards of utilization are employed, differences in tree volumes among species are often of no practical consequence. Excellent examples of composite volume tables are Beers's (1973) for hardwoods in Indiana, and Gevorkiantz and Olsen's (1955) for timber in the Lake states. These tables have been tested extensively and have been found to replace individual species tables, especially for the estimation of volume on large tracts. Adjustment factors can be used for individual species that vary from the average.

Why have so many volume tables been constructed? Why has so much research gone into the development of volume tables? The answer is that foresters have been looking for methods that are simple, objective, and accurate. However, because trees are highly variable geometric solids, no single table, or set of tables, could possibly satisfy all of these conditions, regardless of the method of construction. Consequently, one by one the older methods of

volume table construction have been abandoned. For example, the once popular harmonized-curve method (Chapman and Meyer, 1949), which requires
large amounts of data to establish the relationships and considerable judgment
to fit the curves, is rarely used today. The alignment-chart method, another
subjective method, has generally been discarded. Other discarded methods
have been described by Spurr (1952). Today, interest has focused on the use
of mathematical functions, or models, to prepare volume tables. There is no
advantage for the majority of foresters in using any other method.

In mathematical models the volume of the stem of trees is considered a
function of the independent variables, diameter, height, and form in the expression

$$V = f(D, H, F)$$

where V = volume (cubic units or board feet)
      D = dbh
      H = total, merchantable, or height to some specific limit
      F = measure of form such as the Girard form class or absolute form
        quotient

6-3.1 Local Volume Functions

Local volume functions utilize the single independent variable D, generally
dbh, or some transformation of this variable. The simplest model for a local
volume table is

$$V = b_0 D^{b_1} \qquad\qquad (6\text{-}16)$$

where V and D are as above
      b_i = constants

This can be linearized using the logarithmic transformation

$$\log V = b_0 + b_1 \log D$$

Other local volume functions, which have been used principally in Europe, as
reported by Prodan (1965) and Prodan et al. (1997), include

$$V = b_0 + b_1 D^2$$
$$V = b_0 + b_1 D + b_2 D^2$$
$$V = b_0 + b_1 g$$

In the last model, g is basal area. This model has been called the *volume line*
since the use of basal area has linearized the volume–diameter relationship.

6-3.2 General Volume Functions

These functions estimate volume according to diameter and height and, in some cases, the addition of form. Behre (1935) and Smith et al. (1961) concluded that no practical advantage is gained from the use of a measure of form in addition to dbh and height. Clutter et al. (1983) have given the following reasons that models using only diameter and height are preferred:

1. Measurement of upper stem diameters is time-consuming and expensive.
2. Variation in tree form has a much smaller impact on tree volume or weight than does height or dbh variation.
3. With some species, form is relatively constant regardless of tree size.
4. With other species, tree form is often correlated with tree size, so that the dbh and height variables often explain much of the volume (or weight) variation actually caused by form differences.

Shown below are some commonly used general volume functions (also applicable as tree weight functions):

$$\text{Constant form factor:} \quad V = b_1 D^2 H \tag{6-17}$$

$$\text{Combined variable:} \quad V = b_0 + b_1 D^2 H \tag{6-18}$$

$$V = b_1 D^{b_2} H^{b_3} \tag{6-19}$$

$$\text{Log transformed:} \quad V = \log b_1 + b_2 \log D + b_3 \log H \tag{6-20}$$

$$\text{Honer's transformed variable:} \quad V = \frac{D^2}{b_0 + b_1 H^{-1}} \tag{6-21}$$

Models that include form as a variable are

$$V = b_0 + b_1 D^2 H F \tag{6-22}$$

$$V = b_0 D^{b_1} H^{b_2} F^{b_3} \tag{6-23}$$

The constants b_i are obtained using regression analysis techniques. Clutter et al. (1983) and Prodan et al. (1997) summarized the recommended techniques for fitting these regressions.

6-3.3 Derivation of Local Volume Table from Standard Volume

A local volume table may be derived from a standard volume table by "localizing" the heights by dbh classes using the following procedure.

1. Measure the heights and dbh values of a sample of trees representative of those to which the local volume table will be applied. Record dbh to the nearest tenth of an inch, and height to the nearest even foot (nearest centimeter and meter when using the metric system).

2. Prepare a curve of height over dbh by the freehand method (see Section 8-3).

3. Read average heights to the nearest even foot from the curve for each dbh class (usually 2-in. classes).

4. Interpolate from the standard volume table the volume of the tree of average height for each dbh class, or if a standard volume equation is available, substitute the appropriate values in the equation and compute the volume for each dbh class.

6-3.4   Tree Volume Tarif Tables

The term *tarif*, which is Arabic in origin, means tabulated information. In continental Europe, the term has been applied for years to volume table systems that provide, directly or indirectly, a convenient means for obtaining a local volume table for a given stand (Garay, 1961).

British tarifs (Hummel, 1955), which have been quite successful, stimulated the preparation of *Comprehensive Tree-Volume Tarif Tables* by Turnbull et al. (1963). This clever system, which is summarized in Table 6-9, merits wider consideration in all types of inventories.* It requires no curve fitting to obtain a local volume table; it provides a convenient method of converting from one unit of measure to another or from one merchantable limit to another. To determine average annual volume increment per tree in any desired unit of volume and merchantable limit, one simply multiplies the average annual diameter increment in inches by the growth multiplier (GM).

6-3.5   Volume Functions to Upper-Stem-Diameter Limits

The prediction of stem volumes (or weights) to different upper-stem-diameter limits (such as merchantability limit) has until recently required the preparation of separate functions and volume tables for each limit. Models have now been developed that permit the adjustment of volume to the upper-stem-diameter limit specified as follows:

$$V = f(D, H)$$

$$V_u = rV$$

---

*The tarif system is based on the concept that a tree with a dbh of 4 in. (equivalent to a basal area of $0.087\,\mathrm{ft}^2$) has zero volume. The tarif number is the predicted volume for a tree of $1.0\,\mathrm{ft}^2$ of basal area. The volume function is $V = b_1(g - 0.087)$ and the tarif number T is $T = b_1(1.0 - 0.087)$, so that $b_1 = T/0.913$. For a given tarif number T and tree basal area g, the volume of a tree is $V = (T/0.913)(g - 0.087)$.

where $D = $ dbh
           $H = $ total height
           $V = $ total stem volume
           $V_u = $ stem volume to upper stem diameter specified
           $r = $ proportion of volume up to upper stem diameter

The total volume V is multiplied by the adjustment factor r to obtain the volume to the upper diameter limit specified. Several functions have been developed for r, some using only diameter as the independent variable and others with both height and diameter as independent variables. An example of the first approach is the model of Burkhart (1977):

$$r = 1 + b_0 \frac{d_u^{b_1}}{d^{b_2}}$$

where $d = $ dbh
           $d_u = $ upper stem diameter

An example of a function using both diameter and height is that of Mattney and Sullivan (1982):

$$r = b_0 \frac{d_u}{d} + b_1 \left(\frac{d_u}{d}\right)^2 h_u$$

where d and d_u are as above
           $h_u = $ height at upper stem diameter

Models including height as an independent variable can be transformed to determine the height h_u at which a specified upper stem diameter occurs. For the Mattney and Sullivan function this has been done with the restriction that d be at 4.5 ft and that $r = 0$ when $d_u = 0$, yielding the equation

$$h_u = h + \frac{d_u}{d}(4.5 - h) + \frac{576 \, V}{\pi \, d^2} \frac{d_u}{d} \left\{ b_1 \left[\frac{d_u}{d} - 1 \right] + b_2 \left[\left(\frac{d_u}{d}\right)^2 - 1 \right] \right.$$
$$\left. + b_3 \left[\left(\frac{d_u}{d}\right)^3 - 1 \right] + b_4 h \left[\left(\frac{d_u}{d}\right)^2 - 1 \right] \right\}$$

For a number of other models to determine r and h_u, see Prodan et al. (1997).

6-4. VOLUME DISTRIBUTION IN TREES

Knowledge of volume distribution over a tree stem can be used to improve volume estimates and to aid in estimating volume losses from defects. (Volume deduction for defect is treated in Chapter 9.) Table 6-10 illustrates a method of

TABLE 6-9. Specimen of Comprehensive Tree Volume Tarif Table[a]

Height—dbh Access Table for Douglas-fir

Dbh	Total Height (ft)				
	60	62	64	66	68
12.2	22.2	23.1	23.9	24.8	25.7
12.4	22.0	22.9	23.7	24.6	25.5
12.6	21.8	22.7	23.6	24.4	25.3
12.8	21.6	22.5	23.4	24.2	25.1
13.0	21.5	22.3	23.2	24.0	24.9
13.2	21.3	22.1	23.0	23.8	24.7
13.4	21.1	22.0	22.8	23.7	24.5
13.6	20.9	21.8	22.6	23.5	24.3
13.8	20.8	21.6	22.5	23.3	24.2
14.0	20.6	21.4	22.3	23.1	24.0
14.2	20.4	21.3	22.1	23.0	23.8
14.4	20.3	21.1	22.0	22.8	23.6
14.6	20.1	21.0	21.8	22.6	23.5

Instructions

1. Measure height and dbh of sample trees representative of stand.
2. Look up tarif numbers of sample trees in the appropriate height—dbh access table and average them. For example:

Height	dbh	Tree Tarif (No.)
60	12.2	22.2
68	14.3	23.7
⋯	⋯	⋯
	Mean =	24.5

3. In tarif book, find table with mean tarif number.

Tarif Table 24.5

Dbh (in.)	Total Tree Volume						Volume to a 6-in. Top					
	Including Top and Stump (ft^3)		Including Top Only (ft^3)		Volume to a 4-in. Top (ft^3)		(ft^3)		Scribner (board feet)		International $\frac{1}{4}$-in. Rule (board feet)	
	Vol. A	GM A	Vol. B	GM B	Vol. C	GM C	Vol. D	GM D	Vol. E	GM E	Vol. F	GM F
2	0.3	0.2	0.2	0.2	—	—	—	—	—	—	—	—
3	0.7	0.7	0.6	0.6	—	—	—	—	—	—	—	—
4	1.5	1.0	1.4	1.0	—	—	—	—	—	—	—	—
5	2.6	1.4	2.5	1.3	1.4	1.5	—	—	—	—	—	—
6	4.1	1.7	4.0	1.6	3.0	1.8	—	—	—	—	—	—
7	5.9	2.0	5.7	2.0	4.9	2.1	1.9	2.2	6	7.2	9	10.7
8	8.1	2.4	7.8	2.3	7.1	2.4	4.3	2.8	14	9.8	21	13.9
9	10.5	2.7	10.2	2.6	9.6	2.7	7.2	3.1	25	11.9	36	16.2
10	13.3	3.0	12.9	2.9	12.3	3.0	10.5	3.4	38	13.7	53	18.0

Dbh	V/BA Ratio	GM A V/BA Ratio	% of Vol. A	V/BA Ratio	% of Vol. B	V/BA Ratio	% of Vol. C	V/BA Ratio	B/CU Ratio	V/BA Ratio	B/CU Ratio
2	9.3	8.3	89.0	—	—	—	—	—	—	—	—
3	12.5	11.6	92.5	—	—	—	—	—	—	—	—
4	16.3	15.4	94.4	—	—	—	—	—	—	—	—
5	19.0	18.1	95.5	9.7	51.0	—	—	—	—	—	—
6	20.7	19.9	96.1	14.9	71.9	—	—	—	—	—	—
7	22.0	21.2	96.4	18.1	82.1	6.8	37.7	21.1	3.1	32.0	4.7
8	23.0	22.2	96.6	20.1	87.6	12.3	61.1	40.6	3.3	59.9	4.9
9	23.7	23.0	96.7	21.5	90.7	16.3	75.6	56.8	3.5	81.5	5.0
10	24.3	23.6	96.7	22.5	92.6	19.1	84.6	69.6	3.6	97.5	5.1

Source: Adapted from Turnbull and Hoyer (1965).

[a]Volume in cubic feet for entire tree and volume in cubic and board feet to various merchantable limits and volume/basal area ratios for horizontal point sampling and growth multipliers (GMs) to determine growth are given. The letters A, B, C that follow Vol. and GM are used for convenient identification of columns.

TABLE 6-10. Average Distribution of Tree Volumes by Logs According to Log Position

Usable Length (16-ft logs)	Percent of Total Volume in Each Log, by Position					
	1st	2nd	3rd	4th	5th	6th
1	100					
2	59	42				
3	42	33	25			
4	34	29	22	15		
5	29	25	21	15	10	
6	24	23	20	16	11	6

Source: Adapted from Mesavage and Girard (1946).

expressing volume distribution that shows the percentage of volume according to each 16-ft log in trees with heights of one to six logs.

Although the percentages vary slightly with tree diameter and unit of volume, they may be used without serious error for merchantable trees of all sizes that are measured in cubic or board-foot volume. Note that Table 6-10, which is for 16-ft logs, provides a satisfactory guide when heights are measured in 8- or 12-ft lengths. Table 6-11 shows another generalized volume structure of tree stems according to cylindrical form factors and section length of 0.2 height.

In another approach, Honer et al. (1983) developed volume percentages based on both height ratios and diameter ratios. In their model, ratios are predicted using a quadratic equation

$$r = b_0 + b_1 X + b_2 X^2$$

TABLE 6-11. Tree Stem Volume Structure According to Cylindrical Form Factors

Sections of 0.2h	Percentage of Volume for Cylindrical Form Factors									
	0.407		0.442		0.500		0.550		0.600	
	Vol%	Σ	Vol%	Σ	Vol%	Σ	Vol%	Σ	Vol%	Σ
I	49.1	49.1	45.3	45.3	40.0	40.0	36.4	36.4	33.3	33.3
II	29.7	78.8	29.3	74.6	28.2	68.2	29.0	65.4	27.1	60.4
III	15.1	93.9	16.3	90.9	19.6	87.8	20.8	86.2	22.0	82.4
IV	5.5	99.4	7.4	98.3	10.5	98.3	11.6	97.8	14.4	96.8

where $r =$ volume ratio to upper limit specified
       $X =$ either height ratio (h_u/H) or diameter squared ratio (d_u^2/D^2)
       $h_u =$ upper height limit
       $H =$ total height
       $d_u =$ upper diameter limit inside bark
       $D =$ dbh outside bark
       $b_i =$ constants

Table 6-12 shows the volume percentage by diameter ratio and height ratio for the combined species volume predictions based on Honer's transformed variable equation [eq. (6-21)]. The main advantage of this system is that products may be specified by both a minimum upper diameter and length. The proportion of total volume in each product can be determined by using the two volume percentages iteratively. For example, sawlogs might have a minimum upper diameter of 12 in. and are sold in 16-ft lengths. The proportion of sawlog volume contained in a tree with dbh $= 30$ in. and total height of 90 ft would be found using the following steps:

1. Determine the volume percentage to the minimum top diameter:

$$\frac{d_u}{D} = \frac{12}{30} = 0.4$$

$$\% V = 96.22$$

TABLE 6-12. Proportions of Total Stem Volume for Upper Height:Total Height and Upper Diameter:dbk Ratios

Height Ratio, h_u/H	Volume Percentage	Diameter Ratio, d_u/D	Volume Percentage
0.10	21.76	0.10	100.00
0.20	39.60	0.20	99.96
0.30	55.12	0.30	98.88
0.40	68.30	0.40	96.22
0.50	79.12	0.50	91.59
0.60	87.70	0.60	84.07
0.70	93.92	0.70	72.52
0.80	97.80	0.80	55.63
0.90	99.36	0.90	31.87

Source: Adapted from Honer et al. (1983).

2. Using the volume percentage, determine the height ratio to the minimum top diameter:

$$\%V = 96.22$$

$$\frac{h_u}{H} \approx 0.80$$

$$h_u = 0.80(90) = 72$$

3. Subtracting 1 ft for the stump and allowing 0.3 ft for trim, the number of 16-ft logs is determined:

$$L = \frac{72 - 17.3}{16.3} + 1$$

$$= 3.3 + 1 = 4 \, \text{logs}$$

4. The height at the top of the last log is determined and the final volume percentage interpolated from the table:

$$h_u = 1.0 + 16.3 \cdot 4 = 66.2$$

$$\frac{h_u}{H} = \frac{66.2}{90} = 0.73$$

$$\%V \approx 93.92$$

Thus, the percent volume in sawlogs for this tree is 93.92% of total volume. Volume percentages for small products such as pulp could then be determined for this tree. The method is easily automated and applicable to any data set where both diameter and heights are available.

7

DETERMINATION OF TREE WEIGHT

Weight is being used increasingly to express the quantity of wood in a forest as well as for scaling traditional forest products. In addition, the growing interest in complete tree utilization (roots, stump, branches, etc.), the use of residues from the manufacture of forest products, biomass quantities and carbon content, fuel quantity in relation to forest fire conditions, and other topics has increased the use and importance of weight measurement. The basic procedure of weighing at any locality consists of comparing an object of unknown weight with the weight of an object of known mass. Since the force of gravity at any location affects both objects identically, the weight thus determined is a relative value, independent of the gravitational force. Thus, an object would weigh the same at any locality, provided that the standard used for comparison was of the correct mass.

The weight (or more precisely, the force) of objects can be measured by any one of five general methods (Doebelin, 1966):

1. By balancing the object against the gravitational force on a standard mass. This method employs well-known weighing machines: equal-arm balances, unequal-arm balances and pendulum scales.

2. By measuring the acceleration of a body of known mass to which an unknown force is applied. This method, which uses an accelerometer for force measurement, is of restricted application since the force determined is the resultant of several inseparable forces acting on the mass.

3. By balancing against a magnetic force developed by the interaction of a current-carrying coil and magnet.

4. By transducing the force to a fluid pressure and then measuring the pressure. This method is exemplified by a container filled with a liquid, such as oil, under a fixed pressure. Application of a load increases the liquid pressure, which can then be read on a gauge. Instruments of this type can be constructed for measuring large weights.

5. By applying the force to some elastic members and measuring the resulting deflection. This method permits the measurement of both static and dynamic loads, whereas the methods described above are restricted to static or slowly moving loads. By using a deflection transducer, the force applied to some elastic member will cause it to move, and this motion can then be transformed to an electrical signal. The various devices differ principally in the form of the elastic element and in the displacement transducer, which generates the electrical signal. The movement of the elastic element may be a gross, ocularly perceptible motion, or it may be a very small motion that requires the use of strain gauges to sense the force.

All of the methods of weight measurement described above may be applied to some aspect of forestry. However, for weighing large bulky quantities of wood, weighing machines or scales have been the most widely used.

7-1. FACTORS INFLUENCING WOOD WEIGHT ESTIMATES

The determination of the gross weight of wood is comparatively easy, but estimates of dry weight are more difficult because the gross weight is affected by both the *density* and *moisture content* of the wood. When measuring wood products by weight, bark and foreign material must also be deducted (Section 9-8).

7-1.1 Density

The density of a substance is its mass per unit volume. In the International System of Units (SI), density is expressed in kilograms per cubic meter or grams per cubic centimeter. In the English system density is expressed in pounds per cubic foot. Wood density is generally expressed as the dry mass of wood substance per unit of green volume:

$$D = \frac{W_d}{V_g} \tag{7-1}$$

where D = wood density (kg/m^3 or lb/ft^3)
          W_d = oven-dried weight of wood (kg or lb)
          V_g = green volume (m^3 or ft^3)

However, in many parts of the world, density is calculated using total actual weight (wood weight + water weight):

$$D_g = \frac{W_g}{V_g} \tag{7-2}$$

where D_g = wood density (kg m^3 or lb m^3) using green weight of wood
W_g = green weight (kg/m^3 or lb/ft^3)

If the wood is dried to a specific moisture content, density may be calculated based on the volume at the moisture content:

$$D_{MC\%} = \frac{W_d}{V_{MC\%}} \tag{7-3}$$

where $D_{MC\%}$ = wood density of specified percent moisture content
$V_{MC\%}$ = volume at moisture content specified

Since wood density varies with the moisture content, it is essential to specify the moisture content at which volume was determined.

The density of water under standard conditions is approximately 62.4 lb/ft^3, or 1 g/cm^3 (1000 kg/m^3). These figures are standards to which the densities of solids and liquids are compared. When the density of a substance is divided by the density of water, the quotient is referred to as the *specific gravity S*:

$$S = \frac{D}{D_w} = \frac{W}{V}\frac{1}{W_w} \tag{7-4}$$

where D = density of liquid or solid
D_w = density of water
W = weight of liquid or solid
V = volume of liquid or solid
W_w = weight of unit volume of water (62.4 lb/ft^3 or 1000 kg/m^3)

Similar to density, there are three methods to calculate the specific gravity (SG) of wood, depending on how volume is determined. In each method, the oven-dry weight W_d is the numerator. Current-volume specific gravity (SG) uses green volume V_g in the denominator:

$$SG = \frac{W_d}{V_g}\frac{1}{W_w} \tag{7-5}$$

Dry-volume specific gravity (SG$_d$) uses the oven-dried volume in the numerator:

$$SG_d = \frac{W_d}{V_d}\frac{1}{W_w} \tag{7-6}$$

where V_d = oven-dried volume

The third method calculates specific gravity using volume at a specific moisture content:

$$SG_{MC\%} = \frac{W_d}{V_{MC}} \frac{1}{W_w} \qquad (7\text{-}7)$$

where $SG_{MC\%}$ = specific gravity at MC% moisture content

To illustrate these calculations, consider the following example block of wood:

		Green	12% MC	Oven-Dry
Volume	English (ft^3)	0.65	0.57	0.50
	metric^a (m^3)	0.0184	0.0161	0.0142
Weight	English (lb)	22.6	18.5	18.0
	metric (kg)	10.3	8.4	8.2

^{a}To convert lb/ft^3 to kg/m^3, multiply by 16.0185. To convert kg/m^3 to lb/ft^3, multiply by 0.062 428 0.

The density and specific gravity can be expressed correctly in the following ways:

$$D_g = \frac{W_g}{V_g} = \frac{22.6\,\text{lb}}{0.65\,\text{ft}^3} = 34.77\,\text{lb/ft}^3$$

$$= \frac{10.3\,\text{kg}}{0.0184\,\text{m}^3} = 556.9\,\text{kg/m}^3$$

$$D = \frac{W_d}{V_g} = \frac{18\,\text{lb}}{0.65\,\text{ft}^3} = 27.69\,\text{lb/ft}^3$$

$$= \frac{8.2\,\text{kg}}{0.0184\,\text{m}^3} = 443.6\,\text{kg/m}^3$$

$$D_{MC12\%} = \frac{W_d}{V_{MC12\%}} = \frac{18.0\,\text{lb}}{0.57\,\text{ft}^3} = 31.58\,\text{lb/ft}^3$$

$$= \frac{10.3\,\text{kg}}{0.0161\,\text{m}^3} = 505.8\,\text{kg/m}^3$$

$$SG = \frac{W_d}{V_g} \frac{1}{W_w} = \frac{18.0\,\text{lb}}{0.65\,\text{ft}^3} \left(\frac{1\,\text{ft}^3}{62.4\,\text{lb}}\right) = 0.444$$

$$= \frac{8.2\,\text{kg}}{0.0184\,\text{m}^3} \left(\frac{1\,\text{m}^3}{1000\,\text{kg}}\right) = 0.444$$

$$SG_d = \frac{W_d}{V_d}\frac{1}{W_w} = \frac{18.0\,\text{lb}}{0.50\,\text{ft}^3}\left(\frac{1\,\text{ft}^3}{62.4\,\text{lb}}\right) = 0.577$$

$$= \frac{8.2\,\text{kg}}{0.0142\,\text{m}^3}\left(\frac{1\,\text{m}^3}{1000\,\text{kg}}\right) = 0.577$$

$$SG_{MC12\%} = \frac{W_d}{V_{MC12\%}}\frac{1}{W_w} = \frac{18.0\,\text{lb}}{0.57\,\text{ft}^3}\left(\frac{1\,\text{ft}^3}{62.4\,\text{lb}}\right) = 0.506$$

$$= \frac{8.2\,\text{kg}}{0.0161\,\text{m}^3}\left(\frac{1\,\text{m}^3}{1000\,\text{kg}}\right) = 0.506$$

Unless otherwise specified, the term *specific gravity* means current-volume specific gravity. Procedures for determining specific gravity are described in Besley (1967), Wenger (1984), and Haygreen and Bowyer (1996).

Because the cell wall substance of woody plants is quite uniform, the specific gravity is about 1.5. Solid wood with no air spaces would thus weigh about 93.6 lb/ft³ or 1500 kg/m³. However, the density of wood never attains this figure because wood is a porous structure. The specific gravities of commercial woods in North America range between 0.3 (19 lb/ft³) and 0.8 (50 lb/ft³). For specific gravities of commercial woods in the United States, see Wenger (1984), Haygreen and Bowyer (1996), and Alden (1997). The range of specific gravities of woods from other parts of the world is much wider, ranging from 0.1 (6 lb/ft³) to 1.1 (69 lb/ft³). Specific gravities for most tropical timbers of the world are given in Chudnoff (1984). One should note that there is considerable variation in density between trees of the same species.

For most species there is a tendency for the specific gravity to decrease from base to tip of stem. It appears that this variation is small in comparison to the difference between trees. The density of the wood in the cross section of stems tends to increase from the pith to the cambium. Large variations of specific gravity within individual annual rings have also been found.

7-1.2 Moisture Content

The moisture content of wood varies by species, by location in the tree, and by length of time since cutting. The practical determination of this variability constitutes a major problem in the use of weight as a measure of wood quantity. Moisture occurs in wood as free water in cell cavities and as absorbed water in the cell wall. The condition that exists in a cell when the cell cavity contains no free water and the cell wall is saturated with bound water is known as the *fiber saturation point*. Its value will vary from 27 to 32 percent of the dry weight for most species. Customarily, the moisture content of wood is expressed as a percentage of dry weight. The dry weight is obtained by drying a sample of wood at $103 \pm 2°C$ until a stable weight is obtained.[*] The moisture content, as a percentage, is calculated from

$$MC_d = 100\left(\frac{W_g - W_d}{W_d}\right) \qquad (7\text{-}8)$$

where MC_d = moisture content as percentage of oven-dried weight
$\qquad W_g$ = green weight of wood
$\qquad W_d$ = oven-dried weight of wood

In the pulp and paper industry, moisture content is often expressed as a percentage of the wet weight:

$$MC_g = 100\left(\frac{W_g - W_d}{W_g}\right) \qquad (7\text{-}9)$$

where MC_g = moisture content as percentage of wet weight

For example, the moisture contents from the example above are

$$MC_d = 100\left(\frac{22.6 - 18.0}{18.0}\right) = 25\%$$

$$MC_g = 100\left(\frac{22.6 - 18.0}{22.6}\right) = 20\%$$

The moisture content of wood varies with location in standing trees (Besley, 1967; Nylinder, 1967; Koch, 1972). The moisture content in the heartwood of conifers is usually appreciably lower than in the sapwood; in hardwoods there is variation, but it is less pronounced. For a compilation of moisture contents of most North American tree species, see Wenger (1984). The wood in the upper portion of conifers usually has higher moisture content than in the lower sections because of the larger proportion of sapwood. Again, there are differences in moisture content at varying heights on the stems of hardwoods, but they are less pronounced. There are also variations in moisture content by seasons; studies indicate higher moisture content in winter and spring than at other times of the year (Marden et al., 1975).

---

[*]There are numerous methods of determining moisture content, including: oven drying, vacuum drying, distillation, electric moisture meters, electric hygrometers, microwave absorption, nuclear magnetic resonance, and nuclear radiation.

7-2. TREE WEIGHT RELATIONSHIPS

The increasing use of weight to measure forest products and tree and stand biomass has developed a need to estimate the weight of wood in standing trees. Since the early 1960s, studies have been conducted to estimate (1) weight of the merchantable portion of a standing tree, and (2) weight of the whole tree.

In the past, only the merchantable stems of trees were taken from the woods. This is also true for most present-day operations. The unutilized material in roots, stumps, and branches constitutes a sizable portion of the total volume of cut trees. Young et al. (1964) show the proportions of the entire tree made up of the various components (Table 7-1).

7-2.1 Tree Weight Functions

The same mathematical models for construction of volume tables as discussed in Section 6-3 can be used to construct tree weight tables. In this case, the dependent variable is weight, either green or oven-dry, or biomass for the main stem, for live and/or dead branches, for foliage, and for roots.

TABLE 7-1. Example of Proportional Weights of a Tree in Eight Components

	Weight[a]			
	Red Spruce 12-in. dbh, 70 ft Total Height		Red Maple 12-in. dbh, 70 ft Total Height	
Tree Component	Pounds	Percent	Pounds	Percent
Roots less than 1 in. in diameter	55	3	62	3
Roots from 1 to 4 in. in diameter	115	6	96	5
Roots larger than 4 in. to base of stump	115	6	115	6
Stump—from 6 in. above ground to large roots	109	5	159	8
Merchantable stem from stump to 4 in. upper diameter	1218	60	1224	63
Branches larger than 1 in. in diameter	76	3	109	6
Branches smaller than 1 in. in diameter, including leaves	320	16	118	6
Stem above merchantable portion	20	1	58	3
Total tree	2028	100	1941	100

Source: Adapted from Young et al. (1964).

The following models or their logarithmic transformations have been used for these relations:

$$Y = b_0 + b_1 D^2$$

$$Y = b_0 + b_1 D + b_2 D^2$$

$$Y = b_0 + b_1 D + b_2 D^2 + b_3 D^2 H$$

$$Y = b_0 + b_1 D^2 H$$

$$Y = b_0 + b_1 D^2 + b_2 H$$

$$Y = b_0 + b_1 D^2 + b_2 D^2 H$$

$$Y = b_0 + b_1 D^2 + b_2 H + b_3 D^2 H$$

$$Y = b_0 + b_1 D^{b_2} H^{b_3}$$

$$Y = b_0 D^{b_1} H^{b_2}$$

$$Y = b_0 D^{b_1}$$

where Y = weight of component (kg or lb)
   D = dbh (cm or in.)
   H = total height (m or ft)
   b_i = regression coefficients

Parresol (1999) presents an analysis of several regression models and their statistics for evaluating goodness of fit and for use in comparing alternative biomass models. In his study he used the following "best" models for willow oak (*Quercus phellos*):

$$\hat{Y}_{\text{wood}} = b_0 + b_1 D^2 H$$

$$\hat{Y}_{\text{bark}} = b_0 + b_1 D^2$$

$$\hat{Y}_{\text{crown}} = b_0 + b_1 \frac{D^2 H(\text{LCL})}{1000} + b_2 H$$

For total tree biomass the "best" individual equation was

$$\hat{Y}_{\text{total}} = b_0 + b_1 D^2 H$$

where $\hat{Y}_i$ = weight of component (kg)
   D = dbh (cm)
   H = total height (m)
   LCL = live crown length (m)

He pointed out that a desirable feature of tree component regression equations is that the predictions for the components (bole, bark, crown) sum to the prediction for the total tree.

To obtain the basic data to develop the weight functions, a sample of trees covering the ranges of dbh and height (and, if needed, form) is selected and their measurements are made. The felled trees are cut into sections and the lengths, diameters, and green weights of the sections are measured. Weights can be obtained using a weighing machine, such as platform scales or spring balances. Sample disks are cut from the ends of sections, placed in plastic to prevent moisture loss, and taken to the laboratory. These disks are used to estimate the weight of bark and wood portions of the sections. Moisture content and weights of oven-dried bark and wood portions of each section are also estimated from the sample disks. The following total weights for all trees are then obtained by summing the weights of the sections of a tree: oven-dried wood; green wood, oven-dried bark, and green bark.

Using such a methodology, Husch (1962) in an early study developed tree weight relationships to estimate the oven-dry weight of wood in the merchantable stem of standing white pine (*Pinus strobus*) trees in southeastern New Hampshire (Fig. 7-1). A similar study of the green weight of red pine (*P. resinosa*) in New York yielded the results shown in Table 7-2 (Cody, 1976).

A study by Schroeder et al. (1975) showed the weights of the stem of longleaf pine to different top diameters, and the weights of bark residue, sawdust,

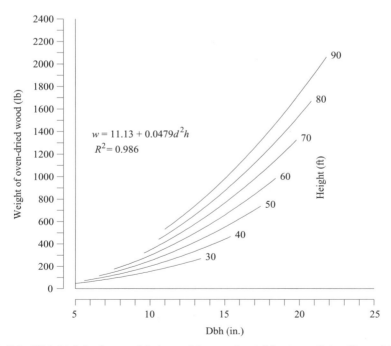

FIG. 7-1. Weight (w) of oven-dried wood in merchantable stem of standing white pine trees according to dbh (d) and total height (h). Weight included stem without bark from stump to top dob of 3 in. (adapted from Husch, 1962.)

TABLE 7-2. Weight in Pounds of Green Wood in Merchantable Stem of Red Pine to a 4-in. Top[a]

Dbh (in.)	Total Tree Height (ft)					
	16	24	32	40	48	56
6	122	168	215	261	307	—
8	194	276	358	441	523	605
10	—	415	543	672	800	929
12	—	—	769	954	1139	1324
14	—	—	1037	1288	1540	1792
16	—	—	1345	1674	2002	2331

Source: Adapted from Cody (1976).

lumber, and chippable residue. Weight tables for yellow poplar (*Liriodendron tulipifera*) were prepared by Clark and Schroeder (1977). A compilation up to 1979 of weight functions for many trees and shrubs in North America can be found in Hitchcock and McDonnell (1979).

Clark (1979) summarized the procedures for measuring tree biomass recognizing the following components:

- *Complete tree*: all component parts of the tree, including roots, stump, total stem, branches, foliage, and fruit
- *Stump and roots*: stump plus all roots (stump height dictated by local practice)
- *Total tree above stump*: all components of the tree except stump and roots
- *Total stem or full bole*: trunk of the tree from stump to tip, minus all foliage, branches, and fruit
- *Stem or bole*: trunk of tree from stump to some specified minimum top, preferably 4 in. (10 cm) dob or as dictated by local practice
- *Stem topwood*: portion of total stem above 4 in. (10 cm) dob or specified top diameter to tip of stem
- *Crown*: all branches, foliage, and stem topwood
- *Branches*: all limbs and twigs, excluding foliage
- *Foliage*: all needles, leaves, and fruit

Weights of stem components can be measured as explained previously. Green and dry weights of crown, branches, and foliage can be determined by separating these components from the entire tree. Weighing stumps and roots is difficult and costly, requiring mechanized equipment and washing to clean the roots before weighing.

Clutter et al. (1983) indicated that the weight of any section of a tree stem could be estimated if the green and dry weight densities for sample disks cut from both ends of a section have been obtained. Using an adaptation of Newton's formula [eq. (6-9)] the green weight of wood and bark W_g for a section is

$$W_g = \frac{L}{6}\left(A_1 D_{gu} + 2A_1 D_{g1} + 2A_u D_{gu} + A_u D_{g1}\right) \qquad (7\text{-}10)$$

and for an estimate of the dry weight of wood W_d of a section is

$$W_d = \frac{L}{6}\left(A_l' D_{du} + 2A_l' D_{dl} + 2A_u' D_{du} + A_u' D_{dl}\right) \qquad (7\text{-}11)$$

where
A_l = cross-sectional area of wood and bark at lower end of section
A_u = cross-sectional area of wood and bark at upper end of section
D_{gl} = green-weight density at lower end of section
D_{gu} = green-weight density at upper end of section
L = length of section
A_l' = cross-sectional area of wood only at lower end of section
A_u' = cross-sectional area of wood only at upper end of section
D_{dl} = dry-weight density at lower end of section
D_{du} = dry-weight density at upper end of section

7-2.2 Conversion of Volume Tables to Weight Tables

Weight tables can be constructed using the tree weight equations as discussed above. Table 7-2 is an example of a weight table constructed from a tree weight equation. Weight tables can also be obtained using volume tables or equations if reliable weight–volume conversions can be established. For example, a volume table can be converted to green weight using mean specific gravity and moisture content estimates:

$$W_g = SG_d W_w \left(1 + \frac{MC_d}{100}\right) \qquad (7\text{-}12)$$

where
W_g = green wood weight (lb or kg) per unit volume (ft^3 or m^3)
W_w = weight of unit volume of water (62.4 lb/ft^3 or 1000 kg/m^3)
SG_d = dry volume specific gravity [eq. (7-6)]
MC_d = dry weight moisture content [eq. (7-8)]

The applicability of a weight table, whether derived from tree weight equations or converted from existing volume tables, should be verified using the methods outlined in Section 6-2.3 for verifying volume tables.

8

STAND PARAMETERS

A *stand* is a group of trees that occupy a given area and that has some common characteristic or combination of characteristics, such as origin, species composition, size, or age that set it apart from other groups of trees. A number of stands taken together form a *forest*. *Stand structure* is the distribution of species and tree sizes within a stand or forest area. A stand's structure is the result of the species' growth habits and of the environmental conditions and management practices under which the stand originated and developed. Traditionally, stand structures have been broadly classified on the basis of tree ages: even-aged versus uneven-aged. An *even-aged stand*, as the name implies, is a stand where all trees have roughly the same age. Even-aged stands are composed of trees that originated within a short period of time, generally following a major disturbance such as wildfire or clearcut harvesting. *Uneven-aged stands* are composed of trees having many different ages. These stands are generally the result of smaller-scale disturbances, such as windthrow, selective harvesting, natural senescence, and intertree competition, that influence single trees or small groups of trees.

Stand structure can also be described using species composition, diameter distribution, height distribution, and crown classes (Oliver and Larson, 1996). For example, stands might be composed of a single species or a mixture of species. These stands might consist of a single predominant canopy layer or be vertically stratified into two or more distinct canopy layers. For a more detailed treatment of stand structure and the processes that produce these structures, see Oliver and Larson (1996).

The most important stand parameters characterizing structure include age, species composition, diameter and basal area, height and crown closure, density and stocking, volume, weight, and site quality. In this chapter the most common methods of expressing these parameters are presented. For details of the measurement of these parameters, refer to Chapters 5 and 10, and for information on sampling and estimation, refer to Chapters 11 and 13.

8-1. AGE

An even-aged stand is a group of trees that originated within a short period of time. The trees in an even-aged stand thus belong to a single age class. The limits of the age class may vary, depending on the length of time during which the stand formed. A natural stand may seed-in over a period of several years. Rarely will an age class be only 1 year, except in plantations. More commonly, the age class for an even-aged stand will extend to 10 or 20 years. In some cases, a stand may appear even-aged because the trees show size uniformity. For example, stands growing slowly on poor sites may consist of trees of widely diverse ages, yet have little variation in size. Even-aged stands may be composed of shade-tolerant or shade-intolerant species, although even-aged stands of intolerant species are more common. Even-aged stands arise out of, or are perpetuated by, environmental conditions that allow trees to become established within a comparatively short, definable period. An even-aged forest may consist of several even-aged stands belonging to different age classes.

If a stand, such as a plantation, is absolutely even-aged, a count of the annual rings of a single tree will give the age. Stands originating through natural reproduction, which generally takes 5 to 15 years or more, contain trees of various ages. There are several conceptions of the age of such a stand. The average age of all the trees in the stand, as determined by sampling, is sometimes used. The objection to this concept is that younger trees should not be given the same weight as the larger, older trees that make up the major part of the basal area or volume of the stand. One method suggested is to take the age of several sample trees whose volume is the average for the stand. However, a simpler concept, with many advantages, is to consider the age of the stand to be the average age of the dominant and codominant trees (i.e., the largest individuals).

A stand consisting of trees of many ages and corresponding sizes is said to be uneven-aged (sometimes called *all-aged*). The trees in an uneven-aged stand originate at different times, in contrast to the single or short reproductive period characterizing an even-aged stand. This continuing source of new trees produces, in a stand free of major disturbance, trees of ages varying from germinating seedlings to overmature veterans. Consequently, one cannot speak of the *age* of an uneven-aged stand. Stands that consist of two or more age groups are often called *multiaged*.

Because the ages of individual trees vary within uneven-aged stands, age is often not considered an important stand parameter. If age is summarized at all for these stands, it is generally expressed as an average age by diameter class, height or canopy position, or by species or species group. Occasionally, the age distribution might be shown in the form of a frequency polygon or histogram (Fig. 8-1). As shown in the figure, the frequency polygons, while similarly shaped, are different for age determined at breast height (4.5 ft or 1.3 m) versus age determined at ground level.

8-2. SPECIES COMPOSITION

The species present in a stand has always been an important parameter in describing forest stands. Different species represent not only different forest products and values, but are also important indicators of wildlife habitat, site quality, and past disturbance history. Environmental issues such as global climate change and the apparent declining biodiversity have required foresters to be more explicit in documenting the species present. Forest certification procedures and monitoring protocols require foresters to document what species are present and how forest management activities are modifying their abundance and distribution.

Typically, foresters express species composition as the distribution of individuals among the different species present in a stand. Species composition may be expressed using number of individuals, basal area, or volume and can be

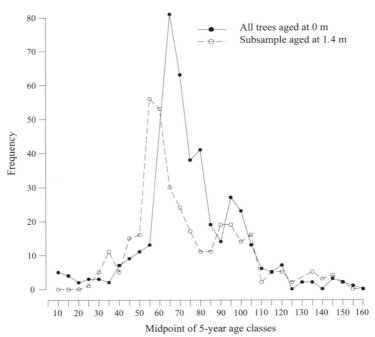

FIG. 8-1. Age distribution at root collar and breast height for a mixed oak–maple–birch–hemlock stand in New England. (Adapted from Oliver and Stephens, 1977.)

either the sum of these parameters or a percentage of the total. The resulting species composition values can vary greatly depending on which stand parameter is used. For example, Table 8-1 shows species composition for a mixed species stand in New Brunswick, Canada. Beech (*Fagus grandifolia*) makes up 43% of the species, in terms of number of stems, but only 22% of the basal area and 16% of the volume. Red spruce (*Picea rubrum*), on the other hand, makes up only 2% of the species, in terms of number of stems, but 12% of the basal area and 14% of the volume.

The choice of which parameter to use to express species composition depends on data availability and the use and interpretation of the composition values. For example, if species composition is going to be used as a parameter to stratify stands into classes for harvesting or other silvicultural activities, volume might be a more meaningful measure of composition than number of stems.

From an ecological perspective, species composition can be viewed as having three components: frequency, abundance, and dominance. *Frequency* is the number of sampling units in which a species is found. *Abundance* is the number of individuals in a population, and *dominance* is an expression of the size of individuals in a population. Each of these parameters is often expressed on a relative basis as a percentage of the totals for a stand or forest area.

Importance value has been widely used as a measure of species composition that combines frequency, abundance, and dominance (Greig-Smith, 1957):

$$I_j = 100\left(\frac{n_j}{N} + \frac{d_j}{D} + \frac{x_j}{X}\right) \tag{8-1}$$

TABLE 8-1. Species Composition for a Mixed Species Stand in New Brunswick, Canada

Species	Trees (number/ha)		Basal Area (m²/ha)		Volume (m³/ha)	
	Number	% Total	Sum	% Total	Sum	% Total
Fagus grandifolia	269	43.0	6.1	22.4	43.9	15.8
Betula papyrifera	31	5.0	2.7	9.9	26.7	9.6
Acer saccharum	56	9.0	4.8	17.6	44.7	16.0
Acer rubrum	238	38.0	9.9	36.3	120.3	43.2
Acer pensylvanicum	13	2.0	0.5	1.7	3.0	1.1
Picea rubra	13	2.0	3.2	11.7	39.0	14.0
Abies balsamea	6	1.0	0.1	0.5	1.0	0.3
Total	625		27.2		278.5	

where I_j = importance value of jth species

$\quad\quad\quad n_j$ = number of sampling units where jth species is present

$\quad\quad\quad N$ = total number of sampling units

$\quad\quad\quad d_j$ = number of individuals of jth species present in sample population

$\quad\quad\quad D$ = total number of individuals in sample population ($D = \sum d_j$)

$\quad\quad\quad x_j$ = sum of size parameter (generally basal area or volume) for jth species

$\quad\quad\quad X$ = total of size parameter across all species ($X = \sum x_j$)

Importance has a range of 0 to 300. The value 300 would occur in stands composed of a single species. In many situations, importance is calculated using relative frequency (n_j/N) and either relative density (d_j/D) or relative dominance (x_j/X). In this case, importance has a range of 0 to 200.

With the increased interest in biodiversity and monitoring the impacts of forest management on species diversity, numerous other measures and indices of species composition have been proposed. For a discussion of these indices, the reader is referred to Pielou (1966), Peet (1974), and Krebs (1989).

8-3. DIAMETER

Diameter is the most widely used descriptor of stand structure. Diameter may be summarized into a single parameter, generally the average diameter, or used to compute cross-sectional area and summed to yield an estimate of basal area. The distribution of diameters might be summarized into a stand table (Section 11-2.5) depicting number of trees per unit area by diameter class or used to obtain parameter estimates for mathematical distribution functions, which are subsequently used to describe stand structure.

8-3.1   Expressions of Mean Diameter

The average diameter (dbh) of a stand may be expressed by the arithmetic mean or the quadratic mean (Curtis and Marshall, 2000). If the primary interest is to obtain an average for the calculation of stand basal area and volume, the quadratic mean is more appropriate. If trees are selected with equal probability (i.e., using fixed area plots; see Section 11-2), the arithmetic mean stand diameter is

$$\bar{d} = \frac{\sum_{i=1}^{n} d_i}{n}$$

and the quadratic mean stand diameter is

$$\bar{d}_Q = \sqrt{\frac{\sum_{i=1}^{n} d_i^2}{n}}$$

where d_i = dbh of ith tree

       n = number of trees measured

The quadratic mean diameter can also be calculated using

$$\bar{d}_Q = \sqrt{\frac{\text{BA/unit area}}{c(\text{trees/unit area})}}$$

where   BA/unit area = basal area per unit area (m^2/ha or ft^2 acre)

     trees/unit area = number of trees per unit area

                c = conversion factor for diameter in centimeters or inches to cross-sectional area in m^2 or ft^2 ($c = 0.000\,078\,54$ in metric system and $c = 0.005\,454$ in English system)

The arithmetic mean of trees selected using horizontal point sampling (Section 11-3.1) is actually an unbiased estimate of the basal area weighted mean because trees are selected with probability proportional to their basal area. A weighted mean using the tree factor as the weight should be used to obtain an estimate of the mean unweighted diameter.

8-3.2   Basal Area

The total basal area of all trees, or of specified classes of trees, per unit area is a useful characteristic of a forest stand. For example, basal area is related directly to stand volume and biomass, and is a good measure of stand density and competition. The parameter incorporates the number of trees in a stand and their diameters. Stand basal area can be calculated from measurements of the dbh of all trees or of those of particular interest in a known area such as a fixed-area plot or using horizontal point sampling where tree dbh need not be measured (Section 11-3.1).

8-3.3   Diameter Distributions

A stand table shows the number of trees per unit area (or for a total area) according to designated characteristics. The most common form is a table that shows the number of trees per unit area by species and dbh class (Table 8-2). Knowledge of stand structure is useful for deciding on silvicultural measures and for estimating the yield of different products that may be obtained from a stand.

The trees in an even-aged stand are fairly consistent in height, with variations depending on their crown position (Fig. 8-2). Diameters, however, show wider variation. Most trees cluster near the average diameter, with decreasing frequencies at larger and smaller diameters. As even-aged stands grow older, the diameter class distribution changes. The total number of trees in the stand

TABLE 8-2. Number of Trees per Hectare by Species and 2-cm dbh Classes for a Mixed Species Stand

Dbh Class (cm)	Species[a]							
	Fgrd	Bpap	Asac	Arub	Apen	Prub	Abal	Total
10	81	0	0	25	0	0	0	106
12	25	6	0	19	0	0	0	50
14	31	0	6	31	0	0	0	68
16	44	0	0	38	0	0	6	88
18	25	0	0	50	6	0	0	81
20	19	6	0	6	0	0	0	31
22	19	0	13	13	0	0	0	45
24	13	0	6	6	6	0	0	31
26	0	0	6	19	0	0	0	25
28	0	0	6	0	0	0	0	6
30	6	0	0	13	0	0	0	19
32	0	6	0	0	0	0	0	6
34	0	0	0	0	0	0	0	0
36	6	0	0	0	0	0	0	6
38	0	0	0	0	0	0	0	0
40	0	6	0	6	0	0	0	12
42+	0	6	19	13	0	13	0	51
Total	269	30	56	239	13	13	6	625

[a]Fgrd, *Fagus grandifolia*; Bpap, *Betula papyrifera*; Asac, *Acer saccharum*; Arub, *Acer rubrum*; Apen, *Acer pensylvanicum*; Prub, *Picea rubra*; Abal, *Abies balsamea*.

decreases, with trees appearing in larger-diameter classes not represented previously. Figure 8-2 shows the diameter distribution of an even-aged mixed oak stand at several ages. The diameter distribution for a typical pure even-aged stand is *unimodal*, as shown in the figure, with a tendency to asymmetry or skewness toward the right side of the curve. The diameter distribution in an even-aged stand may be *bimodal* in stands of mixed species, especially if one is tolerant and the other intolerant or if the species differ in growth rates.

In an uneven-aged forest, the trees are of many heights, resulting in an irregular stand profile as viewed from a vertical cross section (Fig. 8-3a). The more shade-tolerant species tend to form uneven-aged stands. Cutting methods that remove only scattered individuals at short intervals maintain forest conditions favorable to shade-tolerant species and an uneven-aged stand. The typical diameter distribution for an uneven-aged stand is a large number of small trees in the smaller-diameter classes with decreasing frequency as the diameter increases, as shown in Fig. 8-3b.

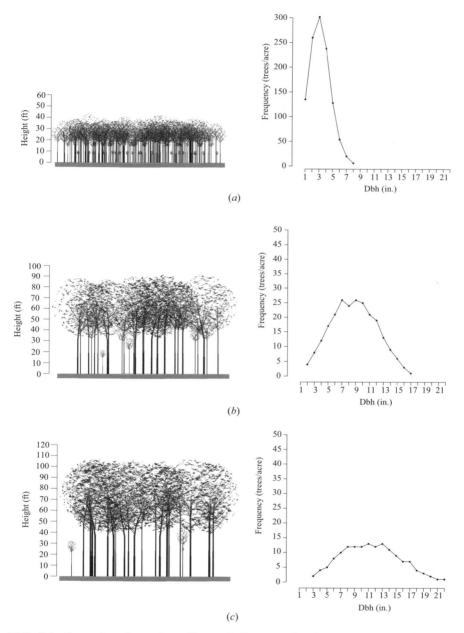

FIG. 8-2. Examples of stand profiles and diameter distributions for even-aged oak stands at three different ages: (*a*) 20-year-old stand; (*b*) 60-year-old stand; (*c*) 100-year-old stand (stand data for site index 80; Schnur, 1937).

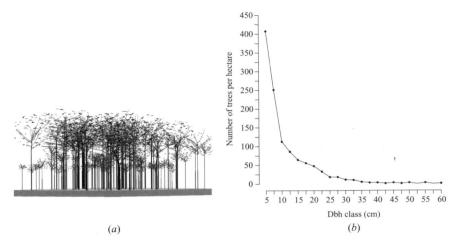

(a)　　　　　　　　　　　　　　　　　　　(b)

FIG. 8-3. (*a*) Stand profile and (*b*) diameter distribution for an uneven-aged stand of oak–mixed hardwoods in Missouri. (Adapted from Loewenstein et al., 2000.)

Diameter distributions for small areas of uneven-aged forests may show considerably greater irregularity. As the area of the uneven-aged stand or forest increases, the irregularities tend to even out and the inverse J-shaped diameter distribution of an uneven-aged forest becomes apparent. For the forest shown in Fig. 8-3, the inverse J-shaped distribution was apparent on a scale of about 0.24 ha (Loewenstein, 1996).

Early investigations of stand diameter distributions for uneven-aged forests were carried out by De Liocourt, a French forester, in 1898. He found that the ratios of number of trees in successive diameter classes were quite consistent. Meyer (1953), basing his work on the investigations of De Liocourt, studied the structure of what he termed a *balanced uneven-aged forest*. His definition was "one in which current growth can be removed periodically while maintaining the diameter distribution and initial volume of the forest." Meyer stated that a balanced uneven-aged forest tends to have a diameter distribution whose form can be expressed by the negative exponential equation

$$Y = ke^{-aX} \tag{8-2}$$

By taking the logarithm of both sides, a linear form of the equation is obtained:

$$\ln Y = \ln k - aX$$

where　Y = number of trees per diameter class
　　　　X = dbh class
　　　　e = base of natural logarithms

$$a, k = \text{constants for characteristic diameter distribution}$$
$$\ln = \text{natural logarithm}$$

A balanced distribution implies that the number of trees in successive diameter classes follows a geometric series of the form $m, mq, mq^2, mq^3, \ldots$, where q is the ratio of the series and m is the number of trees in the largest diameter class considered. The constant q is the ratio of trees in successive diameter classes.

If the logarithm of number of trees is plotted over diameter class, a balanced distribution will show a linear trend line (Fig. 8-4). The parameters a and k are obtained by fitting to the log-transformed data using regression analysis. Excluding the trees greater than 42.5 cm dbh, the resulting equation for the data shown in Fig. 8-4 is $\ln N = 6.4786 - 0.1399\text{dbh}$. The current value of the constant q can be obtained using the estimated value of a and the diameter class width:

$$q = e^{aW} \tag{8-3}$$

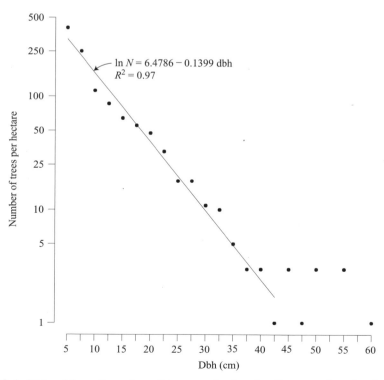

FIG. 8-4. Natural log of number of trees per hectare by diameter class for the forest depicted in Fig. 8-3. (Diameters greater than 42.5 cm were excluded for illustration purposes.)

where a = estimated slope coefficient
          W = diameter class width

In Fig. 8-4, the diameter class width is 2.5 cm, so $q = e^{0.1399 \cdot 2.5} = 1.42$.

For many silvicultural applications, foresters are interested in determining the diameter distribution for a specified q value, maximum diameter class, and basal area. Brender (1973) gives a numeric example for calculating m for the series $m, mq, mq^2, mq^3, \ldots$

$$m = \frac{g}{c \sum_{i=1}^{n} D_i^2 q^{i-1}} \tag{8-4}$$

where m = number of trees in largest diameter class
          g = specified basal area (ft^2/acre of m^2/ha)
          c = cross-sectional area conversion factor (0.005 454 in English system, 0.000 078 54 in metric system)
          D_i = diameter class midpoint (D_1 = class midpoint of largest class and D_n = class midpoint of smallest class)
          q = series ratio [eq. (8-3)]

Moser (1976) presented a generalized methodology for calculating the parameters a and k of eq. (8-2) given a specified q value, maximum diameter class, and stand density specified as either basal area, tree-area ratio (Section 8-5.3), or crown competition factor (Section 8-5.4).

Stand diameter distributions may be represented mathematically by *probability density functions*. A number of functions have been used or tried, including the normal, exponential, binomial, Poisson, Charlier, Fournier series, normal logarithmic, Johnson's S_B, Pearl, Reed, Schiffel, gamma, beta, and Weibull. For detailed treatments of probability density functions in forest mensuration, see Loetsch et al. (1973), Schreuder et al. (1993), Prodan et al. (1997), and Johnson (2001). Of the numerous functions used to describe diameter distributions, the Weibull function has received the greatest attention.

The probability density function for the Weibull distribution is

$$f(D) = \frac{c}{b} \left(\frac{D-a}{b} \right)^{1/c} e^{-[(D-a)/b]^c} \tag{8-5}$$

where $f(D)$ = probability density
          a = location parameter (theoretical minimum population value)
          b = scale parameter
          c = shape parameter
          D = diameter

The cumulative probability distribution function is given by

$$F(d \leq D) = 1 - e^{-[(D-a)/b]^c} \qquad (8\text{-}6)$$

where $F(d \leq D)$ = probability of observing a value d less than or equal to D

Equations (8-5) and (8-6) are often referred to as the *three-parameter Weibull distribution* because three parameters (a, b, and c) are required to specify the distribution. The *two-parameter Weibull model* is a special case of the three-parameter model where a, the location parameter, is assumed to equal 0. The *one-parameter Weibull model* is the case where $a = 0$ and the shape parameter (c) is assumed known.

The Weibull distribution has been widely applied in forest mensuration because of its flexibility. The Weibull distribution can exhibit a variety of shapes, depending on the value of c.

Value of c	Shape of Curve
$c < 1$	Inverse J-shape
$c = 1$	Exponential decreasing
$1 < c < 3.6$	Positive asymmetry
$c = 3.6$	Symmetric
$c > 3.6$	Negative asymmetry

By fitting the Weibull distribution to the data shown in Figs. 8-2 and 8-3, this flexibility can be observed (Fig. 8-5).

The parameters of the Weibull distribution can be estimated directly from a list of diameter measurements or from stand table summaries (number of trees by diameter class). In many cases, the location parameter is assumed known. Since the location parameter is the minimum value of the distribution, it is logical to set this parameter to equal the smallest value observed or the lower limit of diameter measurement. When diameter measurements are grouped into classes, the lower bound of the smallest diameter class is often used as the location parameter. For example, if diameters were measured in 2-cm classes with 10 cm as the smallest midpoint, the location parameter would equal 9.0 cm.

The other two parameters can be estimated using parameter prediction, parameter recovery, or percentile estimation techniques. The parameter prediction technique involves directly predicting the parameters based on stand characteristics such as age, site index, mean dbh, quadratic mean dbh, density, or total basal area (Bailey and Dell, 1973). An efficient algorithm for moment-based parameter recovery is given by Burk and Newberry (1984). Zarnock and Dell (1985) discuss the use of percentile estimators for obtaining Weibull parameters. Using the estimators specified by Zanakis (1979), they compared per-

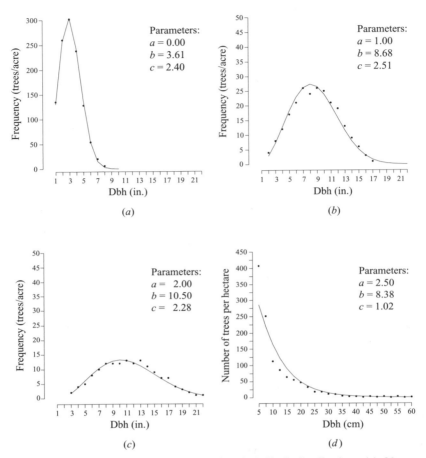

FIG. 8-5. Observed number of trees and fitted Weibull distribution: (*a*) 20-year-old stand; (*b*) 60-year-old stand; (*c*) 100-year-old stand; (*d*) uneven-aged stand.

centile estimators to moment-based estimators. Although the moment-based estimators were superior in terms of accuracy, the percentile estimators are simpler to obtain, and when $c < 2$, are as accurate as moment-based estimators, especially if sample size is small.

8-4. HEIGHT

Height is another widely used stand structure parameter. Height is an important factor in determining individual and total stand volumes. Height is widely used as a measure of site quality and stand productivity. Vertical structure (i.e., the height distribution) is an important factor in many silvicultural prescriptions and in assessing wildlife habitat.

For an even-aged stand, the variation in heights is typically less than the variation in diameter (Fig. 8-2). For uneven-aged stands, the height distribution is often similar to the diameter distribution, although generally not as wide (Fig. 8-3).

The vertical structure can be described using the actual heights or using a classification based on crown position. The mean height may be calculated or the height distribution can be specified using many of the same models as used for diameter. Kraft [1884; cited in Assmann (1970) and Oliver and Larson (1996)] proposed the following definitions that are still widely used today:

- *Dominant.* Crowns extend above the general level of crown cover of others of the same stratum and are not physically restricted from above, although possibly somewhat crowded by other trees on the sides.
- *Codominant.* Crowns form a general level of crown stratum and are not physically restricted from above, but are more or less crowded by other trees from the sides.
- *Intermediate.* The trees are shorter, but their crowns extend into the general level of dominant and codominant trees, free from physical restrictions from above, but quite crowded on the sides.
- *Suppressed* (*overtopped*). Crowns are entirely below the general level of dominant and codominant trees and are physically restricted from immediately above.

In even-aged stands composed of a single canopy layer, the crown classes generally reflect relative height, with the dominants being the tallest and the suppressed being the shortest (Fig. 8-6a). In uneven-aged stands and some even-aged stands, the trees often form distinct canopy layers referred to as *strata* (Oliver and Larson, 1996). Within each of these strata, dominant, codominant, intermediate, and suppressed trees are found (Fig. 8-6b).

8-4.1 Expressions of Mean Height

A single value to characterize the height of a stand is useful in estimating stand volume or biomass from a stand volume or biomass function and to determine site index from a curve or equation. The following are methods that have been used to obtain the average height of a stand.

1. Measure and average the heights of all trees, or a sample of trees, regardless of their size or relative position in the stand. This corresponds to an unweighted mean stand height.
2. Measure and average the heights of dominant trees, or of dominant and codominant trees. (In Australia and New Zealand these are called the

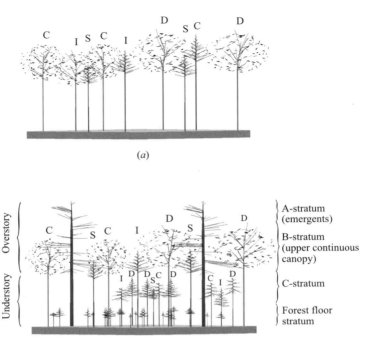

FIG. 8-6. Crown class and (*a*) single-stratum and (*b*) multistrata canopy. D, dominant; C, codominant; I, intermediate; S, suppressed. (Adapted from Oliver and Larson, 1996.)

predominant height and *dominant height*, respectively.) Since the selection of a dominant or codominant tree is subjective, different observers often obtain different results. The average height of dominant and codominant trees is the expression commonly used in determining the site index in North America.

3. Measure and average heights of a fixed number of the largest trees (usually, largest in diameter, although it could be largest in height) per unit area. (In Australia and New Zealand the mean total height of the *n* trees per hectare with the largest dbh values is called the *top height*.)

4. Determine the average height weighted by basal area, called *Lorey's mean height* h_L:

$$h_L = \frac{n_1 g_1 h_1 + n_2 g_2 h_2 + \cdots + n_z g_z h_z}{G} = \frac{\sum_{i=1}^{z} n_i g_i h_i}{\sum_{i=1}^{z} n_i g_i} \qquad (8\text{-}7)$$

where G = total basal area per unit area
n_i = number of trees in ith diameter class
g_i = average basal area of ith diameter class
h_i = average height of trees in ith diameter class

The arithmetic average height of the trees selected in horizontal point sampling (Section 11-3.1) yields Lorey's mean height, as shown by Kendall and Sayn-Wittgenstein (1959), and later by Beers and Miller (1973).

In addition to the above, several expressions of average stand height have been developed that utilize a height–diameter curve constructed from sample tree data representative of the stand. After preparing the curve, one decides what average diameter is representative of the stand and reads the height of the tree of this diameter from the curve. For example, the diameter of the tree of average basal area might be used (symbolized h_g); the arithmetic mean diameter might be used (symbolized h_d); the median diameter might be used (symbolized h_{dM}); or the diameter of the tree of median basal area might be used (symbolized h_{gM}). In New Zealand, the quadratic mean diameter of the largest 100 trees is determined. The corresponding height for this diameter tree is then estimated from a height–diameter curve.

8-4.2 Height–Diameter Curves

Height–diameter curves are often needed for preparing local volume tables. They are often plotted free hand, although the relationship can be expressed by mathematical functions and fitted using regression analysis. Since the curve form may vary from one forest stand to another, numerous functions have been developed. Some examples are

$$h = 4.5 + b_1 D + b_2 D^2 \qquad \text{(Trorey, 1932)}$$

$$\log h = b_0 + b_1 \log D \qquad \text{(Stoffels and Van Soest, 1953)}$$

$$h = b_0 + b_1 \log D \qquad \text{(Hendricksen, 1950)}$$

$$\log h = b_0 + b_1 D^{-1} \qquad \text{(Avery and Burkhart, 2002)}$$

Prodan et al. (1997) describe these additional models:

$$h - 1.3 = \frac{D^2}{(b_0 + b_1 D)^2}$$

$$h = b_0 D^{b_1} \quad \text{or} \quad \log h = \log b_0 + b_1 \log D$$

$$h = b_0 (1 - e^{-b_1 D})$$

$$h - 1.3 = b_0 \left(\frac{D}{1+D} \right)^{b_1}$$

$$h - 1.3 = b_0 e^{-b_1/D}$$

$$\ln(h - 1.3) = \ln b_0 - b_1 \frac{1}{D}$$

$$h = b_0^{b_1 \ln D - b_2 \ln(D)^2}$$

$$\frac{1}{(h - h_b)^{0.4}} = b_0 + \frac{b_1}{D} \quad \text{or} \quad h = 1.4 + \left(b_0 + \frac{b_1}{D} \right)^{-2.5} \qquad \text{(Petterson 1955)}$$

where b_i = constants
$\quad h$ = total height
$\quad D$ = dbh
$\quad e$ = base of natural logarithms
$\quad h_b$ = breast height
$\quad \ln$ = natural logarithm

In any of these models, height may be expressed in feet or meters and diameter in inches or centimeters.

Although numerous functions have been proposed, the parabolic equation $h = 4.5 + b_1 D + b_2 D^2$ can be used to describe the height–diameter relationships of many forest stands. However, if one desires to use a mathematical function to describe the height–diameter relationship for a particular stand, one should test to see which function is most applicable.

8-5. DENSITY AND STOCKING

Measures of stand density and forest stocking are both used to depict the degree to which a given site is being utilized by the growing trees or simply to indicate the quantity of wood on an area. However, a distinction is usually made between the two terms. Gingrich (1967) describes the distinction in this way: "*Stand density* is a quantitative measurement of a stand in terms of square feet of basal area, number of trees or volume per acre. It reflects the degree of crowding of stems within the area. *Stocking*, on the other hand, is a relative term used to describe the adequacy of a given stand density in meeting the management objective. Thus, a stand with a density of 70 square feet of basal area per acre may be classified as overstocked, or understocked, depending on what density is considered desirable."

Stand density can be expressed, as above, in absolute units per unit land area according to such stand parameters as volume, basal area, crown coverage, number of trees, and so on, but often it is expressed on a relative scale as a percentage of "normal" (full or desirable) density or as a percentage of average density. When expressed in this form, it should be clear that *relative density* exists as a term transitional between *stand density* and *stocking* as above.

8-5.1   Relative Density

For many forestry purposes, volume has been the ultimate expression of stand density. Relative density in terms of volume is determined by comparing the volume of an observed stand with the volume of a standard, such as the volumes of fully stocked stands for specified ages and site qualities as given in a yield table. For example, a 50-year-old stand of white pine with a site index of 58 in Massachusetts was measured and its volume was found to be 4500 board feet per acre. A normal yield table showed theoretically that the full stocking for this age and site was 6290 board feet. The relative density is then $100(4500/6290) = 71.5$ percent. Note that relative density percentages using volume depend on the volume unit chosen. For example, board-foot density percentages will differ from cubic-foot density percentages for the same stand.

Density as measured by relative volumes has several disadvantages. Volumes as expressed for the standard or fully stocked stand may be based on different merchantability limits, different log rules, or different volume units from the stand under investigation, making valid comparison difficult. In addition, stand volume estimates are too expensive if only a measure of relative density is needed. The advantage of basal area is that it is easily determined and is quite consistent for fully stocked stands of specified ages and sites. Since relative density depends on the unit of volume used, even for the same stand, relative density using basal area will not necessarily be the same as that using volume.

8-5.2   Stand Density Index

The number of trees per unit land area can be used as another measure of stand density. At any age, there can be a wide range in the number of trees per unit land area, so that frequency by itself is of little value. For a useful descriptive measure of stand density, number of trees must be qualified by tree size. The stand structure as shown in a stand table (Table 8-2) describes this but is too cumbersome for practical use as a stand density description. A useful measure of density for even-aged stands based on number of trees is *Reineke's stand density index* (Reineke, 1933). This stand density index is the number of trees per unit area that a stand would have at a standard average dbh. In the English system, the standard dbh is generally 10 in., and in the metric system the standard dbh is 10 cm. The stand density index for a stand can be obtained by referring to a stand density index chart for the species. As shown in Fig. 8-7, the chart consists of a series of lines representing the relationship between number of trees per acre and average stand diameter.

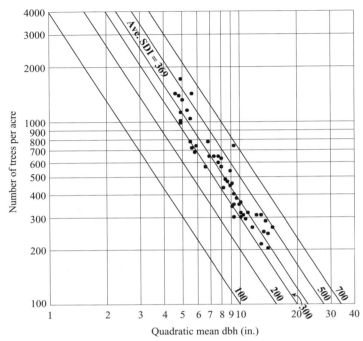

FIG. 8-7. Stand density index (SDI) chart for white pine in southeastern New Hampshire. Equation is $\log N = -1.598 \cdot \log \overline{D}_Q + 4.165$. Based on 53 sample plots.

The chart can be constructed by plotting the logarithm of number of trees per acre over the logarithm of the average stand dbh on rectangular coordinate paper. Alternatively, as shown in Fig. 8-7, the natural values can be plotted on logarithmic paper, yielding the same results. The number of trees and the average stand diameters are obtained from a series of sample plots. Average stand diameter is taken as the diameter of the tree of arithmetic mean basal area (i.e., quadratic mean diameter). Reineke (1933) defined the stand density index relationship as

$$\log N = b \log \overline{D}_Q + a \qquad (8\text{-}8)$$

where N = stand density (trees per unit area)
     $\overline{D}_Q$ = quadratic mean diameter (diameter of tree of average basal area)

Reineke (1933) found that the b constant was -1.605 for several species and was independent of site quality and age. Other investigators note that the linear relationship expressed by the equation holds for many species and that the slope (b) differs little, although the constant a (i.e., the intercept) varies considerably.

An average SDI relationship for the observations is obtained by fitting the stand data to eq. (8-8) using regression analysis. This line represents the average stocking of all plots. For the data shown in Fig. 8-7, this line is $\log N = -1.598 \cdot \log \overline{D}_Q + 4.165$. The number of trees indicated by the intersection of this line and the ordinate at the standard dbh is the average stand density index. In Fig. 8-7, the 10-in. ordinate is taken as the standard. The average line intersects the 10-in. ordinate at $N = 369$, so the average SDI is 369. A series of parallel lines is then constructed to intersect the standard diameter ordinate at specified numbers of trees per acre. The numbers at these intersections are the stand density index values for the set of parallel lines.

Any two stands falling on the same line have the same stand density index (i.e., the same relative density). For example, in Fig. 8-7, a stand with 300 trees/ acre and a quadratic mean dbh of 8 in. and a stand with 900 trees/acre and a quadratic mean dbh of 4 in. would both have an SDI = 200 (i.e., the same relative density as a stand with 200 trees/acre and a quadratic mean dbh of 10 in.).

The stand density index for any stand can be determined by plotting the position of the observed number of trees/acre and the quadratic mean dbh on the stand density chart for the species. The stand density index is indicated by the closest line to the plotted point or can be found by interpolation between the index lines. Alternatively, the stand density index can also be calculated from the formula

$$\log \text{SDI} = \log N - b \cdot (\log \overline{D}_Q - \log \overline{D}_I) \tag{8-9}$$

where   SDI = Reineke's stand density index
   N = number of trees per unit area
   $\overline{D}_Q$ = quadratic mean diameter (diameter of tree of average basal area)
   $\overline{D}_I$ = standard diameter

The formula is derived from eq. (8-8) by setting $\overline{D}_Q$ equal to 10. Consequently, in this case $\log N = \log \text{SDI}$. For the example, a stand with 265 trees/acre and a $\overline{D}_Q = 14.6$ would have an SDI of

$$\log \text{SDI} = \log 265 - (-1.598)(\log 14.6 - \log 10)$$
$$= 2.423 + 1.598(1.164 - 1)$$
$$= 2.423 + 1.598(0.164)$$
$$= 2.686$$
$$\text{SDI} = 10^{2.686}$$
$$= 485$$

8-5.3   Tree-Area Ratio

The tree-area ratio is a measure of density proposed by Chisman and Schumacher (1940) as a measure independent of stand age and site quality and appropriate for even- or uneven-aged stands. It is based on the concept that if the space on the ground Y, occupied by a tree of diameter at breast height d, can be expressed by the parabolic relation

$$Y = b_0 + b_1 d + b_2 d^2 \qquad (8\text{-}10)$$

then the total area of growing space represented on a plot or unit of ground area can be found by summing over all the trees on the plot or unit area. Thus, a measure of growing space utilization can be obtained by adding over all trees (n) on a unit area, leading to

$$\text{tree area} = b_0 n + b_1 \sum d + b_2 \sum d^2 \qquad (8\text{-}11)$$

After the constants b_0, b_1, and b_2 are obtained by least squares, the contribution to tree area of a single tree of diameter d can be found by letting $n = 1$, $\sum d = d$, and $\sum d^2 = d^2$.

Using data obtained from sample plots adjusted to the appropriate unit area basis and setting the tree area value to 1, the constants in eq. (8-11) are obtained using regression analysis. If the data used to derive the coefficients b_0, b_1, and b_2 in eq. (8-11) came from stands that were deliberately chosen to be "fully" or "normally" stocked, application of the regression equation to other stands and substitution of n, $\sum d$, and $\sum d^2$ will provide a tree-area figure that will reflect the proportion of *full stocking* demonstrated by that stand. On the other hand, if the data used to derive the coefficients came from stands having a range of densities, substitution into the equation for a given stand will reflect the proportion of stocking compared to the *average stocking* of the basic data.

8-5.4   Crown Competition Factor

A measure of stand density, which in final form is similar to the tree-area ratio, although considerably different in derivation, is the crown competition factor (CCF) proposed by Krajicek et al. (1961). The CCF is considered independent of site quality and stand age and can be used in both even- and uneven-aged stands.

The development of a CCF formula for a given species or species group would proceed as follows, using the example given by Krajicek et al. (1961).

1. Measurements of crown width and dbh are taken on a satisfactory number of truly open-grown trees, selected carefully to ensure that they have developed in an undisturbed, competition-free environment.

2. For this measured sample, the relationship between crown width (CW) and dbh (d) is found by least squares. For example, Krajicek et al. (1961) used the relationship $CW = b_0 + b_1 d$ and obtained the equation $CW = 3.12 + 1.829d$.

3. A formula for the crown area of individual trees expressed as a percentage of unit area (A) is derived and is called *maximum crown area* (MCA), since it indicates the maximum proportion of an area that the crowns of trees of a given dbh can occupy:

$$MCA = 100 \left[\frac{\pi(CW)^2}{4} \right] \frac{1}{A} \qquad (8\text{-}12)$$

In the English system, $MCA = 0.0018(CW)^2$; in the metric system, $MCA = 0.0078(CW)^2$.

4. The regression relating CW to dbh is then substituted into eq. (8-12) to obtain an expression of MCA as a function of dbh:

$$MCA = 100 \left[\frac{\pi(b_0 + b_1 d)^2}{4} \right] \frac{1}{A}$$

$$= \frac{100\pi}{4A} \left(b_0^2 + 2b_0 b_1 d + b_1^2 d^2 \right)$$

In Krajicek et al.'s example:

$$MCA = 0.0018(3.12 + 1.829d)^2$$

$$= 0.0175 + 0.02050d + 0.0060d^2$$

5. By adding the MCAs for all trees on a per unit area basis of forestland, an expression of stand density, called the *crown competition factor* (CCF), is obtained:

$$CCF = \sum_{i=1}^{m} (n_i MCA_i)$$

$$= \sum_{i=1}^{m} \left[n_i \frac{100\pi}{4A} \left(b_0^2 + 2b_0 b_1 d_i + b_1^2 d_i^2 \right) \right]$$

$$= \frac{100\pi}{4A} \left(b_0^2 \sum_{i=1}^{m} n_i + 2b_0 b_1 \sum_{i=1}^{m} d_i n_i + b_1^2 \sum_{i=1}^{m} d_i^2 n_i \right) \qquad (8\text{-}13)$$

where CCF = crown competition factor
$\qquad m$ = number of dbh classes

n_i = number of trees per unit area in ith dbh class
d_i = midpoint diameter of ith dbh class
b_i = crown width coefficients
A = unit area ($43{,}560\,\text{ft}^2$ or $10{,}000\,\text{m}^2$)

For the example above, the CCF for a specific stand is determined by

$$\text{CCF} = \left(0.0175 \sum n_i + 0.0205 \sum d_i n_i + 0.0060 \sum d_i^2 n_i \right) \qquad (8\text{-}14)$$

In eq. (8-14), it is assumed the n_i are expressed on a per acre basis. If the n_i are for the total stand, eq. (8-14) must be divided by stand area to obtain CCF on a per acre basis.

Any combination of MCAs that sum to 100 (CCF = 100) represents a closed canopy and reflects a situation where the tree crowns just touch and are sufficiently distorted to cover each acre of ground completely. However, the authors of this index state: "It should be emphasized that CCF is not essentially a measure of crown closure. Theoretically, complete crown closure can occur from CCF 100 to the maximum for the species (e.g., in oaks, approximately CCF 200). Instead of estimating crown closure, CCF estimates the area available to the average tree in the stand in relation to the maximum area it could use if it were open grown."

8-5.5 Relative Spacing

Another expression of stand density is *relative spacing*. RS_H is the average spacing between trees, assuming square spacing, divided by the average height of the dominant trees:

$$\text{RS}_H = \frac{A/N}{H_D} \qquad (8\text{-}15)$$

where A = unit area ($43{,}560\,\text{ft}^2$ or $10{,}000\,\text{m}^2$)
N = number of trees per unit area (acre or ha)
H_D = average height of dominant trees (ft or m)

Relative spacing can also be expressed in terms of diameter:

$$\text{RS}_D = \frac{A/N}{D_D}$$

where D_D = average dbh of dominant trees (in. or cm)

The relative spacing indices for RS_H or RS_D will be numbers such as 10, 11, or 12. The formula for RS_H has also been written as

$$RS_H = \frac{\sqrt{A/N}}{H_D} \tag{8-16}$$

In this case the index numbers will usually be decimals such as 0.15. Equation (8-16) is referred to as the spacing–top height factor (Wilson, 1946). The RS index is higher when N is larger. Thus, for even-aged stands, RS decreases as the stand grows older and the number of trees decreases due to mortality.

8-5.6 Point Density and Competition Indices

The measures of density described previously are usually employed to determine density of a stand in general or "on average." More specific measures of density have been developed to describe the degree of competition at a given point or tree in the stand. These measures have been referred to as either point density estimates or competition indices. The basic idea of these indices is to describe the degree to which growth resources (light, water, nutrients, and physical growing space) available to an individual tree are limited by neighboring trees. The increased interest in modeling individual tree growth and yield has produced a number of competition indices. These indices can be broadly classified into two categories: distance-independent measures and distance-dependent measures.

Distance-independent measures describe the competitive status of a tree or class of trees relative to all trees in the stand. An example of a distance-independent index is the basal area index proposed by Glover and Hool (1979):

$$G_i = \frac{\pi(D_i/2)^2}{\pi\left[\left(\sum_{j=1}^{n} D_j/n\right)/2\right]^2} = \frac{D_i^2}{\overline{D}^2} \tag{8-17}$$

where G_i = basal area index for ith tree
$\quad\quad D_i$ = diameter of ith tree
$\quad\quad \overline{D}$ = mean plot or stand diameter

An alternative expression of this index is the ratio of a tree basal area to the mean basal area (Daniels et al., 1986):

$$G_{Bi} = \frac{\text{BA}_i}{\overline{\text{BA}}} = \frac{D_i^2}{\left(\sum_{j=1}^{n} D_j^2\right)/n} = \frac{D_i^2}{\overline{D}_Q^2}$$

Other indices have been calculated based on ratios of tree height to mean height, tree height to dominant height, and tree volume to mean volume. The main advantage of distance-independent indices is that time-consuming measures of tree location are not required. The main disadvantage is that these indices measure a tree's status relative to average stand conditions rather than the immediate conditions surrounding the tree.

Distance-dependent indices attempt to describe a tree's competitive status based on the immediate conditions surrounding the tree. Distance-dependent indices fall into three broad classes (Tomé and Burkhart, 1989): area overlap indices, distance-weighted size ratios, and area potentially available indices.

Area overlap indices are based on the idea that each tree has a potential area of influence over which it obtains or competes for site factors (Opie, 1968). All trees whose area of influence overlaps with a subject tree's area of influence are considered competitors (Fig. 8-8a). Spurr's (1962) point density is an example of an area overlap index. Spurr (1962) adapted Bitterlich's point basal area to be used as a point density measure. All trees included in a basal area sweep are considered competitors. The estimate of point density is given by

$$\text{PD} = k \frac{\frac{1}{2}(D_1/L_1)^2 + \frac{3}{2}(D_2^2/L_2)^2 + \cdots + \left(n - \frac{1}{2}\right)(D_n/L_n)^2}{n} = k \frac{\sum_{i=1}^{n}\left(i - \frac{1}{2}\right)(d_i/L_i)^2}{n}$$

$$(8\text{-}18)$$

where PD = point density

k = unit area conversion factor ($k = 43{,}560/(144 \times 4) = 75.625$ in English system and $k = 10{,}000/(10{,}000 \times 4) = 0.25$ in metric system)

D_i = diameter

L_i = distance from point to tree

n = number of trees in basal area sweep

Trees are entered into the formula starting with the largest angle subtended from the viewing point (i.e., largest D/L), followed by the next largest, and so

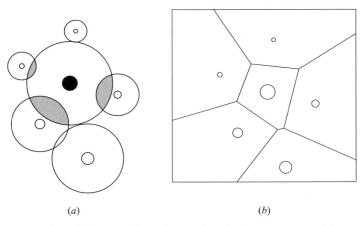

(a)   (b)

FIG. 8-8. Examples of distance-dependent point density measures: (a) area overlap concept; (b) area potentially available.

on. As Spurr (1962) points out, the tree with the largest angle is not necessarily the largest tree or the closest tree.

Distance-weighted size ratios are calculated as the sum of the ratios between the dimensions of each competitor and to the subject tree, weighted by a function of intertree distance (Tomé and Burkhart, 1989). An example is the competition index proposed by Hegyi (1974):

$$C_i = \sum_{j=1}^{n} \frac{D_j/D_i}{L_{ij}} \tag{8-19}$$

where C_i = competition index for subject tree
  D_j = diameter of jth competitor
  D_i = diameter of subject tree
  L_{ij} = distance from subject tree to jth competitor
  n = number of competitors

Hegyi (1974) defined n as the number of trees within a fixed radius of the subject tree. Daniels (1976) modified the index by defining n as the number of trees within a fixed-angle gauge sweep.

The *area potentially available index* utilizes polygons created by the intersections of the perpendicular bisectors of the distance between a subject tree and its competitors (Fig. 8-8*b*). The polygon area, as calculated from the coordinates of the vertices, is the area potentially available for tree growth (Brown, 1965). Moore et al. (1973) modified the index so that the division was weighted by tree size:

$$I_{ij} = \frac{D_i^2}{D_i^2 + D_j^2} L_{ij} \tag{8-20}$$

where I_{ij} = distance from subject tree to weighted midpoint between subject tree and competitor
  D_i = diameter of subject tree
  D_j = diameter of jth competitor
  L_{ij} = distance between subject tree and jth competitor

As mentioned above, numerous indices have been developed. Each index is derived based on certain assumptions about how the competitive process is manifested. Daniels (1976) suggests that the utility of an index be judged based on correlation with observed tree growth and computational simplicity. Several studies have investigated the efficacy of these measures for predicting individual tree growth (e.g., Opie, 1968; Gerrard 1969; Johnson 1973; Daniels, 1976; Alemdag, 1978; Noone and Bell, 1980; Martin and Ek, 1984; Daniels et al., 1986; Tomé and Burkhart, 1989; Biging and Dobbertin, 1995). The results are variable and no single index has emerged as universally superior. The choice of an index depends primarily on the use and the data available.

8-5.7   Forest Stocking and Density Management Diagrams

In an excellent discussion of stocking and density, Bickford et al. (1957) accept the Society of American Foresters' definition of stocking as "an indication of the number of trees in a stand as compared to the desirable number for best growth and management: such as well-stocked, over-stocked, partly stocked." Although they point out that there are varying shades of meaning for the silviculturist, economist, or forest manager, the most common connotation of *forest stocking* is in the sense of "best growth." That is, the terms *overstocked* and *understocked* represent the upper and lower limits of site occupancy within which there exists a degree of stocking where forest growth will be optimum. Ideally, forest managers should be able to recognize this optimum stocking point under the complete range of stand composition conditions that they encounter. Many attempts have been made to quantify forest stocking so that its relationship to growth can be determined more readily.

Basal Area Stocking Diagrams. Based on the repeatedly shown concept that gross increment varies very little over a wide range of stand density, the work of Gingrich (1964, 1967) culminated in a stocking chart (Fig. 8-9) that has found considerable use in applied forest management in the central United States.

The chart was developed using (1) a tree-area equation (see Section 8-5.3) derived from data for stands that were deliberately chosen to be "fully stocked," and (2) an equation based on the crown competition factor (see Section 8-5.4), using data from open-grown trees. Thus, in Fig. 8-9, the A-line (100 percent stocking) represents a normal condition of maximum stocking for undisturbed stands of upland hardwoods of average structure, and the B-line represents the lower limit of stocking for full site occupancy (Gingrich, 1967). The entire range of stocking between A and B is called fully stocked because the growing space can be fully utilized. It follows that stands having a combination of basal area per acre falling outside the range will demonstrate a gross increment less than the potential of the site, because of either overstocking or understocking.

Application of the stocking chart to determine a prescription of silvicultural treatment is in itself simple. For example, if stand measurements indicate a basal area per acre of 80 ft^2 and 175 trees per acre, an average diameter of 9.2 in. is indicated in Fig. 8-9. Following the 9.2 line down to the point where it crosses the B-line, one finds that a basal area of 65 ft^2 is the minimum basal area to maintain full stocking at that average diameter. Therefore, a silvicultural treatment that removes 15 ft^2 of basal area without materially changing the average stand diameter leaves a stand that will still fully utilize the site and produce wood efficiently. For greater detail on application, the reader is referred to the handbooks written by Roach and Gingrich (1962, 1968) and Roach (1977).

Stand Density Management Diagrams. Drew and Flewelling (1979) developed a stand density management diagram for Douglas-fir based on the

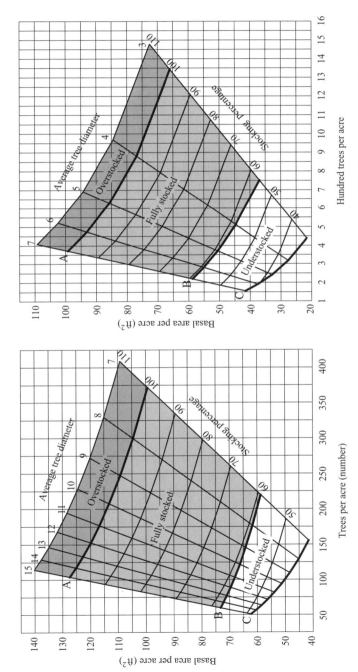

FIG. 8-9. Basal area stocking guide for upland hardwood stands. The area between curves A and B indicates the range of stocking where the trees can fully utilize the growing space. Curve C shows the lower limit of stocking necessary to reach the B level in 10 years on average sites. (Adapted from Gingrich, 1967.)

maximum size–density relationship and the $-\frac{3}{2}$ rule of self-thinning. The maximum size–density relationship is a general principle of plant population biology which postulates that for even-aged pure species stands, the maximum mean tree size attainable for any density can be determined from the $-\frac{3}{2}$ power rule:

$$\overline{V} = aN^{-3/2} \qquad (8\text{-}21)$$

where $\overline{V}$ = mean tree volume
a = species specific constant
N = trees per unit area

The maximum size–density line represents maximum stocking. *Relative density* is defined as the ratio of actual density to the maximum density attainable in a stand with the same mean tree volume:

$$R = \frac{N}{N_{\max}}$$

where R = relative density
N = actual stand density
$N_{\max}$ = maximum density attainable: $N_{\max} = (a/\overline{V})^{2/3}$

In addition to the relative density lines, the lower limit of competition-induced mortality (Drew and Flewelling, 1977) and crown closure lines are drawn on their diagram. The lower limit of competition-induced mortality is approximately 55 percent of the maximum size–density relationship and crown closure is approximately 15 percent of the maximum. The resulting stand density management diagram is shown in Fig. 8-10.

Similar diagrams utilizing either the $-\frac{3}{2}$ power rule, stand density index [eq. (8-9)], or relative spacing [eq. (8-15)] have been developed for several species worldwide [e.g., McCarter and Long (1986) for lodgepole pine and Wilson (1979) for red pine]. Like the basal area stocking diagrams, these diagrams are widely used as a means of assessing thinning needs and predicting stand development and yields. For a complete description of the application of density management diagrams, see Drew and Flewelling (1977, 1979) and McCarter and Long (1986).

8-6. VOLUME AND WEIGHT

8-6.1 Volume

An estimate of the total volume of trees in a stand is an important parameter for providing information necessary for making decisions on the management of a forest. Those components of the stand included in the volume must be

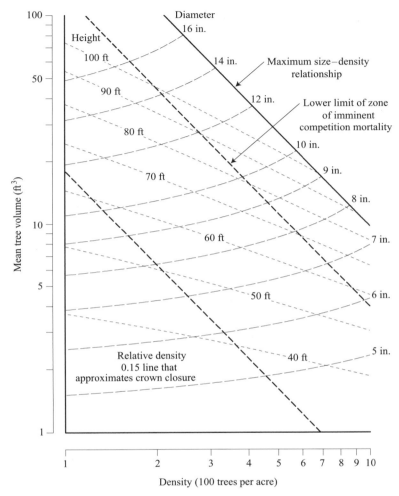

FIG. 8-10. Douglas-fir stand density management diagram. (Adapted from Drew and Flewelling, 1979.)

specified (e.g., species, minimum dbh and top diameter of the main stem, branches). For even-aged stands, the age should be specified. Note that in even-aged forests, stand volume at a given age is indicative of the site quality.

Stand volume can be estimated by various procedures:

- *Ocular estimates.* Rough estimates of stand volume can be made by experienced foresters or timber cruisers who have worked in similar stands with known volumes.

- *Average tree procedures.* Determining the tree of average volume and multiplying by the number of trees can estimate the volume of a stand. In principle, the method is simple and direct. The practical difficulty in applying this procedure is to determine what is the tree of mean volume. Of course, it would be possible to measure a number of sample trees and calculate their mean volume, but the benefit of a quick estimate is lost as the number of sample trees measured increases and the procedure becomes the same as taking forest inventory plots. A variation of the mean tree volume procedure is to divide the volume of what is chosen as the average tree by its basal area and then multiply this ratio by the basal area of the stand $V = (\bar{v}_t/g_t)G$, where V is the stand volume, $\bar{v}_t$ the mean tree volume, g_t the mean tree basal area, and G the stand basal area. Estimation of stand basal area and the average basal area per tree is readily obtainable by point sampling (see Section 11-3 and Chapter 14). The volume of the tree of average basal area can then be estimated from a basal area–volume relationship.[*] The use of average tree methods was developed and used primarily in European forestry. Several procedures for the application of this technique using dbh or forest classes are described by Prodan (1965).

- *Inventory procedures.* Of course, stand volume may be estimated by the sample plot procedures discussed in Chapter 11.

- *Stand volume equations.* The cubic volume of a stand can be estimated as the product of the total stand basal area, the average stand height, and some expression of the stand form factor. Then $V = \text{GHF}$, where V is the total stand cubic volume, G the total basal area of the stand, H the average stand height, F the form factor for the stand (e.g., cylindrical form factor).[†] The objective is to obtain a stand volume estimate rapidly without the necessity of measuring all trees or obtaining their volumes from tables. The accuracy of this method depends on how representative the values of basal area and average height and form factor are for a specific stand. Stand volume functions can also be developed using several of the models for tree volume equations, substituting stand basal area for dbh^2 and stand height for tree height [e.g., see eq. (6-17)].

8-6.2 Weight

Stand weight as a stand parameter has increased in importance as interest has grown in the measurement of biomass. Just as with stand volume, the compo-

---

[*]The linear regression of the volumes of individual trees on their respective basal areas is called the *volume-line* (Hummel, 1953, 1955). From a volume-line relationship, the volume of the tree of mean basal area can be estimated.

[†]In Australian forest practice, stand form factors F have been determined empirically for *Pinus radiata* plantations from the relationship $F = V/HG$ where H is stand height and G is stand basal area (Brack, 1988).

nents included in an expression of the weight of a stand must be specified. Weight can be determined for the timber in a forest stand or for the stand's biomass (see Section 10-4).

8-7. SITE QUALITY

The productivity of a site for tree growth is usually evaluated on a stand basis. Considered in this way, site quality expresses the average productivity of a designated land area for growing forest trees. A common way of expressing relative site quality is to set up from three to five classes, or ordinal ranks, such as site I, site II, and site III, designating comparative productive capacities in descending rank. The characteristics of each class must be defined to enable any area to be classified. To a large extent, the definitions are in qualitative terms, so that the ranking of a site is quite subjective. Wherever possible, attempts are made to introduce numerical definitions to improve the precision of site-quality ranking.

Site quality can be evaluated in two general ways:

1. By the measurement of one or more of the individual site factors that are considered closely associated with tree growth. This approach evaluates site quality in terms of the environmental causal factors themselves.
2. By the measurement of some characteristics of the trees or lesser vegetation that are considered expressive of site quality. This approach assesses site quality from the effects of the environment on the vegetation.

8-7.1 Measurement of Site Factors

Knowledge of the growth responses of forest trees to factors of the environment is important to forest management. The forester can use this knowledge to encourage the establishment and growth of desirable species, either by modifying the environment or by concentrating on sites having desirable environmental characteristics. In the past, foresters have been restricted by their inability to modify the environment on a given site in order to change stand density and structure. With the use of fertilization and irrigation practices, it is possible to modify some soil characteristics, especially fertility and moisture content. However, most applications of site–growth relationships consist of encouraging the growth of a species on sites where its establishment is readily achieved or where its growth potential can be fully realized.

The relationship of the growth of forest trees to their environment, or, as it is commonly referred to, their *site*, is difficult to measure. The factors of the site and the plants themselves are interacting and interdependent, making it difficult to assign cause-and-effect relationships. The environmental factors of the site can be grouped as edaphic, climatic, topographic, and competitive. The most important elements of each are shown below.

- *Edaphic*: soil depth and texture, nutrient levels, pH, moisture, drainage
- *Climatic*: air temperature, precipitation, humidity, length of growing season, available light, wind
- *Topographic*: altitude, slope angle, position and length, aspect
- *Competitive*: other trees and vegetation

A considerable amount of effort has been directed towards investigating the characteristics of the soil in an attempt to find a single environmental factor to serve as a reliable indicator of site quality. This approach has been found practical but frequently leaves unexplained a sizable amount of the variation in the growth parameter employed. To understand fully the growth of trees in relation to the environment, individual site factors cannot be studied in isolation. The interdependencies and influences of the other factors may be masked and, consequently, not recognized. Even if the primary interest is the study of one factor of the site, it must be done with recognition of the effects of other factors.

The usual form of a soil–site quality investigation has consisted of a multiple regression analysis with height or site index as the dependent variable and a number of soil and other environmental characteristics as the independent variables. A commonly used model has been

$$\log H = b_0 + b_1 \frac{1}{A} + b_2(B) + b_3(C) + \cdots + b_n(N)$$

where H = height
             A = age
$B, C, \cdots, N$ = soil or other environmental factors
             b_i = constants to be determined by regression analysis

A major difficulty in this type of analysis pertains to the numerical coding of qualitative variables to use in the regression analysis. Such a procedure can lead to difficulty because the arbitrary assignment of numbers to discrete variables and subsequent computations, by assuming the continuous scale, implies a scale of equal units that may not represent the actual relationship between the original discrete classes. The thoughtful assignment of numerical codes to qualitative variables will make the subsequent regression analysis more meaningful. For an example of this type of coding, refer to Beers et al. (1966) and Stage (1976).

8-7.2   Measurement of Vegetative Characteristics

The characteristics of the vegetation that can be used to express the quality of a site include (1) the quantity of wood produced (commonly called the *site productivity*), (2) the size characteristics of the trees, and (3) the species of plants naturally occurring on the area.

Since the concept of site quality refers to productivity, its most direct measures are the quantity of wood grown on an area of land within a given period or mean annual increment of the stand. However, since little information of this type is available for most forest sites, this measure of site quality has had limited application. The use of volume growth to assess site quality will have greater application as data accumulates on forest growth for different sites and species.

Since the size that trees will attain according to their age is also affected by site quality, the most widely used tree-size characteristic for site evaluation is tree height. Diameter is less reliable since it is more sensitive to stand density. The relationship of tree height to age, called *site index*, has been used for many years in evaluating site quality for even-aged stands of single species or nearly pure composition. The height of the dominant and codominant trees has usually been taken as representative of stand height for site index work. This choice is not without its limitations. It relies on subjective decisions about which are dominants and which are codominants. In addition, the crown position of a tree and its height growth may be affected by stand alterations such as cuttings. Other stand measures, such as the average height of a specified number of the largest trees or the height of the tallest tree, have been suggested as alternative parameters. Unless otherwise specified, site index is generally defined as the average height that the dominant and codominant trees in an area will attain at key ages such as 50 or 100 years. For example, site index 70 on a 50-year basis means that the dominants and codominants reach an average height of 70 ft in 50 years. Site index 120 on a 100-year basis means an average height of 120 ft in 100 years. Site index curves are prepared for even-aged stands as shown in Fig. 8-11 to allow site classification for a stand at any age.

To assess the site quality of an area, it is necessary to determine the average height of the dominant and codominant trees and their average age. The position of these coordinates is then located on the site index chart for the species. The site index for the stand can be read from the closest curve. For example, a stand with an average height of the dominants and codominants of 65 ft and 40 years of age would have a site index of 80 for white pine in the southern Appalachians. Total age or age at breast height (dbh level) can be used in the preparation of site index curves. Husch (1956) has pointed out several advantages of using age at dbh instead of total age. Measuring age at dbh eliminates the necessity of adding arbitrary corrections to convert age at increment-boring level to total age; it measures tree age after the initial period of establishment and adjustment has passed; it also utilizes a standard and conventional point for age determination.

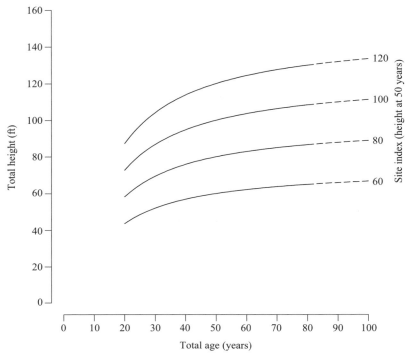

FIG. 8-11. Site index curves for natural stands of white pine in the southern Appalachians. (Adapted from Doolittle and Vimmerstedt, 1960.)

It is important to understand that site index varies according to species. Site index charts are prepared for individual species or for typical forest types, such as the charts prepared by Schnur (1937) for mixed oak forest in the central United States. A single forest area may have different site index values depending on the species and site index chart. To help solve this problem, regression formulas can be derived that relate the site index or height of one species with that of another. Examples of this type of study are those of Foster (1959), Deitschman and Green (1965), and Norman and Curlin (1968).

The relationship of age and total height expressed by site index has enjoyed widespread popularity for several reasons. Height has been found closely correlated to the ultimate measure—volume. In addition, the two requisite measurements, height and age, are determined quickly and easily. It is generally considered that height growth is only slightly affected by stand density, although some studies have shown that stand height and site index in some cases are related to stand density (Gaiser and Merz, 1951; Husch and Lyford, 1956). Finally, site index has been popular because it provides a numerical expression for site quality rather than generalized qualitative description.

In uneven-aged stands of several species, height in relation to age cannot be used to express site quality. The height growth of a species in this type of stand is not closely related to age but more to the varying stand conditions by which it has been affected during its life. The classic concept of site index has consequently been restricted to species normally occurring in even-aged stands. McClintock and Bickford (1957) considered several alternatives for evaluating site quality in uneven-aged stands in their study of site quality for red spruce in the northeastern United States. They concluded that the relationship between height and dbh of the dominant trees in a stand was the most sensitive and reliable measure of site quality. Site index according to this concept is then defined as the height attained by dominant trees at a standard dbh. The site index for a tree of any age can be read from the height–dbh curves for the range of site indexes as shown in Fig. 8-12. This chart utilizes a standard dbh of 14 in.

Another approach to site-quality evaluation makes use of the composition of plant communities on an area of land. This system is based on the theory that certain key "indicator" species in the forest reflect the overall quality of the site for a tree species or forest type. As Westveld (1954) pointed out some time ago: "The concept recognizes that plant communities are distinct entities

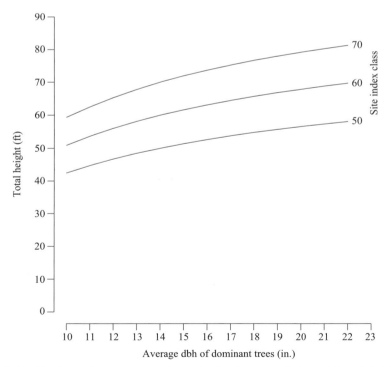

FIG. 8-12. Site index for uneven-aged stands of red spruce. (Adapted from McClintock and Bickford, 1957.)

developed and arranged in accordance with definite biological laws; they are not mere aggregations of plants brought together by chance. Such communities are well differentiated and are very constant for the same site." Site classification systems based on this concept have been most successful in relatively undisturbed northern forests in Finland and eastern Canada where the forests are extensive and the species few. These systems utilize measures of presence and relative abundance of characteristic species in the minor forest vegetation, called *plant indicators*, as indicative of the quality of the site for specified tree species. An additional premise is that these shorter-lived plants are more useful site-quality indicators than the trees themselves, since they are more sensitive and will, after a disturbance of the forest, return to equilibrium with site conditions more rapidly than will trees.

In summary, it has been proven that there exists a valid correlation between plant indicators and site quality, but it must be kept on broad terms. The general applicability of plant indicator systems has several limitations. It is restricted to forests of simple composition such as occur in northern latitudes; it requires considerable ecological knowledge on the part of the forester; and it must be recognized that the lesser vegetation is affected by forest composition, stand density, and past management as well as site quality. In addition, the lesser vegetation is shallow-rooted and does not indicate conditions in deeper soil horizons, although these soil conditions affect tree growth. Despite these limitations, indicator plants can be of general assistance in site-quality evaluation.

8-7.3   Preparation of Site Index Curves

The preparation of site index curves for even-aged stands is based on average height and age measurements of the dominant and codominant trees on a series of sample plots. When temporary sample plots are used, there should be a sufficient number and distribution to cover equally the range of age and site classes found under natural conditions. For reliable relationships, a total of at least 100 plots is necessary, although more are desirable.

Site index curves can be prepared using anamorphic or polymorphic techniques. The anamorphic techniques assume that the curves of height over age for different sites all have the same form and shape. This assumption does not always hold, so anamorphic site index curves may not represent the true forms of curves for different site indexes. Polymorphic site index curves eliminate this limitation by showing different shapes of curves for different site indices.

In the past, graphical techniques have been used to construct the desired series of anamorphic site index curves. In very brief form, this method plotted average height over age found on each sample plot on graph paper. A curve was then fitted freehand to these plots [see Husch (1963) for freehand curve fitting]. The average site index for all plots is the height as read from this curve for the key age. Based on the average curve, curves for other site index classes are constructed. The assumption is made that these other curves will have a trend and shape similar to those of the average site index curve. Under this assumption, the other curves are spaced above or below the average curve in proportion to their height at the key age. For example, the average site index curve might have a height of 65 ft at a 50-year key age. The site index 60 curve would be $[(65 - 60)/65]100 = 7.7\%$ below the average site index curve. The ordinates of the site index 60 curve would be obtained by reducing the ordinate of the average curve at any age by 7.7 percent. The same procedure would be followed for all other site index curves.

In recent years, regression techniques have been employed to remove the subjectivity involved in the freehand fitting of curves. One commonly used approach is described in the following paragraphs. Using field plot data involving total tree height and tree age (plot averages or individual tree data) obtained from selected dominant and codominant trees, site index curves similar to those shown in Fig. 8-11 can be derived. The procedure for preparing anamorphic site index equations is as follows[*]:

1. Transform the height and age data to a logarithm of height H and reciprocal of age A and fit a simple linear regression, obtaining numerical values for the constants a and b in the model

$$\log H = a + b\left(\frac{1}{A}\right) \tag{8-22}$$

The resulting equation represents the average site index curve for the data.

2. Locate points needed to draw a specified site index curve by moving the Y-axis to the key age (by mathematical translation) and then, by definition, the Y-intercept is the log of site index S. For example, if the key age is 50 years, eq. (8-22) is translated to become

$$\log H = \log S + b\left(\frac{1}{A} - \frac{1}{50}\right) \tag{8-23}$$

For example, if the regression coefficients for eq. (8-22) are $a = 1.950$ and $b = -4.611$, the translated equation for key age of 50 years is

$$\log H = \log S - 4.611\left(\frac{1}{A} - \frac{1}{50}\right)$$

$$= \log S - \frac{4.611}{A} + \frac{4.611}{50}$$

$$= \log S - \frac{4.611}{A} + 0.092\,22$$

---

[*]This technique is referred to as the *guide curve* method (Clutter et al., 1983).

The curve for each site index is found by substituting in the desired site index value for S and computing the height for various ages. For example, the curve for site index 80 would be

$$\log H = \log 80 - \frac{4.611}{A} + 0.092\,22$$

$$= 1.90309 - \frac{4.611}{A} + 0.092\,22$$

$$= 1.99531 - \frac{4.611}{A}$$

3. Locate other site index curves by substituting the pertinent site index number in eq. (8-23) and proceeding as described in step 2.

It is often useful to calculate site index from the fitted equation rather than to read a graph. For this purpose, eq. (8-23) is rearranged by solving for the log site index to become

$$\log S = \log H - \frac{b}{A} + \frac{b}{A_S} \qquad (8\text{-}24)$$

where A_S is the key age. For the example used in step 2, the resulting equation is

$$\log S = \log H + \frac{4.611}{A} - \frac{4.611}{50}$$

$$= \log H + \frac{4.611}{A} - 0.09222$$

For a given plot, one can substitute values of average tree height (as a logarithm) and average tree age and obtain the logarithm of the site index; then, by using antilogs, the site index can be estimated.

Polymorphic site index curves fall into two broad classes: disjoint and nondisjoint. *Disjoint polymorphic curves* are a set of site index curves in which even though the form and shape of each site index curve differs, the individual lines representing the different site indices do not cross within the age range of interest. *Nondisjoint polymorphic curves* do cross one another within the age range of interest. Clutter et al. (1983) discuss the procedures for fitting polymorphic disjoint site index curves. Newberry and Peinaar (1978) provide an example of fitting polymorphic nondisjoint curves.

9

MEASUREMENT OF PRIMARY FOREST PRODUCTS

An important task in forest mensuration is proper measurement of forest products. In this chapter we describe the units of measurement used in determining their quantities, rules used to estimate log volume, and scaling of primary products by both volume and weight.

9-1. UNITS OF MEASUREMENT

9-1.1 Board Foot

The *board foot*, which is still widely used to express the volume of trees, logs, and lumber, is defined as a piece of rough green lumber 1 in. thick, 12 in. wide, and 1 ft long, or its equivalent in dried and surfaced lumber. Thus a board foot is a nominal volume unit. For example, in the purchase of lumber the standard finished size of a kiln-dried 1 in. × 12 in. board would be $\frac{3}{4}$ in. × $11\frac{1}{4}$ in.; a kiln-dried 2 in. × 4 in. board would be $1\frac{1}{2}$ in. × $3\frac{1}{2}$ in; and so on. However, the board-foot volume of a piece of lumber would be computed from the nominal thickness and width, not the exact dimensions, by the following formula:

$$\text{board feet} = \frac{WTL}{12} \qquad (9\text{-}1)$$

where W = nominal width (in.)
$\quad\quad\quad T$ = nominal thickness (in.)
$\quad\quad\quad L$ = actual length (ft)

When log and lumber volumes in commercial transactions, inventory reports, and so on, involve large quantities of material, the volumes are normally given in thousands of board feet. In this case, the abbreviation M.B.F. (thousand board feet) or M.B.M. (thousand feet, board measure) is used. For example, 11,234,000 board feet = 11,234 M.B.F. Occasionally, especially in Canada, the abbreviation F.B.M (foot board, thousands) is used.

The board foot is the standard unit of lumber measurement in the United States (and is used in many other countries). Lumber that is thinner than 1 in. is usually sold on the basis of surface measure. Finished lumber, such as trim and molding, is sold by the linear foot.

Although there is an inexactness in the measurement of the board-foot volume of lumber, board-foot log rules showing the estimated number of board feet of lumber that can be sawed from logs of given lengths and diameters are frequently used to estimate the contents of logs and trees. This is rather unique. Few raw materials are measured in terms of the finished product. It is somewhat like trying to measure the yield of a field of corn in terms of boxes of cornflakes.

The number of board feet that can be produced from a log depends primarily on its length and diameter. In addition, there are other factors that affect the yield of a log. Among these are:

1. Efficiency of the sawmill machinery and, in particular, the thickness of the kerfs cut by the various saws
2. Efficiency of the workers, particularly the sawyers, edgers, and trimmers
3. Market conditions (when markets are good, efforts will be made to utilize small pieces, and the output will be raised; when the ratio of thick lumber cut to 1-in. lumber cut increases, output will be raised)
4. Amount of defect and taper in logs

Other units, which have largely disappeared, are the Hoppus foot and the Blodgett foot. The *Hoppus foot* is a cubic volume unit that has been used in the United Kingdom, Australia, New Zealand, and many of the Caribbean Islands. The formula to determine Hoppus feet, often called the *quarter-girth formula*, is

$$\text{Hoppus feet} = \left(\frac{C}{4}\right)^2 \frac{L}{144}$$

where C = girth (i.b. or o.b.) = circumference (in. at center of log)
L = length (ft of log)

The Hoppus formula gives 78.5 percent of the actual cubic volume of a log, and a Hoppus foot is considered equivalent to 10 board feet. To obtain cubic volume, a divisor of 113 is used in place of 144 in the quarter-girth formula.

The *Blodgett foot*, formerly employed in the northeastern United States, is defined as a cylindrical block of wood 16 in. in diameter and 1 ft in length. It is equivalent to $1.4\,ft^3$.

9-1.2 Volume Units for Stacked Wood

The *cord* is a unit of measure widely utilized in North America to express the volume of stacked wood. The need to measure relatively small pieces of rough, low-value wood stacked at scattered locations in the woods gave rise to this unit.

A *standard cord* is a pile of stacked wood 8 ft long and 4 ft high that is made up of 4-ft pieces (the standard cord occupies $128\,ft^3$). The actual solid wood content is generally less than $100\,ft^3$ and varies by species, method of stacking, form of wood, length and diameter of wood, bark thickness, and other factors.

A *long cord* measures 8 ft long and 4 ft high and is made up of pieces longer than 4 ft. Long cords commonly consist of pieces 5 ft long, or 5 ft 3 in. long, and occupy 160 or $168\,ft^3$, respectively.

A *short cord* or *face cord* is a unit smaller than the standard cord and is usually used to measure fuelwood that is cut less than 4 ft long. A *rick* of fuelwood is often considered to be an 8 ft × 4 ft pile made up of 12-in. pieces (four ricks per standard cord), or an 8 ft × 4 ft pile made up of 16-in. pieces (three ricks per standard cord).

A *pen*, which was used in the southern United States, consists of sticks stacked to a height of 6 ft in the form of a square enclosure with two sticks to a layer. Five pens of 4-ft sticks are assumed to equal a standard cord; five pens of 5-ft sticks are assumed to equal a long cord of $160\,ft^3$.

The *stere* or metric cord, which is used in some countries that employ the metric system, is a pile of stacked wood 1 m long and 1 m high that is made up of 1-m pieces (the stere occupies $1\,m^3$ of space).*

9-2. LOG RULES

A *log rule* is a table or formula that gives the estimated volume of logs of specified diameters and lengths. In North America most log rules give volumes in board feet of lumber, although tables that give volumes in cubic units are available. In nations where the International System of Units is used, expression of volume in board feet is still common, although many log rules give volume in cubic meters.

The cubic volume of a log may be determined by any of the methods described in Section 6-1. However, for log scaling, gross cubic volumes are

---

*Other units to measure stacked wood are employed in different countries. For example, the unit of stacked wood in Chile is the *metro ruma*, which consists of a 1 m × 1 m pile of 2.44-m sticks occupying $2.44\,m^3$ of space. The solid wood content is approximately $1.66\,m^3$.

usually computed by Huber's or Smalian's formula. Bell and Dilworth (1993) mention other formulas used on the West coast of the United States (two-end conic rule, subneiloid rule, and the Bruce butt log formulas). Traditionally, log rules have been presented in tabular form; however, the formulas can be used directly. Formulas are generally used in computer processing of inventory data rather than lookup tables that occupy large amounts of computer memory and are generally slower than direct computation.

In the preparation of cubic meter tables, volumes are most often computed for 2-cm diameter classes and 0.2-m length classes. In the preparation of cubic foot tables, volumes are most often computed for 1-in. diameter classes and 1-ft length classes. Diameter is often given as the midpoint-diameter inside bark. (When the midpoint diameter cannot be measured, the average of the diameters inside bark at the two ends of the log is generally used for midpoint diameter.) In some cases, volume is given in terms of small-end-diameter inside bark.

9-3. BOARD-FOOT LOG RULES

It is not easy to prepare a board-foot log rule that is universally applicable, because of variations in the dimensions of lumber produced from logs, the equipment used to saw logs, the skill of operators, computer programs used to saw logs, and the logs themselves. In the early years of the lumber industry in the United States and Canada, there were a number of independent marketing areas, and no industrial organization or governmental agency had control over the measurement of lumber and logs. As a result, different areas devised rules to fit specific operating conditions. Freese (1973) pointed out in his excellent report on log rules, "In the United States and Canada there are over 95 recognized rules bearing about 185 names." (Most of these "over 95 recognized rules" have long since been forgotten. Only five or six rules are important in present-day use. There are perhaps half a dozen others that may be encountered in certain localities.)

Board-foot log rules are used to estimate the contents of logs. This constitutes an attempt to estimate, before processing, the amount of lumber in logs. Thus we must distinguish between the measurements of the board-foot contents of sawn lumber, the *mill tally*, and the estimation of the board-foot contents of logs, the *log scale*. The board-foot mill tally, although not exact, is a well-defined unit; the board-foot log scale is an ambiguous unit. Consequently, the amount of lumber sawed from any run of logs rarely agrees with the scale of the logs. This variation O_v may be expressed in board feet:

$$O_v \text{ (in board feet)} = \text{mill tally} - \text{log scale}$$

When O_v is positive, a mill has produced an *overrun*; when O_v is negative, a mill has produced an *underrun*.

O_v is generally expressed as a percentage of log scale:

$$O_v = 100\left(\frac{MT - LS}{LS}\right) = 100\left(\frac{MT}{LS} - 1\right) \qquad (9\text{-}2)$$

where   MT = mill tally
         LS = log scale

The quantity MT/LS is commonly referred to as the *overrun ratio*, the number of board-feet mill tally per board-foot scale.

In the construction of all known board-foot log rules, three basic methods have been used: mill study, diagram, and mathematical. For the board-foot log rules in present-day use, generally the yield of logs V in board feet is estimated in terms of lumber 1 in. thick from average small-end-diameter inside bark D in inches and log length L in feet.

9-3.1   Mill-Study Log Rules

In the mill study method of constructing log rules, a sample of logs is first measured prior to sawing. Then, as each log is sawed, the boards are measured to determine the board-foot volume yield of each log. The log rule is prepared by relating board-foot yields, the dependent variable, with log diameters and lengths, the independent variables. The problem may be solved graphically or by the method of least squares.

A rule of this type should give good estimates for mills that cut timber with certain characteristics, or for those that use specific milling methods. The method, however, has never been widely used. The Massachusetts log rule, one of the few constructed by this method that is still in use, was based on 1200 white pine logs. This rule was constructed for round- and square-edged boards sawed from small logs ($\frac{1}{4}$ in. saw kerf). Some boards over 1 in. thick were included, so the values are slightly high for 1 in. boards.

9-3.2   Diagram Log Rules

The procedure for the construction of a diagram log rule is simple:

1. Draw circles to scale to represent the small ends of logs of different diameters inside bark. Assume that logs are cylinders of a specific length, such as 8 ft.
2. Use definite assumptions on saw kerf and shrinkage and board width, and draw boards (rectangles) 1 in. thick within the circles.
3. Compute the total board-foot content for each log diameter.
4. Determine the board-foot contents of other log lengths by proportion.

When a diagram log rule is prepared for any given log length, it will be found that increases in volume from one diameter to the next will be slightly irregular. Preparing a freehand curve or a regression equation to predict volume from diameter for each length may eliminate these irregularities.

The Scribner log rule, the most widely used diagram log rule, was first published in 1846 by J. M. Scribner, a country clergyman. The rule was prepared for 1-in. lumber with a $\frac{1}{4}$-in. allowance for saw kerf and shrinkage. The minimum board width is unknown. The original table gave board-foot contents for logs with scaling diameters (diameter inside bark at small end) from 12 to 44 in. and with lengths from 10 to 24 ft. Log taper was not considered. A few years after the original rule was published, Scribner modified the rule by increasing the slab allowance on larger logs. This is the rule in use today. The Scribner rule gives a relatively high overrun (up to 30 percent) for logs under 14 in. Above 14 in. the overrun gradually decreases and flattens out around 28 in. to about 3 to 5 percent.

A regression equation was prepared from the original table by Bruce and Schumacher (1950). The equation, which gives volume in board feet V in terms of scaling diameters in inches D and log length in feet L is

$$V = \left(0.79D^2 - 2D - 4\right)\frac{L}{16} \qquad (9\text{-}3)$$

Some *Scribner tables* contain values based on this equation. Values in this table differ slightly from the original Scribner values because Scribner did not smooth the values he obtained from his diagrams. Note that the values in Table 9-1 are from the original Scribner table.

Since calculating machines were not generally available in the nineteenth century, scalers found the adding of long columns of figures laborious. Consequently, the Scribner rule was often converted into a *decimal rule* by dropping the units and rounding the values to the nearest 10 board feet. Thus the value for 114 board feet was written as 11 and for 159 board feet was written as 16.

Because the original Scribner rule did not give values for logs less than 12 in. in diameter, a number of lumber companies extrapolated to derive volumes for small logs. Finally, the Lufkin Rule Company prepared three tables using different assumptions to extend the rule to cover small logs. They published these as decimal rules and called them Scribner decimal A rule, Scribner decimal B rule, and Scribner decimal C rule. The decimal C rule is the only one of these rules still widely used.

There are other log rules based on diagrams. The best known are the *Spaulding rule*, which was devised by N. W. Spaulding of San Francisco in 1868, and the *Maine rule*, which was devised by C. T. Holland in 1856. The Spaulding rule is used on the Pacific coast of the United States; the Maine rule is used in northeastern United States. The Spaulding rule, which closely approximates the values of the Scribner rule, may be expressed by the following regression equation, where V is volume in board feet, D is scaling diameter in inches, and L is log length in feet:

$$V = \left(0.778D^2 - 1.125D - 13.482\right)\frac{L}{16} \qquad (9\text{-}4)$$

9-3.3 Mathematical Log Rules

In the mathematical method of constructing log rules, one makes definite assumptions on saw kerf, taper, and milling procedures and prepares a formula that gives board-foot yield of logs in terms of their diameters and lengths.

Doyle Log Rule. This is one of the most widely used, one of the oldest, and one of the most cursed log rules. It was first published in 1825 by Edward Doyle. The rule states: "Deduct 4 inches from the scaling diameter of the log, D, in inches, for slabbing, square one-quarter of the remainder, and multiply by the length of the log, L, in feet." As Herrick (1940) pointed out, when Doyle deducted 4 in. from the diameter of the log for slabbing, he was squaring the log. Then he calculated the board-foot contents of the squared log or cant, as follows:

$$(D - 4)(D - 4)\frac{L}{12}$$

To allow for saw kerf and shrinkage, he reduced the volume of the cant by 25 percent to obtain the final rule:

$$V = \frac{(D - 4)^2 L}{12}(1.00 - 0.25) = \left(\frac{D - 4}{4}\right)^2 L \qquad (9\text{-}5)$$

For 16-ft logs the *Doyle rule of thumb* is

$$V = (D - 4)^2$$

The simplicity and ease of application are the reasons for the wide acceptance of this rule.

When the Doyle rule is applied to logs between 26 and 36 in. in diameter, it gives good results. When the rule is applied to large logs, it gives an underrun; when the rule is applied to small logs, it gives a high overrun. This comes about because the 4-in slabbing allowance is inadequate for large logs and excessive for small logs.

International Log Rule. This is one of the most accurate mathematical log rules. It was developed by J. F. Clark and published in 1906 (Clark, 1906). In the derivation of the original rule one first computes the board-foot contents of a 4-ft cylinder in terms of cylinder diameter in inches D, assuming that the cylinder will produce lumber at the rate of 12 board feet per cubic foot. The solid board foot contents of a 4-foot cylinder is

$$\frac{\pi D^2}{4(144)}(4)(12) = 0.262D^2$$

To allow for saw kerf and shrinkage one assumes that for each 1-in. board cut, $\frac{1}{8}$ in. will be lost in saw kerf and $\frac{1}{16}$ in. in shrinkage. Thus the proportion lost from saw kerf and shrinkage is

$$\frac{3/16}{1+3/16} = 0.158$$

When reduced by 0.158, the volume of the 4-ft cylinder becomes

$$0.262D^2(1.000 - 0.158) = 0.22D^2$$

Thus the losses from saw kerf and shrinkage are proportional to the end area of the log (i.e., to D^2).

Clark determined that losses from slabs and edgings constitute a ring-shaped collar around the outside of the log and that they are proportional to the surface area, or the diameter D of the log. From a careful analysis of the losses occurring during the conversion of sawlogs to lumber, Clark found that a plank 2.12 in. thick and D in. wide would give the correct deduction. [The thickness of the collar T is about 0.7 in. for all values of D. This can be determined from the equation

$$2.12D = \pi\frac{D^2}{4} - \frac{\pi(D - 2T)^2}{4}$$

which leads to $T^2 - DT + 0.6748D = 0$.] Therefore, in terms of cylinder diameter in inches D, the board-foot deduction is computed using eq. (9-1):

$$\frac{2.12(D)(4)}{12} = 0.71D$$

Thus the net board-foot volume V of a 4-ft cylinder is

$$V = 0.22D^2 - 0.71D \qquad (9\text{-}6)$$

After studying a number of tree species, Clark decided to allow a taper of $\frac{1}{2}$ in. for each 4-ft section. With this assumption, the basic formula was expanded to cover other log lengths.

$$V(8 - \text{ft logs}) = 0.44D^2 - 1.20D - 0.30 \qquad (9\text{-}7)$$

$$V(12 - \text{ft logs}) = 0.66D^2 - 1.47D - 0.79 \qquad (9\text{-}8)$$

$$V(16 - \text{ft logs}) = 0.88D^2 - 1.52D - 1.36 \qquad (9\text{-}9)$$

$$V(20 - \text{ft logs}) = 1.10D^2 - 1.35D - 1.90 \qquad (9\text{-}10)$$

Lengths over 20 ft are scaled as two or more logs.

The following equation, developed by Grosenbaugh (1952) using the method of least squares, can be used for the determination of the board foot volume (International rule, $\frac{1}{4}$ in. kerf) for logs of any length:

$$V = 0.049\,7621 LD^2 + 0.006\,220 L^2 D - 0.185\,476 LD + 0.000\,259 L^3$$
$$- 0.011\,592 L^2 + 0.042\,222 L$$

The original International log rule may be modified to give estimates for saw kerfs other than $\frac{1}{8}$ in. For example, for a kerf of $\frac{1}{4}$ in. (shrinkage of $\frac{1}{16}$ in.), the proportion lost is

$$\frac{5/16}{1 + 5/16} = 0.238$$

So the original rule may be converted to a $\frac{1}{4}$-in. rule by multiplying the values by the factor

$$\frac{1.000 - 0.238}{1.000 - 0.158} = 0.905$$

The factor to convert to a $\frac{7}{64}$-in. rule is 1.013; the factor to convert to a $\frac{3}{16}$-in. rule is 0.950.

When Clark (1906) published his log rule in table form, he rounded all values to the nearest multiple of 5 board feet. This is the form that most International log rule tables appear today.

The *Brereton log rule* is another rule based on a mathematical formula:

$$V = 0.0654 D^2 L$$

where D is the average of the large and small end diameters of the log. This rule makes no deduction for saw kerf or slabs. This rule really calculates the cubic content of the log, which is then converted to board feet on the basis of 12 board feet per cubic foot.

9-3.4 Combination Log Rules

This type of rule combines values from different log rules. Such a rule takes advantage of the best, or the worst, features of the rules used. For example, the *Doyle–Scribner rule*, a combination of the Doyle and Scribner rules, was prepared for use in defective and overmature timber. Since the Doyle rule gives an overrun for small logs, its values were used for diameters up through 28 in. Since the Scribner rule gives an overrun for large logs, its values were used for diameters greater than 28 in. Thus, the Doyle–Scribner rule gives a consistently high overrun that is supposed to compensate for hidden defects. The *Scribner–Doyle rule*, exactly opposite to the Doyle–Scribner rule, gives a consistently low overrun.

9-3.5 Comparison of Log Rules

Because different methods and assumptions are used in the construction of log rules, different rules give different results, none of which will necessarily agree with the mill tally for any given log (Table 9-1). This points out that the board-foot log scale, by any rule, is a unit of estimate, not a unit of measure.

9-4. CUBIC-VOLUME LOG RULES

The cubic volume of a log may be determined by any of the methods given in Section 6-1.1 [eqs. (6-1) to (6-9)]. However, for log scaling, gross cubic volumes are generally computed by Smalian's or Huber's formulas. The latter has the disadvantage of requiring inside- and outside-diameter measurements at the

TABLE 9-1. Comparison of Volumes of 16-ft Logs from Different Log Rules

Log Diameter (in.)	Mill Tally[a] (board feet)	Log Scale				
		Scribner	Maine	International $\frac{1}{4}$-in. Rule	Doyle	Spaulding
6		18	20	20	4	
10	75	50	68	65	36	
14	145	114	142	135	100	114
18	229	213	232	230	196	216
22	382	334	363	355	324	341
26	578	500	507	500	484	488
30	665	657	706	675	676	656
34	862	800	900	870	900	845
38	1037	1068	1135	1095	1156	1064

[a]Average yield of logs sawed in an Indiana bandmill.

midpoint of the log length. The formulas could be used directly, but it is more convenient to prepare tables. In the preparation of cubic meter tables, volumes are most often computed for 2-cm diameter classes and 0.2-m length classes. In the preparation of cubic-foot tables, volumes are most often computed for 1-in. diameter classes and 1-ft length classes. Diameter is often given as the midpoint-diameter inside bark. (When the midpoint diameter cannot be measured, the average of the diameters inside bark at the two ends of the log is generally used for midpoint diameter.) In some cases, volume is given in terms of small-end-diameter inside bark. For other formulas used principally in the Pacific Northwest of the United States, see Bell and Dilworth (1993). These formulas include the two-end conic rule, the subneiloid rule, and the Bruce butt log formula.

9-5. LOG SCALING

Scaling is the determination of the gross and net volumes of logs in board feet, cubic feet, cubic meters, or other units. The determination of gross scale consists of measuring log length and diameter and determining the volume using a log rule. The gross volume may be read from a table or from a *scale stick*: a flat stick that has volumes for different log diameters and lengths printed on its face. Deductions are then made for defects to obtain the net volume.

9-5.1 Board-Foot Scaling

In board-foot scaling, a maximum length of 40 ft is standard for the western regions of the United States; 16 ft is standard for the eastern regions. When logs exceed the maximum scaling length, they are scaled as two or more logs. If a log does not divide evenly, the butt section is assigned the longer length. The scaling diameter for the assumed point of separation can be estimated from the taper of the log. Although logs are most commonly cut and measured in even lengths (i.e., 8, 10, 12, 14, and 16 ft), they may be cut and measured, particularly with hardwood logs, in both odd and even lengths (i.e., 8, 9, 10, 11, and 12 ft). Logs must be cut longer than standard lumber lengths because it is impossible to buck logs squarely and because there is logging damage to log ends. This extra length, which will range from 3 to 6 in., depending on the size of timber, products sawed, and logging methods, is called *trim allowance*.

Most board-foot log rules call for diameter measurements inside bark, to the nearest inch, at the small end of the log. When a log is round, one measurement is enough. When a log is eccentric, as most logs are, the usual practice is to take a pair of measurements at right angles across the long and short axes of the log end and to average the results to obtain the scaling diameter.

To determine net scale one must deduct from gross scale the quantity of lumber, according to the log rule used that will be lost due to defects. These deductions do not include material lost during manufacturing, or defects that affect the quality of the lumber. Instead, they include those defects that reduce the volume of lumber.

Detailed procedures have been worked out to estimate the volume of deductions in defective logs [see a summary in Bell and Dilworth (1993)]. Grosenbaugh (1952) proposed a logical and generally applicable system. In this method, the amount of material lost in defect is estimated by multiplying the gross scale by the proportion of the log affected. The system works, with minor modifications, regardless of the units in which the log is measured: board feet by any log rule, cubic feet, cubic meters, cords, pounds, kilograms, and so forth. The procedure for common defects can be summarized in the following five rules, where scaling diameter is defined as the average inside bark diameter at the small end, and measurements are in English units.

1. When a defect affects an entire section, the proportion P lost is

$$P = \frac{\text{length of defective section}}{\text{log length}}$$

Example:

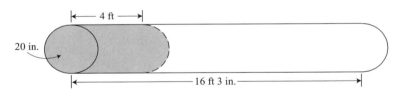

Gross scale, Scribner decimal C rule =   28

$$\text{Cull} = \left(\frac{4}{16}\right)(28) = 7 \quad -7$$

$$\text{Net scale} \qquad\qquad\qquad \overline{21}$$

2. When a defect affects a wedge-shaped sector:

$$P = \frac{\text{Length of defective section}}{\text{log length}} \cdot \frac{\text{central angle of defect}}{360°}$$

Example:

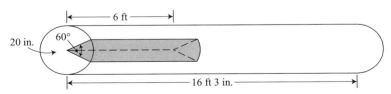

Gross scale, Scribner decimal C rule =   28

$$\text{Cull} = \left(\frac{6}{16}\right)\left(\frac{60}{360}\right)(28) = 2 \quad -2$$

Net scale $\overline{26}$

3. When a log sweeps (ignore sweep less than 2 in.):

$$P = \frac{\text{maximum departure} - 2}{\text{scaling diameter}}$$

Example:

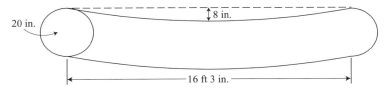

Gross scale, Scribner decimal C rule =   28

$$\text{Cull} = \left(\frac{8-2}{20}\right)(28) = 8 \quad -8$$

Net scale $\overline{20}$

4. When a log crooks:

$$P = \frac{\text{maximum deflection}}{\text{scaling diameter}} \cdot \frac{\text{length of deflecting section}}{\text{log length}}$$

Example:

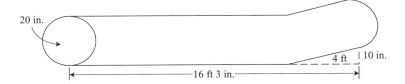

Gross scale, Scribner decimal C rule =   28

$$\text{Cull} = \left(\frac{10}{20}\right)\left(\frac{4}{16}\right)(28) = 3 \quad -3$$

Net scale $\overline{25}$

5. When the average cross section of interior defect is enclosable in an ellipse or circle:

$$P = \frac{(\text{major diameter} + 1)(\text{minor diameter} + 1)}{(\text{scaling diameter} - 1)^2} \cdot \frac{\text{defect length}}{\text{log length}}$$

[Defect in peripheral inch of log (slab collar) can be ignored.]

Example (Defect diameters: major $= 9$ in., minor $= 7$ in.):

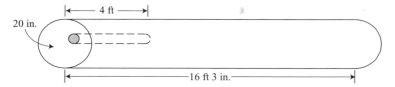

Gross scale, Scribner decimal C rule $=$ 28

$$\text{Cull} = \frac{(9 + 1)(7 + 1)}{(20 - 1)^2} \left(\frac{4}{16}\right)(28) = 2 \quad -2$$

Net scale $\overline{26}$

9-5.2   Cubic Volume Scaling

Cubic volume scaling estimates the total contents of a log rather than the products that can be obtained, as is the case with board-foot scaling. The total cubic contents of a log can then be converted to the unit of measure appropriate to each manufacturing plant with less uncertainty than in converting board-feet log scale to board feet of lumber, or from board-feet log scale to square feet of veneer.

In cubic volume scaling, log diameters and log lengths are measured as explained in Section 9-4. In making deductions for defects, the five rules given in Section 9-5.1 are applicable. If cubic feet are used, diameter is average small-end diameter in inches and length is in feet and the rules are used without modifications. If cubic meters are used, diameter is average small-end diameter in centimeters and length is in meters, and the third and fifth rules are changed as follows.

3. When a log sweeps (ignore sweep less than 5 cm):

$$P = \frac{\text{maximum departure} - 5}{\text{scaling diameter}}$$

5. When the average cross section in the interior defect is enclosable in an ellipse or circle:

$$P = \frac{(\text{major diameter} + 2)(\text{minor diameter} + 2)}{(\text{scaling diameter} - 2)^2} \cdot \frac{\text{defect length}}{\text{log length}}$$

where P equals the proportion lost due to defect.

For cubic foot scaling rules prepared by the U.S. Forest Service, see USDA (1991).

9-5.3 Unmerchantable Logs

The definition of a cull, or unmerchantable, log is largely a local matter. Merchantability varies with species, economic conditions, and other factors. However, no matter what units are employed, specifications for a merchantable log should give the minimum length and minimum diameter allowed, and the minimum percent of sound material left after deductions are made for cull. For example, a cull log might be defined as any log less than 8 ft long, less than 6 in. in diameter, or less than 50 percent sound.

9-5.4 Sample Scaling

Under conditions where the scaling operation interferes with the movement of the logs, or where scaling costs are high, sample scaling should be considered. Sample scaling is generally feasible when (1) logs are fairly homogeneous in species, volume, and value; (2) logs are concentrated in one place so they can be scaled efficiently; and (3) the total number of logs is large. Sampling can be applied to individual logs or to truckloads.

Once one has decided to use sample scaling, there are two basic questions:

1. How many logs or truckloads must be scaled to determine the total scale within limits of accuracy acceptable to both buyer and seller?
2. How should the sample log or truckloads be selected?

The number of logs or truckloads to measure can be calculated from eq. (3-21), the minimum-sample-size formula applicable to a finite population:

$$n = \frac{t^2 \cdot CV^2 \cdot N}{N(E\%)^2 + t^2 \cdot CV^2}$$

where CV = coefficient of variation of volume of logs or truckloads, expressed as percent
   t = t value corresponding to probability chosen
   N = total number of logs or truckloads in population
   $E\%$ = desired error of mean expressed as percent of mean (acceptable sampling error)

As an example, assume that CV is 50 percent for a population N of 10,000 logs, and the acceptable sampling error is 3 percent (both CV and N are estimates), then if we let $t = 2$, giving approximately 20:1 odds that a chance discrepancy between the estimated and true value will not exceed 3 percent, we obtain

$$n = \frac{50^2(2^2)(10,000)}{10,000(3^2) + 50^2(2^2)} = 1000$$

A practical procedure to obtain the 1000-log sample would be to scale every tenth log: that is, take a systematic sample. Of course, to obtain total volume, every log must be counted since the total number of logs used to calculate the sample size n is an estimate. The same procedure can be applied to truckload sampling, where N is the total number of truckloads, CV is the variation in volume among truckloads, and n is the number of truckloads to be scaled.

Although random sampling is required if one desires to calculate valid sampling errors, it is not essential if the sole purpose of sampling is to obtain an unbiased estimate of the average volume per log or per truckload and the total volume. Johnson et al. (1971) described how a $3P$ sample selection procedure (see Section 14-3) could be applied to sample log scaling.

9-6. SCALING STACKED VOLUME

Stacked volume (Section 9-1.2) has traditionally been obtained for firewood, pulpwood, excelsior wood, charcoal wood, and other relatively low-value products that are assembled in stacks. In scaling a stack of wood in cords, one first records the length—the average of measurements taken on both sides of the stack—to the nearest 0.1 ft. Then stack height is obtained by averaging measurements taken at intervals of about 4 ft. The height, which is reduced about 1 in./ft by some scalers to compensate for settling and shrinkage, is recorded to the nearest 0.1 ft. Finally, piece lengths are checked to see if they vary from the lengths specified in the sale or purchase contract (standard lengths for pulpwood cut in the United States are 4 ft, 5 ft, 5 ft 3 in., and 8 ft 4 in.). If they do, the procedure given in the contract should be followed.

The volume in standard cords V_c of a stack of wood is calculated as follows:

$$V_c = \frac{L_s H_s L}{128} \qquad (9\text{-}11)$$

where L_s = stack length (ft)
   H_s = stack height (ft)
   L = stick length (ft)

If stacks are piled on slopes, the length and height measurements should be taken at right angles to one another.

If the stacked volume is measured in cubic meters (1 cubic meter = 1 stere), stack length and height are usually measured in 2-cm classes, and piece lengths are checked as described above. Then gross volume of a stack in cubic meters V_m is[*]

$$V_m = LHW \qquad (9\text{-}12)$$

where L = stack length (m)
          H = stack height (m)
          W = stick length (m)

Since the procedure above gives gross stacked volume, to obtain net volume, deductions must be made for defective wood and poor stacking. The definitions of defects and procedures for allowing for defects will vary from one organization to another. In general, deductions are made for *defective sticks* and *loose piling*. Defective sticks include rotted, burned, undersized, and peeled sticks with excessive bark adhering. Loose piling may occur when knots have been trimmed improperly, when excessively crooked wood is present, and when sticks have been carelessly piled.

When making deductions for defective sticks, the scaler examines each stick in a pile and notes which sticks do not meet specifications. These sticks are then culled by deducting the cubic space they occupy from the gross cubic space occupied by the pile—either a stick is acceptable or it is not acceptable. Estimating the cubic space that would be occupied by sticks that could be included in the loose pile and subtracting this volume from the gross cubic space occupied by the pile makes deductions for loose piling.

The term *rough wood* is used to designate wood with bark, in contrast to the term *peeled wood*, which refers to wood with bark removed. It should be made clear in a sales contract whether wood is to be measured rough or peeled. If the sale price is based on rough wood volume, then if peeled wood must be measured, volume must be increased 10 to 20 percent, depending on bark thickness (Section 6-1.4).

9-7. VOLUME UNIT CONVERSION

Board foot–cubic foot conversions for logs vary by log rule, log and tree size, and form. Table 9-2 illustrates the nature of these variations for 16-ft logs. In general, the ratios increase rapidly from small to large diameters and level off

[*]Other units of stacked volume may be used in different countries.

TABLE 9-2. Board Foot–Cubic Foot Ratios for 16-ft Logs by Taper Rate and Scaling Diameter

Scaling Diameter (in.)	2 in. per Log				4 in. per Log			
	Volume[a] (ft³)	International $\frac{1}{4}$-in.	Scribner	Doyle	Volume[a] (ft³)	International $\frac{1}{4}$-in.	Scribner	Doyle
10	10.6	6.710	5.166	3.381	12.9	5.532	4.259	2.787
12	14.8	7.221	5.781	4.314	17.5	6.138	4.914	3.667
14	19.7	7.598	6.229	5.071	22.7	6.604	5.414	4.407
16	25.3	7.887	6.569	5.690	28.6	6.974	5.808	5.031
18	31.6	8.117	6.836	6.205	35.3	7.273	6.126	5.560
20	38.6	8.303	7.052	6.637	42.6	7.520	6.387	6.012
22	46.2	8.457	7.229	7.005	50.6	7.728	6.606	6.402
24	54.6	8.586	7.378	7.322	59.3	7.904	6.792	6.741
26	63.7	8.697	7.504	7.598	68.8	8.057	6.952	7.039
28	73.5	8.792	7.613	7.839	78.9	8.189	7.091	7.302
30	83.9	8.875	7.707	8.053	89.7	8.305	7.212	7.536
32	95.1	8.948	7.790	8.242	101.2	8.408	7.320	7.745
34	107.0	9.013	7.863	8.412	113.4	8.500	7.416	7.933
36	119.6	9.071	7.928	8.565	126.4	8.582	7.501	8.104
38	132.8	9.122	7.987	8.704	140.0	8.656	7.578	8.259
40	146.8	9.169	8.039	8.830	154.3	8.723	7.648	8.400

[a]Solid wood volume determined by Smalian's formula.

once the larger diameters have been reached. Although any fixed conversion factor should be used with care, a rule-of-thumb factor generally used is 6 board feet (Scribner log rule) per cubic foot.

Cubic foot–cubic meter conversions can be accomplished easily by using an exact mathematical relationship:

$$1 \text{ cubic foot} = 0.028\,317 \text{ cubic meter}$$

$$1 \text{ cubic meter} = 35.3145 \text{ cubic feet}$$

See Appendix Table A-1 for a complete list of conversion factors.

Cubic foot–cord conversions vary greatly. Approximations of between 60 to 94 ft^3 per standard cord are generally used for unpeeled wood, depending on species, method of stacking, size of wood, and bark thickness. The average bark volume will vary from 10 to 20 percent of unpeeled volume for most species. Good working averages are between 75 and 85 solid cubic feet per standard cord for green, unpeeled southern pine, between 80 and 90 solid cubic feet per standard cord for green, unpeeled Douglas-fir or western hemlock, and between 73 and 85 solid cubic feet per standard cord for green, unpeeled hardwoods.

Board foot–cord conversions are unreliable and are used infrequently. However, a conversion factor used at times is 1000 board feet (Scribner log rule) equals 2 standard cords of unpeeled stacked wood. For more accurate conversion, however, consideration must be given to diameter and length of logs, bark thickness, and other factors. For example, one might obtain a variation in yield, per 1000 board feet, of 1.8 cords with logs of 30-in. diameter and larger to 3.3 cords with logs of 6-in. diameter.

Cubic meter–stere conversions are analogous to cubic foot–cord conversions. On a percentage basis, the solid cubic contents of a stere can be expected to vary, as does the cord. For example, if averages are between 73 and 85 solid cubic feet per standard cord for green, unpeeled hardwoods—that is, between 57 and 66 percent of the 128 ft^3 occupied by the cord is solid wood—averages would be between 0.57 and 0.66 solid cubic meter per stere for green, unpeeled hardwoods.

For *conversion of volume per unit area*, the following conversion factors can be used for cubic conversions between the metric and English systems:

$$1 \text{ cubic foot per acre} = 0.069\,97 \text{ cubic meter per hectare}$$

$$1 \text{ cubic meter per hectare} = 14.29 \text{ cubic feet per acre}$$

An approximate conversion from cubic meters/ha to board feet/acre (assuming 5 board feet per cubic foot) is $1 \text{ m}^3/\text{ha} = 14.3 \text{ ft}^3/\text{acre} = 75$ board feet/acre.

9-7.1   Determination of Solid Cubic Contents of Stacked Wood

It is often necessary to know the solid cubic contents of wood that is stacked (standard cord, stere, etc.) on the ground or on trucks. Although average conversion factors, such as those given above, are often used, better factors are generally required. These can be determined by the following methods.

1. *Direct measurement.* The cubic volume of individual sticks, or of groups of sticks, can be determined by displacement (Section 6-1.2). Using Huber's, Smalian's, or Newton's formula can also compute the cubic volume of individual sticks. In any case, when the cubic space occupied by a pile is known, the ratio of solid cubic volume to total cubic volume can be calculated from the equation

$$f = \frac{\text{solid cubic volume of pile}}{\text{total cubic volume of pile}}$$

   The factor f multiplied by the space occupied by a cord, or by an entire pile, will give the solid cubic volume of wood in the stack.

2. *Photographic methods.* The factor f can be estimated from photographs of the ends of the sticks in a pile. The camera is located a fixed distance from the pile with the optical axis of the lens perpendicular to the side of the pile. Normally, only a portion of a stack or truckload is included in a single photograph. After a photograph is developed, a transparent grid with systematically spaced dots is superimposed on the photograph and the number of dots falling on air space can be counted (Fig. 9-1). The factor f (percent solid wood) is computed as follows:

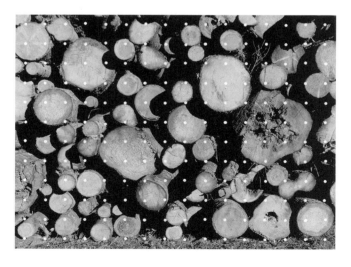

FIG. 9-1. Photographic method of determining solid wood content in stacked wood.

$$f = 1 - \frac{\text{total dots in air spaces}}{\text{total dots in photograph}}$$

In Fig 9-1, there are 67 dots falling in air spaces and a total of 182 dots on the photograph. The percent solid wood $f = 1 - (67/182) = 0.63$ and the solid wood volume per stacked cord $= 0.63(128) = 81\,\text{ft}^3$. Although one photograph of a truckload will usually give an adequate sample, several photographs of large stacks may be required. For example, Garland (1968) determined that a 20 percent photo sample was required to estimate the solid wood content to within ± 2.4 percent accuracy at 95 percent confidence. With the advent of affordable high-quality digital cameras and image analysis software, the photographic method is an affordable and easily implemented method of determining solid wood content.

3. *Angle-gauge method.* By "projecting" an angle of about 23° parallel to the face of a stack from randomly selected points, the conversion factor f may be obtained quickly and efficiently. This method, which is a modification of horizontal point sampling, is discussed by Loetsch et al. (1973).

9-8. SCALING BY WEIGHT

When a tree is felled and cut into logs, the wood immediately begins to lose moisture. If permitted to air-dry, its moisture content will reach about 12 percent. The rates of drying for logs vary with air temperature, humidity, species, log size, knottiness, method of stacking, presence of bark, and other factors. Besley (1967), Nylinder (1967), and Adams (1971) reported varying weight losses over time for several species in North America and Scandinavia. The results of Adams's study to determine the weight loss of red-oak logs are shown in Fig. 9-2.

If only the weight of wood is desired, bark and foreign material such as ice, snow, mud, and rocks must be removed before measurement, or their weight must be deducted from the gross weight to obtain the wood weight. Green bark was found to be between 9 and 19 percent of the weight of green, rough (i.e., unpeeled) hardwood pulpwood in Maine (Hardy and Weiland, 1964). Oven-dry bark was found to be between 3.8 and 9.1 percent of the weight of green, rough logs for several species in Minnesota (Marden et al., 1975).

9-8.1 Weight Measurement of Pulpwood

The use of stacked measure (e.g., cord or stere) has long been used to measure bulk forest products, such as fuelwood and pulpwood. Although stacked measure is not an accurate measure of the solid cubic contents, when measurements

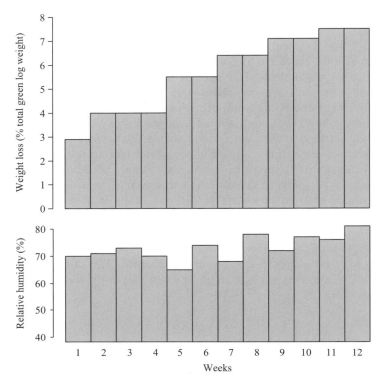

FIG. 9-2. Cumulative weekly weight loss due to moisture loss for 21 red oak sawlogs and the associated relative humidity record. (Adapted from Adams, 1971.)

must be made in the woods, particularly at scattered locations, it is often a necessary compromise. However, if measurement can be done on trucks, and weighing facilities are available, weighing provides a cheaper, more accurate, and more objective method of scaling.

The green weight and moisture content of wood provide good measures of the wood available for pulp. Despite some problems in obtaining moisture content, weight as a measure of pulpwood quantity has several advantages:

1. It permits an accurate determination of the yield of pulp, which is measured in weight.
2. It encourages wood suppliers to deliver wood to the mill promptly to reduce weight loss (fresh, green pulpwood is preferred at the mill).
3. It encourages better loading of trucks since there is no advantage in loose piling.
4. It is faster and more economical than volume scaling.
5. It eliminates personal judgment.

When weight scaling is employed, a dependable procedure for obtaining moisture content is essential. If unpeeled wood is being handled, estimates of bark weight must also be made. There are two ways to deal with these problems.

1. *Develop average moisture and bark percentages for green wood at the time of cutting and at intervals since cutting.* To use the percentages for reducing fresh, green-wood weight, it is best that weighing be done immediately following cutting. In practice, the conversion from green weight with bark to dry weight without bark is often not made. Instead, the wood is weighed immediately after cutting, and prices are based on this weight. Although the quantity of dry wood is not determined explicitly, it is implicit in its effect on the price per unit weight. Some moisture percentages for several species used for pulpwood in the southern and northeastern parts of the United States are shown in Table 9-3. The percentages shown are based on freshly cut green wood without bark. When weighing is done at varying times following cutting, moisture and bark percentages are required at intervals of time since cutting. Percentages for the moisture component are more variable and less reliable than those for fresh green wood, since season, weather, method of stacking, and so on, affect moisture content.

2. *Determine current moisture and bark percentages at the time of weighing.* This approach requires that an estimate be made at the time of weighing of the contribution of moisture and bark to the total weight. Sampling procedures must be utilized to provide these estimates. When moisture percentages have been determined, the dry weight of wood can be calculated using eq. (7-8) or (7-9). The relationship expressed by eq. (7-8) is shown in Fig. 9-3. Nylinder (1958) found that sample disks cut 10 cm from the ends of logs gave satisfactory estimates of the moisture content of logs. Braathe and Okstad (1967) found that a thin triangular segment of the log cross section cut with a chain saw, or a sample taken from the log radius with a drill, gave satisfactory estimates of the moisture content of logs. Electrical moisture meters are available, but they have not been too satisfactory for moisture determination of pulpwood or sawlogs.

Large platform scales capable of determining the gross weight of a truck and its load are commonly used for weight scaling. The gross weight of the truck and load minus the weight of the empty truck, the *tare weight*, equals the weight of wood, including bark and moisture. The dry weight of wood can be estimated by applying corrections for moisture and bark. Since pulpwood quantity in terms of stacked volume may be desired after the wood has been weighed, estimates of weight per cord are available, such as shown in Table 9-3.

TABLE 9-3. Sample Weights[a] and Moisture Contents of Some Species Used for Pulpwood

	Weight per Cord Green (lb)			Oven-Dry Weight Barked Wood (lb)	Barked Wood Moisture Content (%)
Species	Unbarked	Bark	Barked		
Longleaf pine	6374	660	5714	2920	95.8
Shortleaf pine	5669	675	4994	2037	145.1
White ash	5031	795	4236	2992	41.5
Beech	5584	446	5138	3157	62.7
Gray birch	5690	677	5013	2700	85.6
White birch	5731	705	5026	2788	80.3
Yellow birch	6090	786	5304	3013	76.0
Elm	5857	763	5094	2627	93.9
Red maple	5482	720	4762	2877	65.5
Sugar maple	5977	801	5176	3178	62.0

Source: Derived from Taras (1956) and Swan (1959).

[a]All weights are per cord.

9-8.2 Weight Measurement of Sawlogs

Weight scaling of sawlogs can be used to (1) estimate the amount of lumber, veneer, and so on, in logs, and (2) to estimate the total quantity of wood in logs. In both cases, the determination of weight is an intermediate step in the

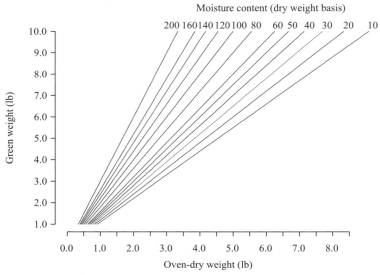

FIG. 9-3. Relationship between green weight, moisture content, and oven-dry weight of wood.

estimation of volume, because the wood-using industries, particularly in North America, customarily measure sawlogs in volume units. Weight scaling of sawlogs therefore normally consists of weighing and converting the weight to volume. The same problems with moisture content, bark, and foreign material that pertain to weight scaling of pulpwood pertain to weight scaling of sawlogs.

Generally, weights of entire truckloads are determined and converted to volume equivalents, although weights of individual logs can be determined. Weight scaling in truckload lots is most suitable for logs of a single species, with uniform diameter, uniform length, and uniform quality. This is the reason that weight scaling has been most widely used for southern pine in the southeastern United States.

Weight scaling of truckloads eliminates the need for measurement of individual logs, speeds up scaling, and reduces errors of judgment. It also encourages the delivery of freshly cut logs, since price is almost always based on green weight. When logs are variable in size and quality, however, prices must be adjusted for these factors. Consequently, objections have been raised to weight scaling of hardwood logs, because they vary more than softwood logs in size, shape, and quality.

In North America, weight scaling of sawlogs has generally been viewed as a more rapid method than conventional log scaling of obtaining volume estimates. Thus the main efforts have been to develop volume–weight relationships. Relationships of this type can be developed from studies that relate volume of a sample of sawlogs to their weights (volumes may be estimated from log rules or obtained from mill studies). Guttenberg et al. (1960) developed a regression equation showing the relationship of the board-feet mill tally to weight in pounds for individual shortleaf and loblolly pine sawlogs in Arkansas and Louisiana (Table 9-4). Yerkes (1966) developed a regression equation showing the relationship of cubic feet to weight in pounds for Black Hills ponderosa pine sawlogs: cubic foot volume $= -2.09 + 0.020W$, where W is total log weight in pounds.

For an industrial application of sawlog weight scaling, it is desirable to develop relationships of volume to weight for truckloads of logs (Row and Fasick, 1966; Row and Guttenberg, 1966; Timson, 1974; Adams, 1976; Donnelly and Barger, 1977). Donnelly and Barger found that the accuracy of conversion from weight to volume was improved by including number of logs per load as an additional independent variable.

In applying truckload weighing, sampling procedures are generally used to determine, or adjust, the conversion factors. The number of truckloads to measure is first determined for an acceptable sampling error. Each load sampled is chosen randomly or systematically, weighed, and scaled log by log for volume. Average volume–weight ratios are then calculated for converting weight to volume for all the truckloads in the operation (Chehock and Walker, 1975; Adams, 1976; Donnelly and Barger, 1977).

TABLE 9-4. Board Foot Lumber Yields from Loblolly and Shortleaf Pine

Log Weight (lb)	Predicted Green Lumber Yield[a] (board feet)
200	9
600	91
1000	94
1400	134
1800	184
2000	207
2200	231
2600	278
3000	328

Source: Adapted from Guttenberg et al. (1960).

[a]Based on the equation

$$\text{board feet} = \frac{\text{weight}_{lb}}{9.88} + \frac{\text{weight}_{lb}^2}{254,362} - 10.96$$

9-8.3 Weight Measurement of Pulp

In the United States, pulp is usually measured in air-dry tons (English system). The air-dry ton consists of 90 percent, or 1800 lb, of dry pulp, and 10 percent, or 200 lb, of water. The oven-dry ton consists of 2000 lb of oven-dry pulp. The air-dry metric tonne consists of 90 percent, or 900 kg, of dry pulp and 10 percent, or 100 kg, of water. The oven-dry metric tonne, also known as bone–dry metric tonne (BDMT), consists of 1000 kg of oven-dry pulp (dried to 0 percent humidity at 103°C for 24 hours).

To convert the oven-dry weight of pulp to cubic volume of wood equivalent, the oven-dry weight of pulp is divided by the yield factor to obtain the oven-dry weight of wood. This figure is then divided by the species' density (oven-dry weight per green cubic unit) to give the green volume equivalent:

$$W_r = \frac{W_p}{Y}$$

$$V_g = \frac{W_r}{SG_d}$$

where W_r = oven-dry weight of raw material
W_p = oven-dry weight of pulp
Y = yield factor
V_g = green volume equivalent
SG_d = species density (oven-dry weight per green cubic unit)

For example, assume that we desire to determine the number of cubic feet of solid green wood of a given species that is required to produce 1 air-dry tonne (1800 lb) of unbleached kraft pulp. Assuming that the yield of oven-dry unbleached kraft pulp is 54 percent of oven-dry wood and that the oven-dry weight is 25 lb per green cubic foot, then

$$W_r = \frac{1800}{0.54} = 3333 \, \text{lb}$$

$$V_g = \frac{3333}{25.0} = 133 \, \text{ft}^3$$

To express the wood requirement in cords, one simply divides the cubic-foot volume by the appropriate number of solid cubic feet per cord. For example, assume that a cord of unpeeled pulpwood contains 80 solid cubic feet of wood. The cord equivalent for the example above would be: $133/80 = 1.66$ cords per air-dry ton of pulp.

9-8.4   Weight Measurement of Other Forest Products

The weights of sawn lumber, plywood, veneer, wood chips, and sawmill residues may be desired. Such weights may be determined by weighing, or indirectly by estimating volume and converting to weight. The process of determining weight indirectly can be illustrated by an example. Assume that we desire to know the weight of 1000 board feet of rough 2 in. × 4 in. lumber with a moisture content of 18 percent. Since the cubic foot equivalent of 1000 board feet of this lumber is 64.8, and the density of this lumber at 18 percent moisture content is 35.7 lb/ft^3, the estimated weight per 1000 board feet is $64.8(35.7) = 2313$ lb. The weights of other products can be estimated in a similar manner.

10

NONTIMBER FOREST VEGETATION PARAMETERS

As a result of the increased need for more comprehensive information on natural resources, forest inventories have expanded their scope from only the measurement of timber quantities to other parameters of interest. Forests are not only sources of wood for traditional timber products but also for wood fiber for new industrial products. In addition, forest resources play an important role with respect to wildlife habitat, plant diversity, nutrient recycling, biogeochemical interchange, and repositories for carbon. This emphasizes the need for forest mensuration to consider measurements beyond those of traditional timber quantities. Schreuder and Geissler (1998) have indicated that the following variables associated with forest resources are measurable and useful for forest vegetation and inventory monitoring:

1. Forest vegetation
    a. Trees: number of trees, tree basal area, length, diameter, and frequency of down woody material, tree mortality and regeneration, number of diseased and insect-infested trees, removals by species
    b. Understory: number, mortality, height, percent seedlings, percent saplings, and percent mature shrubs by species
    c. Forbs, grasses: number of species, aerial extent
2. Soil
    a. Depth of organic matter, depth of A-horizon, soil series, soil quality (SQ), pH
    b. Other characteristics: erosion rate, slope, and aspect

3. Animals, relative abundance of:
   a. Birds
   b. Small ground vertebrates (mammals, reptiles, and amphibians)
   c. Ground insects
4. Water
   a. Quality, depth, and extent

In this chapter we concentrate on the forest vegetation parameters employed in multiple resource inventories, forest health monitoring, and biomass and carbon estimation which are not covered in other chapters: understory vegetation, regeneration, dead standing trees and woody detritus, total forest biomass, and carbon quantities. For description and measurement of nonvegetation parameters (soils, animals, water, air, etc.) the reader should consult references dedicated to those topics (e.g., Sutherland, 1996).

10-1. UNDERSTORY VEGETATION

Understory or lesser vegetation consists of species of nontimber value: mosses, lichens, ferns, herbs, shrubs, and natural tree regeneration. Information on the amount and characteristics of regeneration and other understory vegetation and its biomass is required for forest management decisions, evaluating forest health, and for the estimation of total vegetation biomass and its carbon content. These components are generally not measured in operational forest inventories to estimate timber quantities.

The most important characteristics of understory vegetation to measure are:

● Species composition
● Relative cover by species or species groups
● Density (number of stems or plants per unit area)
● Frequency (the proportion of samples in which a species occurs)
● Abundance (number of stems or plants per sample)
● Sizes (height, diameter), especially for tree regeneration

Table 10-1 summarizes the sampling techniques commonly applied to understory vegetation. In this chapter we review some of the more common techniques employed in estimation of these parameters. For a more complete treatment of understory vegetation measurement and sampling, refer to Kershaw and Looney (1985), Bonham (1989), or Sutherland (1996). Examples of integrated multiresource forest inventories and their design and analysis can be found in O'Brien and Van Hooser (1983), Schreuder et al. (1993), and Tallent-Halsell (1994).

TABLE 10-1. Methods^a for Sampling Understory Vegetation

Method	Vegetation Type					
	Saplings	Seedlings	Shrubs	Herbs and grasses	Bryophytes	Fungi and Lichen
Counts						
Fixed-area plots	*	*	+	?	—	—
Point samples	+	?	?	?	—	—
Transects	*	*	*	*	?	?
Distance sampling	*	*	*	?	?	?
Cover						
Visual estimation	*	*	*	*	*	*
Frame quadrats	+	*	+	*	*	*
Point quadrats	—	+	+	*	*	*
Point samples	?	?	*	*	—	—
Transects	*	*	*	*	*	*
Biomass						
Harvesting	+	*	*	*	*	*
Reference units	+	+	+	?	?	—
Allometric relationships	*	*	*	*	?	?

Source: Adapted from Bullock (1996).

^{a} *, Usually applicable; +, often applicable; ?, sometimes applicable; −, generally not applicable

10-1.1   Estimation of Frequency and Density

Frequency is based on the presence or absence of a species in sample units (plots, transects, or points) and is defined as the number of times a species is present in a given number of sample units (Raunkiaer, 1934). Frequency is usually expressed as a percentage of the total number of sample units. Percent frequency is sometimes referred to as the *frequency index* (Bonham, 1989). Density is a quantitative expression of the number of plants per unit area. Depending on the size of the plants, density is expressed as number of individuals/ft^2 or individuals/m^2 for small plants and number of individuals/acre or individuals/hectare for larger plants.

The most common method for estimating understory vegetation frequency or density utilizes fixed-area square or circular plots which can vary in size, depending on the class of vegetation to be studied. For example, Cain and de Oliveira Castro (1959) suggested the following plot areas: for the moss layer, 0.01 to 0.1 m^2; for the herb and small seedling layer, 1 to 2 m^2; for tall herbs and low shrubs, 4 m^2; for tall shrubs and low trees, 10 m^2; and for trees, 100 m^2. However, the selection of an appropriate plot size for measurement is a subjective decision and should be based on the size and spacing of individuals of a species (Bonham, 1989). Curtis and McIntosh (1950) proposed that a plot should be no larger than one or two times the mean area per individual of the most common species. Bartlett (1948) determined the most efficient size of plots for density estimation corresponded to a 20 percent absence rate (frequency $= 80$ percent). A number of researchers have examined efficiency in terms of sampling error and time requirements for various plot sizes and shapes (e.g., Evans, 1952; Van Dyne et al., 1963; Eddlemann et al., 1964; Hyder et al., 1965). Frequencies and densities can also be estimated using line transects (Section 11-2.2) and distance methods (Section 11-4). Density estimates for larger shrubs and small trees may be obtained using point sampling techniques (Section 11-3 and Chapter 14).

For frequency estimates, only the presence of a species on a plot needs to be noted. For density estimates, all individuals within the plot boundary need to be counted. Plot counts are expanded to per unit area counts using the ratio of unit area to plot area:

$$\text{expansion factor} = \frac{\text{unit area}}{\text{plot area}} \tag{10-1}$$

For example, if the number of individuals on 5-ft^2 plots are counted, the number of individuals/ft^2 is obtained by multiplying the count by 0.2 (1 ft^2/5 ft^2). If 100-m^2 plots are used, the number of individuals per hectare is obtained by multiplying the count by 100 [(10,000 m^2/ha)/(100 m^2/plot)].

To estimate density, each individual plant on a plot needs to be identified and counted. One of the greatest difficulties in estimating density of understory vegetation is identification of individual plants (Bonham, 1989). Strickler and

Stearns (1962) defined an individual as the aerial parts corresponding to a single root system. For single stem species, like most trees and annuals, this definition is simple to apply; however, for many grass species, clonal herbs, and multistemmed shrubs, where the number of individual plant stems per root system vary considerably, this definition is not easily applied. While the only practical counting unit for density estimation is the individual, the value of carefully defining the individual depends on the purpose of the study, definition of the unit, and precision of the count (Bonham, 1989). The number of individual stems or shoots may be more highly correlated with other parameters of interest, such as biomass and cover, than with the number of individual plants.

10-1.2 Estimation of Cover

The simplest definition of *cover* is the percentage of ground surface covered by vegetative material. Cover is generally expressed as a fraction or percentage of total area. Cover of a species or life-form expressed as a percentage of total vegetation is referred to as *relative cover*. Cover is generally measured as the vertical projection of vegetative material on to the ground surface (see Fig. 5-17 for an example of crown projection area). Cover is one of the most commonly measured vegetation parameters. Because cover is an expression of vertical projection, its measurement does not require identification of individual plants, thus estimation of cover is generally easier than estimation of density. Cover also has the advantage of being able to express measures of different life-forms (e.g., mosses, grasses, forbs, shrubs, and trees) in comparable terms. If the vegetation occurs in distinct layers (e.g., trees, shrubs, and undergrowth), then depending upon the objectives of the sample, cover of each species can be measured separately by layer (Bonham, 1989).

Cover may be estimated by measuring plant dimensions and applying formulas for regular geometric shapes. For example, crown area is often calculated by measuring crown diameter along one or more axes and applying the formula for a circle (see Section 5-5.1). For understory vegetation, cover is often estimated visually using small fixed-area plots. A frame quadrat (Fig. 10-1a) can be used to facilitate visual estimation. A frame quadrat divides a larger fixed-area plot into smaller subplots. The example illustrated in Fig. 10-1a has divided the larger plot into 100 equal-area subplots. Cover can be estimated visually for each subplot, or the subplot can be classified as either covered or not covered by a species. Cover for the larger plot is then obtained by summation of the cover values of the smaller plots.

Photographic frame quadrats (Fig. 10-1b) are an efficient method of estimating cover. Vertical photographs are obtained at a constant height above the vegetation or ground. A grid is superimposed on the image either by using a filter at the time of image capture or by manually overlaying a grid on the developed image. As with the normal frame quadrat, cover can be estimated visually for each subplot, or the subplot can be classified as covered or not covered. For example, a subplot can be considered covered if 50 percent of its

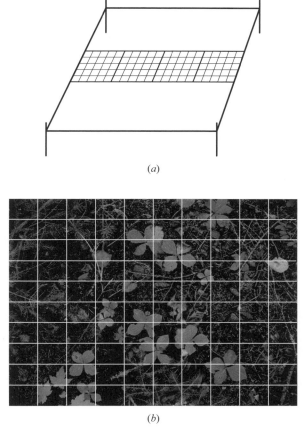

(a)

(b)

FIG. 10-1. Frame quadrat method for estimating vegetation cover: (a) frame quadrat; (b) photo frame quadrat.

area is occupied by a given species. Using this definition, the number of sub-plots in Fig 10-1b covered by bunchberry (*Cornus canadensis*) is 16 and the percentage cover is estimated to be $100(16/100) = 16$ percent. The availability of reasonably priced high-quality digital cameras and powerful image analysis software makes photographic frame quadrats an easier and less time consuming method of obtaining cover estimates.

Visual estimation of cover has the disadvantages of potential variation among different observations and the potential for high observer bias (Bonham, 1989). A number of intercept methods have been developed which eliminate much of the potential observer variation and bias. Two commonly employed intercept methods are the point intercept technique and the line intercept technique.

The *point intercept technique* involves lowering a pin through the vegetation canopy and recording the number of hits (interceptions) by species (Fig. 10-2). Percent cover is obtained by dividing the number of hits by the total number of pins. For example, in Fig. 10-2b, a forb is hit by 4 out of 10 pins; therefore, the percent cover for forbs is 100(4/10) = 40 percent. Similarly, grass had one hit, representing 10 percent cover, and bare ground had 5 hits, representing 50 percent cover. The point intercept technique can also be applied to vertical photographs (Fig. 10-3). As with the photo frame quadrat, a dot grid can be

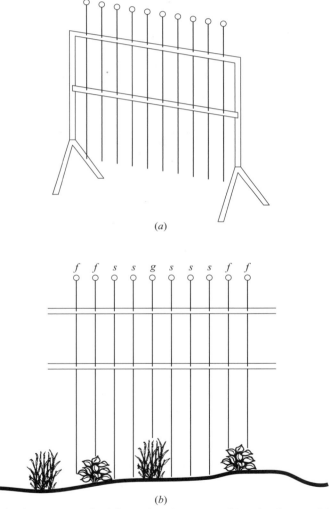

FIG. 10-2. Point intercept method for estimating cover: (*a*) point frame with 10 pins; (*b*) point frame intersections. *f*, First hit on forb; *g*, first hit on grass; and *s*, first hit on soil.

FIG. 10-3. Photographic point intercept method.

superimposed on the photograph and the number of dots falling on a given species counted. In Fig. 10-3, 13 dots fall on bunchberry, thus the percentage cover is estimated as $100(13/100) = 13$ percent.

The *line intercept technique* utilizes a transect and measures the length of the transect intercepted by the vertical projection of a species (Fig. 10-4a). The percentage cover is estimated as the ratio of interception length to total transect length:

$$\text{percent cover} = 100 \frac{\sum I}{L} \qquad (10\text{-}2)$$

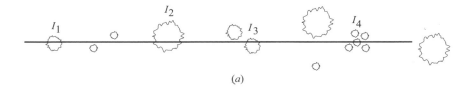

(a)

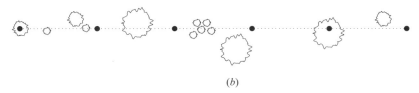

(b)

FIG. 10-4. (a) Line intercept technique for cover estimation; (b) point transect method.

where I = interception length
       L = total transect length

For some species, such as trees and larger shrubs, the determination of intercepted distance can be difficult and subject to observer bias (Bonham, 1989). A
point transect (Fig. 10-4b) is a modification of the line intercept technique.

The *point transect technique* is similar to the point intercept technique.
Points along a transect are established at predetermined intervals. Each
point is assessed to determine if it is covered or not covered. The percent
cover is estimated as the number of covered points divided by the total number
of points.

Bonham (1989) describes another technique for estimating cover using a
modification of sampling with probability proportional to size (Section 14-1).
An angle gauge (Fig. 10-5a) is built using two sticks. The gauge constant is
determined from the ratio of stick length to crossbar length:

$$K = \frac{L}{I} \tag{10-3}$$

where K = gauge constant
       L = stick length
       I = crossbar length

This gauge constant, K, is the reciprocal of the gauge constant k used in
horizontal point sampling (Section 11-3.1). Plants are counted if the diameter
of their associated crown cross section is greater than the projected crossbar
length (Fig. 10-5b and c). The percent cover represented by each plant counted
is determined from the ratio of the area of a circle whose diameter equals the
crossbar length to the area of a circle whose radius equals the stick length:

$$\text{percent cover} = 100\frac{\pi(I/2)^2}{\pi L^2} = 100\frac{I^2}{4L^2} = 25\frac{I^2}{L^2} = \frac{25}{K^2} \tag{10-4}$$

If $K = 5$, each plant counted represents 1 percent cover. Total cover is obtained
by counting all plants in a $360°$ search around the sample point.

10-1.3   Estimation of Biomass

Interest in *understory biomass* has increased because of its role in biodiversity, global climate change, carbon sequestering, wildlife habitat evaluation, and forest fuel assessment. Understory biomass may be measured
directly using harvest techniques or measured indirectly using a variety of
nondestructive measurements and regression equations relating biomass to
these measures.

Harvest methods may employ either complete removal of vegetation within
a sample unit or some sort of proportional harvesting scheme. When using

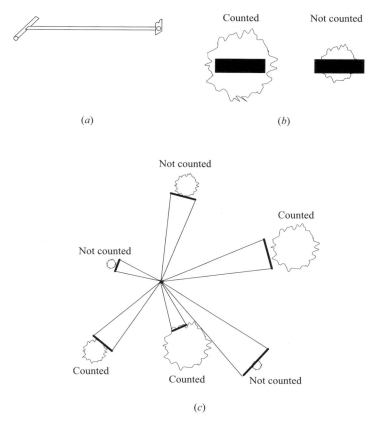

FIG. 10-5. Sampling cover with probability proportional to size: (*a*) angle gauge; (*b*) counting cover; (*c*) cover point sample. (Adapted from Bonham, 1989.)

complete removal methods, all vegetation within a predefined sample area is removed. Often, the plot boundaries are projected vertically and only vegetation within the plot space is removed. Portions of plants rooted within the plot boundary but projecting out of the plot space are discarded from the sample. Similarly, parts of plants not rooted within the plot boundary, but projecting into the plot space, are counted. The clipped vegetation may be weighed fresh or dried and may be separated into components (foliage, branches, stems), depending on the requirements of the survey. In some surveys, clipped vegetation may be weighed fresh in the field and a fixed proportion of the material selected and dried. A ratio between the fresh weight and dried weight of the subsample is then used to estimate dried weight for the entire sample. Biomass per unit area is obtained by expanding the plot measurement to per unit area values using an appropriate expansion factor [eq. (10-1)].

Proportional harvesting schemes utilize either a fixed percentage removal or simply sample individual plants or individual plant parts. Sampling individual plant parts is often referred to as *reference unit sampling*. Reference unit sampling is commonly used on multistem shrub species. One stem is randomly harvested and its biomass determined. Total biomass for the plot is obtained by multiplying the reference unit weight by the number of reference units on the plot. See Bonham (1989) or Pitt and Schwab (1988) for detailed discussions of implementing reference unit sampling.

The most common approach to understory biomass determination is to predict biomass from nondestructive measurements of plants. A variety of regression models have been developed to predict biomass from plant measurements. The most common equation forms include

$$Y = b_0 + b_1 X \qquad \text{linear}$$

$$Y = b_0 + b_1 X + b_2 X^2 \qquad \text{quadratic}$$

$$Y = b_0 e^{b_1 X} \qquad \text{exponential}$$

$$Y = b_0 X^{b_1} \qquad \text{allometric}$$

$$\log Y = b_0 + b_1 \log X \qquad \text{logarithmic}$$

where Y = biomass
  X = nondestructive plant measure
  b_1 = regression coefficients

Regression equations have been developed that utilize stem diameter at the ground, stem diameter at some height above ground, crown area, plant height, or a combination of these variables. Examples of biomass equations can be found in Brown (1976), Smith and Brand (1983), and Wharton and Griffith (1998).

10-1.4 Regeneration Surveys

Information on regeneration is important in forest management to determine its current status, survival, and whether or not it is sufficient, to predict its future, to decide on silvicultural treatments, to forecast future stand yields, and to see if it complies with legislative requirements (Stage and Ferguson, 1984; Stein, 1984a).

Regeneration studies or inventories should first define what constitutes the population of interest. The population may consist of:

- All tree species or only chosen ones
- All individuals (seedlings, sprouts, saplings) or only healthy ones

If all individuals are included, indications may be made of their health or condition, such as browsed by animals. The heights and/or diameters may be measured for the individuals in the regeneration population.

Natural tree regeneration consists of seedlings, sprouts, and saplings. The definitions and size characteristics of these components of regeneration vary in different studies, although in general terms, seedlings are small plants of tree species originating from seed; sprouts are stems that have originated from a dead or cut tree stem or from roots; and saplings are young trees that have not attained a given dbh or height. In the Forest Health Monitoring Guide Program (Tallent-Halsell, 1994) seedlings are individuals of tree species at least 1 ft (0.3 m) tall but less than 1.0 in. (2.5 cm) dbh. Saplings are individuals from 1.0 in. (2.5 cm) to 4.9 in. (12.4 cm) dbh. In a study of biomass in Maine (Wharton and Griffith, 1998), seedlings were defined as trees less than 1.0 in. dbh, and saplings were trees at least 1.0 in. but less than 5.0 in. dbh. The *Forestry Handbook* defines a *seedling* as a woody plant of either a shrub or tree species that is less than 3.0 ft (91.4 cm) tall, a *shrub* as a woody plant greater than 3.0 ft (91.4 cm) tall that will not become a dominant or codominant in the canopy, and a *sapling* as a woody plant with a dbh less than 4.0 in. (10.2 cm) but greater than or equal to 1.0 in. (2.5 cm). The same size definitions may be applied to sprouts, although their origin should be noted.

Several methods have been developed to estimate the amount of regeneration in a forest area. The most important methods are total stocking methods and the stocked-quadrat method. *Total stocking* or *plot-count methods* use small fixed-area plots, such as a circular or square milacre plot. Tree counts on each plot are made by species, type of regeneration, health, or condition. In more detailed studies, the heights and diameters may be recorded for each individual on a plot. Counts are then converted into per unit area values using appropriate expansion factors [eq. (10-1)]. For example, if milacre (1/1000 acre) plots are used, the count is multiplied by 1000 to convert to a per acre basis.

Counts of this kind are useful measures of the density of regeneration but are often insufficient. In addition to density, a complete characterization of regeneration should include some measure of spatial distribution. Loetsch et al. (1973) present a summary of methods to measure this characteristic. They describe an *index of heterogeneity*, which is the ratio of the variance to the population mean of the number of individuals per sample plot:

$$I_H = \frac{\sigma^2}{\mu} \tag{10-5}$$

where I_H = index of heterogeneity
σ^2 = population variation of number of individuals per plot
μ = population mean of number of individuals per plot

If individuals are randomly distributed (i.e., Poisson distributed), $I_H = 1$. If $I_H < 1$, the distribution is more systematic (i.e., equally spaced). The smaller the value of I_H, the more regular the spacing. If $I_H > 1$, the distribution is clustered.

Vertical sampling (Section 11-3.4) is an overlooked alternative to using small fixed-area plots to obtain regeneration counts. Descriptions of the application of vertical sampling to regeneration assessment are found in Beers and Miller (1976) and Eichenberger et al. (1982).

In the *stocked-quadrat method*, a sample plot is stocked if it has at least one seedling of the species of interest. The presence or absence of a tree on the plot, not the total number, is the primary focus of the stocked-quadrat method. The method emphasizes the evaluation of tree distribution rather than tree density. The basic idea is to divide an area into small squares of a size such that one tree per square represents full stocking at maturity. Stein (1984b) pointed out that the size of the quadrat can be determined as the reciprocal of the number of stems per unit area that constitute full stocking. Thus, if full stocking is 250 stems per acre, the presence of trees should be checked on plots $1/250$ acre in size; if full stocking is 2000 stems per hectare, plot size should be $1/2000$ ha. Plot size can also be determined from ideal spacing. For example, if full stocking is 2500 stems per hectare, the ideal tree spacing is $\sqrt{10,000/2500} = \sqrt{4} = 2\,\text{m}$. The corresponding plot size is $(\text{spacing})^2$. However, Kershaw (in review) found that circular quadrats, where size is determined as the reciprocal of full stocking density, significantly underestimated stocking percentage. Circular plots with a radius equal to half of the diagonal spacing (spacing $\times \sqrt{2}/2$) were the optimal size for obtaining an unbiased estimate of stocking percentage.

The number of stocked quadrats in relation to the total number of plots gives the *stocking percentage*:

$$\% \text{ stocking} = 100 \frac{\text{number of stocked quadrats}}{\text{total number of quadrats}} \tag{10-6}$$

A regression of the form $Y = b_0 + b_1 X^2$ can be prepared where Y is the seedlings per unit area, X the stocking percentage, and the b values are constants. With this function the percentage of stocked quadrats can be used to estimate the number of seedlings per unit area.

Dennis (1984) describes *distance-sampling methods* as an alternative to the use of fixed-area sample plots for evaluating forest tree regeneration. He summarized the several forms of distance sampling as:

1. Measuring the distance from a randomly located point to the nearest tree
2. Measuring the distance from a randomly selected tree to its nearest neighbor

3. Measuring the point-to-tree distance as in form 1, then measuring the distance to the nearest neighbor lying beyond a line through the first tree drawn perpendicular to the original point-tree line (*T-square sampling*)
4. Measuring the distances from a randomly located point to the first, second, third, ..., jth nearest tree

All of these methods require several repetitions to obtain an adequate sample size. These distance methods permit estimation of the number of trees per unit area (density) and an assessment of the spatial pattern of the trees. The use of distance methods for estimation of density and other stand parameters is discussed in Section 11-4.

Regeneration can also be obtained from initial plantation establishment. The original density of a plantation (number of stems per unit area) is determined by the spacing used in planting. The density is

$$N = \frac{A}{LR} \tag{10-7}$$

where N = number of plants per unit area
A = size of area unit (hectare = $10,000\,m^2$; acre = $43,560\,ft^2$)
L = distance between plants in a row (m or ft)
R = distance between rows (m or ft)

For example, the density per acre for spacing of 6 ft × 6 ft is

$$N = \frac{43,560}{6(6)} = 1210 \text{ plants/acre}$$

Estimation of the survival or density of the plantation at some age can be determined by sampling as described in Chapter 13. Tree nurseries may require an inventory of the total number of seedlings and their health or condition. Estimates can be made using small sample plots and counting the number of seedlings, measuring their heights, and determining their health and their suitability for planting. From the sample plots, estimates can be made of total amounts in the nursery.

10-2. WOODY DETRITUS

The Forest Inventory Assessment (FIA) field guide (FIA, 2001) has emphasized that down woody debris is an important component of forest ecosystems of interest to wildlife biologists, ecologists, mycologists, foresters, and fuel specialists. Information on down woody debris helps describe:

- Quality and status of wildlife habitats
- Structural diversity within a forest
- Fuel loading and fire behavior
- Carbon sequestration—the amount of carbon stored in dead wood
- Storage and cycling of nutrients and water—important for site product-
  ivity
- Quantity available for possible commercial utilization

Harmon and Sexton (1996) have prepared guidelines for measurements of woody detritus in forest ecosystems. They recommend that the terms *woody detritus* and *woody debris* include all forms of dead woody material above- and belowground. Aboveground woody detritus can be divided into coarse or fine fractions. Minimum dimensions for coarse woody detritus are usually 10 cm diameter at the large end and 1.5 m in length. Smaller pieces than these are usually considered fine woody detritus. *Coarse fractions* can in turn be divided into *snags* (or *standing dead*) and *logs* (or *dead and downed*).* The separation of snags from logs is usually at a 45° angle. In addition to snags, stumps should be recognized in managed settings. They recommend that the short vertical pieces resulting from natural processes always be called snags, and that the term *stump* be reserved for short vertical pieces created by cutting. *Fine fractions* can also be divided into suspended or downed fractions. In the case of sus-pended fine wood, one must distinguish between that attached to living woody plants and that attached to dead woody plants. Woody branches, twigs, and bark pieces less than 1 cm in diameter can be very numerous and are treated as fine litter. They recommend that dead fine roots be separated from dead coarse roots at a diameter of 1 cm. Belowground woody detritus has rarely been studied, but they recommend that it be divided into buried wood (very decayed material in the mineral soil or forest floor) and dead coarse roots.

10.2.1 Fixed-Area Plots

Fixed-area plots are the simplest and most direct method of inventorying woody detritus, although line intercepts and variable radius plots have been used (see Harmon and Sexton, 1996). The volume of coarse woody detritus consisting of snags, stumps, logs, and piles of decomposed bark and wood accumulated at the base of snags (referred to as *blobs*) can be measured on fixed-area plots of from 0.05 to 0.20 ha, depending on the forest type. For logs, the diameters at both ends and midpoint and length are measured to calculate volumes (hollows are deducted). For snags, the dbh is measured for intact boles

---

*Salvageable dead trees are dead trees with intact bark. This does not include snags that have lost their bark and for the most part contain no solid wood. Nevertheless, dead snags of unusable timber must also be included in the biomass.

and the diameters at the base and top and length for boles that have broken. The base and top diameters and length are recorded for stumps (or a midpoint diameter). The diameter at the base is measured for blobs. These volumes must be converted to weight using estimates of wood specific gravity (g/cm^3). Downed fine wood can be weighed directly on portable scales and samples taken to estimate moisture content for conversion of the field weights to dry weight. Harmon and Sexton (1996) give detailed instructions for the estimation of attached dead wood, buried wood, and dead coarse roots.

10-2.2 Line Intersect Sampling for Woody Debris

Line intersect sampling (LIS) was developed initially to estimate the amount of woody debris or slash; for example, residue after logging, or to estimate the amount of fuel wood and inflammable material on the ground. As Shiver and Borders (1996) explain, the procedure to carry out a line intersect sample for this purpose consists of two steps:

1. Establish a line of a given length across the area of interest.
2. Traverse the line, maintaining the initial direction and record the diameter(s) of every piece of woody material that intersects the line. Diameter(s) may be measured at the midpoint of the piece, at both ends, or where the line crosses the piece.

With this procedure, the estimate of total amount $\hat{T}$ (number, volume, or weight) of material per unit area is

$$\hat{T} = \frac{\pi}{2L} \sum_{i=1}^{n} \frac{x_i}{l_i} \tag{10-8}$$

where L = length of sample line
l_i = length of ith intersecting sample element
x_i = characteristic of interest on ith sample element

If l_i and L are measured in feet, $\hat{T}$ estimates x per square foot. If l_i and L are measured in meters $\hat{T}$ estimates x per square meter. If the characteristic of interest is cubic volume, the cubic volume of the ith element is

$$x_i = \pi \left(\frac{d_i}{2}\right)^2 l_i \tag{10-9}$$

where x_i = cubic volume of ith element
d_i = diameter of ith element where it intersects line
l_i = length of ith element (note that d_i and l_i are measured in the same units, feet or meters)

Substituting eq. (10-9) into eq. (10-8) and simplifying, the total volume of material per unit area (square foot or square meter) is

$$\hat{T} = \frac{\pi}{2L} \sum \frac{\pi(d_i/2)^2 l_i}{l_i} = \frac{\pi^2}{8L} \sum_{i=1}^{n} d_i^2 \tag{10-10}$$

The volume of woody debris per acre (ft^3/acre) is obtained by multiplying $\hat{T}$ by 43,560 (1 acre = 43,560 ft^2):

$$\hat{T}/\text{acre} = 43{,}560\hat{T} = 43{,}560\frac{\pi^2}{8L} \sum_{i=1}^{n} d_i^2 = \frac{5445\pi^2}{L} \sum_{i=1}^{n} d_i^2 \tag{10-11}$$

where $\hat{T}/\text{acre}$ = cubic feet of woody debris per acre
$\quad\quad d_i$ = diameter of ith element (ft)
$\quad\quad L$ = transect length (ft)

If d_i is measured in inches and L in feet, the volume of woody debris per acre (ft^3/acre) becomes

$$\hat{T}/\text{acre} = \frac{5445\pi^2}{L} \sum_{i=1}^{n} \left(\frac{d_i}{12}\right)^2 = \frac{5445\pi^2}{144L} \sum_{i=1}^{n} d_i^2 = \frac{373.2}{L} \sum_{i=1}^{n} d_i^2 \tag{10-12}$$

The volume of woody debris per hectare (m^3/ha) is obtained by multiplying $\hat{T}$ from eq. (10-10) by 10,000 (1 ha = 10,000 m^2):

$$\hat{T}/\text{ha} = 10{,}000\hat{T} = 10{,}000\frac{\pi^2}{8L} d_i^2 = \frac{1250\pi^2}{L} \sum_{i=1}^{n} d_i^2 \tag{10-13}$$

If d_i is measured in centimeters and L is measured in meters, the estimate becomes

$$\hat{T}/\text{ha} = 10{,}000\hat{T} = 10{,}000\frac{\pi^2}{8L} \sum_{i=1}^{n} \left(\frac{d_i}{100}\right)^2 = \frac{10{,}000\pi^2}{80{,}000L} \sum_{i=1}^{n} d_i^2$$

$$= \frac{\pi^2}{8L} \sum_{i=1}^{n} d_i^2 = \frac{1.2337}{L} \sum_{i=1}^{n} d_i^2 \tag{10-14}$$

where $\hat{T}/\text{ha}$ = cubic meters of wood debris per hectare
$\quad\quad d_i$ = diameter of ith element (cm)
$\quad\quad L$ = transect length (m)

As it happens, eq. (10-14) for m^3/ha is the same as eq. (10-10) for m^3/m^2; the difference is that d is measured in centimeters in eq. (10-14) and in meters in eq.

(10-10). For detailed treatment of this method of sampling and an estimate of variance, see Shiver and Borders (1996).

The FIA (2001) method measures coarse and fine woody debris using transects established on each subplot of a four-plot cluster. Each transect starts at the subplot center and extends to the edge of the subplot (58.9 ft). Each transect is segmented according to the length of different condition classes. Individual pieces of coarse and fine woody debris are tallied or counted if they meet the rules for these types of debris. The diameters and lengths of coarse woody debris that is crossed by the transect are measured. On the fine woody debris transects, counts are made of three size classes. Depth measurements are made of the duff and litter layers and fuel bed at two points along each transect. In addition, a microplot (6.8 ft radius) is established in each of the four subplots. On microplots, the percent cover and height of live and dead shrubs, live and dead herbs, and litter are measured.

10-2.3 Other Methods

Gove et al. (2001) describe a *point relaskop sampling* (PRS) method for sampling that portion of coarse woody debris consisting of downed logs. The method is analogous to horizontal point sampling with an angle gauge. In PRS the angle gauge at a sampling point is sighted on the downed log lengths to determine whether a log is "in" or "out." The angle of the gauge determines a squared length factor (L) such that each "in" log represents L square units (feet or meters) of squared length per unit area.[*] Any quantity that can be associated with a log can be expanded to a per unit area estimate. For PRS, the equation for the estimate $\hat{y}$ (quantity per unit area) on any given sample point where m logs have been found to be "in" is

$$\hat{y} = L \sum_{i=1}^{m} \frac{y_i}{l_i^2} \tag{10-15}$$

where L = squared length factor for angle of gauge
$\quad\quad y_i$ = quantity of interest (number, volume, biomass) of ith log
$\quad\quad l_i$ = length of ith "in" log

A simple relaskop can be constructed from a wooden slat and two nails (Fig. 10-6a). The relaskop angle v is formed from the ratio of reach length r and

---

[*]Logs are selected with probability proportional to the square of their length. This is analogous to horizontal point sampling (Section 11-3), where standing trees are selected with probability proportional to their basal area (i.e., diameter squared).

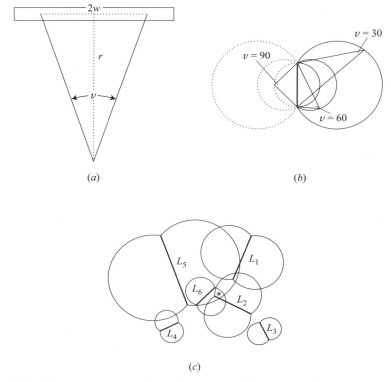

FIG. 10-6. Point relaskop sampling of down logs (a) geometry; (b) inclusion zones; (c) example (∗, plot center; "in" logs, L_2, L_5, and L_6). (Adapted from Gove et al., 2001.)

width w between the two nails (nails are $2w$ apart). The gauge constant ϕ is given by

$$\phi = \frac{\pi(1 - v/180) + \sin v \cos v}{2 \sin^2 v} \tag{10-16}$$

The inclusion area (Fig. 10-6b) is obtained from

$$A_i = \phi l_i^2 \tag{10-17}$$

The squared length per unit area factor L is derived by expanding the squared length per plot A_i to a per unit area basis:

$$L_i = l_i^2 \text{ (expansion factor)}$$

$$\text{expansion factor} = \frac{\text{unit area}}{\text{plot area}}$$

$$\text{plot area} = A_i = \phi l_i^2 \tag{10-18}$$

$$\text{expansion factor} = \frac{\text{unit area}}{\phi l_i^2}$$

$$L_i = l_i^2 \frac{\text{unit area}}{\phi l_i^2} = \frac{\text{unit area}}{\phi}$$

where L_i = squared length per unit area factor for ith log
unit area = 43,560 ft²/acre or 10,000 m²/ha
A_i = plot area [from eq. (10-17)]
l_i = length of ith log

Since L_i is a constant independent of log length, all logs will have the same squared length per unit area factor L. ϕ is independent of measurement system (English or metric), and L is obtained by substituting in the appropriate unit area, 43,560 ft²/acre for English and 10,000 m²/ha for metric. Table 10-2 shows L for both the English and metric systems for various reach/width ratios. A log is counted as "in" if its inclusion area includes the sample point (Fig. 10-6c). This is determined by sighting one nail at one end of the log, and then sighting the second nail down the length of the log. If the log is longer than the projected angle, the log is "in." To calculate the number of logs per unit area $\hat{y}$ represented by the value of L, one assigns a value of 1 to y_i and

$$\hat{y} = L\frac{1}{l_i^2} \tag{10-19}$$

TABLE 10-2. Some Useful Reach/Width Ratios and Their Associated Relaskop Angles v and Squared Length Factors L

Relaskop Reach/Width	v (deg)	L (ft²/acre)	L (m²/ha)
1:1	90.00	55,462	12,732
2:1	53.13	20,694	4,751
3:1	36.87	10,531	2,418
4:1	28.07	6,291	1,444
5:1	22.62	4,155	954
6:1	18.92	2,939	675
7:1	16.26	2,185	502
8:1	14.25	1,686	387

Source: Adapted from Gove et al. (2001).

Per unit area values for other quantities are calculated in like manner by letting y_i be the quantity of interest (e.g., volume or length).

Brown (1974) described an older method for estimating the volume and weight of downed woody material, fuel, and duff depth. Using a planar inter-sect technique, downed material is inventoried by 0–0.25-in., 0.25–1-in., and 1–3-in. diameter classes; and by 1-in. classes for sound and rotten pieces over 3 in. The method involves counting downed woody pieces that intersect vertical sampling planes and measuring the diameters of pieces larger than 3 in. in diameter. The piece counts and diameters permit calculations of tons per acre. Arcos et al. (1996) devised a method for the volume estimation of large woody debris that uses stereoscopic photo images.

10-3. FOREST VEGETATION FOR WILDLIFE MANAGEMENT

The determination of forest and vegetative types, their areas and patterns of distribution (extensive areas or fragmented, amount of edges), and the char-acteristics of the vegetation on an area are important components of wildlife habitat evaluation. The species of plants and their sizes, density, and spacing determine the availability, adequacy, and quality of food (forage, browse, fruits, seeds), den and nest sites (snags, dead trees), and resting and bedding grounds. Different animal species have different habitat requirements, and observations of these habitat characteristics must be keyed to the animal species of interest. Ripley and Halls (1966) have pointed out that vegetation measurements are usually made for one or all of the following reasons:

- To find out how much food is available
- To find out how much and what kinds of plants are being eaten
- To determine the condition of the range and whether it is getting better or worse
- To describe interrelations between plants, animals, and the environment

The kind of information, which must be obtained for evaluating wildlife habitat, depends on the species of wildlife of interest. As an example, Rennie et al. (2000) indicate the variables that must be measured to evaluate habitat suitability for five species of fauna. Many of these are obtained in standard forest inventories, but others must be obtained from additional sources and additional variables observed during a forest inventory. They indicate that information on the following variables must be obtained from other sources and additional measurements during the inventory: elevation; proximity to streams, human activity, roads, trails, and evergreen shrub thickets; history of vegetation disturbance; slope; aspect; fire history; stump biomass; canopy height, percent shrub, herbaceous, and grass cover. Rudis (1991) prepared a compendium of references regarding wildlife habitat analysis from forest inventories. Information on these and other nontimber variables may be obtained from multiple forest resource inventories discussed in Chapter 12.

One of the more popular approaches used to relate vegetation and other environmental variables to wildlife populations is the *habitat suitability index* (HSI). HSI models identify critical components of habitat in terms of the life cycle of the target species (e.g., food, cover, and breeding requirements). In most HSI models, each critical habitat component is scaled to a quality index between 0 (very poor quality) and 1 (excellent/optimum quality). The overall habitat quality is then expressed as a function of the indices of the critical components. Generally, these functions result in an expression of overall HSI as an index between 0 (very poor habitat) and 1 (excellent/optimum habitat).

For example, in an HSI model developed for the black-capped chickadee (Schroeder, 1983), two critical components of habitat are identified: food and reproduction. The food component is a combination of percent tree canopy closure (V_1) and average height of overstory trees (V_2). The index values for V_1 and V_2 are interpolated from the corresponding graphs in Fig. 10-7. The overall index for the food component is computed as $I_F = \sqrt{V_1 V_2}$. Quality of reproduction habitat is based on the availability of snags for nesting. The index value for reproduction, I_R, is interpolated from the corresponding graph in Fig. 10-7. The overall habitat suitability index is computed as the minimum of the two critical indices, $\text{HSI} = \min(I_F, I_R)$.

Based on this model, a stand with 75 percent crown closure and an average overstory height of 12.5 m would have index values $V_1 = 0.90$ and $V_2 = 0.8$. The corresponding index value for food would then be $I_F = \sqrt{(0.9)(0.8)} = 0.85$. If the average number of snags per hectare is 1.5, the index value for reproduction, $I_R = 0.75$ and the $\text{HSI} = \min(0.85, 0.75) = 0.75$. Forest-level averages are computed using weighted means with stand area as the weight (Schamberger et al., 1982).

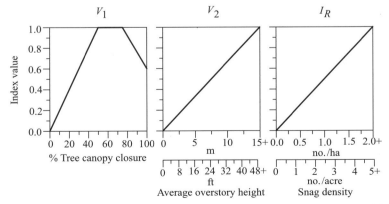

FIG. 10-7. Index values for habitat suitability model for black-capped chickadee. (Adapted from Schroeder, 1983.)

The U.S. Department of Interior (USDI) Fish and Wildlife Service has developed an extensive library of HSI models for over 100 species (Schamberger et al., 1982). HSI models are used extensively by the USDI Fish and Wildlife Service and other resource management groups and are some of the most influential wildlife management tools in use (Brooks, 1997). These models are useful because they represent in a simple and under-standable form the major environmental factors thought to most influence occurrence and abundance of a wildlife species; however, HSI models have been criticized because they do not provide information on population size, trend, or behavioral response by individuals to shifts in resource conditions (Morrison et al., 1992). Despite the wide application of these models, many models have not been evaluated adequately or consistently (Roloff and Kernohan, 1999). Brooks (1997) and Roloff and Kernohan (1999) discuss approaches for improving and evaluating HSI models. Bender et al. (1996) discuss two techniques for estimating confidence intervals for HSI models.

For the forest mensurationist and other forest managers, HSI models are very useful because many of the parameters required are collected during normal forest inventories, and the additional variables can easily be incorpo-rated or obtained using other management tools, such as GIS. Many of the models can easily be incorporated into existing forest growth and yield models and forest management planning systems, thus giving forest managers a tool to evaluate the impacts of management decisions on wildlife habitat.

10-4. FOREST BIOMASS

Brown (1997) defined *forest biomass* as the total amount of aboveground living organic matter expressed as oven-dry tons per unit area. In this book we limit this to vegetative matter and do not include other types of living matter. There is an increasing need to improve the accuracy of total forest biomass quantities, for several reasons:

- The need to make estimates of carbon pools in forests (United Nations, 1992)
- For studying other biogeochemical cycles

Schreuder et al. (1997) note that changes in forest biomass density are brought about by natural succession; human activities such as silviculture, harvesting, and degradation; and natural impacts caused by wildfire and cli-mate change. Thus they use biomass density as a useful measure for assessing change in forest structure and estimation of carbon content. They also point out that biomass density is a useful variable for comparing structural and functional attributes for forest ecosystems across a wide range of environmen-tal conditions.

Wharton and Griffith (1998) distinguish between biomass of timber and forest biomass. They define *timber biomass* as the merchantable stems of growing stock trees and the additional sources of biomass in these trees: bark, branches, foliage, and the stump–root system; cull trees; and salvageable dead trees. To the biomass of timber are added the biomass of seedlings, saplings, and shrubs and other vegetation, which constitutes the *forest biomass*.

Wharton and Griffith (1998) summarized the timber biomass into percentage tables for northeastern tree species (Table 10-3). The table summarizes the percentage of aboveground biomass found in the foliage and branches; the main stem biomass percentage is obtained by subtraction. For example, one can ascertain from this table that in small saw timber of deciduous species, the foliage constitutes 2.7 percent and branches 9.9 percent of the aboveground biomass. The remaining 87.4 percent is in the main stem. The table shows that stump and roots constitute 20.1 percent of the complete tree biomass.

For a complete estimate of forest vegetation biomass, the tree biomass must be added to the biomass of other types of vegetative material. This is made up of the understory vegetation of mosses, lichens, ferns, herbs, and natural tree regeneration together with their belowground roots and rhizomes. Most of the belowground biomass of forests is contained in coarse roots, generally defined as < 2 mm. The largest part of the total root biomass is found within 30 cm of the soil surface (IPPC, 1999).*

The most economical approach for estimating aboveground forest biomass is to use data from forest inventories. Obviously, forest volume inventories do not generally characterize all forest biomass; they usually indicate the volume of commercially valuable wood in the main stem. Brown (1997) pointed out that the following additional problems might arise in using conventional forest inventories for biomass estimation.

1. The minimum dbh of trees in the inventory is often greater that 10 cm and sometimes as large as 50 cm; this excludes smaller trees which can account for a large proportion of the biomass.
2. The maximum dbh class in stand tables generally lumps the very large trees in a single class.
3. Frequently, only commercial tree species are included in the inventory volume.
4. The definition of inventory volume is not always consistent.

To use inventory volume data to estimate aboveground biomass density (defined as aboveground biomass in trees per unit area) it is necessary to take into account a reduction factor for rot and an expansion factor to account

*Numerous estimates of aboveground biomass density have been made. On the other hand, estimates of root biomass density are far less common. For a summary of these estimates, see Cairns et al. (1997).

TABLE 10-3. Branch Biomass and Foliage Biomass as a Percentage of Aboveground Tree Biomass, and Stump-Root Biomass as a Percentage of Complete Tree Biomass, Dry-Weight Basis

Stand-Size Class	Foliage		Branches		Stump-Root	
	Evergreen	Deciduous	Evergreen	Deciduous	Evergreen	Deciduous
Pole timber	11.26	3.48	14.02	10.93	20.83	21.09
Small saw timber	9.60	2.68	14.10	9.91	20.30	20.13
Large saw timber						
≤ 21.0 in. dbh	8.60	2.24	14.27	9.32	20.32	19.43
≥ 21.0 in. dbh	7.68	1.75	14.57	8.60	20.40	18.44

Source: Adapted from Wharton and Griffith (1998).

for the additional components of trees, such as branches, twigs, bark, stumps, foliage, and seedlings and saplings. A reduction factor F_r, may be determined from the expression

$$F_r = \frac{B_n}{B_g} \qquad (10\text{-}20)$$

where B_n = net biomass excluding amount of rot
B_g = gross biomass that includes amount of rot

To develop reduction factors requires that special studies be carried out involving the felling and weighing of sample trees to determine their net and gross weights. For example, a study of the net and gross biomass in trees of *Nothofagus pumilio* in southern Argentina showed that the reduction factors varied from 0.88 to 0.96 (Loguercio and Defossé, 2001). Expansion factors to take into account the other components of a tree's aboveground biomass were found in this study to vary from 2.2 for small diameter trees to 1.1 for large trees, with an average of 1.4 for all trees. (Of course, in the estimate of total carbon content in an area of forest it is also necessary to include the other elements of understory vegetation and dead material discussed previously.)

Schreuder et al. (1997) developed the following aboveground biomass regressions for eastern U.S. hardwoods with diameters from 1.3 to 85.1 cm:

$$B_h = 0.5 + \frac{25{,}000\text{dbh}^{2.5}}{\text{dbh}^{2.5} + 246{,}872} \qquad (10\text{-}21)$$

and for conifers with diameters from 2.52 to 71.6 cm:

$$B_c = 0.5 + \frac{15{,}000\text{dbh}^{2.7}}{\text{dbh}^{2.7} + 364{,}946} \qquad (10\text{-}22)$$

where B = oven-dry tree biomass (kg)

The coefficients of determination were 0.99 and 0.98, respectively.

Using these equations and stand table data of the forest inventory analysis database of the U.S. Forest Service for the eastern United States, they calculated the aboveground biomass density (AGBD) of these forests. They then determined a type of biomass expansion factor (BEF) to take into account that the diameter limit for the aboveground biomass density equations differed from the limits for the growing stock volume (GSV) of the forest inventory. The BEF they used was the ratio of AGBD/GSV. For these forests, the BEF varied from 1.0 to 4.5, depending on the forest type.

Brown (1999) has pointed out that a number of biomass regression equations exist for specific species and that others are more generic in nature. As an example for a single species, Veiga et al. (2000) prepared aboveground biomass equations for the following components of *Acacia mangium* in Brazil: total stem wood dry weight outside bark, total foliage dry weight, total branch dry weight, and total crown dry weight using dbh_{ob} and total height as the independent variables. With these equations it is possible to estimate directly the biomass of trees sampled and not use the procedure of converting inventory volumes. Of course, it would be possible to carry out studies to generate these regression equations for a given species or forest area, but this would be time consuming and costly. For this reason, generic equations such as those shown in eqs. (10-21) and (10-22) are frequently used, although unknown error may result in the biomass estimate.

10-5. CARBON CONTENT

The Kyoto Protocol and its follow-ups recognize that the actions of sequestering, storing, and reducing carbon dioxide associated with forest ecosystems are important mechanisms for regulating anthropogenetic emissions of this gas and can contribute importantly to the mitigation of global warming. The protocol established a mechanism whereby the quantity of carbon captured or sequestered by a forestry project can be sold to countries or companies to count against the reductions that they are obligated to effect. The procedure for carrying out such a project and how to determine the amount of carbon that can be sold is given in Brown (1999) and IPCC (1999). With increasing use of this mechanism, much interest has been generated in the estimation of the carbon content in forest ecosystems [see Harmon (2001) and Johnsen et al. (2001a)].

These estimates must include measurements of the aboveground live biomass described in Section 10-4, the dead biomass described in Section 10-2, and roots and soil (MacDicken, 1997). Estimates of the carbon stock in a forest ecosystem require the following measurements:

- An inventory of the biomass of live standing timber. If biomass regressions are available for the entire tree, weights can be estimated directly from plot measurements of dbh and height of the trees. If such regressions are not available, inventory volumes must be converted to weight and adjusted to include biomass in branches, crown, and foliage (see Section 10-5.1).
- An inventory of the biomass of understory vegetation (including trees below the minimum dbh for timber).
- An estimate of dead biomass commonly referred to as *necromass* (see Section 10-2).
- Estimates of total root biomass and soil carbon pools.

Well-developed techniques and methodologies are available for the first two measurements and are covered in Chapters 12 and 13.

Estimations of root biomass and soil carbon are more difficult. Inclusion of these components is important since more than half of the assimilated carbon in forest vegetation eventually enters the soil through the incorporation and decay of fallen leaves and woody detritus and root growth and exudations. Studies have shown that soils generally contain over half the carbon stock in forest ecosystems. For estimates of root biomass carbon based on above-ground biomass carbon, see Cairns et al. (1997). Belowground biomass can be measured directly by taking soil cores for fine roots and by digging a pit to sample coarse roots. In this procedure, all woody roots above a minimum diameter (e.g., 5 mm) are collected from a known volume of soil from the pit. The dry mass is determined and then converted to a per hectare estimate. However, this does not permit sampling directly beneath stumps and consequently, is an underestimate of woody root biomass. Detailed studies can be carried out to develop equations of root mass by dbh, but this requires excavation and washing of roots and stumps. For methodologies to determine the carbon content of soils, see Post et al. (1999).

10-5.1 Estimation of Carbon Stock from Forest Inventories

Frequently, the results of a traditional forest inventory form the initial basis for the estimation of the quantity of carbon in a forest ecosystem. Clearly, information from a timber inventory is insufficient for a complete estimate of carbon stock since inventories of this type normally express volume of the main stems of commercial value, ignoring volume in the other components of the trees and other carbon pools in the ecosystem. As a consequence, information from a traditional inventory must be adjusted by an expansion factor to include these quantities. To convert green cubic volumes from an inventory to dry weight, the following procedure can be used: Obtain the specific gravity in kilograms per cubic meter at different moisture contents for the species in question, as shown in the following example. [It may be available as air-dry weight at 12 percent moisture, see Haygreen and Bowyer (1996).] An example for three species is shown below.

Specific Gravity (kg/m^3)

Species	Moisture Content (%)						
	120	100	80	60	40	20	12
1	1307	1185	1069	950	832	693	665
2	1052	956	860	765	669	568	535
3	1054	958	862	766	671	575	536

The dry weights in kg/m^3 can be obtained from the expression

$$\text{dry weight (tonnes/m}^3) = \frac{100(\text{wet weight})}{100 + \text{moisture percent}} \qquad (10\text{-}23)$$

Using this expression, the dry weight at 0 percent moisture content in tonnes/m^3 for the species are:

Dry Weight

Species	Tonnes/m^3
1	0.594
2	0.478
3	0.479

It may be convenient to use a weighted average of the tonnes/m^3 of the species that constitute the forest using the volumes of the species as weights.

The weight of carbon is estimated by multiplying the weight of the biomass by a factor that varies between 0.45 and 0.55, indicating the proportion of carbon in the vegetative material. If no specific information is available, a value of 0.50 is most often used. Again a weighted average for all the species may be used. The equivalent weights of carbon per cubic meter at three percentages of carbon content are shown below.

Tonnes of Carbon per Cubic Meter

Species	Dry Weight (tonnes/m^3)	Percent Carbon		
		50	52	55
1	0.594	0.297	0.309	0.327
2	0.478	0.239	0.249	0.263
3	0.479	0.240	0.249	0.264

The dry weights per cubic meter and carbon contents for different volumes per hectare can now be calculated. As an example, these are shown for different volumes per hectare in the following table.

Dry Weight and Carbon Content

Volume per Hectare (m^3)	Equivalence in Tonnes of Dry Wood per Hectare at Tonnes/m^3 of:			Carbon Content in Tonnes/ha Assuming 50% for Dry Wood at Tonnes/m^3 of:		
	0.450	0.500	0.550	0.450	0.500	0.550
100	45.0	50.0	55.0	22.5	25.0	27.5
150	67.5	75.0	82.5	33.7	37.5	41.2
200	90.0	100.0	110.0	45.0	50.0	55.0
250	112.5	125.0	137.5	56.3	62.5	68.8
300	135.0	150.0	165.0	67.5	75.0	82.5

The per hectare and total volumes from an inventory can be converted to dry weights of wood and weights of carbon in a similar manner.

To include the weight of the other components of the biomass (branches, foliage, roots, understory vegetation, and detritus on the forest floor), the weight of the commercial volume generated by the inventory is multiplied by an expansion factor. Of course, it would be possible to carry out a study to determine these quantities directly. However, to reduce costs and time and to make acceptable approximations, expansion factors determined from other studies are generally used. In general, allometric relations have been developed which show that these expansion factors vary from 1.3 to 2.5, depending on species, age of the forest, average dbh of the stand, and amount of necromass. As an example, using an expansion factor of 1.9, the per hectare carbon content for the volume per hectare classes is as shown below

Total Carbon Content in Tonnes per Hectare

Volume[a] per Hectare (m^3)	Dry Wood Content (tonnes/m^3)		
	0.450	0.500	0.550
100	42.7	47.5	52.3
150	64.3	71.3	78.3
200	85.5	95.0	104.5
250	107.0	118.7	130.7
300	128.3	142.5	156.7

[a]With an expansion of 1.9 to include other components of the trees and other carbon pools in the ecosystem.

11

SAMPLING UNITS FOR ESTIMATING PARAMETERS

To obtain information regarding parameters of a stand or forest area, the most common practice is to use sample plots. The sample plot is the unit for recording information and measurements. In most cases, this corresponds to the basic sampling unit. In cluster sampling, the basic sampling plot is subdivided into several subplots.

For many years, the most common sample plot has been a unit of fixed area. This results in a probabilistic procedure for selecting trees around a sample point; the probability of selection is constant and equal for all individuals that make up the population of the fixed-area plot. It is also possible to use a sampling procedure in which the probability of selecting a tree is variable and depends on some dimension of the tree. This is the case for sampling with *probability proportional to size*, commonly known as *PPS sampling*. Distance methods, which typically measure only the n closest trees, are another example of sampling procedures where the probability of selecting trees varies.

The choice of using plots of fixed or variable size depends on the practicality of their use in addition to theoretical considerations. In general, it is more efficient to use a plot where trees are selected with a probability proportional to the variable of interest. For example, if one is interested in the estimation of volume of a stand, it will be more efficient to use PPS sampling since the selection of sample trees is proportional to their basal area, which is closely related to volume. On the other hand, if one is interested in determining the number of trees in a stand, it will be more efficient to use fixed-area plots.

11-1. THE FACTOR CONCEPT

In most analyses of forest inventory data, measurements are summarized and expressed on a per unit area basis (per acre for the English system and per hectare for the metric system). Sample measurements are scaled to per unit area measurements using a ratio of unit area to associated sample area:

$$TF_i = \frac{\text{unit area}}{\text{sample area}_i} \tag{11-1}$$

where TF_i = expansion factor of ith sample tree
        unit area $= 43{,}560 \text{ ft}^2$ (1 acre) or $10{,}000 \text{ m}^2$ (1 ha)
        sample area$_i$ = size of sampling unit (ft^2 or m^2) associated with ith tree

Each tree selected for measurement represents TF trees per unit area. For example, if 0.2-acre fixed-area plots are used, each tree sampled will represent $(1/0.2) = 5$ trees per acre as, illustrated in Fig. 11-1.

The expansion factor shown in eq. (11-1) is often referred to as the *tree factor* since it gives the number of trees per unit area that each sample tree represents. Depending on the type of sampling unit used, the tree factor may be constant or may vary by tree size or some other factor. The number of trees per unit area is obtained by summing the tree factors for each tree on the plot. If tree factor is constant for all sample trees, trees per unit area may be obtained by multiplying the constant tree factor by the number of trees per plot.

The expansion factors for other tree characteristics (XF_i), such as basal area or volume, are obtained by multiplying the value of the characteristic, X_i, by the tree factor:

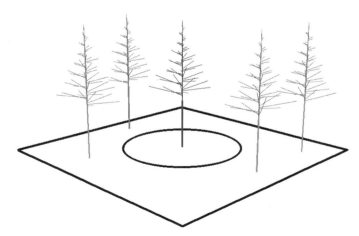

FIG. 11-1. The factor concept. Each tree on a 0.2-acre plot represents 5 trees per acre.

$$XF_i = X_i \cdot TF_i \qquad (11\text{-}2)$$

For example, the basal area factor for an individual tree is

$$BAF_i = BA_i \cdot TF_i = cD_i^2 \cdot \frac{\text{unit area}}{\text{sample area}}$$

where BAF_i = basal area factor of ith tree
      BA_i = basal area of ith tree
      TF_i = tree factor associated with ith tree [eq. (11-1)]
        c = basal area conversion factor (0.005 454 in English system, 0.000 078 54 in metric)
      D_i = dbh of ith tree

Per unit area estimates for a single plot are obtained by summing the factors:

$$
\begin{aligned}
X/\text{unit area} &= XF_1 + XF_2 + XF_3 + \cdots + XF_n \\
&= X_1(TF_1) + X_2(TF_2) + X_3(TF_3) + \cdots + X_n(TF_n) \\
&= \sum_{i=1}^{n} XF_i = \sum_{i=1}^{n} X_i(TF_i) \qquad (11\text{-}3)
\end{aligned}
$$

For example, basal area per unit area is obtained by summing the BAF values for each sample tree. If TF is constant for each tree, basal area per unit area may be obtained by summing the basal area of each tree and multiplying that sum by the constant tree factor:

$$\text{BA per unit area} = \sum BAF_i = \sum TF \cdot BA_i = TF \sum BA_i$$

Factors for other stand parameters are obtained in a similar manner.
The factors derived using this method lead to the following definitions:

- *Tree factor*: the number of trees per unit area represented by each tree tallied
- *Basal area factor*: the number of units of basal area per unit area represented by each tree tallied
- *Volume factor*: the number of units of volume per unit area represented by each tree tallied
- *Height factor*: the number of units of height per unit area represented by each tree tallied

The factor concept provides a simple and unified approach to forest inventory analysis. By focusing on the derivation of tree factor, all other factors are simply obtained by multiplying the value of that parameter by the tree factor. In the following sections, various sampling units are described and the factors important to foresters derived for each type of sampling unit.

11-2. FIXED-AREA PLOTS

Fixed-area sampling units in a forest inventory or study are called *plots* or *strips*, depending on their dimensions. The term *plot* is loosely applied to sampling units of small areas of square, rectangular, circular, or triangular shape. The term *strip* is generally used to refer to a rectangular plot whose length is many times its width.

11-2.1 Circular Plots

Circular plots have been used widely since a single dimension, the radius, can be used to define the perimeter. The dimensions of commonly used circular sample plots are shown in Table 11-1. Circular plots have two advantages:

1. A circle has the minimum perimeter for a given area, which implies fewer decisions for trees near the plot boundary.
2. A circular plot has no predetermined orientation, which in some cases, especially in plantations, can be a cause of appreciable bias.

TABLE 11-1 Dimensions of Commonly Used Fixed-Area Plots

Plot Area as a Fraction of Per Unit Area	English System			Metric System		
	Plot Area (ft^2)	Circular Radius (ft)	Square Side (ft)	Plot Area (m^2)	Circular Radius (m)	Square Side (m)
1/1000	43.56	3.7	6.6	10	1.78	3.16
1/500	87.12	5.3	9.3	20	2.52	4.47
1/250	174.24	7.4	13.2	40	3.57	6.32
1/100	435.6	11.8	20.9	100	5.64	10.00
1/50	871.2	16.7	29.5	200	7.98	14.14
1/25	1,742.4	23.6	41.7	400	11.28	20.00
1/20	2,178	26.3	46.7	500	12.62	22.36
1/10	4,356	37.2	66.0	1,000	17.84	31.62
1/5	8,712	52.7	93.3	2,000	25.23	44.72
1/4	10,890	58.9	104.4	2,500	28.21	50.00
1/2	21,780	83.3	147.6	5,000	39.89	70.71
1	43,560	117.8	208.7	10,000	56.42	100.00

The main disadvantage of a circular plot is the error that may arise if the plot boundary is not observed carefully and if ocular estimations of limiting trees are not well done.

In general, small circular plots are more efficient than large ones. With large plots, the decision regarding trees near the plot boundary is often difficult. Consequently, it is advisable to use plots of a size that allows easier control of trees near plot limits. An experienced person standing at plot center if the radius of the plot is no greater than about 5 m can do this with confidence. Of course, one can determine more precisely if a tree near the perimeter is in the plot by measuring the distance from plot center to the tree using a tape or electronic distance measurement device (Chapter 4).

Circular plots on slopes can make decisions difficult regarding including a tree in a plot. To resolve this difficulty, a special technique described by Beers (1969) for horizontal point samples can be used to delimit fixed-area plots. With this technique one can establish a circular plot on a slope (which is elliptical in its horizontal projection) of an area equivalent to the preestablished size of the plot.

A circular plot of radius r on flat terrain has an area of $a = \pi r^2$. If the circular plot is located on terrain with a slope of α degrees, its horizontal projection will generate an elliptical plot with major radius r_{max} and minor radius r_{min}. The area of the elliptical plot is less than the area of the circular plot in a horizontal plane.

Since the area of an ellipse is $a' = \pi r_{max} r_{min}$, one can calculate the area of the projected ellipse in a horizontal plane observing that the major radius is equivalent to the radius of the circle on the slope ($r_{max} = r$), and the minor radius $r_{min} = r \cos \alpha$. Thus the area of the ellipse projected in a horizontal plane a' is

$$a' = \pi r (r \cos \alpha) = \pi r^2 \cos \alpha$$

Since $a = \pi r^2$, then $a' = a \cos \alpha$.

Up to here we have shown the area of the horizontal projection of a plot on a slope. Since $\cos \alpha$ is always less than 1 (if $\alpha > 0$), the area of the horizontal projected ellipse is always less than the area of the circular plot on the slope. If we want the area of the circular plot on the slope to be always of the preestablished fixed area a, it will be necessary to adjust the radius of the circular plot on the slope. This radius r_c will vary depending on the slope. The constant area $a = \pi r_c^2 \cos \alpha$. The radius of a circular plot on a slope, which will give the constant area, is

$$r_c = \sqrt{\frac{a}{\pi \cos \alpha}} \tag{11-4}$$

For example, if we are using circular plots of 0.05 ha (500 m^2), the radius of a circular plot on a slope of 20° to give a horizontal projected area of 500 m^2 would be

$$r_c = \sqrt{\frac{500}{\pi \cos 20°}} = 13.01 \text{ m}$$

instead of the normal plot radius of 12.62 m.

11-2.2 Square and Rectangular Plots

The advantage of square plots is the somewhat greater ease of deciding if trees are in or out of the plot because plot boundaries are straight lines. The plot limits can easily be established by measuring diagonals at right angles from the plot center. Using a compass or right-angle prism to establish the direction of the diagonals, one measures and marks the distance from plot center to the corners of the square. The trees or plants are then measured systematically in the four triangles formed by the diagonals and periphery of the plot. Of course, the plot boundaries can be established by marking the corners using compass and tape directly. The dimensions for commonly used square plots are shown in Table 11-1.

In rectangular plots the width and length are not equal (the term *length* is generally applied to the longer dimension). Rectangular plots are usually established from the central axis of a given length. The width is measured from this axis and corners can be established. Rectangular plots are especially useful in natural forests with difficult topography and large altitudinal variation. In these situations the axis of the rectangular plot should be oriented to cross the maximum slope so that it may sample the maximum variability of the forest.

A strip is a type of rectangular plot whose length is many times its width. For recording purposes, the continuous strip may be subdivided into smaller recording units. It is important to remember, however, that the entire strip is still considered the ultimate sampling unit and is the basis for the number of degrees of freedom in subsequent statistical computations. [If interrupted strips are used (e.g., alternate lengths of a strip tallied), the individual units of the strip tallied should be treated like plots in subsequent calculations.]

An advantage of a continuous strip over plots is that a tally is taken for the entire strip traversed so that there is no unproductive walking time between sampling units. However, continuous strips have a disadvantage: The number of sampling units, and thus the degrees of freedom, is small. Comparing strip sampling to plot sampling of equal intensity, the size of the sampling unit is larger and the number of sampling units smaller. The larger sampling unit results in a reduction in the variability, but the smaller number of sampling units counteracts this advantage. For this reason, the sampling error of a strip sampling design is usually larger than for plot sampling, assuming the same sampling intensity.

11-2.3 Subplots

With fixed-area plots such as circular plots, the different size classes of trees or plants (e.g., dbh or height) are sampled in proportion to their frequency in the population. Normally, in forest stands there are more small trees than large ones (this is typical in natural forests—not necessarily in plantations). Since each tree has the same probability of selection, there will be many small trees in the sample. This has the disadvantage that it will be necessary to measure many more small trees than large ones despite the fact that many times they will be of less importance, especially if volume is the parameter of interest. To remedy this situation, it is possible to modify the sampling plan so that more large trees and fewer small ones are measured in the sampling process. This modification consists of using different sizes of plots for different size classes or attributes of trees or vegetation. The common approach is to use a large plot for big trees and small plots for small trees and lesser vegetation. This can be accomplished by nesting or subdividing the large plot into subplots of different sizes. For example, one could establish a circular plot of $1000\,m^2$ (0.1 ha) with radius of 17.84 m, for measuring trees greater than 25 cm dbh. Within this plot, a concentric plot of $500\,m^2$ (0.05 ha) having a radius of 12.62 m can be established at the same center for trees with a dbh up to 25 cm. Meersschaut and Vandekerkhove (2000) used a plot design of four concentric circular sample plots with areas of 16, 64, 255, and $1018\,m^2$ to measure seedlings, shrubs, and trees (living and dead) of different size limits. They also established a 16 m × 16 m plot for measuring lesser vegetation and lying deadwood. Other systems of subplots can be established, such as small circular or square subplots established at some fixed design within a large circular plot or square plot. Subplots of different shapes and locations can be used with any plot shape.

11-2.4 Selection of Plots and Trees

To respect the laws of probability and obtain unbiased estimates of the parameters of a stand or forest, the sample plots should be selected at random from the total population of plots. All the trees or individual plants that are within the limits of the plot are measured to obtain information regarding the attributes of interest, such as dbh, height, or basal area.

With fixed-area plots, the tendency is to think of the tree selection process as the result of establishing a plot center and boundary, then measuring all the trees contained within that boundary, as illustrated for a circular plot in Fig. 11-2a. This view is often referred to as the *plot–centered approach* (Grosenbaugh, 1958; Beers and Miller, 1973; Oderwald, 1981a). It is also possible to view the selection process by visualizing an imaginary fixed-area

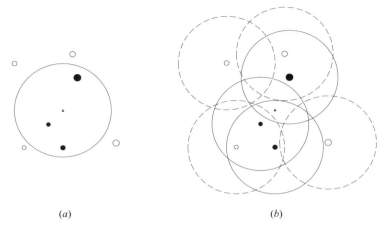

(a)   (b)

FIG. 11-2. Selection of trees in fixed-area plot sampling: (a) plot-centered approach; (b) tree-centered approach.

plot around each tree (Fig. 11-2b). A plot center is established, and trees are included in the sample if this plot center is included in the area of their imaginary plot. This view is often referred to as the *tree–centered approach* (Grosenbaugh, 1958; Beers and Miller, 1973; Oderwald, 1981a).

The tree-centered approach aids in understanding the probability of a tree being selected for inclusion in a plot. A tree is included in a plot if its imaginary plot contains the established plot center (Fig. 11-2b). If random sampling is used, the probability of selection P_j is equal to the plot area divided by the area of the stand:

$$P_j = \frac{\text{plot area}}{\text{stand area}} \tag{11-5}$$

Because the plot area is the same for all trees, the probability of being selected is constant for all trees.

11-2.5   Stand and Stock Tables

Plot measures are scaled to per unit area measures using the expansion factors described in Section 11-1. Average per unit area values and total values are obtained using the methods described in Chapters 3 and 13. While estimates of the averages per unit area and total values for various stand parameters are important, foresters often desire more detailed summaries. Typically, foresters will summarize data into stand and stock tables. A *stand table* gives the number of trees by species and dbh class. A *stock table* gives volumes (or weights) by similar classifications. In many cases, basal area and average height are included. Occasionally, tables may be subdivided by height class as well as dbh class. A *combined stand and stock table* gives density and volume by species and dbh class. Values within stand and stock tables are normally expressed on a per unit area basis; however, total values for the stand may be given.

The construction of stand and stock tables from fixed-area plot data will be illustrated using the following example. Four 20 m × 20 m plots were measured and the following total tally obtained:

Dbh Class	10	12	14	16	18	20	22	24	26	28	30	32	34	36	38	40	42+
No. Tallied	9	6	17	8	9	4	8	7	5	6	2	5	3	1	3	0	2

Table 11-2 shows the combined stand and stock table. Column 1 shows the dbh classes corresponding to the tally. The number of trees tallied are in column 5. Columns 2, 3, and 4 contain the average per-tree values for height, basal area, and volume. Total height was measured on all trees shown in the tally above, and average height (column 2) was calculated for each dbh class. The basal area per tree (column 3) is found by calculating the cross-sectional area of a circle corresponding to the diameter class:

$$BA_{tree} = \pi \left(\frac{D}{2 \cdot 100} \right)^2$$

$$= \frac{\pi}{40,000} D^2$$

$$= 0.000\,078\,54 D^2$$

Volume per tree (column 4) can be estimated using a variety of methods, including a local volume table, a standard volume, or a volume equation. For this example, trees were assumed to be paraboloids [eq. (6-2)] and volume per tree is obtained by multiplying form (0.5) by basal area per tree (column 3) by average height (column 2). For example, the volume per tree for the 10-cm dbh class is

$$Vol_{10} = \tfrac{1}{2}(A_b H)$$

$$= \tfrac{1}{2}(BA \cdot H)$$

$$= \tfrac{1}{2}(0.0079)(11.0)$$

$$= 0.043\,m^3$$

TABLE 11-2. Combined Stand and Stock Table for a Northern Hardwood Stand Located in Central New Brunswick[a]

[1]	[2]	[3]	[4]	[5]	[6]	[7]		[8]	[9]	[10]	[11]
	Per Tree Averages					Factors[b]			Per Hectare Averages		
Dbh Class (cm)	Height (m)	BA (m²)	Volume (m³)	Number of Trees Tallied	Tree (number)	BA (m²)	Volume (m³)	Volume (m³)	Trees (number)	BA (m²)	Volume (m³)
10	11.0	0.0079	0.043	9	25	0.1964	1.080		56.25	0.44	2.4
12	11.7	0.0113	0.066	6	25	0.2827	1.654		37.50	0.42	2.5
14	12.9	0.0154	0.099	17	25	0.3848	2.482		106.25	1.64	10.5
16	13.8	0.0201	0.139	8	25	0.5027	3.468		50.00	1.01	6.9
18	13.9	0.0254	0.177	9	25	0.6362	4.421		56.25	1.43	9.9
20	16.5	0.0314	0.259	4	25	0.7854	6.480		25.00	0.79	6.5
22	16.8	0.0380	0.319	8	25	0.9503	7.983		50.00	1.90	16.0
24	17.3	0.0452	0.391	7	25	1.1310	9.783		43.75	1.98	17.1
26	19.8	0.0531	0.526	5	25	1.3273	13.141		31.25	1.66	16.4
28	18.0	0.0616	0.554	6	25	1.5394	13.854		37.50	2.31	20.8
30	20.0	0.0707	0.707	2	25	1.7672	17.672		12.50	0.88	8.8
32	18.2	0.0804	0.732	5	25	2.0106	18.297		31.25	2.51	22.9
34	21.0	0.0908	0.953	3	25	2.2698	23.833		18.75	1.70	17.9
36	19.0	0.1018	0.967	1	25	2.5447	24.175		6.25	0.64	6.0
38	19.7	0.1134	1.117	3	25	2.8353	27.928		18.75	2.13	20.9
40	20.0	0.1257	1.257	0	25	3.1416	31.416		0.00	0.00	0.0
42	20.0	0.1385	1.385	2	25	3.4636	34.636		12.50	1.73	17.3
Total				95					593.75	23.17	203.0

[a]Based on four 20 m × 20 m fixed-area plots.
[b]Factors are the value per unit area represented by each tree tallied.

267

Tree factor (column 6) is constant for fixed-area plots and is obtained using eq. (11-1):

$$TF = \frac{\text{unit area}}{\text{plot area}}$$
$$= \frac{10,000}{20(20)}$$
$$= 25$$

The basal area factor (column 7) and the volume factor (column 8) are obtained by multiplying the tree factor (column 6) by the corresponding per tree value [eq. (11-2)]. For the 10-cm class, the basal area factor is

$$BAF_{10} = BA_{10} \cdot TF_{10}$$
$$= (\text{column 3})(\text{column 6})$$
$$= 0.0079(25)$$
$$= 0.1964$$

and the volume factor is

$$VF_{10} = Vol_{10} \cdot TF_{10}$$
$$= (\text{column 4})(\text{column 6})$$
$$= 0.043(25)$$
$$= 1.080$$

Average per unit area values for each parameter is obtained by multiplying the corresponding factor by the number of trees tallied and dividing by the number of plots. Tree per hectare (column 9) is then obtained by multiplying the tree factor (column 6) by the number of trees tallied (column 5) and dividing by the number of plots:

$$\text{trees/ha} = \frac{TF \cdot (\text{no. tallied})}{\text{no. plots}}$$

For example, there were 9 trees tallied in the 10-cm class; therefore, the trees/ha for the 10-cm class becomes

$$\text{trees/ha} = \frac{\text{TF} \cdot (\text{no. tallied})}{\text{no. plots}}$$

$$\text{column } 9 = \frac{(\text{column 6})(\text{column 5})}{\text{no. plots}}$$

$$= \frac{25(9)}{4}$$

$$= 56.25$$

Similarly, basal area per hectare (column 10) is

$$\text{BA/ha} = \frac{\text{BAF} \cdot (\text{no. tallied})}{\text{no. plots}}$$

$$\text{column } 10 = \frac{(\text{column 7})(\text{column 5})}{\text{no. plots}}$$

$$= \frac{0.1964(9)}{4}$$

$$= 0.44$$

and volume per hectare (column 11) is

$$\text{volume/ha} = \frac{\text{VF} \cdot (\text{no. tallied})}{\text{no. plots}}$$

$$\text{column } 11 = \frac{(\text{column 8})(\text{column 5})}{\text{no. plots}}$$

$$= \frac{1.080(9)}{4}$$

$$= 2.4$$

11-2.6   Plots near Stand Borders

Single Fixed-Area Plots. When a forest area is bounded by nonforest or other land-use classes, the trees near the border will usually be somewhat different than those in the interior of the forest. If the perimeter proportion of a forest area is large, it will be necessary to take precautions that this zone is adequately represented in the sample. In addition, very frequently, sample plots are located near the border of a forest area so that a portion of the plot falls outside the limits of the forest or stand or portions of the plot fall in different forest conditions or types.

To assure adequate representation of the border areas and take into consideration the part of the plot that may be partially outside the forest or in different forest conditions, several methods have been developed. These methods may modify the location, size, or form of those plots whose center is within the forest or given stand condition, but a portion of the plot is outside. These methods are shown diagrammatically in Fig. 11-3.

a. The plot is displaced so that it falls completely within the forest. This method is questionable and can potentially lead to significant bias if the stand has a large proportion of its area as edge. By moving the plot away from the edge, edge trees are undersampled. When edge is a relatively small proportion of the stand, the bias is small but still present.

b. The radius of the plot is increased so that the increased size is equivalent to the part of the original plot outside the stand. Although an improvement over method a, edge trees are still undersampled using this method.

c. The area of the plot within the stand is determined and one measures the trees only in the part of the plot within the stand. This method can be extremely time consuming since determining the portion of the plot within the stand can be complex. Ratio estimation (Section 13-3.1) is employed to obtain valid estimates of the mean and total.

d. The plot is divided into two, and a half-plot is established exactly on the stand edge. Trees within the half-plot are measured. Plot characteristics are determined as usual and the results doubled. In this method, edge trees are oversampled, thus producing biased results similar to methods a and b.

e. Use of a reflection or mirage method in which the part of the plot that is outside the border of the stand is "reflected" toward the interior of the plot that is within the stand. The trees or plants in the reflected part are counted and measured twice. This method was originally proposed by Schmid-Haus (1969) and is relatively easy to implement in the field. All trees in the original plot that are inside the stand are measured. A second plot center is established the same distance from the edge as the current plot center but on the opposite side of the boundary. All trees in this plot that are inside the stand boundary are then measured.

Cluster Plots. When clusters are used, some of the subplots may fall in non-forest areas or in different forest stands. For a description of several techniques to solve this problem, see Birdsey et al. (1995). The Forest Health Monitoring program uses the method described by Scott and Bechtold (1995). In this method, the areas in the different condition classes of a subplot are calculated and their proportions estimated. The attributes of interest of any tree characteristic are measured on these condition class areas, and the population total and its variance can be estimated for each of the condition classes.

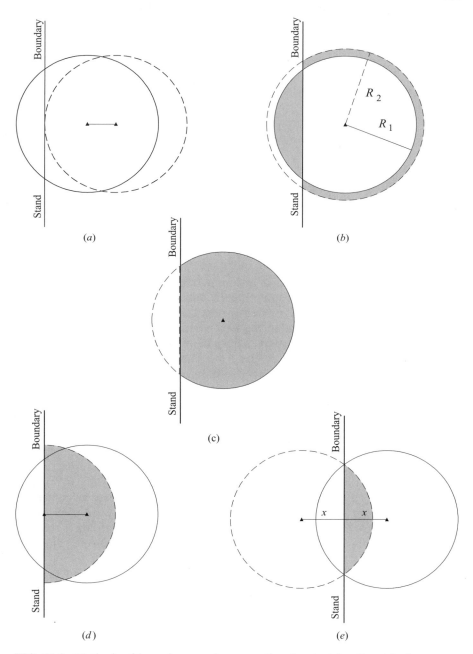

FIG. 11-3. Methods of boundary overlap correction (see text for discussion).

11-3. SAMPLING UNITS WITH VARIABLE PROBABILITY

Up to now we have considered plots where their size or area is fixed and constant. As illustrated in Fig. 11-2, the imaginary circular plots around each tree are of the same size, regardless of tree size. This means that the probability of selecting any tree is constant regardless of tree size. It is also possible to devise selection procedures where the probability of selecting a tree varies according to some characteristic of that tree: for example its dbh or height. In this case, we can visualize circular plots around each tree where the size of the imaginary plot depends on the size of the tree characteristic. Trees of large size will have larger imaginary circles, and smaller trees will have smaller circles. In other words, the probability of selecting a tree is proportional to its size.

11-3.1 Horizontal Point Samples

The idea of selecting individuals in a sample in proportion to some characteristic has been recognized for a long time in statistics, but it was not applied in forest mensuration until an Austrian forester, Walter Bitterlich, invented an ingenious method of determining the basal area of a stand (Bitterlich, 1947). Originally, it was not realized that this was a form of sampling with variable probability until another forester, the American, Lewis Grosenbaugh, recognized it (Grosenbaugh, 1955, 1958). He pointed out that the Bitterlich method was really an application of selecting samples with probability proportional to size (commonly called PPS). Development and use of this type of sampling has been an important landmark in forest mensuration.

The most used application of sampling with probability proportional to size in forestry is called *horizontal point sampling*. This is a type of sampling where the probability of selecting a tree is proportional to its basal area. In this application, a series of sampling points, similar to the centers of circular fixed-area plots, are located in the forest area. The observer occupies the point and projects a horizontal angle with an instrument toward each tree at the dbh level. As shown in Fig. 11-4a, all the trees that appear larger than the projected angle are counted. Trees that are smaller than the projected angle are not counted.

The circles represent the cross sections of trees at dbh level and the lines indicate the angle projected from the sampling point. One can measure any attribute of the trees selected, as in fixed-area plots (dbh, height, crown, health, etc.). These measures are scaled to per unit area values using the factor concept discussed in Section 11-1. From eq. (11-1), we know that the tree factor is determined using

$$TF_i = \frac{\text{unit area}}{\text{sample area}}$$

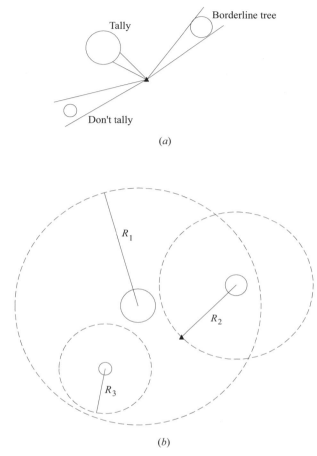

FIG. 11-4. Selection of trees in horizontal point sampling: (*a*) point-centered approach; (*b*) tree-centered approach.

In fixed-area plots, the sample area was constant; however, in horizontal point sampling, the sample area varies as a function of tree cross-sectional area. This is illustrated in Fig. 11-4*b* using the imaginary tree circles. Each of the three trees has a different plot radius (R_i) that is proportional to each tree's cross-sectional area. To determine the tree factor, we must determine each tree's plot radius. It is helpful to consider a tree at the borderline condition, where the gauge angle is precisely tangent to the breast height cross section (Fig. 11-5), and to keep in mind the following:

1. The angle gauge is projecting a fixed horizontal angle θ.

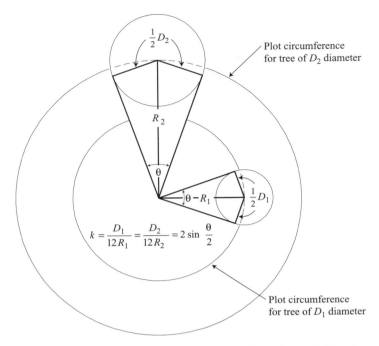

FIG. 11-5. Gauge constant k where D is tree diameter in inches and R is plot radius in feet.

2. At any sampling point, a series of concentric circular plots is conceptually established, a different plot radius being associated with every different tree diameter.

3. The radius of each concentric plot is determined by each different tree diameter and is not influenced by the actual spatial location of the tree; therefore, for the purpose of development, all trees can be considered in the "borderline" condition, as shown in Fig. 11-5.

4. At the borderline condition, the ratio of tree diameter to plot radius is a constant. Thus, for a given angle θ, tree diameter in inches D, and plot radius in feet R, we can define the gauge constant k to be

$$k = \frac{D}{12R} = 2\sin\frac{\theta}{2} \tag{11-6}$$

Therefore, the plot radius is

$$R = \frac{D}{12k} \tag{11-7}$$

Since the plot area $= \pi R^2$, the tree factor is determined to be

$$TF = \frac{43{,}560}{\pi R_i^2} = \frac{43{,}560}{\pi(D_i/12k)^2}$$

$$= \frac{43{,}560k^2}{(\pi/144)D_i^2}$$

By dividing the top and bottom by 4, we obtain

$$TF_i = \frac{(1/4)43{,}560k^2}{(1/4)(\pi/144)D_i^2} = \frac{10{,}890k^2}{0.005454D_i^2} = \frac{10{,}890k^2}{BA_i} \tag{11-8}$$

In the metric system, tree diameter D is measured in centimeters and plot radius R is measured in meters. For a given angle θ, the gauge constant is

$$k = \frac{D}{100R} = 2\sin\frac{\theta}{2} \tag{11-9}$$

the plot radius becomes

$$R = \frac{D}{100k} \tag{11-10}$$

and the tree factor is

$$TF = \frac{10{,}000}{\pi R_i^2} = \frac{10{,}000}{\pi(D_i/100k)^2}$$

$$= \frac{10{,}000k^2}{(\pi/10{,}000)D_i^2}$$

Dividing the top and bottom by 4, we obtain

$$TF_i = \frac{(1/4)10{,}000k^2}{(1/4)(\pi/10{,}000)D_i^2} = \frac{2500k^2}{0.000\,07854D_i^2} = \frac{2500k^2}{BA_i} \tag{11-11}$$

As discussed in Section 11-1, other factors are obtained by multiplying the tree factor by the value of the tree characteristic. In horizontal point sampling, the basal area factor is of particular interest. In the English system, the basal area factor is

$$BAF_i = TF_i \cdot BA_i = \frac{10{,}890k^2}{0.005454D_i^2}(0.005454D_i^2) = 10{,}890k^2 \tag{11-12}$$

and for the metric system

$$\text{BAF}_i = \text{TF}_i \cdot \text{BA}_i = \frac{2500k^2}{0.000\,07854D_i^2}(0.000\,078\,54D_i^2) = 2500k^2 \qquad (11\text{-}13)$$

By examining eqs. (11-12) and (11-13), an outstanding aspect of horizontal point sampling is observed. The basal area factor is dependent only on k. Since k is constant for a given sample, this implies that the basal area per unit area represented by each tree tallied is constant. Thus basal area per unit area is estimated by counting the number of trees tallied and multiplying by eqs. (11-12) or (11-13). *No tree measurements are required to estimate basal area per unit area.*

The value of BAF depends on the value of k, which in turn depends on the angle chosen. Generally, the gauge constant k is chosen such that $10{,}890k^2$ or $2500k^2$ is a convenient number. Once the BAF is fixed, the diameter to plot radius ratio is fixed, which, in turn, implies a plot radius for every tree diameter. Consequently, all trees of the same diameter that are located less than their "plot-radius distance" from a given sampling point will be "on the plot" (Fig. 11-6). The plot is completed by rotating 360° about the plot center and determining all "in" trees.

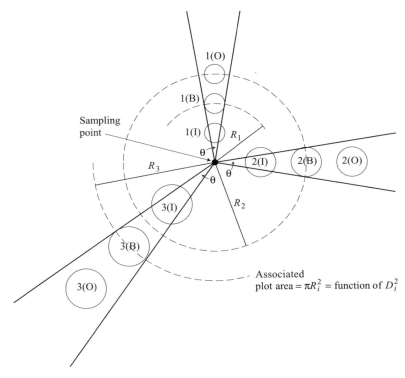

FIG. 11-6. Tree size and plot radius. I, "in" trees; B, border trees; O, out trees.

By fixing BAF, the diameter/plot radius ratio, the gauge constant, and the horizontal angle can all be calculated. For example, if we want the value of BAF to be 10, in English units, then

$$10 = 10,890k^2$$

$$k^2 = 0.000\,918$$

$$k = 0.030\,303$$

The angle corresponding to k is

$$k = 2 \sin \frac{\theta}{2}$$

$$\sin \frac{\theta}{2} = \frac{k}{2}$$

$$\theta = 2 \sin^{-1} \frac{k}{2}$$

$$\theta = 2 \sin^{-1} \frac{0.030303}{2}$$

$$= 2(52')$$

$$= 1°44'$$

Suppose that we want to use a value of BAF $= 4$ for metric units. Then

$$4 = 2500k^2$$

$$k^2 = 0.0016$$

$$k = 0.04$$

and

$$\theta = 2 \sin^{-1} \frac{0.04}{2}$$

$$= 2(1°9')$$

$$= 2°18'$$

Table 11-3 gives the diameter/plot radius ratios, gauge constants, and horizontal angles for some common English and metric BAF values. Types of angle gauges and their calibration and use in forest inventory are discussed in Section 14-1.

TABLE 11-3. Diameter/Plot Radius Ratios, Gauge Constants, and Angles for Common English and Metric BAF Values

English Units				Metric Units			
BAF (ft^2/acre/tree)	DR[a] (in.:ft)	Gauge Constant k	Angle	BAF (m^2/ha/tree)	DR[a] (cm:m)	Gauge Constant k	Angle
5	1:3.9	0.0214	1°14′	1	1:0.50	0.0200	1°9′
10	1:2.8	0.0303	1°44′	2	1:0.35	0.0283	1°37′
15	1:2.2	0.0371	2°8′	3	1:0.29	0.0346	1°59′
20	1:1.9	0.0429	2°27′	4	1:0.25	0.0400	2°18′
25	1:1.7	0.0479	2°45′	5	1:0.22	0.0447	2°34′
30	1:1.6	0.0525	3°	6	1:0.20	0.0490	2°48′

[a]In English units, the diameter/plot radius ratio gives the plot radius in feet per inch of diameter. For example, a 10-in. tree when using BAF = 10, would have a corresponding plot radius of 10(2.8) = 28 ft; in the metric system, plot radius is given in meters per centimeter of diameter.

11-3.2 Stand and Stock Tables

Stand and stock tables can be constructed from horizontal point data using a process similar to constructing stand and stock tables from fixed-area plot data (Section 11-2.5). An example will be used to illustrate the construction of stand and stock tables from horizontal point data. Four horizontal points were sampled from a northern hardwood stand in central New Brunswick, Canada using a 2M (m²/ha/tree) BAF prism. The following tally was obtained:

Dbh Class	10	12	14	16	18	20	22	24	26	28	30	32	34	36	38	40	42+
No. Tallied	1	2	5	3	2	3	6	6	6	5	3	6	5	1	5	1	3

Table 11-4 shows the combined stand and stock table. Columns 1 through 5 are similar to those in Table 11-2, the stand and stock table based on fixed-area plots (Section 11-2.5). Total height was measured on each sample tree and Lorey's average height (Section 8-4.1) calculated (column 2). Column 5 is the number of trees tallied.

The basal area factor (column 7) is constant for horizontal points and was 2 for this sample. Because plot size varies with tree diameter, the tree factor (column 6) varies and is determined using

$$TF_{dbh} = \frac{BAF}{BA_{dbh}}$$

For this example, the tree factor will be

$$TF_{dbh} = \frac{2.0}{0.00007854(dbh)^2}$$

For example, the tree factor for the 10-cm dbh class is

$$TF_{10} = \frac{2.0}{0.000\,078\,54(10)^2} = \frac{2.0}{0.007\,854} = 254.6$$

The volume factor is obtained by multiplying the volume per tree (column 4) by the tree factor (column 6):

$$VF_{dbh} = V_{dbh} \cdot TF_{dbh}$$

and volume factor for the 10-cm class is

TABLE 11-4. Combined Stand and Stock Table for a Northern Hardwood Stand Located in Central New Brunswick[a]

[1]	[2]	[3]	[4]	[5]	[6]	[7]	[8]	[9]	[10]	[11]
Dbh Class (cm)	Per Tree Averages			Number of Trees Tallied	Factors[b]			Per Hectare Averages		
	Height (m)	BA (m²)	Volume (m³)		Tree (number)	BA (m²)	Volume (m³)	Trees (number)	BA (m²)	Volume (m³)
10	11.0	0.0079	0.043	1	254.6	2.0	11.0	63.66	0.50	2.8
12	12.0	0.0113	0.066	2	176.8	2.0	12.0	88.42	1.00	6.0
14	14.2	0.0154	0.099	5	129.9	2.0	14.2	162.40	2.50	17.8
16	16.0	0.0201	0.139	3	99.5	2.0	16.0	74.60	1.50	12.0
18	16.3	0.0254	0.177	2	78.6	2.0	16.3	39.30	1.00	8.2
20	17.7	0.0314	0.259	3	63.7	2.0	17.7	47.75	1.50	13.3
22	18.0	0.0380	0.319	6	52.6	2.0	18.0	78.92	3.00	27.0
24	18.7	0.0452	0.391	6	44.2	2.0	18.7	66.31	3.00	28.1
26	19.0	0.0531	0.526	6	37.7	2.0	19.0	56.50	3.00	28.5
28	19.0	0.0616	0.554	5	32.5	2.0	19.0	40.60	2.50	23.8
30	19.3	0.0707	0.707	3	28.3	2.0	19.3	21.22	1.50	14.5
32	19.0	0.0804	0.732	6	24.9	2.0	19.0	37.30	3.00	28.5
34	19.3	0.0908	0.953	5	22.0	2.0	19.3	27.54	2.50	24.1
36	19.3	0.1018	0.967	1	19.6	2.0	19.3	4.91	0.50	4.8
38	19.4	0.1134	1.117	5	17.6	2.0	19.4	22.04	2.50	24.3
40	19.7	0.1257	1.257	1	15.9	2.0	19.7	3.98	0.50	4.9
42	20.6	0.1385	1.385	3	14.4	2.0	20.6	10.83	1.50	15.5
Total				63				846.29	31.50	283.8

[a]Based on four 2M BAF points.
[b]Factors are the value per unit area represented by each tree tallied.

$$VF_{10} = V_{10} \cdot TF_{10}$$

$$= 0.043(254.6)$$

$$= 11.0$$

By comparing average height (column 2) with the volume factor (column 8), an interesting and powerful feature of horizontal point sampling can be observed. In this example, volume per tree was estimated using the formula for a paraboloid [eq. (6-2)], which is a constant form factor equation (i.e., $V_i = f \cdot BA_i \cdot H_i$). By substituting this formula for volume into the volume factor equation, we get

$$VF_{dbh} = V_{dbh} \cdot TF_{dbh}$$

$$= f \cdot BA_{dbh} \cdot H_{dbh} \cdot \frac{BAF}{BA_{dbh}}$$

$$= f \cdot BAF \cdot H_{dbh}$$

Thus, if volume can be estimated using a constant form factor equation, height is the only tree variable that needs measured. In this particular example, because form $= \frac{1}{2}$ and $BAF = 2$, the $VF_i = H_i$ and volume per hectare is simply the sum of the heights of the "in" trees. A further discussion of volume estimation using horizontal point sampling is found in Section 14-1.8.

Trees per hectare (column 9) are obtained by multiplying the number of trees tallied (column 5) by the tree factor (column 6) and dividing by the number of points:

$$\text{trees/ha} = \frac{TF \cdot (\text{no. tallied})}{\text{no. points}}$$

For the 10-cm dbh class, the number of trees per hectare is

$$\text{trees/ha} = \frac{TF \cdot (\text{no. tallied})}{\text{no. points}}$$

$$\text{column } 9 = \frac{(\text{column } 6)(\text{column } 5)}{\text{no. points}}$$

$$= \frac{254.6(1)}{4}$$

$$= 63.66$$

Similarly, basal area per hectare (column 10) is obtained by multiplying the BAF (column 7) by the number of trees tallied (column 5), and dividing by the number of points and volume per hectare (column 11) is obtained by multiplying the volume factor (column 8) by the number of trees tallied (column 5) and dividing by the number of points.

11-3.3 Points near Stand Borders

As with fixed-area plots, horizontal point samples can be located near stand boundaries, where a portion of the sweep falls outside the stand. Any of the methods discussed in Section 11-2.6 can be applied to horizontal point samples. The mirage method, originally developed by Schmid-Haus (1969) and later described by Beers (1977), is the easiest and most commonly employed method of boundary overlap correction.

The following guidelines are used when the mirage method is applied in horizontal point sampling:

1. Determine if overlap exists. This is the case when the plot radius R_i associated with any qualifying tree exceeds the shortest (i.e., perpendicular) distance B from the sample point to the boundary. This can readily be checked for the "in" tree of largest diameter D_i. If $R_i > B$, overlap exists. R_i may be determined using eq. (11-7) or (11-10) or using the diameter/plot radius ratios shown in Table 11-3, where $R_i = D_i \cdot DR$. The ratio of diameter/plot radius is also referred to as the *horizontal distance multiplier* HDM and can be calculated using:

$$\text{English units:} \quad \text{HDM} = \frac{33\sqrt{10}}{12\sqrt{\text{BAF}}} \qquad (11\text{-}14)$$

$$\text{metric units:} \quad \text{HDM} = \frac{1}{2\sqrt{\text{BAF}}} \qquad (11\text{-}15)$$

2. If overlap exists, a new point is established B units across the boundary along a line perpendicular to the boundary and passing through the original point.

3. Trees within the stand determined to be "in" from this new point are again tallied. Thus some trees may be tallied twice, representing the adjustment for the plot being undersized.

In cases where the area beyond the stand boundary is inaccessible, another method must be used. The *direct weighting procedure* (Beers, 1966) is generally the most practical.

11-3.4 Other Forms of Sampling Proportional to Size

Other forms of sampling with probability proportional to size include horizontal line sampling, vertical point sampling, and vertical line sampling. None of these techniques are as widely applied as horizontal point sampling and are summarized only briefly below. For a complete explanation of sampling theory and estimation procedures, see Husch et al. (1982).

- *Vertical point sampling.* Vertical point sampling is implemented by projecting a vertical angle ϕ from a point location. Trees are selected for sampling if the angle to the tip of the tree is greater than the projected angle (Fig. 11-7a). The gauge constant q is

$$q = \frac{H_i}{R_i} = \tan\phi$$

  and the associated plot radius is given by

$$R_i = \frac{H_i}{q}$$

- *Horizontal line sampling.* In horizontal line sampling, a horizontal angle θ is projected perpendicular to a line of length L (Fig. 11-7b). Trees are tallied on both sides of the line. The gauge constant k and the radius R_i are the same as in horizontal point sampling. The associated plot area is $L \cdot 2R_i$.
- *Vertical line sampling.* In vertical line sampling, a vertical angle ϕ is projected perpendicular to a line of length L (Fig. 11-7c). Trees are tallied on both sides of the line. The gauge constant q and the radius R_i are the same as in vertical point sampling. The associated plot area is $L \cdot 2R_i$.

The tree factors and factors for other characteristics can be derived for each PPS sampling technique using the same process shown for horizontal point sampling and the associated plot areas (Fig. 11-7). When using horizontal point sampling, basal area per unit area is estimated directly from tree counts only. With horizontal line sampling, the sum of diameters per unit area is estimated directly from tree counts. With vertical point sampling the sum of heights squared per unit area is estimated directly from tree counts and with vertical line sampling, the sum of heights per unit area is estimated directly from tree counts. Table 11-5 summarizes these sampling aspects for each PPS sampling strategy.

11-4 DISTANCE-BASED SAMPLING UNITS

Many studies of biological populations require estimates of population densities. *Distance sampling* is a group of methods that permits estimation of this fundamental parameter of interest: density or number of individuals of interest per unit area and totals for an entire area. The methods are frequently employed in estimating population densities of wildlife species. The methods can also be applied in estimating the densities of plant populations.

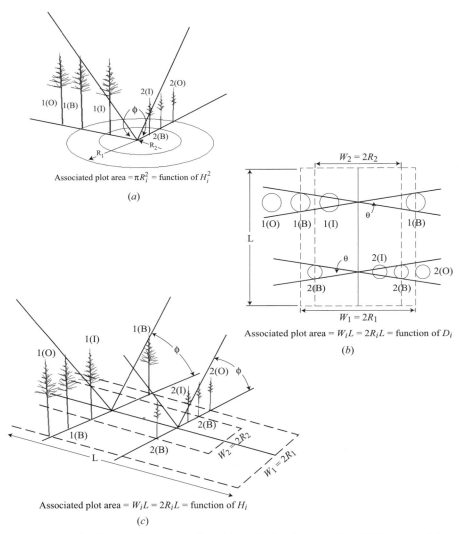

FIG. 11-7. Other forms of PPS sampling: (*a*) vertical point sampling; (*b*) horizontal line sampling; (*c*) vertical line sampling.

Although distance estimators have been widely used in plant ecology (Pielou, 1977), they have rarely been used in forest inventories, especially in North America. Dennis (1984) discusses a variety of distance-based estimators for assessing regeneration. Payandeh and Ek (1986) assess the relative performance of five different distance–density estimators. Jonsson et al. (1992) describe a forest inventory system using density-adapted circular plot sizes.

TABLE 11-5. Summary of PPS Sampling Strategies

PPS System	Trees Selected with Probability Proportional to:	Stand Characteristic Estimated Directly from Tree Counts
Horizontal point	Basal area or diameter squared	Basal area per unit area
Horizontal line	Diameter	Sum of diameters per unit area
Vertical point	Height squared	Sum of heights squared per unit area
Vertical line	Height	Sum of heights per unit area

In their system, the number of trees n per plot is fixed and plot size varies based on the distance to the nth nearest tree. Lessard et al. (1994) compared n-tree distance sampling with point and fixed-area plots in northern hardwood stands in Michigan. They found that if biased-corrected estimators are utilized, n-tree sampling produced estimates comparable to point and fixed-area plot samples. Lynch and Rusydi (1999) found similar results for teak plantations in Indonesia.

With n-tree distance sampling, the number of trees n per plot is fixed and the distance L to the nth nearest tree is measured. In Fig. 11-8, this is illustrated for $n = 4$. The distance L_i is the plot radius for the ith plot, and if circular plots are used, plot size is $a_i = \pi L_i^2$. Since the nth tree lies exactly on the plot boundary

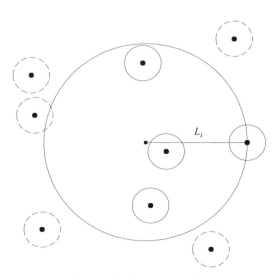

FIG. 11-8. N-tree sampling.

(Fig. 11-8), the plot is considered to have $n - \frac{1}{2}$ trees and the estimate of density for the ith plot was suggested by Prodan (1968b) as

$$N_i = \frac{A(n - 0.5)}{\pi L_i^2}$$

where $A = 43,560\,\text{ft}^2$ (English units) or $10,000\,\text{m}^2$ (metric units). Mean density is estimated as

$$\overline{N} = \frac{\sum_{i=1}^{m} N_i}{m} = \frac{1}{m} \sum_{i=1}^{m} \frac{A(n - 0.5)}{\pi L_i^2} = \frac{A(n - 0.5)}{m\pi} \sum_{i=1}^{m} \frac{1}{L_i^2} \tag{11-16}$$

where $\overline{N}$ = mean density (trees per unit area)
A = unit area ($43,560\,\text{ft}^2$ or $10,000\,\text{m}^2$)
n = fixed number of trees per plot
m = number of plots
L_i = distance (ft or m) to nth nearest tree

The estimated density from eq. (11-16) is biased except possibly when sampling from a population with a random spatial pattern (Payandeh and Ek, 1986). Moore (1954) suggested the use of $(n - 1)/n$ as a bias correction for n-tree sampling. In this case, the mean density is estimated as

$$\overline{N} = \frac{n-1}{n} \frac{1}{m} \sum_{i=1}^{m} \frac{An}{\pi L_i^2} = \frac{n-1}{n} \frac{An}{m\pi} \sum_{i=1}^{m} \frac{1}{L_i^2} = \frac{A(n-1)}{m\pi} \sum_{i=1}^{m} \frac{1}{L_i^2} \tag{11-17}$$

Equation (11-17) suggests that the nth tree is used only to establish the plot radius (Jonsson et al., 1992). Estimation of other parameters, such as basal area or volume are made using

$$\overline{X} = \frac{n-1}{n} \frac{1}{m} \sum_{i=1}^{m} \frac{AX_i}{\pi L_i^2} = \frac{n-1}{n} \frac{A}{m\pi} \sum_{i=1}^{m} \frac{X_i}{L_i^2} \tag{11-18}$$

where X_i = sum of the values of X (basal area, volume, etc.) for the n trees of the ith plot: $X_i = \sum_{j=1}^{n} X_{ij}$

The amount of bias present in these estimates depends on the spatial distribution and the number of trees measured per plot. Prodan (1968b) used $n = 6$ trees. Lessard et al. (1994) and Lynch and Rusydi (1999) found that $n \geq 5$ generally produces acceptable results. Payandeh and Ek (1986) recommended using $n = 7$.

To achieve the same standard error, distance-based estimators require many more sample plots than traditional fixed-area plots or PPS points. However, because a fixed number of trees per plot are being measured, distance-based sampling requires less time per plot and may require fewer total trees measured to obtain the same level of standard error. Lynch and Rusydi (1999) found that n-tree sampling with $n = 5$ was more efficient than either horizontal point sampling (BAF $= 1M$ and 2M) or 0.1-ha fixed-area plots (efficiency was measured in terms of the coefficient of variation and the time required to make measurements). Lessard et al. (1994) found n-tree sampling to be a cost-competitive alternative to traditional point or plot methods. For a complete treatment of the theory and application of distance sampling, see Buckland et al. (2001).

11-5. SELECTING APPROPRIATE SAMPLING UNITS

When selecting a sampling unit, one must consider both the type of sampling unit and its size and shape. In general, the most efficient sampling unit is the one that samples proportional to the variance of the stand parameters of interest. If density (trees per unit area) is the primary variable of interest, fixed-area plots are generally more efficient than PPS sampling. Fixed-area plots sample proportional to frequency, and since the tree factor is constant for a given plot size, no additional individual tree measurements are required. If basal area or volume is the primary variable of interest, horizontal point samples are generally more efficient than fixed-area plots. Horizontal point samples sample proportional to tree basal area. No additional individual tree measurements are required to estimate basal area. In many cases, estimates of volume can be obtained from basal area and measurements of average height and form (Section 14-1.8).

Unbiased estimates of timber quantities and other stand parameters can be obtained from any plot type and size, although the precision and cost of the survey or study may vary significantly. Smaller sampling units are frequently more efficient than larger ones. In a fairly homogeneous forest, the precision for a given sampling intensity tends to be greater for small sampling units than for large ones because the number of independent sampling units is greater. However, the size of the most efficient unit is also influenced by the variability of the forest. When small sampling units are taken in heterogeneous forests, high coefficients of variation will be obtained. In such cases, large sampling units are more desirable.

For a given sampling intensity (the total area of all sampling units), the smaller the plots, the greater will be the precision because there will be more units. On the other hand, the greater the number of units, the higher will be the cost of sampling. In general, the cost of sampling will be greater for a large number of small sampling units than for fewer plots of larger size. In addition, each sampling unit should be large enough so that it will reasonably represent the composition and structure of the forest. If the plot is too small, the probability that it will not be representative of the population increases.

The guiding principle in the choice of plot size should be to have a plot large enough to include a representative number of trees, but small enough so that the time required for measurement is not excessive. For dense stands of small trees, plots should be relatively small; for widely spaced stands of large trees, plots should be relatively large.

When using horizontal point samples, the desired BAF can be determined using an estimate of mean basal area per unit area and the desired number of trees m to be included at each point:

$$\text{BAF} = \frac{\text{BA/unit area}}{m} \qquad (11\text{-}19)$$

For example, if a forest averages $125\,\text{ft}^2$/acre of basal area and we want to count 10 trees on average, the appropriate BAF would be $125/10 = 12.5$. A similar process, based on average density, can be used to determine the size of fixed-area plots.

The relative efficiency of different-sized plots can be measured by

$$e = \frac{(s_{\bar{x}})_1^2 t_1}{(s_{\bar{x}})_2^2 t_2} \qquad (11\text{-}20)$$

where $(s_{\bar{x}})_1$ = standard error in percent for one sampling unit as basis for comparison

$(s_{\bar{x}})_2$ = standard error in percent for the other sampling unit to be compared

t_1 = cost or time for base sampling unit

t_2 = cost or time for sampling unit compared

The equation gives the efficiency of sampling unit 2 relative to sampling unit 1. If e is less than 1, sampling unit 1 is more efficient than 2. If e is greater than 1, sampling unit 2 is more efficient than 1. Procedures for investigating optimum sampling units are given by Mesavage and Grosenbaugh (1956), Freese (1962), Tardif (1965), O'Regan and Arvanitas (1966), Zeide (1980), Oderwald (1981b), and Shiver and Borders (1996).

Zeide (1980) presented a procedure for determining optimal plot size in one-stage systematic or random sampling designs. The optimal plot size was proposed to be the one that minimizes total time required for location and measurement to achieve a given precision. Zeide then developed the following formula for calculating optimal plot size:

$$\text{optimal plot size} = P_1 \left(\frac{t}{m}\right)^2 \qquad (11\text{-}21)$$

where P_1 = size of plot used in preliminary sample to assess time and variation

t = average travel time between two neighboring plots of size P_1 (the
distance between these plots should be for the number of plots
that provides the desired precision)

m = average plot measurement time for plot size P_1

The formula indicates that the greater the distance between plots, the larger
they must be. When plot size is optimal, equal amounts of time will be spent on
travel and on plot measurement.

12

FOREST INVENTORY

A forest inventory is the procedure for obtaining information on the quantity, quality, and condition of the forest resource, associated vegetation and components, and many of the characteristics of the land area on which the forest is located. Most forest inventories have been, and will continue to be, focused on timber estimation. However, the need for information on forest health, water, soils, recreation, wildlife and scenic values, and other nontimber values has stimulated the development of integrated or multiresource inventories. When nontimber information is required, specialists in the pertinent fields should cooperate in planning and executing the inventory.

12-1. TIMBER ESTIMATION

A complete forest inventory for timber evaluation provides the following information: estimates of the area, description of topography, ownership patterns, accessibility, transportation facilities, estimates of timber quantity and quality, and estimates of growth and drain. The emphasis placed on specific elements will differ with the purpose of the inventory (Husch, 1971). For example, if the purpose of an inventory is for the preparation of a harvesting plan, major emphasis should be put on a description of topography, determination of accessibility and transportation facilities, and estimation of timber quantity. The other elements would be given little emphasis or even be eliminated. If the purpose of an inventory is for the preparation of a management plan, major emphasis would be put on timber quantity, growth, and drain with lesser detail on other elements.

Information is obtained in a forest inventory for timber evaluation by measuring and assessing the trees and various characteristics of the land. The information may be obtained from measurements made on the ground or on remote-sensed imagery (aerial photographs, satellite imagery, radar, etc.). When measurements are made on all trees in a forest, the inventory is a complete or 100 percent inventory. When measurements are made for a sample of the forest, it is a sampling inventory. The terms *cruise* in North America and *enumeration* in other English-speaking areas are frequently used instead of inventory.

In executing a forest inventory for timber evaluation, it is impossible to measure directly quantities such as volume or weight of standing trees. Consequently, a relationship is established between directly measurable tree or stand characteristics (e.g., dbh, height) and the desired quantity. This may be done as follows:

1. Make detailed field measurements of trees or stands and compute the desired quantities from these measurements. For example, one might make detailed diameter measurements at predetermined heights along the stem of standing trees and determine volumes by formulas or graphical methods (Section 6-1).
2. Estimate the desired quantities in trees or stands by utilizing relationships derived previously from other trees or stands. For example, one might measure tree or stand characteristics such as dbh, height, and form and determine the corresponding volume or weight from an equation or a table (Section 6-2).

12-1.1 Estimation of Net Usable Volume

Timber inventories can estimate gross and net quantities, normally volume. An estimate of *gross volume* shows the volume of wood, usually without bark, based on the exterior measurements of the trees: dbh, height, and form, without any deductions for defects. An estimate of *net volume* reduces the gross volume due to defects such as rot, diseased portions, and stem irregularities. The reduction for defect can be determined in two ways: (1) at the time of measurement of each tree, the external defects can be noted, internal defects estimated (or directly determined by boring) and recorded, and the loss in volume estimated per tree; and (2) by applying a cull factor expressed as a percentage that will reduce the gross volume of the inventory to net volume. This cull percentage can be determined directly by carrying out a study that requires the felling of a sample of trees and determining their gross and net volumes to determine cull percentages. Frequently, cull percentages are used based on previous experience in the kind of timber being inventoried.

Inventories can be designed to estimate net volumes or quantities by product classes such as poles, pulpwood, sawtimber, and veneer logs. Of course, this requires specifying the criteria such as minimum diameter and length, form and extent of defect, to be used at the time of measurement of sample trees during fieldwork.

Another factor in estimating net usable quantity of timber depends not on the defects in the trees themselves but on the following external causes:

- Accessibility
- Legal restrictions (protected areas, silvicultural requirements)
- Nonutilizable species
- Minimum quality characteristics and sizes of logs
- Losses due to breakage in logging and transport

Estimates of the reduction in timber quantity due to these causes are required to obtain an estimate of the net usable volume.

12-2. NONTIMBER ESTIMATION

As Hassan et al. (1996) have pointed out "the need to look into non-wood benefits of forestry is... becoming an increasingly important component of forest management planning in view of the fact that the contribution of forestry goes beyond wood production." Inventories that include estimates of nontimber parameters in a forest are called *multiple resource inventories*. The parameters measured in this type of inventory vary, depending on the information required. These parameters may include timber estimates together with data on nontimber vegetation and/or the other characteristics of the forest area. For example, the U.S. Forest Service, in their resource inventories, collects the following nontimber information (USDA, 1992):

1. Nontree vegetation
   a. Species abundance
   b. Vegetation profile
   c. Biomass
2. Wildlife habitat
   a. Edge
   b. Animal use, browsing
   c. Snags
   d. Down woody material
   e. Cover, shelter
   f. Suitability
3. Forested range for livestock
   a. Grazing

4. Recreation
   a. Opportunity assessment
   b. Use
5. Soils
   a. Landscape context
   b. Physical characteristics
6. Water
   a. Type
   b. Proximity
7. Other data
   a. Logging operability
   b. Spatial coordinates
   c. Residential fuelwood
   d. Fire fuel quantities
   e. Woodland assessment
   f. Resource zone

Multiple forest resource inventories may also collect additional information on such characteristics as biodiversity, forest health, scenic values, carbon storage, and ownership.

12-3. INVENTORY PLANNING

An important step in designing a forest inventory is the development of a comprehensive plan before initiating work. Such a plan ensures that all facets of the inventory, including the data to be collected, financial and logistical support, and compilation procedures, are thought through before the inventory begins. The reader is referred to Husch (1971) for a discussion of inventory planning.

The following checklist includes all, or almost all, items that should be considered in planning a forest inventory. The items do not always have the same importance, and are not needed in all plans.

1. Purpose of the inventory
   a. Timber and nontimber parameters to be estimated
   b. How the information will be used
2. Background information
   a. Past surveys, reports, maps, photographs, etc.
   b. Individual or organization supporting the inventory
   c. Funds available

3. Description of area
   a. Location
   b. Size
   c. Terrain, accessibility, transport facilities
   d. General character of forest
4. Information required in final report
   a. Tables and graphs
   b. Maps, mosaics, or other pictorial material
   c. Narrative report
5. Inventory design
   a. Estimation of area (from aerial photographs, orthophotos, maps or field measurements)
   b. Determination of timber quantity (e.g., volume tables, units of volume)
   c. Methods for estimation of nontimber parameters (e.g., regeneration, lesser vegetation, woody debris, soil, water, scenic and recreational values)
   d. Size and shape of fixed-size sampling units
   e. Probability sampling
      i. Simple random sampling
      ii. Stratified random sampling
      iii. Multistage sampling
      iv. Double and regression sampling
      v. Sampling with varying probability (e.g., PPS, 3P)
   f. Nonrandom sampling
      i. Selective sampling
      ii. Systematic sampling
   g. Setting precision for inventory
   h. Sampling intensity to meet required precision
   i. Times and costs for all phases of work
6. Procedures for interpretation of photo, satellite imagery, or other remote sensing material
   a. Location and establishment of sampling units
   b. Determination of current stand information, including instructions on measurement of appropriate tree and stand characteristics coordinated with fieldwork
   c. Determination of insect damage, forest cover types, forest fuel types, area, and so on, coordinated with fieldwork
   d. Personnel
   e. Instruments

  f. Recording of information

  g. Quality control

  h. Data conversion and editing

7. Procedures for fieldwork

  a. Crew organization

  b. Logistical support and transportation

  c. Location and establishment of sampling units

  d. Determination of current stand information, including instructions on measurement of trees and sample units coordinated with photo interpretation

  e. Determination of growth, regeneration, insect damage, mortality, forest cover types, forest fuel types, area, and so on, coordinated with photo interpretation

  f. Instruments

  g. Recording of observations

  h. Quality control

  i. Data conversion and editing

8. Compilation and calculation procedures

  a. Instructions for reduction of remote sensing and field measurements

    i. Conversion of remote sensing material or field measurements to desired expressions of quantity

    ii. Calculation of sampling errors

    iii. Specific methods and computer programs to use

    iv. Description of all phases from handling of raw data to final results, including programs

9. Final report

  a. Outline

  b. Estimated time to prepare

  c. Personnel responsible for preparation

  d. Method of reproduction

  e. Number of copies

  f. Distribution

10. Maintenance

  a. Storage and retrieval of data

  b. Plans for updating inventory

The decision to conduct an inventory depends on the need for information. An inventory is an information-gathering process that provides one of the bases for rational decisions. These decisions may be required for many reasons, such as the purchase or sale of timber, for preparation of timber-harvesting plans, in forest and wildlife management, for obtaining a loan, and so on. If the purpose is clarified, one can foresee how the information will be used and thus know the relative emphasis to put on the different elements of the inventory.

As a first step in planning an inventory, one should obtain the requisite background information and prepare a description of the area. One should then decide on the information required from the inventory and prepare the outlines of tables that will appear in the final report. Table outlines should include titles, column headings, class limits, measurement units, and other categories needed to indicate the inventory results. These table outlines should be prepared before detailed planning begins because the inventory design will depend on the information required for the final report. Area information is usually shown by such categories as land-use class, forest-type or condition class, and ownership. Timber quantities are usually given in stand and stock tables. A *stand table* gives the number of trees by species, dbh, and height classes. A *stock table* gives volumes or weights according to similar classifications (see Chapter 11 for details on construction of stand and stock tables). Stand and stock tables may be on a per unit area basis (per acre or hectare) or for the total forest area and may be prepared for forest types or other classifications (e.g., compartments, watersheds).

Since a forest is a living, changing complex, the inventory plan should consider the inclusion of estimates of growth and drain. For a discussion of tree and stand growth, see Chapters 15 and 16.

12-4. FOREST INVENTORY DESIGN

There must be wide latitude in designing an inventory to meet the variety of forest vegetation, topographic, economic, and transportation conditions that may be encountered. The required forest inventory information can be obtained by observations and measurements in the field and on aerial photographs, satellite images, and other remote sensing sources. The most useful and practical approach is a procedure in which remote sensing materials are used for forest classification or stratification, mapping, and area determination, while fieldwork is employed for detailed information about forest conditions, timber quantities and qualities, and additional nontimber characteristics. One can design a forest inventory utilizing only fieldwork, but it is less efficient. If aerial photographs and satellite imagery are available, they should be used. (Under some circumstances, it is possible to design a forest inventory based entirely on photographic interpretations and measurements. However, this method will provide only rough approximations of timber species and the quantity, quality, and sizes present and information on the nontimber parameters.)

The funds available and the cost of an inventory will strongly influence the design chosen. The main factors that will affect costs are the type of information required, the standard of precision chosen, the total size of the area to be surveyed, and the minimum size of the unit area for which estimates are required. General information is relatively inexpensive, but the costs increase as more details are required. The standard of precision chosen greatly influences costs; the greater the precision, the higher the costs since this usually requires more intensive sampling. Costs per unit area will decrease as the size of the inventory area increases. If independent estimates are required for subdivisions of a large forest area, this will also raise costs. Descriptions of basic sampling designs applicable to forest inventory are given in Chapter 13.

12-5. INVENTORY FIELDWORK

The size and organization of field crews will vary with sampling procedures, the observations or measurements required, forest conditions, and tradition. For timber inventory work in temperate-zone forests, crews of one or two workers are widely used. If additional nontimber information is required, additional members are needed. Small crews have proved satisfactory in these areas because roads are usually abundant (access by vehicle is good), forest travel is relatively easy (little brush cutting is required), and well-trained technicians are generally available (they require little supervision).

For inventory work in tropical zone forests, large crews are widely used because roads are generally sparse (access by vehicle is poor), forest travel is difficult (workers are required to cut vegetation), and few trained technicians are available (they require considerable supervision). Whatever the crew size or the assigned tasks, however, specific, clear instructions should be given to each crewmember.

A basic rule of forest inventory is to prepare complete written instructions before fieldwork starts. To minimize later changes, instructions should be tested before operations begin. Instructions should be clear and specific enough so that individual judgment by field crews on where and how to take measurements is eliminated. For example, field crews should not be permitted to choose the position of a sampling unit subjectively or to move it to a more accessible position or more "typical" stand. The aim should be to standardize all work to obtain uniform quality and the best possible reliability of the measurements, regardless of which person does the work. The occurrence of mistakes or nonrandom errors must be eliminated or, at least, held to a minimum.

It is best to settle on a standard set of instruments. The use of several kinds of instruments to make the same type of measurements should be avoided. To minimize errors, the instruments should be checked periodically to see if they are in adjustment.

Decisions should be made on the precision required for each measurement. Thus, tree diameters (dbh) may be stipulated to the nearest centimeter, inch, tenth of an inch, and so on, and heights to the nearest foot, meter, one-half log, and so on.

If estimates of timber quantity are to be made by quality or product classes, field instructions must include tree measurement specifications on minimum dbh and upper stem diameter, section lengths, and total usable length and criteria such as crook, scars, catfaces, evidence of rot, and so on, on individual sections and for the entire tree.

Inventory field operations must include a checking or quality control procedure. Whether plots, strips, or points are used, a certain percentage of the sampling units should be remeasured. The results of the remeasurements should be compared to the original measurement to see if the work meets the required standards. If it does not, remedial steps should be taken.

There is no standard form or system for recording field observations. The manner in which measurements are recorded depends in large part on the way they will be processed. Here are four methods that have been used for recording field measurements:

1. The use of forms that are designed without concern for subsequent calculations. The information needed is extracted from the forms and computations done apart from them. This is the least efficient method.
2. The use of forms with space for subsequent calculations. This is useful for small inventories for which limited information is required.
3. The use of forms designed for efficient transfer of data to computer input devices.
4. The use of methods and instruments that permit direct data entry into a computer (electronic data recorders).

12-6. CALCULATION AND COMPILATION

Plans for calculation and compilation of photo-interpretation data and field measurements should be made before fieldwork begins. It is illogical to postpone consideration of these things until data are obtained because foreknowledge of the calculation and compilation procedures can influence collection of data. For example, if volume tables will be used to determine tree volumes, there would be no point in measuring diameters to a tenth of a centimeter in the field if the volume tables give volumes by full centimeter dbh classes.

The statistical formulas or computer programs to be used for estimating means, totals, and standard errors should be selected early in the planning process. It is worthwhile to check the formulas with simulated data to verify the applicability of the program or to work out the optimum sequence of computational steps.

13

SAMPLING DESIGNS IN FOREST INVENTORIES

In a large forest, sampling can provide all the necessary information in less time and at a lower cost than a 100 percent inventory. Indeed, it is impractical for a large forest to measure all the trees or other characteristics of interest. Since fewer measurements are needed, sampling may produce more reliable results than a complete tally because fewer, better-trained personnel can be used and better field supervision of the work can be exercised. In addition, the idea of precision is in the forefront throughout a sampling inventory, whereas a complete tally may give the delusion of the acquisition of information without error.

This chapter is concerned with the application of sampling theory and techniques to forest resource evaluation applicable to both timber and nontimber parameters. The reader is referred to Cochran (1977) for a basic treatment of sampling theory and techniques. Schreuder et al. (1993) and Shiver and Borders (1996) are useful references for sampling in forest inventory.

13-1. BASIC CONSIDERATIONS

In Chapter 3, a comprehensive overview of the basic statistical concepts and methods was given. A few of these basic concepts are reviewed briefly here in the context of forest inventory.

In forest inventory work, sampling consists of making observations on portions of a population (the forest and its characteristics), to obtain estimates that are representative of the parent population. An observation is a recording of information, such as the volume of a fixed-area plot. The sampling units on which observations are made may be stands, compartments, administrative units, fixed-area plots, strips, or points. The aggregate of all possible sampling units constitutes its population. The group of sampling units chosen for measurement constitutes the sample. For purposes of selecting the sampling units, a frame can be prepared that can be a diagram or list of all possible sampling units in the population. Some populations are finite; that is, they consist of a fixed number of sampling units, such as all nonoverlapping 0.2-acre square plots on a 160-acre forest. Other populations, such as all possible points (as used in horizontal point sampling), are infinite; that is, they consist of an unlimited number of sampling units. In the statistical treatment of data, it is important to know whether the population is infinite or finite. As a practical matter, however, very large finite populations can be treated as infinite.

The essential problem in sampling is to obtain a sample that is representative of the population. If the sample is representative of the population, useful statements can be made about the characteristics of the population (volume or weight per unit area, number of trees per unit area, etc.) on the basis of the characteristics observed in the sample observations. The characteristics of the population are referred to as *parameters*. The exact values of the parameters would be known if the entire population was measured. In most situations, however, complete enumerations are too time consuming and costly, and sampling is used to estimate the values of parameters. Such estimates are calculated from a sample and are called *statistics*. A statistic therefore is a summary value calculated from a sample to estimate a population parameter.

A sampling design is determined by the kind of sampling units used, the number of sampling units employed, and the manner of selecting and distributing them over the forest area, as well as the procedures for taking measurements and analyzing the results. The specifications for each of these elements can be varied to yield the desired precision at a minimum specified cost.

Basic inventory designs generally fall into the following categories:

1. Probability sampling
   a. Simple random sampling
   b. Stratified random sampling
   c. Multistage sampling
   d. Multiphase sampling
   e. Sampling with varying probabilities
2. Nonrandom sampling
   a. Selective sampling
   b. Systematic sampling

In this chapter we concentrate on sampling designs using fixed-area plots (Section 11-2), although the basic sampling designs are applicable to sampling units of any type. In Chapter 14 we discuss sample design issues unique to sampling units with varying probability (Section 11-3).

13-1.1   Errors in Forest Inventories

The precision of a forest inventory based on sampling is indicated by the size of the sampling error and excludes the effect of nonsampling errors. Accuracy of an inventory refers to the size of the total error and includes the effect of nonsampling errors. In forest inventory, as in any sampling procedure, we are concerned primarily with accuracy. We try to achieve accuracy by designing and executing an inventory for an acceptable precision and by eliminating or reducing nonsampling errors to a minimum.

Sampling errors result from the fact that the sample is only a portion of the population and may not produce estimates identical to the population parameter. The sampling error is expressed as the standard error of the mean. Nonsampling errors are errors not connected with the statistical problem of the selection of the sample and may therefore occur whether the entire population or a sample of the population is measured. Thus, nonsampling errors are always present; sampling errors are present only when sampling methods are employed.

Nonsampling errors arise from defects in the sampling frame, mistakes in the collection of data due to bias or negligence, and mistakes in the processing stage. When nonsampling errors are large, the total error will be reduced only slightly by taking a large sample (to decrease the sampling error). Indeed, when the nonsampling errors are large, attention should be focused on reducing them before the sample size is increased to reduce the sampling errors.

Prodan et al. (1997) have made a detailed categorization of nonsampling errors as follows:

1. *Design errors.* These are errors that produce bias in the estimations due to the nonobservance of the probability of selection (subjective distribution) or the independence between sample units. The systematic distribution of sampling units may cause bias if the distribution coincides with some specific characteristic of the area, such as all sampling units falling in river bottoms, ridge tops, or on some given contour.

2. *Operational errors.* The principal operational errors are the erroneous location of samples, inaccurate establishment of sample unit boundaries, and errors in the measurement of tree dimensions or nontimber elements. These errors can be minimized with appropriate training of field crews and the exercise of quality control.

3. *Errors in the functions used to quantify the parameters.* For example, inappropriate mathematical models or errors in their coefficients and constants (e.g., errors in or inappropriate functions to estimate tree volumes).

4. *Errors in the determination of areas.* These are errors that may arise in the preparation of maps and the determination of areas from them.

5. *Errors in the management and processing of data.* Examples are the incorrect codification and registering of measurements, errors in their transfer from field forms and errors that may occur in the use of programs for the processing of data.

13-1.2   Confidence Limits

Forest inventory estimates can be expressed as a range—the confidence interval, bounded by confidence limits—within which the population parameter is expected to occur at a given probability (see Section 3-5.2). The confidence interval is expressed by

$$CI = \overline{x} \pm t \cdot s_{\overline{x}} \qquad (13\text{-}1)$$

The value of t for a chosen probability level can be found from Student's t distribution (Appendix Table A-4) using $n - 1$ degrees of freedom, where n is the size of the sample.

If $\overline{x}$ is the mean volume per unit area and $s_{\overline{x}}$ is the standard error of the mean from a sampling inventory, the confidence interval for the total timber volume estimate for a forest area A is

$$CI(\text{total}) = A\overline{x} \pm Ats_{\overline{x}} \qquad (13\text{-}2)$$

(Note that in this case the forest area is assumed known without sampling error.)

As an example, assume that a 5000-acre forest area has been inventoried. Based on a sample of 144 fixed-area plots, the mean volume per acre was estimated as 11,500 board feet, with a standard deviation of 6000 board feet. The 95 percent confidence interval for the per-acre volume would be calculated as follows:

$$s_{\overline{x}} = \frac{s}{\sqrt{n}} = \frac{6000}{\sqrt{144}} = 500$$

and

$$CI(\text{per acre}) = 11,500 \pm (1.96)(500)$$

$$= 11,500 \pm 980$$

$$= 10,520 \text{ to } 12,480 \text{ board feet per acre}$$

The value of $t = 1.96$ was determined from Appendix Table A-4 using the column for probability $= 0.05$ $(1 - 0.95)$, and since 500 was larger than the largest specified degrees of freedom, the row corresponding to degrees of freedom = ∞ .

Assuming that the value for the area, $A = 5000$, is known without error, the confidence interval and its limits for the total timber volume estimate are:

$$CI(\text{total}) = 5000(11{,}500) \pm 5000(1.96)(500)$$

$$= 57{,}500{,}000 \pm 4{,}900{,}000$$

$$= 52{,}600{,}000 \text{ to } 62{,}400{,}000 \text{ board feet}$$

Equation (13-2) assumes that the total forest area A is known without error. This is seldom the case. Usually, the forest area is estimated by some procedure, such as repeated planimeter, dot grid, or GIS measurements, and the standard error computed. Then, considering both the sampling error of volume per unit area and the sampling error of the area estimate s_A.

$$CI(\text{total}) = A\bar{x} \pm t\sqrt{(As_{\bar{x}})^2 + (\bar{x}s_A)^2} \qquad (13\text{-}3)$$

Assuming that the estimate of forest area in the example has a standard error of 75 acres, then

$$CI(\text{total}) = 5000(11{,}500) \pm 1.96\sqrt{[5000(500)]^2 + [11{,}500(75)]^2}$$

$$= 57{,}500{,}000 \pm 5{,}183{,}415$$

$$= 52{,}316{,}585 \text{ to } 62{,}683{,}415 \text{ board feet}$$

The estimate of a forest area A may be determined as a proportion p of a total area using a procedure such as dot counts on aerial photos. In this case, one assumes that the total area A_T is known without error. However, the estimate of the proportion p will have a standard error s_p. The estimate of the confidence interval for the total volume would then be

$$CI(\text{total}) = A\bar{x} \pm t\sqrt{(As_{\bar{x}})^2 + (\bar{x}A_T s_p)^2} \qquad (13\text{-}4)$$

where $A = pA_T$

Assuming that the forest area of 5000 acres in the preceding example was determined from a dot count showing 62.5 percent in forest of a total land area of 8000 acres and that the estimate of $s_p = 0.007$, then

$$A = 0.625(8000) = 5000 \text{ acres}$$

and

$$CI(total) = 5000(11,500) \pm 1.96\sqrt{[5000(500)]^2 + [11,500(8000)(0.007)]^2}$$

$$= 57,500,000 \pm 5,059,965$$

$$= 52,440,035 \text{ to } 62,559,965 \text{ board feet}$$

The width of the confidence interval $ts_{\bar{x}}$ can be considered a measure of the error associated with an estimated mean at the desired level of probability. By dividing this quantity by the mean, the percent error of an estimated mean $E\%$ at the desired probability level is obtained:

$$E\% = 100\left(\frac{ts_{\bar{x}}}{\bar{x}}\right) \tag{13-5}$$

This is also called the *percent sampling error*, and expresses the precision of the inventory. For the example we have been discussing in this section, E (in percent) for the 0.95 probability level would be

$$E\% = 100\left[\frac{1.96(500)}{11,500}\right] = 8.5\%$$

Instead of expressing a timber estimate by its mean and confidence interval, an analogous expression called the *reliable minimum estimate* (RME) can be used (Dawkins, 1957). The RME estimates the minimum quantity expected to be present with its probability:

$$RME = \bar{x} - ts_{\bar{x}} \tag{13-6}$$

The value of t for a probability level is obtained from one side of the distribution. In using a table of t values where the sign is ignored (i.e., "two-tailed" table as shown in Appendix Table A-4), the appropriate value would be obtained using the column for double the probability level required. Thus, the t value for a probability level of 0.05 would be read under the column headed 0.10, recognizing the appropriate degrees of freedom. For the example we have been following, the reliable minimum estimate would be

$$RME(\text{per acre}) = 11,500 - 1.645(500)$$

$$= 11,500 \pm 820$$

$$= 10,678 \text{ board feet per acre}$$

13-1.3 Precision Level and Intensity

The choice of the precision level for a forest inventory depends on the sampling error that one is willing to accept in the estimates. Thus one might ask: What would occur if decisions on investment, forest management, and so on, were based on estimates with sampling errors of ±1, ±5, or ±10 percent? In most forest inventory work, this is not done. Precision levels used are those traditionally employed in similar inventories. The difficulty in attacking this problem comes from the lack of methods of quantifying the effects on decisions of inventory sampling errors of different sizes (Hamilton, 1978; Husch, 1980).

The precision level can be expressed in relative terms as a percent [eq. (13-5)] or as a standard error of the mean. In the following sections of this chapter, the formulas for the determination of sample size utilize these expressions of acceptable precision.

The *intensity* of sampling with fixed-area plots indicates the percentage of the total area of a population that is included in the sample. Thus, if 200 0.2-acre plots are measured in a 1000-acre forest, the sampling intensity I is

$$I = \frac{200(0.2)}{1000}(100) = 4.0\%$$

13-2. SIMPLE RANDOM SAMPLING

Simple random sampling is the fundamental selection method. All other sampling procedures are modifications of simple random sampling that are designed to achieve greater economy or precision. Simple random sampling requires that there be an equal chance of selecting all possible combinations of n sampling units from the population. The selection of each sampling unit must be free from deliberate choice and must be completely independent of the selection of all other units.

In simple random sampling, the entire forest area is treated as a single population of N units. If fixed-area sampling units are used, the population size N has definable limits. If points are used, the population of N can be considered infinite. From the population, a sample of n sampling units with equal probability of selection is randomly chosen.

Simple, or unrestricted, random sampling in forest inventory yields an unbiased estimate of the population mean and the information to assess the sampling error. However, it has the following disadvantages:

1. Requirement of devising a system for randomly selecting the plots or points
2. Difficulties in locating widely dispersed field positions of selected sampling units
3. Time-consuming and expensive nonproductive traveling time between units
4. Possibility of a clumpy distribution of sampling units may result in atypical estimates of the mean, standard deviation, and other measures

Forest inventory using random sampling requires the establishment of a sampling frame, such as maps, aerial photos, or satellite images, from which to draw the sample. Figure 13-1 shows the simple case of a rectangular-shaped forest that can be divided into N sampling units of fixed area. After the number of sampling units n has been determined, they are chosen from the frame using

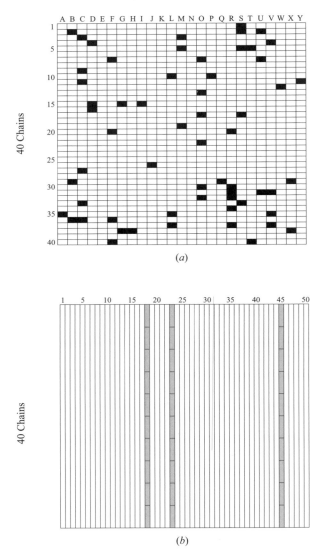

(a)

(b)

FIG. 13-1. Simple random sampling. (a) Using plots. Forest area of 200 acres divided into 1000 sampling units of 0.2 acre (2 × 1 chain). Sixty plots randomly selected. (b) Using strips. Forest area of 200 acres divided into 50 strips 1 chain wide and 40 chains long (4 acres). Three strips randomly selected with recording units of 4 × 1 chains.

any accepted procedure for random selection. The selection can be with or without replacement. If sampling with replacement is followed, since there is a possibility of the same sampling unit being selected more than once, the population can be considered infinite. For large finite populations, the calculation of mean and standard errors can be done as though dealing with an infinite population since the finite population correction factor $(N - n)/N$ [eq. (3-16)] approaches unity. Most sampling with fixed-area plots or strips is done without replacement. Using points, the population is infinite and the sampling is carried out with replacement.

Analysis of the resulting data from the sampling units is summarized below. Note that the formulas are applicable whether dealing with plots, strips, or points. (Separate tallies for each sampling unit in a forest inventory must be recorded to calculate the sampling error.)

Given $n =$ number of sampling units measured

$N =$ total number of sampling units in population (the forest)

$X_i =$ quantity of X measured in ith sampling unit

$\bar{x} =$ mean of X per sampling unit; an estimate of population mean

$s =$ standard deviation of sample

$s_{\bar{x}} =$ standard error of mean

$\hat{X} =$ estimated total of X for population

$CV =$ coefficient of variation [eq. (3-13)]

$E =$ allowable error of X

$E\% =$ allowable error as a percent of mean

$t =$ Student's t for desired level

Then

$$\bar{x} = \frac{\sum_{i=1}^{n} X_i}{n} \tag{13-7}$$

$$s^2 = \frac{\sum_{i=1}^{n}(X_i - \bar{x})^2}{n-1} = \frac{\sum_{i=1}^{n} X_i^2 - \left(\sum_{i=1}^{n} X_i\right)^2/n}{n-1} \tag{13-8}$$

$$s_{\bar{x}}^2 = \frac{s^2}{n}\frac{N-n}{N} \tag{13-9}$$

(For an infinite population, the finite correction factor would be omitted.) The estimate of the population total is

$$\hat{X} = N\bar{x} \tag{13-10}$$

The number of sampling units needed to yield an estimate of the mean with a specified allowable error and probability can be calculated from

$$n = \frac{Nt^2s^2}{NE^2 + t^2s^2} \tag{13-11}$$

For an infinite population

$$n = \frac{t^2s^2}{E^2} \tag{13-12}$$

Expressing the standard deviation and allowable error in percentages gives us

$$n = \frac{Nt^2(\text{CV})^2}{N(E\%)^2 + t^2(\text{CV})^2} \tag{13-13}$$

For an infinite population

$$n = \frac{t^2(\text{CV})^2}{(E\%)^2} \tag{13-14}$$

Note in eq. (13-11) through (13-14) that s and CV refer to the standard deviation and coefficient of variation of a preliminary sample taken to give an indication of the variability of the population. E is for an arbitrarily chosen level and the t value depends on the required probability and degrees of freedom. The t value is determined from Student's t distribution (Appendix Table A-4) with $n - 1$ degrees of freedom, where n refers to the number of sampling units in the preliminary sample. Of course, to be correct, n should be the number of sampling units that is being sought. However, since this is unknown, the n of the preliminary sample can be used. Thus the actual probability level for the indicated number of sampling units will change. If a preliminary sample has not been taken and if the expected sample size is large (over 30), the t-values for an infinite number of degrees of freedom may be used. A detailed explanation of the implementation of these formulas and an example are given in Section 3-6.

If the amount of money for a survey is fixed, the number of sampling units must be determined within this restriction. If the total cost for a survey is given as c_t, then

$$c_t = c_o + nc_1 \tag{13-15}$$

where c_o = overhead cost of survey, including planning, organization, analysis, and compilation
c_1 = cost per sampling unit
n = number of sampling units

The number of sampling units is indicated as

$$n = \frac{c_t - c_o}{c_1} \tag{13-16}$$

If preliminary information on the mean and variance of the population is known from experience or a preliminary sample, it is then possible to estimate the precision that can be obtained for a given cost.

13-3. RATIO AND REGRESSION SAMPLING

Unfortunately, there exists some ambiguity in the term *regression* in the sampling context. It always pertains to the situation where two (or more) variables are under study, but it may be used to indicate the case where the auxiliary variable mean or total is known without error (as opposed to *double sampling*, where an error is involved) or the case where the model assumed has an intercept value (as opposed to *ratio* estimation, where the intercept is zero). By careful use of the words *sampling* and *estimation*, the ambiguity can perhaps be minimized. Thus, we might consider the following classification using the notions presented by Freese (1962).

1. *Regression sampling* (true mean of X known)
    a. *Regression estimation:* $\bar{y}_R = \bar{y} + b(\mu_x - \bar{x})$, where $\bar{y}$, b, and $\bar{x}$ are estimated from the sample and μ_x is the known population mean
    b. *Ratio estimation:* $\bar{y}_R = \hat{R}\mu_x$, where $\hat{R}$ is an estimated ratio obtained from the sample by either $\hat{R} = \bar{y}/\bar{x}$ (ratio of means) or $\hat{R} = \sum(y/x)/n$ (mean of ratios), depending on certain variance assumptions
2. *Double sampling* (true mean of X unknown, and must be estimated from a sample)
    a. *Regression estimation:* $\bar{y}_{Rd} = \bar{y}_s + b(\bar{x}_l - \bar{x}_s)$, where $\bar{y}_s$, b, and $\bar{x}_s$ are determined from a small sample and $\bar{x}_l$ is determined from the large sample
    b. *Ratio estimation:* $\bar{y}_{Rd} = \hat{R}\bar{x}_1$, where $\hat{R}$ is either a ratio of means or a mean of ratios obtained from the small sample and $\bar{x}_1$ is obtained from the large sample

For more details regarding sample sizes needed and formulas for the estimation of means and sampling errors of the various estimates, a text such as Cochran (1977) or Schreuder et al. (1993) should be consulted.

In this book, we discuss only certain applications of these techniques. Specifically, in the following paragraphs we look at the use of ratio and regression estimation to correct irregular-sized sample plots, and in Section 13-7, we consider the use of double sampling in a two-phase inventory such as that encountered when combining aerial photographs or satellite images and ground plot estimations.

When the forest to be sampled, using fixed-area units, is irregular in form, the possibility exists of having fractional plots or irregular length strips. This is illustrated in Fig. 13-2 (the problem in relation to sampling points is discussed in Section 14-1). Situations of this type arise frequently in actual application. Note that to meet the requirement of sampling units of equal size, it has become necessary (as in Fig. 13-2) to sketch imaginary boundaries to enclose the irregular boundaries of the forest. The area within each boundary has been divided into equal-sized sampling units. Some of the plots and strips fall entirely in the forest, and others include both the forest area and a zone beyond. For this reason it is necessary to measure two variables for each plot or strip: the area in the sampling unit that falls in the forest area, and the quantity of the variable, such as volume of timber, in this area. In this case, the mean volume per unit area for the forest must then be calculated using the ratio or regression methods of estimation.

In the majority of cases involving plot sampling, the ratio or regression procedures have been bypassed in the interest of simplifying fieldwork, saving time, and reducing later calculations. Thus, if a plot falls so that it straddles a forest or stratum boundary, instead of measuring both the area and quantities of that portion of the unit in the forest, a number of other procedures have been used (see Section 11-2.6). Older, more questionable procedures involve moving the plots so that they fall entirely within or without the forest or assigning them to the stratum in which the center point falls. To avoid the possibility of bias arising from these procedures, the ratio or regression methods may be used.

When the ratio estimation procedure is employed, the sample should consist of 30 or more units so that the inherent bias of the method becomes negligible. In addition, the method is truly applicable only when the linear relationship between the two variables, quantity and area per sampling unit, passes through the origin. When the linear regression line does not pass through the origin (e.g., volume per unit area can be zero when the plot area is nonzero), the regression method of estimation is preferable.

13-3.1   Ratio Estimation

Given $V_i =$ quantity measured on ith sampling unit
        $X_i =$ area of ith sampling unit

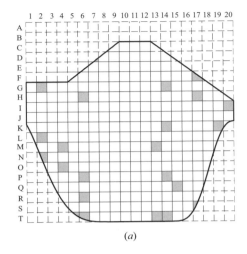

Size of plot = 0.25 ha
Total area of forest = 64.75 ha
$N = 259$
$n = 25$

(a)

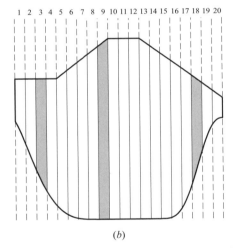

Width of strip = 50 m
Total area of forest = 64.75 ha
$N = 20$
$n = 3$

(b)

FIG. 13-2. Simple random sampling of irregularly shaped forest areas: (a) plot sampling; (b) strip sampling.

$\bar{v}$ = mean of observed V_i on sampling units selected
$\bar{x}$ = mean area of sampling units selected
$\bar{r}$ = estimate of the mean quantity per unit area
$\hat{v}$ = estimate of total quantity (e.g., volume) of forest
X = known total area of forest
N = number of sample units in population
n = number of units in sample

then

$$\bar{r} = \frac{\sum_{i=1}^{n} V_i/n}{\sum_{i=1}^{n} X_i/n} = \frac{\sum_{i=1}^{n} V_i}{\sum_{i=1}^{n} X_i} \tag{13-17}$$

and

$$\hat{v} = X\bar{r} \tag{13-18}$$

If the area is known without any sampling error, the variance of the total estimate of quantity is

$$s_v^2 = X^2 s_{\bar{r}}^2 \tag{13-19}$$

If the total area of the forest is an estimate x and has a sampling error, the variance is

$$s_v^2 = \bar{x}^2 s_{\bar{r}}^2 + \bar{r}^2 s_x^2 \tag{13-20}$$

where s_v^2 = variance of total quantity
 $s_{\bar{r}}^2$ = variance of ratio $\bar{r}$
 $s_{\bar{x}}^2$ = variance of total area estimate

The variance of the ratio $\bar{r}$ is calculated using

$$s_{\bar{r}}^2 = \frac{N-n}{N} \frac{s^2}{n} \tag{13-21}$$

where

$$s^2 = \frac{\bar{r}^2}{n-1} \left(\frac{\sum_{i=1}^{n} V_i^2}{\bar{v}^2} + \frac{\sum_{i=1}^{n} X_i^2}{\bar{x}^2} - \frac{2\sum_{i=1}^{n} V_i X_i}{\bar{v}\,\bar{x}} \right) \tag{13-22}$$

The number of sampling units for a given precision can be estimated by solving eq. (13-21) for n and using a preliminary estimate of s^2. Student's t can be incorporated to vary the probability level.

13-3.2 Regression Estimation

Using this method, an estimate of the mean volume of the sampling units is adjusted by means of a regression coefficient. The regression coefficient indicates the average change in volume per unit change in area between the sampling units in the sample and the population. The total size of the forest area and the total number of sampling units in the population and their average size must be known.

Given X_i, V_i, X, $\hat{v}$, $\bar{v}$, N, and n are as defined for ratio estimation

b = regression coefficient

$\bar{v}_{reg}$ = adjusted estimate of the mean volume per sampling unit in the population

$\overline{X}$ = mean area per sampling unit in population

$\bar{x}_n$ = mean area of sampling units selected

then

$$\bar{v}_{reg} = \bar{v} + b(\overline{X} - \bar{x}_n) \tag{13-23}$$

$$b = \frac{\sum_{i=1}^{n} X_i V_i - \sum_{i=1}^{n} X_i \sum_{i=1}^{n} V_i / n}{\sum_{i=1}^{n} X_i^2 - \left(\sum_{i=1}^{n} X_i\right)^2 / n} \tag{13-24}$$

The estimate of the mean volume per unit area $\bar{r}_{reg}$ is

$$\bar{r}_{reg} = \frac{\bar{v}_{reg}}{\overline{X}} \tag{13-25}$$

The estimate of the variance of the regression $s_{\bar{v}_{reg}}^2$ is

$$s_{\bar{v}_{reg}}^2 = \frac{s^2}{n} \frac{N - n}{n} \tag{13-26}$$

where

$$s^2 = \frac{1}{n - 2} \left[\left(\sum_{i=1}^{n} V_i^2 - \frac{\left(\sum_{i=1}^{n} V_i\right)^2}{n} \right) - b \left(\sum_{i=1}^{n} V_i X_i - \frac{\sum_{i=1}^{n} V_i \sum_{i=1}^{n} X_i}{n} \right) \right] \tag{13-27}$$

The estimate of the variance of the volume per unit area s_{reg}^2 is

$$s_{reg}^2 = \frac{s_{\bar{v}_{reg}}^2}{\overline{X}^2} \tag{13-28}$$

The estimate of the total volume of the population $\hat{v}$ is

$$\hat{v} = \bar{r}_{reg} X \tag{13-29}$$

or

$$\hat{v} = \bar{v}_{reg} N \tag{13-30}$$

and its variance is

$$s_v^2 = X^2 s_{reg}^2 \tag{13-31}$$

13-4. CLUSTER SAMPLING

A cluster consists of a group of smaller recording units that taken together form the sampling unit. The typical cluster consists of a number of subplots (recording units) located around the center in a fixed configuration (Fig. 13-3). The group of subplots forms the sampling unit. Clusters can assume many different configurations, depending on the number of recording units, the distance between units, and the geometric distribution.

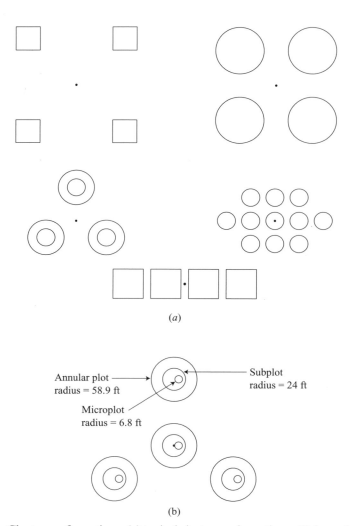

FIG. 13-3. Cluster configurations: (a) typical cluster configurations; (b) four-plot cluster of Forest Health Monitoring Program (Tallent-Halsell, 1994).

Clusters are frequently used in forest inventories of large areas, such as regional or national inventories, especially in remote areas with difficult access or long distances between plots. Instead of a distribution of single plots, which require much time moving from one to another, clusters can be used. When using clusters, fewer sample locations are used and a number of recording units are measured at each location instead of a single plot. The intent is to reduce the time for movement from one sample point to another and reduce the cost of fieldwork.

Cluster sampling is classified into two categories: single-stage and two-stage. In *single-stage cluster sampling* a sample of cluster locations is selected from a set of locations. At each location a fixed set of subunits are measured. In *two-stage cluster sampling* a sample of cluster locations is selected from a set of locations. At each location, a subsample of clusters is selected from a list of clusters and this subset measured. It is also possible to have a situation where the number of clusters per location is not the same and where individual subunits are not equal size (e.g., PPS sampling may be used at the subunit). The analysis discussed below focuses on single-stage clusters of equal size. For a discussion of the analysis of two-stage cluster sampling and clusters of unequal size, see Cochran (1977).

Given n = number of clusters

M = number of subunits per cluster

y_{ij} = value of parameter (e.g., basal area or volume) for jth subunit of ith cluster

$y_i = \sum_{j=1}^{M} y_{ij}$ = total for ith cluster

$\bar{y}_i = y_i/M = \sum_{j=1}^{M} y_{ij}/M$ = mean of subunit of ith cluster

$\bar{y} = \sum_{i=1}^{n} y_i/n$ = estimated sample mean cluster

$\bar{\bar{y}} = \sum_{i=1}^{n} y_i/nM = \bar{y}/M$ = estimated mean subunit

The estimated variation among the subunits has two components and is estimated using

$$s^2 = \frac{(n-1)s_b^2 + n(M-1)s_w^2}{nM - 1} \tag{13-32}$$

where the variation between clusters is estimated using

$$s_b^2 = \frac{\sum_{i=1}^{n}(\bar{y}_i - \bar{\bar{y}})^2}{n - 1} \tag{13-33}$$

and the variance within clusters is estimated using

$$s_w^2 = \frac{\sum_{i=1}^{n} \sum_{j=1}^{M}(y_{ij} - \bar{y}_i)^2}{n(M - 1)} \tag{13-34}$$

The effectiveness of cluster sampling can be assessed using analysis of variance (Cochran, 1977).

If the area of the subunits is a, the area of each cluster is Ma and an estimate of the mean value of y per unit area is given by

$$\frac{\bar{y}}{\text{unit area}} = \frac{A}{Ma}\bar{y} = \frac{A}{a}\bar{\bar{y}} \tag{13-35}$$

where $A =$ unit area (43,560 in English system and 10,000 in metric system)

13-5. STRATIFIED RANDOM SAMPLING

In many cases a heterogeneous forest may be divided by stratification into subdivisions called *strata*. In forest inventory work, the purpose of stratification is to reduce the variation within the forest subdivisions and increase the precision of the population estimate. Stratified random sampling in forest inventory has the following advantages over simple random sampling.

1. Separate estimates of the means and variances can be made for each of the forest subdivisions.
2. For a given sampling intensity, stratification often yields more precise estimates of the forest parameters than does a simple random sample of the same size. This will be achieved if the established strata result in a greater homogeneity of the sampling units within a stratum than for the population as a whole.

On the other hand, the disadvantages of stratification are that the size of each stratum must be known or at least a reasonable estimate be available, and that the sampling units must be taken in each stratum if an estimate for that stratum is needed.

Stratification is achieved by subdividing the forest area into strata on the basis of criteria such as topographical features, forest types, density classes, or volume, height, age, or site classes. If possible, the basis of stratification should be the same characteristic that will be estimated in the sampling procedure. Thus, if volume per unit area is the parameter to be estimated, it is desirable to stratify the forest on the basis of volume classes. Aerial photographs and satellite imagery are of tremendous assistance in stratification for forest inventory.

The different strata into which a forest may be divided can be irregular in shape, of many sizes, and of varying importance. Stratification permits the sampling intensity and precision to be varied for the different strata. An arbitrary form of stratification is often used in sampling large forest areas where there is little basis for some kind of natural subdivision. This often occurs in inventories of large, remote forest areas where maps or photographs are not available or where photo interpretation reveals little basis for stratification. In this case, the forest can be divided into uniform-sized squares or rectangles even though it is known that the resulting blocks may not contain homogeneous subpopulations. However, it is reasonable to assume greater homogeneity within a smaller block than in the entire forest.

Within each of the M strata into which a forest is divided, a number of sampling units are randomly chosen. Figure 13-4 shows a forest divided into three strata of fixed-area sampling units, all of the same size. The analysis of the data obtained from stratified random sampling is summarized below for the situation where the plots or strips are all of a uniform size, as illustrated by Fig. 13-4.

Given M = number of strata in population
n = total number of sampling units measured for all strata
n_j = total number of sampling units measured in jth stratum
N = total number of sampling units in population
N_j = total number of sampling units in jth stratum
X_{ij} = quantity of X measured on ith sampling unit of jth stratum
$\bar{x}_j$ = mean of X for jth stratum
$\bar{x}$ = estimated mean of X for population
P_j = proportion of total forest area in jth stratum = N_j/N

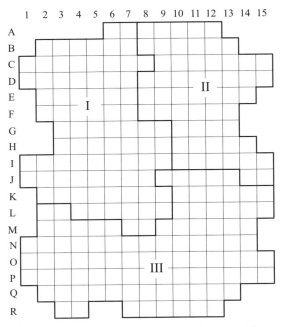

FIG. 13-4. Forest area divided into three unequal-sized strata. All sampling units are 0.5 acre.

$\hat{X}$ = estimated total of X for population
s_j^2 = variance of X for jth stratum
$s_{\bar{x}}^2$ = estimated variance for the mean of population
$s_{\hat{X}}^2$ = estimated variance of $\hat{X}$
E = allowable standard error in units of X

The estimate of the mean per stratum is

$$\bar{x}_j = \frac{\sum_{i=1}^{n} X_{ij}}{n_j} \tag{13-36}$$

The estimate of the mean for the population (i.e., total forest) is

$$\bar{x} = \frac{\sum_{i=1}^{n} N_j \bar{x}_j}{N} = \sum_{j=1}^{M} P_j \bar{x}_j \tag{13-37}$$

The estimate of the total for X for the entire population is

$$\hat{X} = \sum_{j=1}^{M} N_j \bar{x}_j$$

$$= N\bar{x} \tag{13-38}$$

The variance for each stratum in the population s_j^2 is calculated as described for simple random sampling. The variance of the mean for the population is then calculated from

$$s_{\bar{x}}^2 = \frac{1}{N^2} \sum_{j=1}^{M} \left(\frac{N_j^2 s_j^2}{n_j} \frac{N_j - n_j}{N_j} \right) \tag{13-39}$$

If the population consists of strata sufficiently large that the finite correction factor is insignificant or information is available on the relative sizes of the strata, we can estimate the variance from

$$s_{\bar{x}}^2 = \sum_{j=1}^{M} P_j^2 \frac{s_j^2}{n_j} \tag{13-40}$$

The standard error of the total estimate of X is then

$$s_{\hat{X}}^2 = N^2 s_{\bar{x}}^2 \tag{13-41}$$

The n_j sampling units actually chosen and measured per stratum should not be used to estimate the relative size of a stratum. Proportions in the strata should be estimated "a priori" to the actual sampling.

13-5.1   Estimation of Number of Sampling Units

To estimate the number of sampling units needed, it is necessary to have preliminary information on the variability of the strata in the population and to choose an allowable error and probability level. With this information, the intensity of sampling can be estimated. The total number of sampling units can then be allocated to the different strata by either proportional or optimum allocation.

In *proportional allocation*, the number of sampling units in a stratum, out of the total sample, is in proportion to the area of the stratum. In *optimum allocation*, the number of sampling units per stratum is proportional to the standard error of the stratum weighted by area. *Optimum allocation* will give the smallest standard error for a stratified population when a given total of sampling units is taken. If we wish to get the most precise estimate of the population mean for the expenditure of money, optimum allocation should be used. The allocation can be done either if the costs of sampling in all strata are equal or if they differ.

Using proportional allocation, advance knowledge of the variability in the several strata is desirable to determine the total sample size. Where no information on the variability of individual strata is available, it is necessary to estimate the total sample size for the entire population as though simple random sampling was being employed.

Using proportional allocation, the determination of sample size n for a given precision when information on variability per strata is available is

$$n = \frac{Nt^2 \sum_{j=1}^{M} P_j s_j^2}{NE^2 + t^2 \sum_{j=1}^{M} P_j s_j^2} \qquad (13\text{-}42)$$

and

$$n_j = P_j n \qquad (13\text{-}43)$$

If the population can be considered infinite, then

$$n = \frac{t^2 \sum_{j=1}^{M} P_j s_j^2}{E^2} \qquad (13\text{-}44)$$

Using optimum allocation, the determination of sample size n with specified precision is shown in eq. (13-45) for the simplest case when costs per sampling unit are the same in all strata. The sampling intensity is changed in each stratum, according to its variability, to achieve a given precision with the smallest possible number of sampling units:

$$n = \frac{Nt^2 \left(\sum_{j=1}^{M} P_j s_j\right)^2}{NE^2 + t^2 \sum_{j=1}^{M} P_j s_j^2} \tag{13-45}$$

and

$$n_j = \frac{P_j s_j}{\sum_{j=1}^{M} P_j s_j} \tag{13-46}$$

If the population can be considered infinite, then

$$n = \frac{t^2 \left(\sum_{j=1}^{M} P_j s_j\right)^2}{E^2} \tag{13-47}$$

For the determination of sample size by optimum allocation when the costs per sampling unit vary per stratum, or when the total cost of the inventory is fixed, the student is referred to Cochran (1977), Schreuder et al. (1993), and Shiver and Borders (1996).

Frequently, the use of stratified random sampling may result in the boundary lines of strata passing through the uniform sampling units near strata boundaries, resulting in varying areas tallied. (This is analogous to the situation described in Section 13-3.) When this occurs, ratio estimation or regression procedures as described by Loetsch and Haller (1964), Cochran (1977), and Shiver and Borders (1996) should be used.

13-6. MULTISTAGE SAMPLING

In multistage sampling, a population consists of a list of sampling units (primary stage), each of which is made up of smaller units (second stage), which in turn could be made up of smaller units (third stage). A random sample would be chosen from the primary units. A random subsample of the secondary units would then be taken in each of the primary units selected, and the procedure would be continued to the desired stage. In general, this procedure is called multistage sampling. *Two-stage sampling*, the most common application, which is discussed in this section, indicates the sampling stops at the secondary stage. For example, a forest to be inventoried might consist of numerous compartments that could be considered the primary units in a sampling design. Plots chosen in the selected compartments would then form the secondary units. Similarly, an inventory design using plots on randomly chosen lines or strips is a form of two-stage sampling. Another frequently used two-stage sampling design in forest inventory employs clusters of plots or sampling points at randomly chosen locations.

Multistage sampling in forest inventory is not restricted to fixed-area sampling units but can also be employed with variable plot procedures. Thus, a series of primary locations could be randomly chosen in a forest, and at each location, a number of secondary points could be chosen for the selection of trees using the variable plot procedure. In all cases, the group of secondary units selected within each of the primary units can be referred to as a *cluster*.

Multistage sampling has the principal advantage of concentrating the measurement work close to the location of the primary sampling units chosen rather than spreading it over the entire forest area to be inventoried. This is advantageous when it is difficult and costly to locate and get to the ultimate sampling unit, while it is comparatively easy and cheap to select and reach the first-stage unit.

To permit the calculation of unbiased estimates of means and standard errors, random selection of sampling units at all stages should be used. It would also be possible to select primary units such as forest compartments with probability proportional to their sizes and then choose secondary units on a random basis.

Frequent use is made of systematic selection in two-stage sampling (see Section 13-8.1). A common design employed in forest inventory utilizes randomly chosen primary sampling units with systematic selection of secondary units within them.

In two-stage sampling, m sampling units are selected from the M primary units of the population as a first stage. From each of the m units selected, n secondary units are then chosen from the population of N secondary units within each primary sampling unit. Note that if all M primary units are selected, the design is equivalent to stratified random sampling.

The most common cases encountered using two-stage sampling in forest inventory are:

1. Primary units of equal size containing equal numbers of secondary units of uniform size
2. Primary units of unequal sizes containing varying numbers of secondary units of uniform size
3. Primary units of unequal sizes containing varying numbers of secondary units of variable sizes

Case 3 occurs frequently in forest inventory since uniform-sized secondary units falling on forest or strata boundaries will be divided. The analysis requires the use of ratio estimation. Only case 1 is discussed here. The reader is referred to Freese (1962), Cochran (1977), and Shiver and Borders (1996) for analyses of cases when primary units are of unequal sizes. The formulas for estimates of the means, totals, and their variances are shown below.

Given M = total number of primary sampling units in population

N = number of secondary units per primary, equal for all primary units

m = number of primary units in sample

n = number of secondary units per primary in sample, equal for all primary units

X_{ij} = quantity (e.g., volume) measured on ith secondary unit in jth primary unit

$\bar{x}_j$ = estimate of mean of X for jth primary unit

$\hat{X}_j$ = estimate of total of X for jth primary unit

$\hat{X}$ = estimate of total of X for entire forest

$\bar{x}$ = estimate of mean of X for entire forest

$s_{\bar{x}}^2$ = estimate of variance of mean for entire forest

$s_{\hat{X}}^2$ = estimate of variance of total for entire forest

The estimate of the population mean is

$$\bar{x} = \frac{1}{mn} \sum_{j=1}^{m} \sum_{i=1}^{n} X_{ij} \qquad (13\text{-}48)$$

The estimate of the variance of the mean is

$$s_{\bar{x}}^2 = \left(1 - \frac{m}{M}\right) \frac{s_B^2}{m} + \left(1 - \frac{mn}{MN}\right) \frac{s_W^2}{mn} \qquad (13\text{-}49)$$

where s_B^2 = estimate of variance between means of secondary sampling units within primary units

s_W^2 = estimate of variance within groups of secondary sampling units

The values of s_B^2 and s_W^2 are found from

$$s_B^2 = \frac{\sum_{j=1}^{m} \left(\sum_{i=1}^{n} X_{ij}\right)^2 / n - \left(\sum_{j=1}^{m} \sum_{i=1}^{n} X_{ij}\right)^2 / nm}{m - 1} \qquad (13\text{-}50)$$

and

$$s_W^2 = \frac{\sum_{j=1}^{m} \sum_{i=1}^{n} X_{ij}^2 - \sum_{j=1}^{m} \left(\sum_{i=1}^{n} X_{ij}\right)^2 / n}{m(n - 1)} \qquad (13\text{-}51)$$

When the number of primary units in the population is large, the formula for the variance of the mean can be reduced to

$$s_{\bar{x}}^2 = \frac{s_B^2}{m} + \frac{s_W^2}{mn} \qquad (13\text{-}52)$$

Then

$$\hat{X}_j = \frac{N}{n}\sum_{i=1}^{n} X_{ij} \qquad (13\text{-}53)$$

$$\hat{X} = \frac{M}{m}\sum_{j=1}^{m} \hat{X}_j \qquad (13\text{-}54)$$

$$s_X^2 = M^2 N^2 s_{\bar{x}}^2 \qquad (13\text{-}55)$$

Estimates of the numbers of sampling units at the two stages can be made using

$$n = \sqrt{\frac{c_1}{c_2}\frac{s_W^2}{s_B^2}} \qquad (13\text{-}56)$$

where n = optimum number of secondary units per primary
        c_1 = cost of establishing primary unit
        c_2 = additional cost of establishing and measuring secondary unit
        s_W^2 and s_B^2 are estimates from preliminary sample

Then

$$m = \frac{t^2(s_B^2 + s_W^2/n)}{E^2 + (1/M)(s_B^2 + s_W^2/N)} \qquad (13\text{-}57)$$

or, for an infinite population

$$m = t^2 \frac{s_B^2 + s_W^2/n}{E^2} \qquad (13\text{-}58)$$

where m = number of primary units required for estimate of mean with given precision
      E = chosen allowable error in units of X
      t = Student's t for probability level chosen

We can estimate the number of primary units required to obtain optimum precision when we have a fixed total amount of money c available for the inventory. It is first necessary to estimate the optimum number of secondary units per primary as above. Then the number of primary units that should be taken is

$$m = \frac{c}{c_1 + nc_2} \tag{13-59}$$

13-7. DOUBLE SAMPLING

Double sampling is a form of multiphase sampling limited to two phases. In double sampling, an estimate of the principal variable is obtained by utilizing its relationship to a supplementary variable. The method is useful when information on the principal variable is costly and difficult to obtain, whereas the supplementary and related variable can be observed more easily and cheaply. The aim of double sampling is to reduce the number of measurements of the costly, principal variable without sacrificing the precision of the estimate.

The general procedure in double sampling is that in a first phase a large random sample is taken of the secondary or auxiliary variable X that will yield a precise estimate of its population mean or total. In a second phase, a random subsample is selected from the previous sample, and on these sampling units, measurements are taken of the principal variable Y. Note that the first and second phases are mutually dependent since the measurements in the second phase are taken from a portion of the sampling units of the first phase. Thus we have a small sample on which both the supplementary and principal variables, X and Y, have been measured. With these data, a regression can be developed between the two variables that can be utilized with the large sample of the auxiliary variable to make an estimate of the mean and total for the principal variable.

The relationship of Y and X may have one of numerous forms. For illustrative purposes, a simple linear relationship will be demonstrated. However, it is well to bear in mind that in many instances a curvilinear relationship may be required.

In double sampling, the corrected estimate is obtained from a regression of the form

$$\bar{y}_{reg} = \bar{y}_s + b(\bar{x}_l - \bar{x}_s) \tag{13-60}$$

where $\bar{y}_{reg}$ = regression estimate of mean of Y (principal variable) from double sampling

$\bar{y}_s$ = estimate of the mean of Y from second, small sample

$\bar{x}_l$ = estimate of mean of X (auxiliary variable) from first, large sample

$\bar{x}_s$ = estimate of mean of X from second, small sample

b = linear regression coefficient

n = number of sampling units in first, large sample

m = number of sampling units in second, small sample

The regression coefficient is calculated from

$$b = \frac{\sum_{i=1}^{m}(X_i - \bar{x}_s)(Y_i - \bar{y}_s)}{\sum_{i=1}^{m}(X_i - \bar{x}_s)^2} = \frac{\sum_{i=1}^{m} X_i Y_i - \sum_{i=1}^{m} X_i \sum_{i=1}^{m} Y_i / m}{\sum_{i=1}^{m} X_i^2 - \left(\sum_{i=1}^{m} X_i\right)^2 / m} \qquad (13\text{-}61)$$

where X_i = quantity X measured on ith sampling unit of second, small sample
Y_i = quantity Y measured on ith sampling unit of second, small sample

The estimate of the variance of the regression estimate is then

$$s_{\bar{y}_{reg}}^2 = \left[\frac{s_{y \cdot x}^2}{m} + \frac{s_{y \cdot x}^2 (\bar{x}_l - \bar{x}_s)^2}{\sum_{i=1}^{m}(X_i - \bar{x}_s)^2}\right]\left(1 - \frac{m}{n}\right) + \frac{s_{\bar{y}}^2}{n}\left(1 - \frac{n}{N}\right) \qquad (13\text{-}62)$$

N represents the total number of sampling units in the first phase of double sampling (large sample). Note that in eq. (13-62), $(1 - n/N)$ is the finite population correction factor that is dropped if the population is considered infinite or if n is small relative to N.
The values for insertion in the formula for the variance are calculated from

$$s_{y \cdot x}^2 = \frac{\sum_{i=1}^{m}(Y_i - \bar{y}_s)^2 - b^2 \sum_{i=1}^{m}(X_i - \bar{x}_s)^2}{m - 2} \qquad (13\text{-}63)$$

$$s_{\bar{y}}^2 = \frac{\sum_{i=1}^{m}(Y_i - \bar{y}_s)^2}{m - 1} = \frac{\sum_{i=1}^{m} Y_i^2 - \left(\sum_{i=1}^{m} Y_i\right)^2 / m}{m - 1} \qquad (13\text{-}64)$$

An example of double sampling in forest inventory is the procedure using a combination of aerial photographic estimation and field plots. The first phase of sampling consists of estimating the volumes on aerial photographs of a large number of relatively inexpensive sampling units employing photo-interpretation and measurement techniques. Thus, the supplementary variable X could be volume per acre from interpretation of photo plots. In the second phase, a subsample of these plots is selected and visited in the field for direct determination of their volumes. The estimates of the volumes per acre from field plots would be the observation of Y. This subsample is much smaller since field plots are more expensive than photo plots. A regression is then prepared between field-plot volumes and photo-plot volumes, permitting a corrected volume estimate to be made from the large inexpensive sample of the first phase.

Double sampling can also be carried out using ratio estimates, remembering that the ratio estimate is a conditioned regression in which the relationship between the two variables X and Y is such that a zero value of X means a zero value of Y.

13-8. NONRANDOM SAMPLING

Selective and systematic sampling are the two main applications of nonrandom sampling in forest inventory work. In selective sampling, an observer selects a sample of plots that appears to be representative of the forest and measures them. Selective sampling may give good approximations of population parameters, but it is not recommended. Because human choice is often prejudiced by individual opinion, selective sampling may result in bias. In addition, selected samples will not yield a measure of reliability of the estimate because probability theory is based on the laws of chance. Selective sampling was used in the pioneer days of North American forestry but is now rarely used or justified.

13-8.1   Systematic Sampling

In systematic sampling, the sampling units are spaced at fixed intervals throughout the population. Systematic sampling designs, which are widely used, have a number of advantages: They provide reliable estimates of population means and totals by spreading the sample over the entire population. They are usually faster and cheaper to execute than designs based on random sampling because the choice of sampling units is mechanical, eliminating the need for a random selection process. Travel between successive sampling units is easier since fixed directional bearings are followed, and the resulting travel time is usually less than that required for locating randomly selected units. The size of the population need not be known since units are chosen at a fixed interval after an initial point has been selected. In addition, mapping can be carried out concurrently on the ground since the field party traverses the area in a systematic grid pattern. In forest inventory work, the systematic distribution of sampling units can be used with fixed-area plots or strips, or points and lines in PPS sampling.

Since the units for a systematic sample are located at some regular interval, there will be a fixed set of possible samples. If a sampling interval k is chosen, there will be k possible samples. For the mean of a systematic sample to be unbiased, some form of random selection must be incorporated in the sampling process. The only randomization possible is the selection of one of the fixed sets of systematic samples. The set selected will depend on the selection of the initial sampling unit in the population.

The initial sampling unit can be randomly selected out of the entire population of units, or it may be randomly selected from the first k units in the population. In either case, once the first unit is selected, all following units will be selected at the interval k. Many forest inventories start a set of systematically distributed sampling units at some easily accessible, arbitrarily chosen point, assuming negligible bias in the resulting estimate of the mean.

13-8.2   Sampling Error for a Systematic Sampling Inventory

If the total population of sampling units in a forest were randomly distributed, exhibiting no pattern of variation, a systematic sample would be equivalent to a random sample, and the random sampling formulas would be applicable for estimating the sampling error. In biological populations, such as a forest, the components are rarely, if ever, arranged completely independent of each other but, instead, show a systematic or periodic variation from place to place. If sampling units are selected systematically, variation in the observed values may no longer be ascribable to randomness if the interval between sampling units happens to coincide with the pattern of population variation.

The larger the forest area inventoried, the greater the variation that can be expected and the more likelihood that a systematic sample will give a better estimate of the mean than a completely random sample. Even for a stratified population, a systematic sample will probably yield a better estimate of the mean if the strata are large and variable. As the homogeneity of the defined strata increases, the estimates from a random and systematic sample will tend to agree.

Fundamentally, the reason a systematic sample will not yield a valid estimate of the sampling error is that variance computations require a minimum of two randomly selected sampling units. A systematic sample (the entire set of units) consists of a single selection from the population. The sampling interval k divides the population in k clusters or sets of n sampling units, and then only one of these clusters constitutes the sample.

Various methods to approximate the sampling error of a systematic sample have been devised. The systematic sample of equidistant sampling units can be considered as a simple or nonstratified random sample and the sampling error computed as for a random sample. Osborne (1942) has shown that the sampling error computed in this way estimates the maximum sampling error, which may considerably overestimate the actual sampling error. Although a number of approximation procedures have been devised, there is no valid method of estimating the sampling error of a systematic sample.

Shiue (1960) proposed a method of systematic sampling that maintains the advantages of systematic sampling and also provides a reasonable means of estimating the sampling error. In this method several systematic samples are taken, with the initial sampling unit chosen randomly for each start. Using a line-plot procedure, the first sample of systematically located plots constitutes the first cluster. Another systematic sample would be the second cluster, and so on. Based on these clusters, estimates of the mean plot volume and its sampling error can be computed. To avoid a large t value and to maintain a small confidence interval for a given probability, at least five random starts should be used.

13-8.3   Systematic Strip Sampling

By using strips as the sampling unit, the systematic distribution is accomplished by first dividing the forest area into N strips of uniform size. Sampling units would then be taken at intervals of every kth strip to form the sample of n strips. Figure 13-5 shows a forest area divided into 50 strips of uniform length. The selection of n strips at a sampling interval of k strips can be carried out in two ways.

1. A random selection of a number from 1 to N can be made and the corresponding strip chosen as the initial sampling unit. Sampling units at the interval k are then taken in both directions from this initial strip. A practical way of carrying this out is to select some random number between 1 and N, divide by the interval k, and obtain the remainder of the division. This remainder will have the value between 1 and k. Then select the strip with this number as the first sampling unit. All subsequent strips at intervals of k are then selected.
2. Randomly select a number between 1 and k for the first strip. All subsequent strips are taken at intervals of k strips.

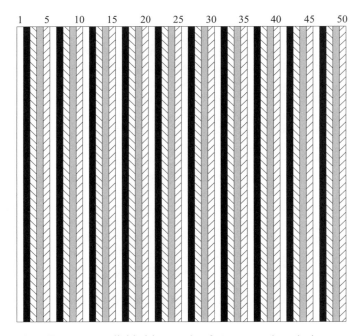

FIG. 13-5. Forest area divided into strips for systematic strip inventory.

Both procedures will yield the probable number of systematic samples. The first procedure will yield an unbiased estimate of the mean, whereas the second procedure may give a slightly biased result if the value of N is not an exact multiple of k. The first procedure should be used if possible. The second procedure, however, must be used if the size of the population is not known, as may occur in sampling a forest where no map is available.

Often, a forest is irregular in shape rather than square or rectangular. If the area is then divided into strips of equal width, the strips will differ in length and consequently in area. Thus the possible systematic samples that could be obtained by taking every kth strip may differ in size. Zenger (1964) has described a method that draws a systematic sample in such a way that the probability of selection of a strip is proportional to its length.

Applying strip sampling, the field party starts from a baseline, or one side of the tract, and runs a straight strip on a compass bearing across the tract stopping at the other side. The party then offsets the determined interval and runs back to the baseline or boundary. The procedure continues until all the strips in the sample have been measured. The measurements of the variables occurring on the strips are tallied and represent the sample of the entire forest. Separate tally sheets may be kept for different forest types or classes so that separate estimates may be made for them.

It is desirable to orient strips at right angles to the drainage pattern in order to increase the likelihood of having the strip intersect all stand conditions. In North America, the common width of strip is 1 chain (66 ft) or less. The width of the strip and the interval between strips determine the intensity or percentage of the total area tallied. The intensity of a systematic strip design is expressed by

$$P = \frac{W}{D} \tag{13-65}$$

where P = proportion of area covered by strips
        W = width of strip in given unit
        D = distance between strips in same units as W

Equation (13-65) is used principally to determine the spacing of strips when the cruise intensity and strip width are known. For example, if a 10 percent cruise ($P = 0.10$) is to be conducted with 1-chain-wide strips, the spacing of strips would be $D = W/P = 1/0.10 = 10$ chains.

The intensity of a systematic design using 1-chain-wide strips spaced at intervals of 10 chains is then $(1/10)100 = 10$ percent. For a given intensity, narrow strips at a closer spacing will give more uniform distribution and better coverage of the stand area than fewer strips that are wider but more distantly spaced, although the cost may be greater.

When all the strips are of equal size, the estimate of the population mean is often calculated from eq. (13-7) and the sampling error from eq. (13-9) under the assumption that the strips constitute a random sample.

When sampling units are not of equal size, as would occur in a strip sample of an irregular-shaped forest area, the ratio method of estimation can be used. Thus, an estimate of the area of each sampling unit X_i and the observation V_i, such as volume, on the units are required to obtain the ratio estimate as described in Section 13-3.1.

13-8.4   Systematic Plot Sampling

If sampling units such as plots or points are used, the sample is systematic in two dimensions—that is, the sampling units are selected at intervals in two directions normal to each other. The following discussion pertains to systematic sampling with fixed-area plots. A discussion of the distribution of sampling points is given in Section 14-1.

As with the strip method, there are a fixed number of possible samples that is determined by the sampling interval chosen. Figure 13-6, illustrating a systematic distribution of plots, shows a rectangular area made up of 60 vertical columns and 40 horizontal rows forming a population of 2400 fixed-area units. If we choose a sampling interval of $k = 10$ in each direction, there will be $(10)(10) = 100$ possible independent samples. The selection of sample plots at sampling interval k can be carried out in a manner analogous to those described for the strip method. The only difference is that there are two dimensions instead of one.

1. A random selection of a number from 1 to the total number of columns is first made. The same procedure is followed for a random selection of one of the rows. The two random numbers indicate the coordinates of the starting point of the grid.

2. Starting at one corner of the tract, a random selection is made from the first $k \times k$ grid. All subsequent sample plots are then taken at a consistent interval of k in both directions.

The more common case will be a forest of irregular shape as shown in Fig. 13-7. The first method of selecting a sample requires establishing an imaginary boundary to enclose the area completely. The initial unit can then be chosen in a fashion similar to that used for Fig. 13-6. Since the number of columns and rows are not exact multiples of the sampling interval, the size of the sample will vary depending on the initial point chosen and the shape of the tract. In this case 18 sample plots form the sample. By using the other method of selecting the sample, we can arbitrarily choose the lower left-hand corner of the tract and out of the first 10×10 squares randomly select one unit. All subsequent

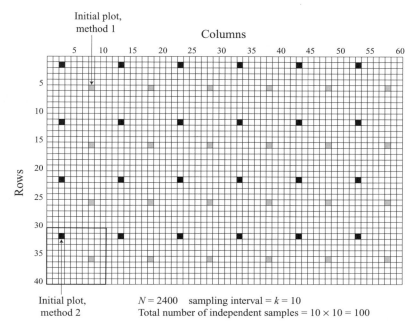

FIG. 13-6. Systematic distribution of equispaced plots for a forest inventory.

units will then be selected at the $k \times k$ interval (square-grid arrangement), resulting in $n = 17$.

When sampling units are spaced in a square-grid arrangement, the calculation of the desired statistics is often carried out as though the units were randomly chosen. Loetsch and Haller (1964) described a method for approximating the true standard error by taking the sum of the squared differences between successive sampling units of one of the two axes of the grid.

For practical reasons, the square-grid arrangement of sampling units is often dropped, resulting in the interval between lines being greater than between units. (If this modification is used with fixed-area plots, it is generally

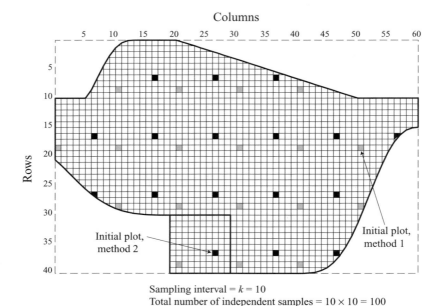

Sampling interval = k = 10
Total number of independent samples = 10 × 10 = 100

Methods for selecting systematic sample:
    1. By selecting random numbers, the initial plot is column 51, row 19.
        All subsequent plots are taken at intervals of 10 in both directions.
        The 18 sampling units are indicated by light shading.

    2. Choosing the lower left-hand 10 by 10 grid, the sampling unit at column
        26, row 37 is randomly selected. The 17 sampling units are indicated by
        dark shading.

FIG. 13-7. Systematic distribution of equispaced plots for forest inventory of irregularly shaped area.

called *line-plot sampling*. However, some foresters also consider the square-grid arrangement of plots as line-plot sampling.) Numerous possible line-plot distributions can be devised, depending on the size of the plot, the distance between plots on a line, and the distance between lines. A line-plot design can be drawn up using the following relationships:

$$n = \frac{AP}{a} \tag{13-66}$$

$$P = \frac{a}{D_l D_p} \tag{13-67}$$

$$P = \frac{a}{D^2} \tag{13-68}$$

where A = total stand area
$\quad\quad P$ = proportion of area covered by plots
$\quad\quad a$ = plot area in square units of D_l and D_p
$\quad\quad n$ = number of plots
$\quad\quad D_l$ = spacing of lines in given unit
$\quad\quad D_p$ = spacing of plots on lines in same units as D_l
$\quad\quad D$ = spacing of lines and of plots on lines for square-grid arrangement ($D_l = D_p$).

For a 5 percent cruise using 0.2-acre plots on lines spaced 10 chains apart, the spacing of plots on the lines is

$$D_p = \frac{a}{D_l P} = \frac{10(0.2)}{10(0.05)} = 4 \text{ chains}$$

(The 10 in the numerator converts acres to square chains: 1 acre = 10 square chains.)

The design for the 10 chain × 4 chain arrangement is shown in Fig. 13-8. For a 5 percent cruise using 0.2-acre plots set out in a square-grid arrangement, the spacing D would be

$$D = \sqrt{\frac{a}{p}} = \sqrt{\frac{10(0.2)}{0.05}} = 6.32 \text{ chains}$$

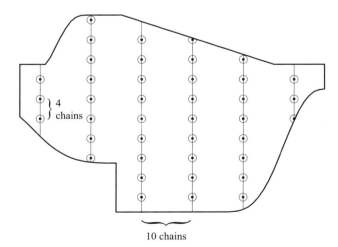

FIG. 13-8. Five percent line plot inventory using 0.2-acre plots spaced 4 chains apart on lines 10 chains apart.

13-9. REPEATED SAMPLING IN FOREST INVENTORY

Repeated sampling (or sampling on successive occasions) in forest inventory has three objectives:

1. To estimate quantities and characteristics of the forest present at the first inventory
2. To estimate quantities and characteristics of the forest present at the second inventory
3. To estimate the changes in the forest during the intervening period

The repetitive process can be continued and, on the occasion of all subsequent inventories, the previous inventory becomes the first and the new inventory becomes the second. Repeated sampling can be carried out in any of the four ways illustrated in Fig. 13-9, as described in the following sections. Of the four approaches, the third—successive sampling with partial replacement—is the most efficient.

13-9.1   New Sample Drawn at Each Inventory

As shown in Fig. 13-9a, sampling units at occasion 2 are different from those at occasion 1. The means, totals, and standard errors would be calculated separately as described in Section 13-2. The estimation of the change or growth would be the difference in the means for the two inventories. The estimate of the variance of this difference s_d^2 is

$$s_d^2 = \frac{s_x^2}{n_1} + \frac{s_y^2}{n_2} \tag{13-69}$$

where s_x^2 = variance at first inventory
             s_y^2 = variance at second inventory
n_1 and n_2 = number of sampling units at first and second inventories

13-9.2   Same Sample Remeasured on Succeeding Occasions

The sampling units measured at the first inventory are remeasured at the second and all succeeding inventories, as shown in Fig. 13-9b. This is the concept of permanent sample plots and the basis of the Continuous Forest Inventory (CFI) developed in North America. The estimates of the means, totals, and standard errors at each inventory would again be found as in the case of the two separate inventories. Similarly, the differences between the means for each inventory would indicate the changes in the forest. However, since the same sampling units are taken on both occasions, the standard error of the difference would be calculated for paired plots as

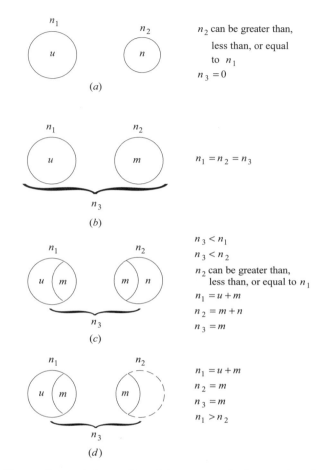

FIG. 13-9. Types of repeated sampling: (*a*) new sample drawn at each occasion; (*b*) same sample remeasured on succeeding occasions; (*c*) successive sampling with partial replacement; (*d*) second sample a subsample of the first. n_1, sample at first inventory; n_2, sample at second inventory; n_3, m sampling units measured at both inventories (matched); u, sampling units measured only at first inventory (unmatched); n, sampling units measured only at second inventory (unmatched).

$$s_d^2 = \frac{s_x^2 + s_y^2 - 2r_{xy}s_xs_y}{n} \tag{13-70}$$

The greater the correlation as expressed by r_{xy} between X and Y, measurements at the first and second inventories, the greater the reduction in the variance. The correlation can be expected to be large for short periods.

However, Hool and Beers (1964) demonstrated that the correlation might remain surprisingly high, even for a 15-year remeasurement interval.

13-9.3   Successive Sampling with Partial Replacement

At the second inventory, a portion of the initial sampling units is remeasured and new ones are measured, as shown in Fig. 13-9c. A detailed account of the development and application of this procedure to forest inventory is given by Ware and Cunia (1962), Cunia (1965), and Frayer (1966). Only a brief summary is presented here. The reader is referred to these references for an explanation of the statistical theory.

At the initial and second inventories, there are three kinds of sampling units (Fig. 13-9c)

u = sampling units measured only at the first inventory

m = sampling units measured at the first and second inventories

n = sampling units measured only at the second inventory

From observations on these sampling units, the quantities present at each inventory and the change or growth over the period can be calculated. Estimates at the initial inventory utilize data from all the u and m units measured. From the m units a relationship can be established between sampling unit quantities found at the initial and second inventories. A regression can then be determined and used to estimate the quantities of the u units at the second inventory and the quantities of the n units as they were at the initial inventory. As a result, there are quantity estimates for all units, some from direct measurement and others from a regression. The value of this procedure is that quantity and growth or change estimates and their variances are obtained from all units, both temporary and permanent.

13-9.4   Sample at Second Inventory: Subsample of the First

At the second inventory, a portion of the sampling units measured at the first inventory is remeasured, as shown in Fig. 13-9d. The estimate of the mean at the first inventory uses the data from the u and m units. At the second inventory, measurements are made only on the m units. From these m units a relationship is again established between the quantities found on units measured at both the first and second inventories. The mean volume at the second inventory is then determined using the data from the n_1 units in a regression based on this relationship.

The growth or change over the inventory period is expressed as the difference between the overall mean at the initial inventory and the regression estimate for the second inventory.

14

INVENTORY USING SAMPLING WITH VARYING PROBABILITY

The sample designs discussed in Chapter 13 are generally applicable to inventories using variable probability. There are, however, several issues unique to sampling with variable probability. In this chapter we focus on these issues.

Three types of variable probability sampling are widely used in forest inventory applications:

1. *Sampling with probability proportional to size (PPS sampling)*. The most frequent application of PPS sampling is horizontal point sampling. Sampling units and basic theory associated with horizontal point sampling are presented in Section 11-3. In this chapter, issues involved with designing and implementing an inventory using horizontal point samples are discussed.

2. *List sampling*. In list sampling, the probability of selecting an individual is proportional to some listed quality associated with the individual. List sampling requires complete enumeration of groups of individuals prior to sample selection. List sampling is similar to cluster sampling and is often discussed in this context in traditional sampling texts.

3. *Sampling with probability proportional to prediction (3P sampling)*. 3P sampling, a term peculiar to forestry literature, is similar to list sampling. 3P sampling does not require a complete enumeration of individuals (or groups) prior to sampling, although each individual (or group) is eventually examined for some attribute.

14-1. HORIZONTAL POINT SAMPLING

In this application, a series of sampling points is chosen, much as one would select plot centers for fixed-area plots (Chapter 13). The observer occupies each sampling point, sights with an angle gauge at breast height on every tree visible from the point and tallies all trees that are greater than the projected angle of the gauge. An estimate of the basal area per unit land area is then the number of trees counted times the basal area factor, as described in Chapter 11.

Any variable associated with the trees selected may be measured, just as in the case of fixed-area plots. These variables are then scaled to per unit area values by multiplying the value of the attribute by the tree factor (Section 11-1). The unique feature of horizontal point sampling is that no tree measurements are needed to obtain an unbiased estimate of basal area per unit land area. This feature arises because, in horizontal point sampling, tree selection is proportional to tree basal area, which leads to the tree factor being inversely proportional to tree basal area:

$$TF_i = \frac{BAF}{BA_i}$$

where BAF = basal area factor of the angle gauge [eq. (11-12) or (11-13)]
     BA_i = tree basal area

Thus, when tree basal area (BA_i) is multiplied by TF_i, a constant is obtained.

14-1.1   Angle Gauges for Horizontal Point Sampling[*]

For horizontal point sampling one needs an angle gauge that will accurately project a small horizontal angle, generally under 5°. A tree that appears larger than the projected angle is considered "in" and a tree that appears smaller than the projected angle is considered "out" (Fig. 11-6). Basically, there are two different ways of projecting the angle:

1. By prolonging two lines of sight from the eye through two points whose lateral separation w is fixed, both of which are in the same horizontal plane and both of which are at the same fixed distance L from the eye (Fig. 14-1a).
2. By deviating the light rays from the tree through a fixed angle (Fig. 14-1b).

---

[*]For vertical point or vertical line sampling, one needs an angle gauge that will accurately "project" a large vertical angle (±40°). A tree that appears larger than the projected angle is considered *in*, and a tree that appears smaller than the projected angle is considered *out*. For additional discussion of vertical angle gauges and their use, see Husch et al. (1982).

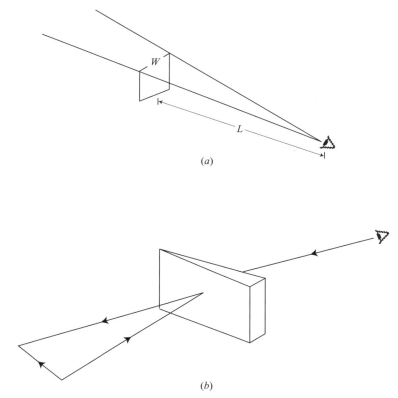

FIG. 14-1. Projecting a horizontal angle (*a*) by prolonging two lines of sight, and (*b*) by deviating the light rays through a fixed angle.

Types of Instruments. Instruments based on the first principle include the stick-type angle gauge and the Spiegel relaskop. To construct a stick-type angle gauge, a device that clearly illustrates the principle behind all of these instruments, one simply provides a stick with a peep sight to position the eye and a cross-arm of predetermined width which is placed on the stick at a predetermined distance from the peep sight (Fig. 14-1*a*). To determine the width of the cross-arm one must know the gauge constant k for the basal area factor BAF to be used, and make a decision on the stick length L. Then cross-arm width will be $w = kL$. A stick-type angle gauge used to estimate canopy cover is illustrated in Fig. 10-5.

The Spiegel relaskop (Fig. 5-7) uses the same basic principle. Instead of using a stick on which to position the cross-arm, the Spiegel relaskop utilizes the principle of the reflector sight to image the scale (cross-arm) that is on a wheel only a short distance from the eye, at a suitable viewing distance. The Spiegel relaskop is available in both English and metric scales. In the English scale, sighting angles for BAF values of 5, 10, 20, and 40 ft^2/acre are provided.

The instrument corrects automatically for slope (Section 14-1.6) and is easy to use. It is relatively expensive (approximately US$1200), and sighting visibility is generally poor in low-light conditions.

Simple angle gauges can also be stamped from lightweight metal. Two examples of the shapes commonly used are shown in Fig. 14-2. These gauges are held a fixed distance L from the eye and the width of the metal or the opening in the metal creates the angle projection. Usually, these gauges come with a chain of length L attached. The end of the chain is held next to the user's eye and the chain pulled tight to ensure that the viewing distance is constant.

The thin prism or optical wedge is the only instrument of the second type that has been used by foresters (Fig. 14-1b). Briefly, a *prism* is a device made of optical glass or plastic in which the two surfaces are inclined at some angle A (the refraction angle) so that the deviation produced by the first surface is increased further by the second. The chromatic dispersion is also increased. However, chromatic dispersion is not a cause of appreciable error unless a telescopic device is used in conjunction with the prism. The cruising prisms that foresters have used in horizontal point sampling generally have a refracting angle of less than $6°$. Such prisms are made in square, rectangular, and round shapes.

Figure 14-3a illustrates the projection of a fixed angle with a thin prism. As shown in the figure, the ray that is tangent to points a, b, and c on the sides of the tree to the observer's right is refracted to E. Thus, when observers at E sight through the prism to points a, b, and c, they will see these points as if they were at a', b', and c'. Of course, all visible points on each tree cross section will be displaced so that each cross section will appear to be displaced as shown in the figure. To use the prism as a gauge, the observer looks *through* the prism at the right side of the trees—that is, at points a, b, and c and, at the same time *over* the prism at the left side of the trees on the line of sight to I. One observes

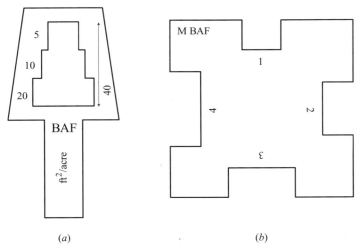

(a)   (b)

FIG. 14-2. (a) Angle gauge; (b) metric relaskop.

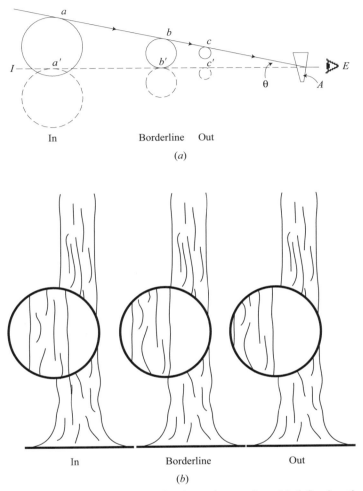

FIG. 14-3. Representation of image deflection using a prism: (*a*) deflection through the cross section of prism and trees; (*b*) deflection as seen by the observer when using a round prism.

if the right side is, or is not, refracted past the left side. The actual "picture" that will be obtained when a round prism is used is shown in Fig. 14-3*b*. Similar pictures are obtained with rectangular prisms.

Prism Calibration. Prisms for use in forest inventories are available as calibrated or noncalibrated. Although the latter are generally less expensive than calibrated prisms, they are more likely to deviate from the stated prism factor. In either case, checking or initial calibration (i.e., determination of BAF, the basal area factor) is imperative before fieldwork begins.

Precise techniques for prism calibration have been described by Beers and Miller (1964) using a collimator and by Stage (1962) using a projector and screen. However, since many situations may not warrant this precision, the following procedure, illustrated in Fig. 14-4, is commonly used:

1. A flat "target" of width w is placed at some distance from the observer holding the prism.
2. The observer moves the prism toward or away from the target until the perpendicular line of sight to the target results in the completely offset picture, obtained when one side of the target seen over the prism precisely lines up with the other side seen through the prism.
3. The perpendicular distance B from the prism to the target is measured carefully in the same units as the target width.
4. The gauge angle θ is then calculated or determined from a table of trigonometric functions since

$$\tan \theta = \frac{w}{B} \tag{14-1}$$

$$\theta = \arctan \frac{w}{B} \tag{14-2}$$

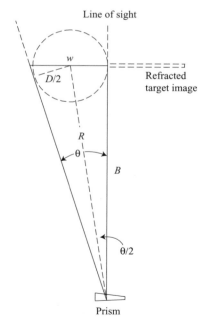

FIG. 14-4. Geometry of prism calibration. Target of width w located at distance B, which will provide the "completely offset" picture. Dashed lines pertain to a hypothetical borderline tree located properly in the generated gauge angle θ.

5. The gauge constant k is then determined from the formula

$$k = 2\sin\frac{\theta}{2} \qquad (14\text{-}3)$$

The basal area factor BAF is determined using eq. (11-12) for English units or eq. (11-13) for metric units. Miller and Beers (1975) give additional details regarding prisms and their calibrations.

14-1.2   Sample Size

In horizontal point sampling, the sampling is performed *with replacement.*[*] (This is contrary to fixed-area plot sampling, which is usually perceived as *sampling without replacement.*) Thus it can be assumed that sampling is being performed in a population that is infinite. Furthermore, the sample units (points or lines) are in a sense without area. This implies that the area of the sample has little meaning, that correction for sampling a finite population is not appropriate, and that the total area of the population has no direct effect on the calculation of sample size. Consequently, for most situations the following formula can be used to determine the number of points to visit:

$$n = \frac{t^2(\mathrm{CV}^2)}{E^2} \qquad (14\text{-}4)$$

where $n =$ number of points required for desired precision E, with probability level implied by value of t
         $t =$ Student's t
    $\mathrm{CV} =$ coefficient of variation (in percent) for forest to be sampled
      $E =$ allowable error or desired precision (in percent) for average volume (or basal area, etc.)

If prior experience or previous data are not available for the value of the coefficient of variation, preliminary inventories might be necessary to establish reasonable approximations. However, when small forest areas are sampled [100 acres: (40 hectares) or less] impractical results may be obtained if the formula is used. For example, for a 40-acre tract where the coefficient of variation is expected to be approximately 70 percent and a desired precision

---

[*]Since horizontal point sampling is based on sampling with replacement, any tree in the forest population may qualify and be tallied from two or more sample points. Provided that the points have been chosen in an unbiased manner, tallying a qualifying tree from two such locations will cause no bias in subsequent estimates of mean stand parameters. In fact, failure to do so will result in biased estimates. If the occurrence of such double-tally trees is high, however, excessive sampling is probably present and the inventory should be modified either by reducing the number of points (increasing spacing if systematic sampling is used), increasing the angle gauge, or both.

of 10 percent is required at the 0.95 probability level ($t \approx 2$), the substitution into the formula leads to

$$n = \frac{(2)^2(70)^2}{10^2} = 196 \text{ points}$$

Locating 196 sample points in a 40-acre woods is unnecessarily intensive. One should note that forest area does not appear in the formula used and that such a problem does not exist when dealing with fixed-area plot sampling, since sampling is performed from a *finite* population, and a correction factor involving forest area is part of the appropriate formula to determine number of plots.

To circumvent these impractical results for small areas, various approaches have been proposed (Shiver and Borders, 1996; Avery and Burkhart, 2002). Often, the procedure is to determine how many fixed-area plots of certain size might be required and then to locate somewhat more (or less) sample points depending on local experience regarding comparative accuracy of plots versus points.

Another approach involves use of a rule of thumb to facilitate the decision. For example, the following has provided reasonable results in the mixed hardwood forests of central United States.

If Area in Acres Is:	Number of Points
Less than 10	10
11–40	1 per acre
41–80	20 + 0.5(area in acres)
81–200	40 + 0.25(area in acres)
Over 200	Found from eq. (14-4)

14-1.3   Choosing a Suitable Gauge Constant

The choice of an appropriate gauge constant for horizontal point sampling is influenced primarily by the nature of the stands to be sampled, and secondarily by the objectives and conduct of the inventory. The choice is frequently based on local experience and other general guidelines, such as: For small trees and open stands, use a small gauge constant; for large trees and dense stands, use a large gauge constant. Since small trees do not always occur in open stands and large trees do not always occur in dense stands, a compromise frequently must be made after assessing both average tree size and stand density. As discussed in Section 11-5, a more definitive approach is first to determine the average number of trees m we wish to tally per location, then after estimating the average stand basal area (in the case of horizontal point sampling), find the basal area factor by division:

$$BAF = \frac{BA/unit\ area}{m}$$

After the basal area factor is determined, the corresponding gauge constant and gauge angle can be calculated as discussed in Section 11-3.1.

Experience has shown that the desired average tree count per sample location should be between 6 and 16. The choice of the desired average number of sample trees is somewhat arbitrary. However, several general concepts must be considered before making a decision about a suitable gauge constant.

1. For small average tree counts there exists a great likelihood of getting many small individual counts (say, less than 5), and conversely, for large average tree counts the likelihood is great for getting large individual counts (say, more than 20).

2. Small or large tree counts can lead to inefficient samples. For very small counts, the forest is *undersampled* and the inventory is economically inefficient since the at-location costs are frequently much less than the between-location costs. Therefore, measuring a few more trees at a location might materially increase the overall statistical precision but not affect cost materially. For very large tree counts the forest is *oversampled* since once a certain level of statistical precision is reached, the precision will be increased negligibly by measurement of additional trees. Then the measurement of additional trees is a waste of time.

3. Estimates of forest parameters may be biased if tree counts are very high. This is the case due to the increased possibility of overlooking borderline trees that qualify as sample trees and the increased difficulty in viewing tree stems. There also is a tendency to be less careful when there are many trees to be scrutinized.

4. In regard to low tree counts, the effect of a mistaken action will lead to a much larger bias (in percentage) than when the tree count is high.

5. In deciding what gauge constant to use, one should remember that the gauge constant, gauge angle, and basal area factor all vary inversely to the expected tree count. Therefore, for horizontal point sampling a large basal area factor implies small tree counts, and a small basal area factor implies large tree counts.

14-1.4   Proper Use of Gauges

Basic to the field application of horizontal point sampling is the requirement that once the necessary factors or constants are developed, there exists a precise method for determining whether a given tree qualifies as a sample tree (i.e., whether it is "in" or "out"). In fixed-area plot sampling, an occasional tree must be checked for inclusion in the plot by lying off the plot radius or plot width. Similarly, in horizontal point or line sampling, an occasional tree will be questionable and must be checked; the plot radius is not fixed for all trees as it is for fixed-area plot sampling. It depends on tree diameter and often requires that questionable trees be checked.

When using a stick-type angle gauge, the Spiegel relaskop, or the angle gauges illustrated in Fig. 14-2, the angle generated has its vertex at the eye of the user; therefore, the user must stand over the sample point so that the angle vertex is positioned vertically above the point. Detailed directions for using the Spiegel relaskop are provided by the manufacturer.

Since the wedge prism is often misused, certain precautions should be observed. Once the observer occupies the sampling point or location, the prism must be positioned properly before each tree is sighted critically; otherwise, bias is likely to occur. The following rules should be followed:

1. Since the gauge angle originates with the prism, the prism must be held vertically above the sample point when sighting; this implies that the observer (not the prism) moves in a small circle about the point.
2. Each tree is sighted at breast height through and over the prism.
3. The line of sight should be perpendicular to the prism bisector (i.e., the plane bisecting the refracting angle of the prism).
4. The distance from the eye to the prism is immaterial provided that a clear picture is obtained. Ten inches (±25 cm) is the normal viewing distance.

With the prism vertically above the designated sampling point, the prism bisector can be oriented perpendicular to the line of sight by the following technique. If the prism is properly oriented at right angles to the line of sight:

- A rotation of the prism in the vertical plane perpendicular to the line of sight will *reduce* the amount of horizontal deflection of the tree (i.e., make the images overlap more).
- A rotation of the prism by "tipping" or "swinging" will *increase* the amount of horizontal deflection of the tree (i.e., make the images overlap less).

The four positions of the prism (unrotated, rotated, tipped, and swung) are shown in Fig. 14-5. The use of prisms or angle gauges for the other forms of PPS sampling are found in Husch et al. (1982).

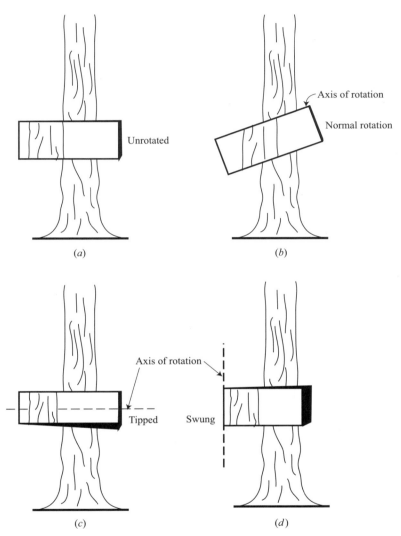

FIG. 14-5. Effect of prism rotation on the amount of horizontal deflection: (*a*) prism in unrotated position on a borderline tree; (*b*) prism rotated in the vertical plane perpendicular to the line of sight—reduced horizontal deflection; (*c*) prism tipped in the vertical plane parallel to the line of sight—increased horizontal deflection; (*d*) prism swung in the horizontal plane—increased horizontal deflection.

14-1.5   Checking Questionable Trees

Any tree that is questionably "in" or "out" (i.e., borderline—Fig. 14-3) as determined by the angle gauge should be measured for dbh and the plot radius (or plot half-width) associated with the tree calculated by multiplying the diameter by the diameter:plot radius ratios in Table 11-3 or by using the horizontal distance multipliers [eqs. (11-14) or (11-15)]. For example (using English units), if the basal area factor BAF is 10.0,

$$\mathrm{HDM} = \frac{33\sqrt{10}}{12\sqrt{10}} = 2.75$$

A 10-in. tree would then have an associated plot radius of 27.5 ft. If the measured horizontal distance to the center of a questionable tree is greater than the plot radius calculated, the tree is "out"; otherwise, it is "in." A table showing plot radii by dbh classes can be prepared. A more efficient method of checking questionable trees makes use of a specially calibrated tape as described by Beers and Miller (1964). Diameters are marked on the tape at the appropriate plot radius for the basal area factor being used, thus avoiding table references or calculations.

14-1.6   Slope Correction

Since the determination of forest stand parameters is on a horizontal land area basis, the projected angle must be corrected if the terrain is not level. Specifically, the gauge constant k must be reduced to a value k_r, where $k_r = k \cos S$, and where S is the slope angle in degrees.

For stick angle gauges based on the principle of projecting a horizontal angle by prolonging two lines of sight as in Fig. 14-1, slope correction can be achieved by reducing the cross-arm width w to the value w_r where $w_r = w \cos S$, or by increasing stick length L to the value L_r, where $L_r = L/\cos S$. The Spiegel relaskop uses an ingenious method of varying cross-arm width. It has a "strip" scale that varies in width directly as the cosine of the slope angle. This scale, mounted on a weighted wheel, is seen "projected" on the target (the tree) and rotates by gravity to the appropriate position as the line of sight is raised or lowered.

Slope correction can be achieved when the wedge prism is used by rotating the prism in a plane perpendicular to the line of sight through an angle equal to the slope angle. Such rotation properly reduces the gauge angle.[*] Instead of making instrument adjustments, a simple procedure for correcting for slope is to measure the dbh of questionable trees and determine the horizontal distance (correcting slope distance using the slope angle) from the observation point to the tree center. If this horizontal distance to the center of the questionable tree is greater than the calculated plot radius, the tree is "out"; otherwise, it is "in."

---

[*]See Husch et al. (1982) for a more detailed discussion of various other methods for correcting for slope.

14-1.7 Leaning and Hidden Trees

Moderate tree lean has little effect on the field procedure. If, however, a tree leans severely to the right or left of the observer and appears to be "just in," a corrected gauge picture should be obtained. This is accomplished by rotating the angle gauge so that the vertical axis of the gauge parallels the axis of the leaning tree. Thus, if a prism is used, the sides of the prism should parallel the sides of the tree; if a stick-type gauge is used, the sides of the blade should parallel the tree sides; if a Spiegel relaskop is used, the sides of the instrument should parallel the tree sides.

A leaning tree that appears "out" with the unrotated gauge need not be checked, since the adjustment described above will lead to a further separation of the actual and refracted image. When a leaning tree is viewed with an unrotated prism, the effective gauge angle is reduced, and rotation of the prism is necessary to obtain the full angle.

On questionable trees and those that lean severely toward or away from the observer, a tape check, as described earlier, should be made. When this is done, the tree center is commonly assumed to be a point vertically above the center of the tree cross section at the ground line.

In dense or brush-choked stands, precautions are necessary to avoid missing or double-counting trees. Trees hidden behind other trees can be detected by swaying from side to side after each obvious tree is examined. There is no error associated with viewing trees from another point as long as the distance from the tree to the observer remains the same as the original distance to the sampling point. Moving from the sample point is also warranted if trees are close enough together that two or more stems are superimposed while being viewed with the angle gauge.

When limbs or underbrush blocks the breast-height point, one can check a visible point higher on the stem for qualification. If a tree qualifies for inclusion at some point above breast height, it will qualify at breast height, unless the tree leans toward the observer and the distance is critical. In any of the situations above, a tape check should be made if a tree is questionable.

14-1.8 Volume Estimation

Volume per unit area can be estimated from horizontal point data using a number of methods. As described in Section 11-3.2, average volume/tree can be estimated for each diameter class and volume per unit area for each diameter class obtained by multiplying trees per unit area and volume per tree:

$$(\text{volume per unit area})_i = (\text{trees per unit area})_i \cdot (\text{volume per tree})_i$$

An estimate of volume per unit area for the stand or point is obtained by summing the volumes per unit area for each diameter class. A mathematically equivalent method is to calculate the volume factor (Section 11-1) for each diameter class:

$$VF_i = TF_i \cdot V_i = \frac{BAF}{BA_i} V_i = \frac{BAF}{cD_i^2} V_i \qquad (14\text{-}5)$$

where VF_i = volume factor for ith dbh class
$\quad TF_i$ = tree factor for ith dbh class
$\quad V_i$ = average volume per tree for ith dbh class
$\quad D_i$ = midpoint diameter of ith dbh class
$\quad c$ = cross-sectional area conversion factor (0.005 454 for English units and 0.000 078 54 for metric units)

Volume per unit area for each diameter class is then obtained from

$$(\text{volume per unit area})_i = \frac{\text{no. trees tallied}_i}{\text{no. points}} VF_i$$

and the total for the stand or point is obtained by summing the values for each dbh class.

The *volume/basal area ratio approach* is an alternative to calculating volume factors or volume per unit area by diameter class. The ratios are obtained by dividing volume estimates from a volume table or equation by basal area:

$$VR_{i,H} = \frac{V_{i,H}}{BA_i} \qquad (14\text{-}6)$$

where $VR_{i,H}$ = volume/basal area ratio for ith dbh class and height H
$\quad V_{i,H}$ = volume per tree for ith dbh class and height H
$\quad BA_i$ = basal area of midpoint of ith dbh class

For example, the volume of a 16-in., two-log (16-ft logs) red oak based on Table 6-7 is 155 board feet. The basal area for a 16-in. tree is $0.00\,5454(16)^2 = 1.396\,\text{ft}^2$. The volume/basal area ratio is then $155/1.396 = 111$ board feet/ft^2. By dividing all entries in a volume table by the associated basal area, a volume/basal area ratio table is derived. Table 14-1 is an example of such a table based on a portion of Table 6-7.

Trees are tallied by dbh and height class and volume per unit area is obtained using

$$\text{volume per unit area} = \frac{\sum_{i=1}^{m} VR_i}{m}(BA) \qquad (14\text{-}7)$$

where VR_i = volume/basal area ratio of ith tree tallied
$\quad m$ = number of trees tallied
$\quad BA$ = basal area per unit area ($BA = m \cdot BAF/n$, where n = number of points)

TABLE 14-1. Board-Foot Volume per Unit Basal Area[a]

Dbh (in.)	Merchantable Height in 16-ft Logs			
	1	2	3	4
12	53	110	166	223
14	54	110	167	223
16	55	111	167	223
18	83	139	195	252
20	83	139	196	252

[a]Based on volumes shown in Table 6-7.

By substituting the formula for basal area per unit area into eq. (14-7), an alternative formula for volume per unit area is derived:

$$\text{volume per unit area} = \frac{\sum_{i=1}^{m} \text{VR}_i}{m} \frac{m \cdot \text{BAF}}{n} = \frac{\sum_{i=1}^{m} \text{VR}_i}{n} \text{BAF} \qquad (14\text{-}8)$$

While the volume/basal area ratio is a valid approach, the computational ease of the factor approach and its adaptability to any form of PPS makes it the preferred method.

A third and extremely powerful method of estimating volume per unit area is *diameter obviation* (Beers, 1964). From eq. (14-5), it is noted that the volume factor can be written as

$$\text{VF}_i = \frac{\text{BAF}}{cD_i^2} V_i$$

If volume per tree V_i can be estimated using a constant form factor equation, $V_i = bD_i^2 H$, the volume factor becomes

$$\text{VF}_i = \frac{\text{BAF}}{cD_i^2} bD_i^2 H_i = \frac{b \cdot \text{BAF}}{c} H_i \qquad (14\text{-}9)$$

where VF_i = volume factor for ith tree (or dbh class)
$\quad D_i$ = dbh of ith tree
$\quad H_i$ = height of ith tree
$\quad b$ = constant form factor
$\quad c$ = cross-sectional area conversion factor

Volume per unit area is then estimated using

$$\text{volume per unit area} = \frac{1}{n} \sum_{i=1}^{m} \left(\frac{b \cdot \text{BAF}}{c} H_i \right) = \frac{b \cdot \text{BAF}}{cn} \sum_{i=1}^{m} H_i \qquad (14\text{-}10)$$

where m = number of tree tallied
n = number of points

From eq. (14-10), it can be seen that volume is estimated from the sum of the height tally and diameter measurements are not required: thus the name *diameter obviation*. Furthermore, since $\overline{H} = \sum H/m$ and $\sum H = m\overline{H}$, eq. (14-10) becomes

$$\text{volume per unit area} = \frac{b \cdot \text{BAF}}{cn} m\overline{H}$$

$$= \frac{b}{c}\frac{m\text{BAF}}{n}\overline{H}$$

$$= \frac{b}{c}(\text{BA per unit area})\,\overline{H}$$

Thus, an estimate of volume can be achieved by estimating basal area per unit area and average height. Since basal area per unit area is estimated directly, horizontal point samples provide an efficient system for estimating volume per unit area when constant form factors can be used. The accuracy of this method depends on the applicability of the assumption of constant form factor. For cubic volume estimation, this is generally a sound assumption.

14-2. LIST SAMPLING

List sampling with varying probabilities can be applied where the listed items are individual elements having different sizes, or where the listed items are clusters having different numbers of elements, or some other appropriate expression of size. In the usual forestry context, we can think of individual trees as the elements, and compartments or stands as clusters. This type of variable probability sampling applied to individual listed trees is usually impractical, because of the necessity of listing each element prior to sampling. Therefore, we discuss the technique for compartments (clusters of trees) having varying but known areas.

The sampling method is carried out first by listing the compartments in any order, along with their measure of size, say area. A sample size is decided on, and sampling is performed in such a way as to give the larger compartments greater chance of being selected. The compartments selected are then visited and measurements are taken on the variable of interest. The analysis of the data, shown subsequently, yields unbiased estimates of means, totals, and their variances, as long as sampling is performed with replacement (i.e., once chosen, a compartment is "put back" in the population and can be drawn again). In application, sampling is often without replacement; in this case, bias (often negligible) in the variance estimate will be incurred if eq. (14-12) is used.

To illustrate the procedure, consider a forest made up of compartments having areas designated by X_i. We want to choose n compartments with selection probability proportional to X_i and measure the variable Y_i on each of the chosen compartments. We must first list the compartments as shown in Table 14-2, obtaining a column of cumulative areas in the process. It is also helpful to show a column of associated numbers that indicates the set of consecutive integers from the one above the previous cumulative total to, and including, the cumulative total of the compartment in question.

If we decide that $n = 5$, five random numbers are appropriately drawn from the range of integers 1 through 419, the total area of the compartments. A compartment is chosen as part of the sample if the random number falls within the interval indicated in the column of associated numbers. Thus, the following might be chosen.

Random Numbers Drawn	Compartments Chosen
153	7
52	3
414	12
283	11
177	8

TABLE 14-2. **List of Compartments and Individual and Cumulative Areas for Use in List Sampling with Varying Probabilities**

Compartment	Area, X_i (acres)	Cumulative Total of X_i	Associated Numbers
1	25	25	1–25
2	10	35	26–35
3	30	65	36–65
4	28	93	66–93
5	15	108	94–108
6	30	138	109–138
7	38	176	139–176
8	51	227	177–227
9	40	267	228–267
10	12	279	268–279
11	60	339	280–339
12	80	419	340–419
Total	419		

After the compartments are visited and measurements are made regarding the variables of interest Y_i, the estimate of the mean value of Y per unit area is

$$\bar{r} = \frac{1}{n}\sum_{i=1}^{n}\frac{Y_i}{X_i}$$

$$= \frac{1}{n}\sum_{i=1}^{n}r_i \qquad\qquad (14\text{-}11)$$

where Y_i = quantity measured on ith compartment (e.g., total compartment volume)

   X_i = size of ith compartment (e.g., compartment area)

   n = number of compartments chosen

   $\bar{r}$ = mean value of Y per unit value of X (e.g., mean volume per unit area)

   r_i = ratio of Y_i to X_i

The variance of $\bar{r}$ can be estimated from

$$s_{\bar{r}}^2 = \frac{\sum_{i=1}^{n}r_i^2 - \left(\sum_{i=1}^{n}r_i\right)^2/n}{n(n-1)} \qquad\qquad (14\text{-}12)$$

The estimate of the total Y for the population then is

$$\hat{y} = \bar{r}X \qquad\qquad (14\text{-}13)$$

with estimated variance

$$s_{\hat{y}}^2 = s_{\bar{r}}^2 X^2 \qquad\qquad (14\text{-}14)$$

where $\hat{y}$ = estimate of total of Y

   X = total of X_i in population

Instead of a complete tally within each compartment as implied above, a more practical procedure would be to take a subsample of secondary sampling units within each of the compartments chosen. This practice implies a two-stage sampling, with secondary sampling units chosen from primary units of unequal size. Although formulas for estimating means are straightforward, those estimating the variance are complex. Reference should be made to sources such as Cochran (1977) and Shiver and Borders (1996) for details.

List sampling with varying probabilities has been used in other forestry applications. For example, Scott (1979) described its use for midcycle updating of permanent inventory plots. The initial plot volumes were used as the listed item from which a sample of n plots was chosen for remeasurement to obtain an estimate of current volume.

14-3. 3P SAMPLING

The necessity of listing the units prior to sampling acts as a severe deterrent to list sampling in many forestry applications, especially those where individual trees are the potentially listed items. Grosenbaugh (1963b), making use of a principle similar to that proposed by Lahiri (1951) to overcome the prior listing requirement, proposed a type of sampling that utilizes the PPS concept, but the element of size considered in his original application was the timber cruiser's on-the-spot estimate of tree volume. The name used by Grosenbaugh for this technique is *sampling with probability proportional to prediction* or *3P sampling*.

The purpose of the present treatment of 3P sampling is to make the reader aware of the general concept and application of the method. For details, reference should be made to the works of Grosenbaugh (1963b, 1964, 1965, 1967, 1979), Mesavage (1971), Bell and Dilworth (1993), and Schreuder et al. (1993). This type of sampling has been applied to timber sales where each tree in the population (all marked trees) is assessed for a crude prediction of volume or value, and a subsample of these trees is selected for more detailed measurements. For this purpose it appears to be very efficient.

Before listing the steps in a simplified application of 3P sampling, it is worthwhile to explain the basic sampling concept that leads to the name *probability proportional to prediction*. The analogy given by Mesavage (1965) is convenient for this purpose. "[S]uppose we have 20 cards numbered one to twenty. If we stipulate that the predicted volume of a sample tree must be equal to or greater than the number on a card subsequently drawn at random, a tree with a prediction of 1 would have only 1 chance in 20 to qualify [as a sample tree to be carefully measured for volume], whereas one with a predicted volume of 15 would have 15 chances in 20. The probability of selection is thus seen to be proportional to prediction."

The steps in conducting a 3P sampling for the purpose of estimating the total volume of timber marked for sale might be as follows:

1. Designate a sample size n, the number of trees to be carefully measured for volume. This can be done using the minimum-sample-size formula for simple random sampling [eq. (13-14)], assuming an infinite population and noting that the coefficient-of-variation figure used should be based on the ratios of actual to estimated tree volume (defined in step 8). This value is typically somewhat smaller than the usual coefficient of variation based on tree volume, which partially explains the usual high efficiency of 3P sampling. Alternatively, for sample size determination, one can make use of a crude guide such as that suggested by Mesavage (1965) for a large timber sale—for trained cruisers, 100 or so trees are usually sufficient for an accuracy of 1.5 percent, and for inexperienced cruisers, approximately 200 trees are needed to achieve the same accuracy. It is worth noting here that it is the consistency (precision) of the cruiser's estimates that leads to high accuracy using 3P, and individual

or volume table bias is of little consequence. Thus the experienced cruiser, although possibly biased, is probably less erratic in estimates than
the beginner and, therefore, is likely to have a more efficient sample.

2. Estimate the sum of volumes for the N trees making up the sale. Thus

$$\hat{x} = \text{estimated} \sum_{i=1}^{N} X_i$$

where X_i = cruiser's estimate of tree volume (this can also be an entry
from a volume table utilizing the cruiser's estimate or measurement of tree diameter and possibly height)

Note that X, the actual sum of estimated volumes, is known only after
the inventory is completed.

3. Designate the maximum individual tree volume expected as K. Thus

$$K = \text{maximum } X_i$$

K, then, is used as the upper limit of the set of integers running from 1
through K, which will act as the means by which each tree will be
checked for qualification as a sample tree to be measured in detail.

4. Adjust the set of integers to ensure that you obtain close to the sample
size desired. That is, define

$$n' = \frac{\hat{x}}{K + Z} \qquad (14\text{-}15)$$

where n' = expected sample size
$\hat{x}$ = estimate of total volume of all trees
Z = number of "rejection symbols" to be randomly mixed with
the set of integers 1 through K

Thus, if we decide on $n' = 200$, and if $\hat{x} = 240{,}000$ board feet and maximum tree volume $K = 1000$ board feet, Z must be 200; otherwise, we
would probably obtain 240 sample trees rather than the desired 200.
Obviously, eq. (14-15) can be solved for Z to streamline the calculations.
In designing a bias-free 3P inventory, it is also worth following the
guidelines suggested by Grosenbaugh (1963b) and cited by Johnson
(1972), as summarized here:

a. $n'K$ must be less than $\hat{x}$
b. $(Z/K)^2$ must be greater than $(4/n') - (4/N)$, where N equals the
anticipated total number of trees in the timber sale.

5. Visit each of the N trees comprising the sale. At each tree follow this
procedure:

a. Estimate directly or indirectly, using a volume table, the tree volume
(or value) of X_i.

b. Record the estimate.

c. Draw a number (or symbol) at random from the set of integers 1 through K having the Z interspersed rejection symbols. A device invented and described by Mesavage (1967) facilitates this operation.

6. If the volume estimate X_i is greater than or equal to the random integer, measure the tree for accurate volume determination. This volume is then recorded as Y_i, the actual volume of the ith tree.

7. If the volume estimate X_i is less than the random integer, or if instead of a number, a rejection symbol is drawn, nothing more is required from the tree and the crew moves on to the next marked or to-be-marked tree.

8. After completion of the inventory, the total volume of the N marked trees can be estimated from the formula

$$\hat{y} = X \frac{\sum_{i=1}^{n}(Y_i/X_i)}{n} = X \frac{\sum_{i=1}^{n} R_i}{n} \qquad (14\text{-}16)$$

where $X = \sum_{i=1}^{N} X_i$ and $R_i = Y_i/X_i$
n = number of sample trees on which Y_i has been measured

In summary, the estimated total marked volume is equal to the sum of the estimates of tree volumes obtained from the complete population, times the average ratio of actual to estimated volume that is obtained from the n sample trees. At the completion of the inventory one should have approximately the sample size n' originally prescribed, but minor variations are possible because of vagaries associated with random numbers in the selection procedure.

9. The variance of the estimate $\hat{y}$ can be estimated, although it was pointed out by Ware (1967) that no exact expression exists for the true variance. The following approximation cited in Grosenbaugh's early work on 3P sampling has most often been applied, perhaps because as shown it is the same as that used for simple random sampling:

$$s_{\hat{y}}^2 = \frac{\sum_{i=1}^{n}[(Y_i X/X_i) - \hat{y}]^2}{n(n-1)}$$

$$= \frac{X^2}{n} s_R^2 = X^2 s_{\overline{R}}^2 \qquad (14\text{-}17)$$

where s_R^2 = variance of ratios Y_i/X_i
$\quad = \sum(R_i - \overline{R})^2/(n-1)$
$s_{\overline{R}}^2$ = square of standard error of ratios
$\quad = s_R^2/n$

Schreuder et al. (1993) describe an inventory procedure called *point-3P* or *point-Poisson* for estimating total stand volume. This method combines point or variable plot sampling with estimated or predicted height of the trees selected in the horizontal point sampling phase. The estimated height of these trees is then compared with a paired number from a random number list. If the random number is less than or equal to the estimated height, that tree becomes a sample and is measured by any of the various dendrometer instruments to compute its volume. Schreuder et al. (1993) show that the total stand volume can readily be computed from

$$\hat{Y}_{pp} = \frac{A \cdot \text{BAF} \cdot H_0}{km} \sum_{i=1}^{m} \frac{y_i}{g_i h_i} \tag{14-18}$$

where A = total area being sampled
          BAF = basal area factor used in horizontal point sampling
$H_0 = \sum_{i=1}^{n} h_0 i$ = sum of estimated heights of n first-stage trees (i.e., those counted as "in" by point sampling)
          k = number of first-stage point samples
          m = actual number of selected trees measured
y_i and g_i = volume and basal area of ith tree

The computation of variance is rather complicated for this estimate.

15

GROWTH OF THE TREE

Tree growth consists of elongation and thickening of roots, stems, and branches. Growth causes trees to change in weight and volume (size) and in form (shape). Linear growth of all parts of a tree results from activities of the primary meristem; diameter growth from the activities of the secondary meristem, or cambium, which produces new wood and bark between the old wood and bark. Total and merchantable height growth, diameter growth at breast height, and diameter growth at points up the stem are elements of tree growth traditionally measured by mensurationists; from these elements, volume or weight growth of sections of the stem, or the entire stem, may be determined. Changes in roots, branches, and crown dimensions, such as crown length, crown width, and height to the base of the crown, are also measured in many situations.

Tree growth is influenced by the genetic capabilities of a species interacting with the environment. Environmental influences include *climatic factors* (air temperature, precipitation, wind, and insolation); *soil factors* (physical and chemical characteristics, moisture, and microorganisms); *topographic characteristics* (slope, elevation, and aspect); and *competition* (influence of other trees, lesser vegetation, and animals). The sum of all these environmental factors is expressed as site quality (Section 8-7). Competition depends on stand structure (Chapter 8) and is somewhat transient since it can be modified by silvicultural treatments. Thus, site quality is generally assessed on dominant trees that have been free of competition for much of their life. When a site has favorable growing conditions, it is considered "good." When a site has unfavorable growing conditions, it is considered "poor." Because species respond differently to various environmental conditions, site quality must be considered by individual species. Extremes exist that provide absolute limits for all species, as exemplified by timberlines on mountains and in polar regions. But since site quality is an effect best expressed by the average reaction of the trees on an area of land, it is more readily measured for stands than for individual trees. Measures of site quality were discussed in Chapter 8.

The increase in a tree (or stand) dimension should be qualified by the period of time during which the increment occurred. The period may be a day, a month, a year, a decade, and so on. When the period is a year, the increase, termed *current annual increment* (c.a.i,), is the difference between the dimensions measured at the beginning and at the end of the year's growth. Since it is difficult to measure some characteristics, such as volume, for a single year, the average annual growth for a period of years, termed *periodic annual increment* (p.a.i.), is often used in place of c.a.i. This is found by obtaining the difference between the dimensions measured at the beginning and at the end of the period, say 5 or 10 years, and dividing by the number of years in the period. If the difference is not divided by the number of years, it is termed *periodic increment*. The average annual increase to any age, termed *mean annual increment* (m.a.i.), is found by dividing the cumulative size by the age.

These increment measures are applicable to individual trees (or stands) for any measurable growth characteristic. However, they have been most commonly applied to the volume growth of stands.

15-1. GROWTH CURVES

When the size of an organism (e.g., volume, weight, diameter, or height for a tree) is plotted over its age, the curve so defined is commonly called the *growth curve* (Fig. 15-1a). Such curves, characteristically S- or sigmoid-shaped, show the cumulative size at any age. Thus they are more descriptively termed *cumulative growth curves*. A true growth curve, which shows increment at any age, results from plotting increment over age (Fig. 15-1b).

The S-shaped form of the cumulative growth curve is evident for individual cells, tissues, and organs, and for individual plants and animals for the full life span. Also, the pattern of growth for short growing periods, such as a growing season, tends to follow the S-shaped curve.

Although the exact form of the cumulative growth curve will change when the tree dimension (height, diameter, basal area, volume, or weight) plotted over age is changed, the cumulative growth curve has characteristics that hold for all dimensions of a tree. With this in mind, an insight into tree growth can be obtained by studying Fig. 15-1a and the derived curves in Fig. 15-1b and c. During youth, the growth rate increases rapidly to a maximum at the point of inflection in the cumulative growth curve, and the acceleration first increases and then drops to zero at the point of inflection in the cumulative growth curve. During maturity and senescence, the growth rate decreases with related changes in acceleration.

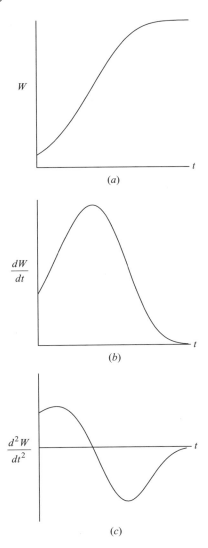

FIG. 15-1. Curve of (*a*) cumulative growth; (*b*) growth rate; and (*c*) growth acceleration. *W*, size; *t*, age.

Curves of current annual increment, periodic annual increment, and mean annual increment may also be derived from a cumulative growth curve by computing increments from sizes read from the cumulative growth curve at chosen ages and by plotting the increments over age. Figure 15-2 shows curves of p.a.i. and m.a.i. derived from a cumulative height growth curve. From Fig. 15-2 we can see that m.a.i. culminates when it equals p.a.i. (this is also true when m.a.i. equals c.a.i.). A formal proof of this could be given, but the reason

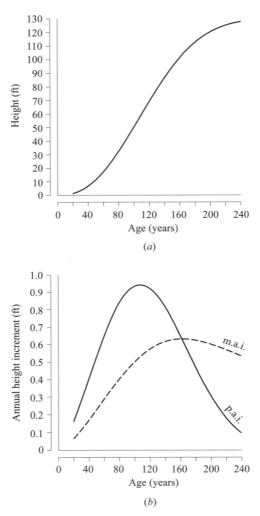

FIG. 15-2. (*a*) Cumulative height growth curve; (*b*) curves of periodic annual height growth (p.a.i.) and mean annual height growth (m.a.i.); p.a.i. and m.a.i. curves derived from cumulative height growth curve.

is obvious; m.a.i. will lag behind p.a.i. if it is smaller than p.a.i. When p.a.i. drops below m.a.i., m.a.i. must decrease; it therefore reaches its maximum when equal to p.a.i. If cumulative growth is expressible as an equation, c.a.i. can be determined analytically by taking the first derivative.

Finally, when working with growth curves, one should realize that each species, perhaps each tree, matures at its own rate. This physiological time varies from one tree species to another and from one stage of development to another. In a sense, then, it is true that a 20-year-old aspen is older (physiologically) than a 20-year-old Douglas-fir because the aspen develops more rapidly than the Douglas-fir.

15-2. HEIGHT AND DIAMETER GROWTH

A cumulative growth curve of height over age for trees shows a juvenile period of less than a decade, a long maturing period when the trend is nearly linear, and a leveling off in old age. A cumulative growth curve of diameter over age shows much the same trend: there is, however, more of a tendency toward curvilinearity during the period of maturity. Since diameter is usually measured at breast height, dbh cannot be measured until a tree is over 4.5 ft tall. Consequently, since some of the early growth is before measurement begins, curves of dbh over age may not reflect early growth patterns.

Past height and diameter growth of individual trees may be determined (1) from repeated measurements of total size at the beginning and at the end of specified growing periods, and (2) from increment measurements of past growth.

15-2.1 Repeated Measurements

Height growth of an individual tree can be obtained by measuring the total (or merchantable) height of a standing tree at the initiation and at the cessation of a specified growing period and by taking the difference. Tree heights up to 75 ft (23 m) can be determined accurately and precisely with telescopic measuring poles that can be purchased from forestry and engineering supply companies. However, for measuring heights over 30 ft, poles are slow and cumbersome; then it is more convenient to use a transit or some precise tripod-mounted instrument that gives height indirectly.

Repeated measurements of trees with mechanical handheld hypsometers (Fig. 5-14) generally do not give sufficiently precise increment measurements. The newer electronic hypsometers (Fig. 5-15) produce height estimates that are extremely precise and repeatable (Skovsgaard et al., 1998). However, these devices tend to underestimate total height in many situations. If the error from these tools is consistent across the range of heights, precise estimates of increment can be obtained from the differences in estimated heights from two periods; however, if the error varies with height, the increment estimates will not be reliable.

Diameter growth of an individual tree can be obtained by measuring the diameter at the beginning and end of a specified period and by taking the difference. Since annual diameter increment is small, when instruments such as calipers and diameter tapes are used, measurements are commonly taken at intervals of several years.

Precise measurement of minute increments in diameter may be required in research. Such changes, which may be for periods as short as an hour, cannot be detected with calipers or diameter tapes. Consequently, dendrometer bands, dial-gauge micrometers, recording dendrographs, and transducers are used to measure minute changes. Dendrometer bands, as described by Liming (1957), Bower and Blocker (1966), and Yocom (1970), consist of aluminum or zinc bands with vernier scales. The band is placed around the stem of a tree and held taut with a spring. Changes in diameter as small as 0.001 in. can be read. Another band dendrometer is the Dial Dendro (Relaskop-Technik, no date). This requires fixing a support bracket to the stem and then a steel strap is hooked onto the level or a dial disk. The instrument can measure changes as small as 0.1 mm.

Reineke (1932) first described a dial-gauge micrometer. This instrument utilized a stationary reference point, a hook screwed into the xylem. The micrometer measures the distance from this fixed point to a metal contact glued to the bark. Changes in diameter as small as 0.001 in. can be read. Daubenmire (1945) modified this instrument by inserting three screws into the xylem as the fixed reference point.

Fritts and Fritts (1955) devised a precision dendrograph. The instrument consists of a pen on an arm bearing on a fixed point on the tree stem. The pen records diameter changes to 0.001 in. on a chart mounted on a drum of an eight-day clock. Phipps and Gilbert (1960) designed an electrically operated dendrograph similar in principle to the dial-gauge micrometer. A potentiometer was fixed to a tree by screws anchored in the xylem. A movable shaft was fixed to the outer bark; any displacement of the shaft was measured by a change in electrical resistance and recorded on a continuous strip chart. Imprens and Schalck (1965) used a variable differential transformer rather than a potentiometer in a similar instrument.

Kinerson (1973) designed a transducer that uses a linear motion potentiometer fixed to an invar plate. When the device is fixed to a tree stem, changes in the stem diameter move the potentiometer shaft.

15-2.2   Increment Measurements

Increment measurements of past height growth can be made quickly if a reference point is marked on a tree or on a pole by the tree. Past increment for intervals during a growing season, for a growing season, or for a specified period may be measured from the reference point. Past height increment may be determined using stem analysis (Section 15-4). For species in which the internodal lengths on the stem indicate a year's growth, past height growth may be determined by measuring these distances (Fig. 5-1)

In regions where tree growth has a seasonal or annual growth pattern, past diameter increment can be obtained from increment borings or cross-sectional cuts (Figs. 5-1 and 5-2). Borings or cross sections can be secured at any point along the stem. However, diameter increment is most often determined at breast height from increment borings. When dealing with high-quality trees, it may be advisable to bore at stump height to eliminate damage to the butt log. In Section 15-3 we discuss the determination of diameter growth from increment cores.

15-3. DETERMINATION OF DIAMETER GROWTH FROM INCREMENT CORES*

Diameter growth is normally desired at breast height. Although most increment borings are made at breast height, diameter increment determined at stump height may be converted to diameter increment at breast height because the relationship between diameter at breast height D and diameter at stump height D_s, for most species or species groups may be expressed by the simple linear regression equation

$$D = a + bD_s$$

Thus diameter increment outside bark at breast height ΔD may be obtained from diameter increment at stump height ΔD_s, as follows:

$$D + \Delta D = a + b(D_s + \Delta D_s)$$

and

$$\Delta D = a + b(D_s + \Delta D_s) - D$$

By substituting $a + bD_s$ for D,

$$\Delta D = a + b(D_s + \Delta D_s) - (a + bD_s)$$

and by simplifying, we obtain

$$\Delta D = b\Delta D_s$$

Therefore, if the diameter growth at stump height for an individual tree is multiplied by the slope coefficient b of D over D_s for the appropriate species or species group, one obtains diameter increment at breast height outside bark.

Increment borings should be taken from trees on sample plots or sample points. For example, if we used $\frac{1}{5}$-acre plots on a cruise, we might establish $\frac{1}{20}$-acre plots within selected $\frac{1}{5}$-acre plots (say, one in four) and bore trees on the $\frac{1}{20}$-acre plots. If we used horizontal point sampling (using BAF = 10), we might use a 40-factor gauge at selected points to choose trees to bore. For each

---

*In this section D = diameter outside bark, and d = diameter inside bark.

species or species group studied, a reliable estimate of average diameter increment by diameter classes can be obtained from a representative sample of
about 100 increment measurements.

A word of warning: Boring one, two, or any predetermined number of trees
per plot, rather than sampling, as explained earlier, will result in an overestimation of growth because in open stands the sample will represent a larger
proportion of the trees than in dense stands—trees in open stands grow faster
than trees in dense stands.

A form for recording the field data is shown in Table 15-1. This table
indicates the recommended degree of accuracy for measurements and calculations. Generally, only columns 1, 2, 3, 4, and 6 are completed in the field.

The constant K, the average ratio of diameter outside bark to diameter
inside bark, is the inverse of the ratio used to calculate bark volume (Section
6-1.4). Thus the equation of the straight line expressing diameter outside bark
D as a function of diameter inside bark d is

$$D = Kd$$

K varies by species and, to some extent, by locality.

Average values of K are calculated as follows:

$$K = \frac{\sum D}{\sum d} \tag{15-1}$$

Thus, for the trees listed in Table 15-1, $K = 1.10$. The calculations for columns
5, 7, and 10 in Table 15-1 are self-explanatory. To calculate column 8 (i.e., past
diameter at breast height outside bark D_p), past diameter at breast height inside
bark d_p is multiplied by K [eq. (15-1)]. To calculate column 9 (i.e., periodic
diameter increment outside bark ΔD), the past 10 years' radial wood growth L
is doubled and multiplied by K because, if in a given period, $2L$ inches of wood
are laid on a given past diameter inside bark d_p, in terms of present diameter
inside bark d, past diameter inside bark will be

$$d_p = d - 2L$$

and

$$2L = d - d_p$$

If in a given period ΔD inches of wood and bark are laid on a given past
diameter outside bark D_p, in terms of present diameter outside bark D, past
diameter outside bark will be

$$D_p = D - \Delta D \tag{15-2}$$

TABLE 15-1. Determination of Diameter Increment from Increment Cores (in.)[a]

[1] Tree No.	[2] Species	[3] Present dbh o.b., D	[4] Double Bark Thickness, $2b$	[5] Present dbh i.b., d	[6] Past 10 Years' Radial Wood Growth, L	[7] Past dbh i.b., d_p	[8] Past dbh o.b., D_p	[9] Periodic dbh o.b. Increment, ΔD	[10] Periodic Annual dbh o.b. Increment, $\Delta D/10$
1	Hard maple	16.2	1.4	14.8	1.32	12.2	13.4	2.90	0.290
2	Hard maple	12.6	1.1	11.5	0.75	10.0	11.0	1.65	0.165
3	Hard maple	10.4	1.0	9.4	0.80	7.8	8.6	1.76	0.176
4	Hard maple	12.2	1.1	11.1	1.08	8.9	9.8	2.38	0.238
⋮	Hard maple	⋮				⋮	⋮	⋮	⋮
100	Hard maple		1.6	16.2	1.04	14.1	15.5	2.29	
Total		1285.0	117.0	1168.0	98.70	970.6	1068.0	217.14	21.714
Average		12.85	1.17	11.68	0.987	9.71	10.68	2.171	0.2171

[a] Data are normally averaged by diameter classes. Averages for columns 5, 7, 8, 9, and 10 can be computed from the averages for columns 3, 4, and 6, and the constant K, without computing the individual values in the columns. $K = 1285/1168 = 1.10$, $d = D - 2b$, $d_p = d - 2L$, $D_p = K(d_p)$, $\Delta D = K(2L)$.

and

$$\Delta D = D - D_p$$
$$= K(d) - K(d_p)$$
$$= K(d - d_p)$$
$$= K(2L) \qquad\qquad (15\text{-}3)$$

When the data are presented as shown in Table 15-1, it is convenient to plot periodic growth or periodic annual diameter growth over present diameter outside bark, or over past diameter outside bark, and thus obtain average diameter growth by diameter classes. When a straight line can represent the relationship, it can easily be fitted by the method of least squares. However, if the trend is curvilinear, Mawson (1982) demonstrated that the following non-linear model could be used to predict diameter growth ΔD from diameter at breast height:

$$\Delta D = b_0 e^{b_1/D} \qquad\qquad (15\text{-}4)$$

where b_0 and b_1 = regression constants
e = base of natural logarithms
D = dbh outside bark

Equation (15-4) can be transformed into a linear equation using the natural logarithm and fitted using linear regression techniques:

$$\ln \Delta D = \ln a + b\frac{1}{D} \qquad\qquad (15\text{-}5)$$

Other useful equations for modeling diameter growth are discussed in Vanclay (1994).

Whether one plots diameter growth over present diameter outside bark or over past diameter outside bark, the final growth determinations will generally be about the same. The second alternative, which assumes that trees of a given diameter will have the same average diameter growth that trees of that diameter had in the past, is preferred to the first alternative, which assumes that future average diameter growth will equal past average diameter growth.

15-4. STEM ANALYSIS

A record of the past growth of a tree may be obtained by a stem analysis. Such a study shows how a tree grew in height and diameter and how it changed in form as it increased in size. In making a stem analysis, one counts and measures the growth rings on stem cross sections at different heights above the ground. Measurements may be taken on a standing tree by using an increment borer, if the tree is not too big or the wood too hard. It is more convenient and more accurate, however, to obtain the measurements from cut cross sections.

The procedure for making a stem analysis on cut cross sections is simple:

1. Fell the tree and cut stem into sections of desired lengths.
2. Determine and record species, dbh, total height, years to attain stump height, and total age.
3. Measure and record the height of the stump, length of each section, and length of tip.
4. Measure and record the average diameter at the top of each section.
5. If only one radius is measured, the average radius should be used. The average radius should be located on each cross section and marked with a line along it with a soft pencil. In many cases, it is desirable to measure more than one radius because of stem eccentricity. For example, the longest and shortest radii or two radii at right angles might be measured. Each radius to be measured should be located and marked with a line using a soft pencil.
6. Along each radius, count the annual rings from the cambium inward, marking the beginning of each ring at the desired interval (e.g., every year, every fifth year, every tenth year). Record the total number of rings at each cross section.
7. From the center of each cross section, measure outward toward the cambium along each radius, recording the distance from the center to each interval. The fractional part of a decade, or other desired period, will be measured and recorded first. The radii on each disk can be averaged using the arithmetic mean or geometric mean (Section 3-3).

Table 15-2 shows how the measurements should be recorded, and Table 15-3 how the height measurements should be summarized.

In making the stem analysis (Fig. 15-3), the first step is to draw a curve of *height* aboveground of section tops over years to attain height at section tops (i.e., *age*) from data in Table 15-3. (This curve appears on the left side of the graph in Fig. 15-3.) Next, diameters for each section (i.e., double the radial measurements) are plotted for the appropriate height from data in Table 15-2 (e.g., the seven radial measurements for section 2 are doubled and plotted at 2.37 m). Finally, diameters within a year (or age) column are connected to form the taper curves for specific years (or ages); the terminal position of each taper curve is estimated from the curve of height over age. For a detailed description of stem analysis methods and data analysis and interpretation, see Duff and Nolan (1953, 1957, 1958) and Forward and Nolan (1961).

TABLE 15-2. Measurements for Stem Analysis of a 39-Year-Old Western Hemlock

Species: Western hemlock
Years to attain base height: 2
Date: November 15, 1990

dbh: 27.8 cm

Total height: 18.5 m
Total age: 39
Measured by: JAK

Section No.	Length (m)	Top dib (cm)	No. of Rings at Top	Average Radial Distance from Pith to Ring Corresponding to nth Year (mm)[a]							
				1955	1960	1965	1970	1975	1980	1985	1990
base	0.37	25.4	37	3	12	29	46	57	73	105	127
1	1.00	25.3	35	0	8	26	45	59	76	107	126
2	1.00	24.6	31	0	1	14	38	54	72	104	123
3	1.00	23.4	29	0	0	7	31	49	68	98	117
4	1.00	22.9	26	0	0	1	23	46	66	97	115
5	1.00	22.3	24	0	0	0	13	35	60	91	111
6	1.00	20.6	23	0	0	0	8	30	51	83	103
7	1.00	19.6	21	0	0	0	2	20	44	77	98
8	1.00	18.0	19	0	0	0	0	13	38	69	90
9	1.00	16.2	18	0	0	0	0	6	29	58	81
10	1.00	15.1	16	0	0	0	0	2	22	51	76
11	1.00	12.0	14	0	0	0	0	0	11	37	60
12	1.00	9.7	12	0	0	0	0	0	2	26	49
13	1.00	7.5	9	0	0	0	0	0	0	14	37
14	1.00	5.4	7	0	0	0	0	0	0	5	27
15	1.00	3.6	6	0	0	0	0	0	0	1	18
16	1.00	2.2	4	0	0	0	0	0	0	0	11
tip	2.16	0.0	0	0	0	0	0	0	0	0	0

[a]Average radius = the geometric mean of the longest and shortest radii; values are doubled to give average diameter when plotting taper curves.

TABLE 15-3. Height Summary for Stem Analysis of a 39-Year-Old Western Hemlock

Section No.	Length (m)	Height above Ground at Top of Section (m)	Ring Count, Top of Section	Years to Grow Section	Years to Attain Height at Top of Section
base	0.37	0.37	37	2	2
1	1.00	1.37	35	2	4
2	1.00	2.37	31	4	8
3	1.00	3.37	29	2	10
4	1.00	4.37	26	3	13
5	1.00	5.37	24	2	15
6	1.00	6.37	23	1	16
7	1.00	7.37	21	2	18
8	1.00	8.37	19	2	20
9	1.00	9.37	18	1	21
10	1.00	10.37	16	2	23
11	1.00	11.37	14	2	25
12	1.00	12.37	12	2	27
13	1.00	13.37	9	3	30
14	1.00	14.37	7	2	32
15	1.00	15.37	6	1	33
16	1.00	16.37	4	2	35
tip	2.16	18.53	0	4	39

15-5. AREAL AND VOLUME GROWTH

Basal area and bole surface area growth (areal growth) and volume (or weight) growth may also be of interest. Although the cumulative growth curves for both areal and volume growth are typically S-shaped, the exact form of the curves is variable. Basal area growth may be estimated from periodic measurements of dbh. Bole surface area growth may be estimated by calculating surface area from periodic measurements of stem diameters at predetermined intervals along the stem. Volume growth, the most important growth determination, may be estimated by taking periodic measurements of dbh; dbh and height; or dbh, height, and form and determining volumes at the beginning and at the end of a period from a local, standard, or form-class volume table as appropriate, and then taking the difference.

Stem analysis may be used to obtain the required measurements and the methods described above and in Section 6-1.1 used. For example, using Smalian's formula [eq. (6-5)] the volume for the tree shown in Table 15-2 was determined to be $0.401\,m^3$ ($14.2\,ft^3$) at age 39 and $0.106\,m^3$ ($3.7\,ft^3$) at

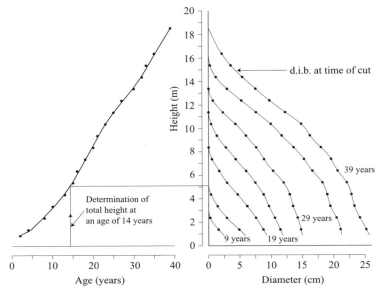

FIG. 15-3. Stem analysis for 39-year-old western hemlock; taper curves at 5-year intervals.

age 29; thus the 10-year volume growth is 0.295 m³ (10.3 ft³) and the average annual growth for this period is 0.03 m³/yr (1.0 ft³/yr).

Baker (1960) called attention to the following simple formula for rapid field computation of current annual volume increment of individual trees, which states that

$$\Delta V = \frac{\text{DHW}}{100} = \frac{\text{DH}}{100\text{RI}} \tag{15-6}$$

where ΔV = current annual increment (ft³)
D = diameter at breast height inside bark (in.)
H = total height (ft)
W = width of last ring at breast height (in.)
RI = rings per inch (based on latest period of growth)

This formula is useful to determine the trees that are growing well and those that should be removed or freed from excessive competition.

Board feet or cords are not good measures of volume growth because of fundamental limitations (see Chapter 9). Thus, growth estimates in board feet or cords are best made by converting cubic volume growth estimates into these units. Although weight growth has not traditionally received much attention, procedures for estimation of weight growth are not difficult. Weight and volume increments of trees are almost parallel in their patterns. Therefore, procedures for weight growth estimation are analogous to procedures for volume growth estimation.

15-6. EFFECTS OF ENVIRONMENTAL FACTORS ON GROWTH

The environmental factors that affect the growth of trees may be stable or transient. *Stable factors*—soil texture, slope, aspect, and soil nutrient level—do not change appreciably during the life of a tree. *Transient factors*—fluctuations in climate and competition among organisms—change cyclically or erratically during the life of a tree.

If past growth is used as a basis for growth predictions, it is important to recognize the magnitude of the effect of transient factors. When cutting alters stand competition, growth will be affected; the changes for a given time are readily related to the cutting. At the same time, climatic variations may also affect growth. These fluctuations, however, are not so recognizable and are not easy to segregate from the total growth response. Yet it may be necessary to estimate and evaluate the growth variation due to climatic changes. For example, if the effect on a tree or stand of a release cutting were under investigation, the periodic volume growth before and after the cutting could be used as a measure of the growth response, except that part of the response may be the result of variation in climate as well as a decrease in competition.

An adjustment can be made when it is necessary to eliminate the effect of climatic variations on growth. H. A. Meyer (1942) devised a procedure for adjusting diameter growth to eliminate these effects. This procedure consists of plotting annual increments for individual trees, or averages for several trees, over time and fitting a trend line to the points. The deviations from the trend line for individual years can then be expressed as percentages of the trend line values and are assumed related to changes in weather conditions. Thus growth estimates for a period of years may be increased or decreased by the magnitude of the average percent deviation for the period. Since the variation in growth due to climate decreases as the length of the growth period increases, most growth measurements are made for periods of 5 or more years. Dendrochronologists have developed several more sophisticated methods for identifying climatic effects. For a description of these techniques, see Fritts (1976) and Cook and Kairiukstis (1990).

15-7. GROWTH PERCENTAGE

Growth percentage is a means of expressing the increment of a tree parameter in relation to the total size of the parameter at the initiation of growth.

Although growth percentage is most frequently used for volume and basal area growth, it is applicable to any parameter. In terms of simple interest, growth percent p is

$$p = \frac{s_n - s_0}{n s_0}(100) \tag{15-7}$$

where s_0 = size of parameter at beginning of growth period
s_n = size of parameter at end of growth period
n = number of units of time in growth period

In this equation, average growth per unit of time is expressed as a percentage of the initial size s_0. To illustrate, if the present volume of a tree is 400 board feet and the volume 10 years ago was 300 board feet,

$$p = \frac{400 - 300}{10(300)}(100) = 3.3 \text{ percent}$$

In terms of compound interest, growth percent p is

$$p = \left(\sqrt[n]{\frac{s_n}{s_0}} - 1 \right) 100 \tag{15-8}$$

In this form, p may be computed by logarithms. But when compound interest tables are available, a more convenient form of the equation is

$$(1 + p)^n = \frac{s_n}{s_0} \tag{15-9}$$

The compound interest rate for the tree mentioned previously is then

$$(1 + p)^{10} = \frac{400}{300} = 1.333$$

$$p = 2.9 \text{ percent}$$

The compound interest rate is based on the premise that the increment for each unit of time is accumulated, resulting in an increasing value of s_0. Thus, as the period increases the simple and compound interest rates will diverge more and more. For short periods, however, they will be almost the same.

To avoid the use of compound interest tables, Pressler based a simple rate of interest on the average for the period, $(s_n + s_0)/2$, which has the effect of reducing the rate to near the compound interest rate. Pressler's growth percent p_p is

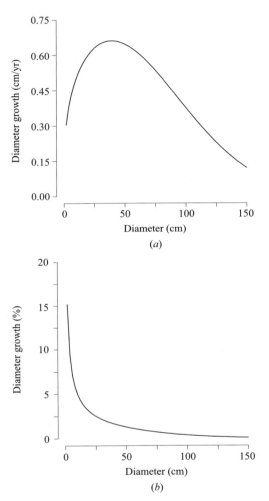

FIG. 15.4. Curves of (*a*) annual diameter growth and (*b*) percent annual diameter growth.

$$p_p = \left(\frac{s_n - s_0}{s_n + s_0}\right)\frac{200}{n} \tag{15-10}$$

For the previous example,

$$p_p = \left(\frac{400 - 300}{400 + 300}\right)\frac{200}{10} = 2.86 \text{ percent}$$

It is essential to remember that growth percentages are ratios between increment and initial size. Thus, percentages change as the amount of increment, and the base on which it is accrued, changes. As trees grow, the base of the percentage increases constantly, and the growth percentage declines even though the absolute increment may be constant or even increasing slightly (Fig. 15-4). In early life, the growth percentage for a tree is at its highest because the base of the ratio is small; the percentage falls as the size of the tree increases. Although young trees may grow at compound rates for limited periods, growth percent is generally an unsafe tool for predicting tree or stand growth, because of the uncertainty in extrapolating growth curves.

16

STAND GROWTH AND YIELD

The structure of a stand—that is, the distribution of trees by species and size classes—changes from year to year because of the birth (regeneration) of new trees and the increase in size, death, and cutting of the individual trees that make up the stand. These changes can be expressed in terms of various stand parameters: volume, weight, basal area, average stand diameter, height, and so on. The net effect of these changes (stand growth) may be positive, indicating increases, or negative, indicating decreases. Yield is thus dependent on a wide variety of factors contributing to a rise or fall in stand growth. Many models are now available for the accurate determination of both growth and yield. In this chapter we discuss the elements of stand growth and review the methodology to model and predict those elements.

16-1. ELEMENTS OF STAND GROWTH

Many problems of stand growth are best understood by considering a stand to be a population of trees and by studying the changes in the structure of the population. For example, consider the even-aged stand in Fig. 16-1, for which two successive 100 percent inventories have been made. If the periodic diameter growth of all trees were 2 in., the periodic growth of this stand would be characterized by a displacement of the diameter distribution 2 in. to the right. The difference between the two inventory volumes represents the gross growth of the volume present at the first inventory. This is depicted in Fig. 16-1, if one omits ingrowth and disregards mortality and cut.

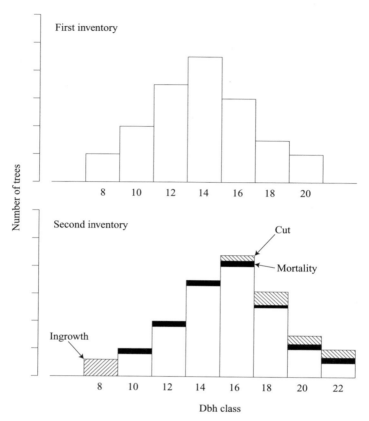

FIG. 16-1. Schematic representation of the changes in stand structure of an even-aged stand due to growth over a 10-year period. (After Beers, 1962.)

The importance of *ingrowth, mortality,* and *cut* in any expression of stand growth is illustrated in Fig. 16-1. Thus, before stand growth is considered, these important terms must be clearly defined. Although volume is the forest parameter stressed in the following definitions, the terms are equally appropriate if another characteristic, such as stand weight or basal area, is considered.

Ingrowth is the number or volume of trees growing periodically into measurable size. There will normally be ingrowth between any two successive inventories, particularly when measurements are made above a minimum diameter, such as 6 or 8 in. The volume of the ingrowth may be 50 percent or more of total cubic volume growth and will be variable from one period to another.

Mortality is the number or volume of trees dying periodically from natural causes such as old age, competition, insects, diseases, wind, and ice. Mortality may be insignificant to catastrophic and may occur at any time during a growth period.

Cut is the number or volume of trees felled or salvaged periodically, whether or not removed from the forest. A cut may be light, medium, or heavy and may occur at any time during the period.

16-1.1 Types of Stand Growth

With the foregoing definitions of ingrowth, mortality, and cut in mind, the generally accepted stand growth terms (Beers, 1962) can be defined by the following equations:

$$G_g = V_2 + M + C - I - V_1 \qquad (16\text{-}1)$$

$$G_{g+i} = V_2 + M + C - V_1 \qquad (16\text{-}2)$$

$$G_n = V_2 + C - I - V_1 \qquad (16\text{-}3)$$

$$G_{n+i} = V_2 + C - V_1 \qquad (16\text{-}4)$$

$$G_d = V_2 - V_1 \qquad (16\text{-}5)$$

where
G_g = gross growth of initial volume
G_{g+i} = gross growth including ingrowth
G_n = net growth of initial volume
G_{n+i} = net growth including ingrowth
G_d = net increase
V_1 = stand volume at beginning of growth period
V_2 = stand volume at end of growth period
M = mortality volume
C = cut volume
I = ingrowth volume

In the equations above, mortality and cut may be defined in two different ways:

1. M and C represent the volume of M and C trees at the time of their death or cutting.
2. M and C represent the volume of M and C trees at the time of the first inventory—that is, the initial volume of M and C trees.

The growth terms above are best considered in the context of repeated measurements of permanent sample plots or entire woodlands. Then it will be clear that the method of inventory generally dictates the most applicable definition of mortality and cut. For example, in inventory systems where the trees are not numbered, it is necessary to measure mortality trees at the time of the second inventory, which amounts to measuring them at the time of death and to measure cut trees at the time of cutting. Under these conditions, definition 1 would apply, and computations of growth that included M and C would then include growth put on by trees that died or were cut during the period between inventories.

If the inventory system utilizes numbered trees, as in continuous forest inventory (CFI) procedures, one can use the initial volume of cut and mortality trees and avoid measuring cut trees at the time of cutting. Under these conditions, definition 2 would apply, and computations of growth that included M and C would not include growth put on by trees that died or were cut during the period between inventories. Of course, if numbered trees are used, cut trees may be measured at the time of cutting and mortality trees at the second inventory, but this practice, which is seldom followed, requires extra care and record keeping.

When gross growth of initial volume [eq. (16-1)] is computed using definition 2 for M and C, it includes only the growth on the trees that survived the period. Then it is often called *survivor growth*. When gross growth of initial volume is computed using definition 1 for M and C, it includes growth on trees that later died or were cut. Then it is often called *accretion*. (Note that growth on trees that later died or were cut may be an important component if cutting or mortality has been heavy, or if the interval between the inventories is long.) Marquis and Beers (1969) recommended that "the terms *survivor growth* and *accretion* be used where appropriate, and that *gross growth of initial volume* be considered a general term applicable only when either of these precise terms is not appropriate."

There is little advantage to using additional terms to qualify the growth terms expressed by eqs. (16-2) to (16-5). When these formulas are used, however, one must understand which definition is used for M and C.

Equations (16-1) to (16-5) apply when tree volumes are first totaled and the resulting sums manipulated. If permanent sample plots are used, such as in the continuous forest inventory system, and observations are made at the individual tree level, the following equations may be used to calculate the various types of growth:

$$G_g = V_{s2} - V_{s1} \tag{16-6}$$

$$G_{g+i} = G_g + I \tag{16-7}$$

$$G_n = G_g - M \tag{16-8}$$

$$G_{n+i} = G_g + I - M \tag{16-9}$$

$$G_d = G_g + I - M - C \tag{16-10}$$

where G_g, G_{g+i}, G_n, G_{n+i}, and G_d are the same variables as defined previously
   V_{s1} = initial volume of survivor trees (i.e., live trees measured at both inventories)
   V_{s2} = final volume of survivor trees (i.e., live trees measured at both inventories)

$$M = \text{initial volume of mortality trees}$$
$$C = \text{initial volume of cut trees}$$
$$I = \text{final volume of ingrowth trees}$$

Since M and C represent the initial volume of mortality and cut trees, gross growth of initial volume G_g is correctly termed survivor growth. Considering this, refer to Table 16-1 to find the differences between eqs. (16-1) to (16-5) and eqs. (16-6) to (16-10).

If the volume totals from Table 16-1 are used, the net growth including ingrowth is obtained from eq. (16-4):

$$G_{n+i} = V_2 + C - V_1 = 749.3 + 241.4 - 744.4 = 246.3$$

Neither mortality volume nor ingrowth volume enters into the calculation. But if the growth per tree is first calculated, the net growth including ingrowth is obtained from eq. (16-9).

$$G_{n+i} = G_g + I - M = 273.8 + 34.6 - 62.1 = 246.3$$

Or, in an approach that typifies the use of permanent sample plots (such as in continuous forest inventory), G_{n+i} may be obtained by totaling the last column in Table 16-1. (Also note that G_g may be obtained by totaling the "survivor growth" column in Table 16-1.)

Clearly, the other growth terms may be computed by the alternative equations, and the same results will be obtained by consistent use of either eqs. (16-1) to (16-5) or eqs. (16-6) to (16-10).

Note that Table 16-1 uses the term *sound volume*. This is done to avoid the use of the terms *net* and *gross* when referring to tree or stand soundness (i.e., amount of defect). This follows the recommendation of Meyer (1953), who suggested that tree or stand volume before defect deduction be termed *total tree volume* (rather than *gross*), and that tree or stand volume after deduction be termed *sound tree volume* (rather than *net*). By employing this terminology, one can have gross and net stand growth in terms of total or sound stand volume.

16-2. GROWTH AND YIELD MODELS

A model is an abstraction or simplified representation of a component of the real world. In forestry, the term *model* generally refers to a table, formula, or computer software package that describes how the forest structure is going to change.

With the increase in readily available, high-powered personal computers, the number and complexity of forest growth and yield models have increased. There are a number of ways to classify growth and yield models based on

TABLE 16-1. Growth Data from a $\frac{1}{5}$-Acre Permanent Sample Plot for a 10-Year Growth Period

Tree No.	Tree Status[a]	First Inventory, V_1	Second Inventory, V_2	Survivor Growth, G_g	Mortality, M	Cut, C	Ingrowth, I	Net Growth, G_n
				Sound Volume (board feet) of:				
1	20	62.1	—	—	62.1	—	—	−62.1
2	24	81.3	—	—	—	81.3	—	—
3	24	66.8	—	—	—	66.8	—	—
4	22	42.4	62.3	19.9	—	—	—	19.9
5	22	63.3	122.5	59.2	—	—	—	59.2
6	22	106.0	163.8	57.8	—	—	—	57.8
7	12	—	34.6	—	—	—	34.6	34.6
8	24	93.3	—	—	—	93.3	—	—
9	22	82.0	119.8	37.8	—	—	—	37.8
10	22	147.2	246.3	99.1	—	—	—	99.1
Plot total		744.4	749.3	273.8	62.1	241.4	34.6	246.3

Source: Adapted from Beers (1962).

[a]Tree status as used here defines the class of tree from a growth-contribution standpoint. Status at each inventory is coded as follows: 0, not present; 1, pulpwood size; 2, sawlog size; 3, cull; 4, cut. By combining the three classes at successive inventories, 20 = sawlog mortality, 22 = sawlog survivor tree, 12 = sawlog ingrowth from pulpwood size, 24 = sawlog cut, and so on.

modeling assumptions, mathematical complexity, and prediction resolution. However, the simple classification proposed by Munro (1974) is still largely applicable today:

1. Stand-level models
2. Distance-independent tree-level models
3. Distance-dependent tree-level models

Stand-level growth and yield models use stand parameters (e.g., age, density, site quality, basal area, volume, etc.) as inputs and predict how these parameters change over time. Examples of stand-level models include yield tables and yield functions. Tree-level models use either stand table data (Sections 11-2.5 and 11-3.2) or individual tree data as inputs. Changes in the attributes of classes or individual trees (e.g., dbh, total height, crown ratio) are predicted and stand-level attributes are obtained by summing the individuals. When stand table data are used as inputs, the models are often referred to as *size-class models*, and when individual trees are used as inputs, the models are referred to as *single-tree models* (Vanclay, 1994). As Leary (1988, 1991) points out, there is really a continuum of models from stand-level to single-tree models.

16-2.1 Yield Tables

Yield tables are an example of a stand-level model. A yield table is a tabular presentation of volume per unit area and other stand characteristics of even-aged stands by age classes, site classes, species, and density. Even-aged yield tables are prepared from yield studies of the relationship between a dependent variable, such as volume, basal area, or number of trees, and independent variables describing stand conditions, such as age, site quality, and stand density. Site quality is most often measured in terms of site index, although discrete site quality classes have been used. Density has most commonly been measured in terms of basal area, although stand density index is often more convenient to use.

Yield tables are valuable in such forest management activities as regulating cut, determining rotation length, making growth estimates, and forest valuation. Although the tabular form of yield relationships has endured years of use in forest management activities, more recent studies have employed the formula form. The construction techniques employed for most of the older yield tables have been supplanted by modern, mathematically sophisticated approaches using computers and statistical analyses.

Almost by definition, yield tables are not applicable to uneven-aged stands, since there is no one representative average age. A similar type of table has been produced for uneven-aged stands showing the volumes produced in growth for given periods with a certain level of growing stock on land of different site qualities (Meyer, 1934). Yield records for uneven-aged stands over long periods are required to prepare this kind of table.

There are several types of yield tables for even-aged stands, depending on the independent variables used to predict growth.

Normal Yield Tables. An example of a normal yield table is shown in Table 16-2. These tables predict stand growth and yield based on stand age and site index. Normal yield tables originated before analytical methods for handling more than two independent variables were available. Since normal yield tables use only two independent variables, they are conveniently constructed by graphical means. Density is held constant by attempting to select sample plots of the same density. The density required has been called *full* or *normal stocking*. Full or normal stocking is supposed to describe the density of a stand that completely occupies a given site and makes full use of its growth potential. Since it is difficult to describe full stocking quantitatively, qualitative and somewhat subjective guides must be used. For example, the guides might include complete canopy closure, no openings in the stand, and regular spacing of the trees. Such specifications leave much to a person's judgment when choosing so-called "fully stocked stands" for samples.

The values of the stand parameters for successive ages shown in normal yield tables are generally prepared from averages of a number of temporary sample plots established in stands considered fully stocked. Each stand in which sample plots are measured might have varying patterns of development. In past years, some stands may have been overstocked or understocked in terms of the definition of normality. When data from these samples are compiled, average relationships are developed that represent the development of a theoretically fully stocked stand over its entire life. It is quite unlikely that any existing stand will show the same pattern as is represented in a normal yield table. In reality, very few stands are encountered that can be called fully stocked. Both understocked and overstocked stands can be encountered, with understocking the usual case.

The volume of an existing stand can be estimated from a normal yield table by measuring its age, site index, and stocking percentage relative to normality. Relative stocking can be measured by comparing the volume, basal area, or number of trees per unit area estimated for a stand with the values predicted from the yield table for a stand of the same age and site index. There is little point in using volume to measure normality when volume is generally the parameter to be estimated. Basal area has been found to be the most satisfactory basis for expressing relative stocking. It is determined easily and quickly and is closely related to volume:

$$RS = \frac{BA_{obs}}{BA_{norm}} \qquad (16\text{-}11)$$

TABLE 16-2. Yield per Acre for Fully Stocked Spruce–Aspen Stands[a]

Spruce Total Age (years)	Tolerant Softwoods (Mainly Spruce)								Intolerant Hardwoods (Mainly Aspen)		Entire Stand
	Average Dominant Height (ft)	Number of Trees	Average dbh (in.)	Basal Area (ft²)	Volume Inside Bark			Basal Area (ft²)	Composition[d] (%)	Volume to Basal Area Factor[e] (units)	Basal Area (ft²)
					Entire Stem (ft³)	Merchantable Stem[b] (12 in.+) (ft³)	Scribner Rule[c] (12 in.+) (bd. ft.)				
30	23	1,091	1.6	16	155	0	0	88	83	16.7	104
40	34	1,379	2.5	49	620	5	0	88	64	19.9	137
50	45	1,344	3.3	79	1,280	20	0	85	52	22.6	164
60	58	1,091	4.1	100	2,010	55	150	82	45	25.0	182
70	70	845	5.0	114	2,740	105	600	79	41	27.1	193
80	80	643	6.0	125	3,445	310	1,540	76	38	28.7	201
90	87	484	7.1	133	4,060	835	3,490	71	35	30.1	204
100	93	376	8.3	140	4,565	1,645	7,020	66	32	31.3	206
110	98	307	9.3	145	4,995	2,520	11,180	60	29	32.3	205
120	102	264	10.2	150	5,370	3,325	15,590	53	26	33.2	203
130	106	238	10.9	153	5,680	3,995	18,980	45	23	34.0	198
140	109	220	11.4	156	5,945	4,460	21,320	36	19	34.7	192
150	112	208	11.8	158	6,165	4,810	23,060	26	14	35.3	184

Source: Macleod and Blyth (1955).

[a]In this study, the site index is defined as the height attained by the average dominant spruce at 80 years of age. This is a good site, ranked 80.
[b]1-ft stump, 4-in. top inside bark.
[c]1-ft stump, 6-in. top inside bark.
[d]Hardwood composition by basal area.
[e]×basal area = total cubic volume.

385

where RS = relative basal area stocking
            BA_{obs} = observed basal area
            BA_{norm} = basal area of normal stand of same age and site index

The stocking or normality percentage times the yield table volume estimates the volume of the existing stand:

$$\hat{V} = RS(V_{norm})\qquad\qquad\qquad(16\text{-}12)$$

where $\hat{V}$ = predicted volume
            RS = relative basal area stocking
            V_{norm} = volume of normal stand of same age and site index

For example, if we had a stand applicable to the yield table shown in Table 16-2, which was 90 years old and had a total basal area of $160\,ft^2$/acre, the relative stocking $RS = 160/204 = 0.78$ and the estimated volume $\hat{V} = 0.78(4060) = 3184\,ft^3$/acre. This naturally assumes that relative stocking in basal area equals relative stocking in volume. This may be a tenable assumption for cubic volume but can lead to serious error for board-foot volume estimation. Normality percentages for the same stand calculated from basal area, cubic volume, and board feet can give widely differing results.

Because of the several subjective decisions necessary in their preparation and use, normal yield tables have been challenged: Indeed, the entire normality concept has been questioned seriously. To overcome the fully stocked assumption of normal yield tables, two other types of tables have been used: the empirical yield table and the variable density yield table.

Empirical Yield Tables. These tables are similar to normal yield tables but are based on sample plots of average rather than full stocking. The judgment necessary for selecting fully stocked stands is eliminated, simplifying the collection of field data.

Variable Density Yield Tables. When stand density is used as an independent variable, variable density yield tables result. These tables show yields for various levels of stocking. This approach also has the advantage of not requiring samples to be fully stocked. Sample plots of any density can be used since the density is measured as a variable for the solution.

Yield studies incorporating stand density as an independent variable were carried out in the 1930s and 1940s as the use of statistical techniques increased. MacKinney et al. (1937) used age, stand density, site index, and a stand composition index as independent variables. This resulted in a more general type of variable density yield table. In a later study, one of the first applications of multiple regression to yield estimation, MacKinney and Chaiken (1939) used age, site index, and stand density as independent variables employing the following model for loblolly pine:

$$\log Y = b_0 + b_1 \frac{1}{A} + b_2 S + b_3 \log \text{SDI} + b_4 C \qquad (16\text{-}13)$$

where Y = volume per acre (ft^3)

A = age (years)

S = site index

SDI = stand density index

C = composition index (basal area of loblolly pine divided by total basal area per acre)

Smith and Ker (1959) used site index, age, maximum height, average stand diameter, basal area per acre, and number of trees per acre in preparing yield equations by multiple regression.

Variable density yield tables are easily created from any yield function (Section 16-2.2) that includes density as a variable. To illustrate this, we will use the yield equation developed by Sullivan and Clutter (1972) for natural loblolly pine stands:

$$\ln V = 2.8837 + 0.01441 S - 21.326 A^{-1} + 0.95064 \ln B$$

where V = total cubic-foot volume, inside bark, per acre

S = site index (ft)

A = stand age (years)

B = basal area per acre (ft^2)

By substituting in values for B and A, the variable density yield table shown in Table 16-3 was created.

TABLE 16-3. Variable Density Yield Table for Loblolly Pine^a (Total ft^3, Inside Bark, Per Acre)

Stand Age (Years)	Basal Area (ft^2/acre)				
	80	100	120	140	160
30	2771	3426	4075	4718	5356
40	3310	4093	4867	5635	6398
50	3683	4553	5415	6269	7118
60	3954	4888	5814	6731	7642
70	4160	5143	6116	7082	8040
80	4322	5343	6354	7357	8352

Source: Sullivan and Clutter (1972).

^{a}Site index 110.

16-2.2   Yield Functions

Most early normal yield tables used in North America were prepared by graphical procedures described by Bruce (1926) and Reineke (1927) and were improved on by Osborne and Schumacher (1935). Departure from the graphical approach was evident in the classic study by MacKinney et al. (1937), who used least squares regression techniques applied to a logarithmic transformation of the Pearl–Reed logistic curve. The multiple regression applications by Schumacher (1939) and Smith and Ker (1959), among others, further demonstrated the superiority of sound statistical techniques over the purely graphical approach for the preparation of yield tables.

The fact that regression techniques provide a "yield formula" as well as a yield table was recognized as a distinct advantage, especially in early computer applications. Through all this development, however, a major problem was ignored or overlooked. Because yield functions (that predict stand volume at a specified age) and growth functions (that predict volume growth over shorter periods) were often derived independently, summation of a succession of periodic *growth estimates* added to an initial volume would not necessarily lead to the final stand volume indicated by the *yield function estimate*.

The application of calculus to growth and yield studies led to the resolution of this inconsistency between growth summation and terminal yield. The independent, essentially simultaneous works of Buckman (1962) and Clutter (1963) began a new era in yield studies. A brief description of their work is appropriate.

Working with even-aged red pine, Buckman (1962) emphasized that growth and yield are not independent phenomena and should not be treated as such. Furthermore, he employed methods of calculus that had been neglected in virtually all previous yield studies of this type. Beginning with a *basal area growth equation* of the form

$$Y = b_0 + b_1 B + b_2 B^2 + b_3 A + b_4 A^2 + b_5 S \qquad (16\text{-}14)$$

where $Y =$ periodic net annual basal area increment (i.e., dB/dA, change in
              basal area with respect to age)
       $B =$ basal area (ft^2/acre)
       $A =$ age (years)
       $S =$ site index

Yield tables were prepared by iterative solution and accumulation; that is, the least squares fit of eq. (16-14) is solved for a particular site, age, and stand density. Basal area growth is then added to the stand density, 1 year is added to age, and the equation is solved again. Addition of the n successive annual growth estimates to the initial basal area provides a yield estimate n years hence.

Clutter (1963) working with even-aged loblolly pine clearly indicated the relationship between growth and yield models by the following definition:

"Such models are here defined as compatible when the yield model can be obtained by summation of the predicted growth through the appropriate growth periods or, more precisely, when the algebraic form of the yield model can be derived by mathematical integration of the growth model." In the research reported by Clutter, a yield model was first prepared of the form

$$\ln V = a + b_1 S + b_2 \ln B + b_3 A^{-1} \qquad (16\text{-}15)$$

where $\ln V$ = logarithm to base e of volume
A = stand age (years)
S = site index (ft)
B = basal area per acre (ft^2)

and differentiated with respect to age, obtaining

$$\frac{dV}{dA} = b_2 V B^{-1} \frac{dB}{dA} - b_3 V A^{-2} \qquad (16\text{-}16)$$

where dV/dA = rate of change of volume with respect to age or instantaneous rate of volume growth
dB/dA = rate of change of basal area with respect to age or instantaneous rate of basal area growth

Since the rate of basal area growth is not ordinarily available, regression analysis was used to obtain dB/dA as a function of age, site, and basal area. The model finally adopted was

$$\frac{dB}{dA} = -B(\ln B)A^{-1} + c_0 A^{-1} B + c_1 B S A^{-1} \qquad (16\text{-}17)$$

Substituting this relation for dB/dA in eq. (16-17) led to the equation

$$\frac{dV}{dA} = -b_2 V(\ln B)A^{-1} + b_2 c_0 V A^{-1} + b_2 c_1 V S A^{-1} - b_3 V A^{-2} \qquad (16\text{-}18)$$

Using the form of this equation as a model, and based on data gathered on permanent sample plots, a least squares regression equation was obtained, thus relating volume growth with present basal area, age, site index, and volume [estimated using eq. (16-18)]. Subsequent integration of this regression equation led to the final yield function, from which volume yield at some future time could be predicted from given initial age, basal area and volume, projected age, and site index. Numerous other yield functions have been developed for even-aged stands. For a review of these equations, see Clutter et al. (1983) and Vanclay (1994).

The majority of yield functions historically have been developed for even-aged stands. Functions for uneven-aged stands are still relatively rare. An example of an uneven-aged growth and yield function is the one proposed by Moser and Hall (1969) for uneven-aged mixed northern hardwood stands. In their model, volume growth was expressed as the first derivative with respect to time:

$$\frac{dV}{dt} = b_1 V B^{-1} \frac{dB}{dt} \tag{16-19}$$

where dV/dt = instantaneous rate of change of stand volume
V = stand volume
B = stand basal area
dB/dt = instantaneous rate of change of basal area
b_1 = constant

For dB/dt, they used the Von Bertalanffy's generalized growth rate equation (Richards, 1959):

$$\frac{dB}{dt} = nB^m - kB \tag{16-20}$$

where dB/dt = instantaneous rate of change of basal area
B = stand basal area
n, m, and k are constants

By substituting eq. (16-20) into eq. (16-19) and integrating, Moser and Hall produced the following yield function:

$$V = \frac{V_0}{B_0^{b_1}} \left[\frac{n}{k} - \left(\frac{n}{k} - B_0^{1-m} \right) e^{-(1-m)kt} \right]^{b/(1-m)} \tag{16-21}$$

where V = future volume
V_0 = initial volume
B_0 = initial basal area
b_1, n, m, k are constants
t = elapsed time
e = natural logarithmic exponent

16-2.3 Stand Table Projection

To apply the method of stand table projection, the following data are required:

1. Diameter growth information
2. Present stand table
3. Local volume table
4. Information to calculate ingrowth

5. Estimates of mortality

Diameter growth information is most commonly obtained from increment borings (Section 15-3). However, excellent diameter growth information may be obtained from repeated measurements of permanent plots. In any case, there are three basic ways that diameter growth information may be applied to the present stand table, in conjunction with a local volume table, to obtain a growth estimate.

1. *Assume that all trees in each diameter class are located at the class mid-point and that all trees will grow at the average rate.* Table 16-4 illustrates this approach.
   - Column 2 is obtained as explained in Section 15-3.
   - Column 3 = column 1 + column 2.
   - Column 4 gives the local volume table values for the diameters given in column 3. The values may be read from a curve of volume over tree diameter (column 6 over column 1) or calculated by an appropriate volume equation.
   - Column 5 is obtained from inventory data.
   - Column 6 gives the local volume table values for the diameters given in column 1.
   - Column 7 = column 4 × column 5.
   - Column 8 = column 6 × column 5.
   - Column 9 = column 7 − column 8.

   Note that the sum of column 9 equals the periodic gross growth of the initial volume. However, if the periodic diameter growth of the 8-in. diameter class had been over 2.00 in., all trees in this class would have grown to measurable size, that is, to the 10-in. class, and would have been *ingrowth*. This, of course, would have increased volume production. Thus, results may be inconsistent if an attempt is made to include ingrowth. But when no attempt is made to determine ingrowth, the method gives good estimates of gross growth of the initial volume.

2. *Assume that trees in each diameter class are evenly distributed through the class and that each tree will grow at the average rate.* Table 16-5 illustrates this approach. In this case a future stand table is predicted by first calculating the movement ratio M for each diameter class:

$$M = \frac{I}{C} \qquad (16\text{-}2)$$

where I = periodic diameter increment
       C = diameter class interval in same units as I

TABLE 16-4. Calculation of 10-Year Predicted Volume Growth per Acre[a]

[1] Present dbh Class (in.)	[2] 10-year dbh Increment (in.)	[3] Future dbh (in.)	[4] Future Volume per Tree (ft³)	[5] Present Stand Table (number)	[6] Present Volume per Tree (ft³)	[7] Future Stock Table (ft³)	[8] Present Stock Table (ft³)	[9] Volume Production (ft³)
6	2.02	8.02	—	41.73	—	—	—	—
8	1.88	9.88	—	28.73	—	—	—	—
10	1.74	11.74	17.0	21.73	12.5	369.4	271.6	97.8
12	1.60	13.60	24.2	17.33	18.4	419.4	318.9	100.5
14	1.46	15.46	31.9	12.87	25.6	410.6	329.5	81.1
16	1.32	17.32	40.7	9.47	34.2	385.4	323.9	61.6
18	1.18	19.18	50.1	8.27	44.1	414.3	364.7	49.6
20	1.04	21.04	62.3	5.00	55.6	311.5	278.0	33.5
22	0.90	22.90	75.3	3.47	68.5	261.3	237.7	23.6
24	0.76	24.76	89.8	2.87	83.5	257.7	239.6	18.1
26	—	—	—	—	100.1	—	—	—
Total				151.47		2829.6	2363.9	465.7

[a] Assuming that all trees in each diameter class are located at the class midpoint and that all trees grow at the average rate.

TABLE 16-5. Calculations of 10-Year Predicted Volume Growth per Acre[a]

[1] Dbh Class (in.)	[2] 10-Year dbh Increment (in.)	[3] Movement Ratio, M	[4] Present Stand Table (number)	[5] Volume per Tree (ft³)	[6] Future Stand Table (number)	[7] Number of Trees Moving — 0 Classes	[8] 1 Class	[9] 2 Classes	[10] Future Stock Table (ft³)	[11] Present Stock Table (ft³)	[12] Volume Production (ft³)
6	2.02	1.01	41.73				41.31	0.42			
8	1.88	0.94	28.73		43.03	1.72	27.01				
10	1.74	0.87	21.73	12.5	30.25	2.82	18.91		378.1	271.6	106.5
12	1.6	0.80	17.33	18.4	22.38	3.47	13.86		411.6	318.9	92.8
14	1.46	0.73	12.87	25.6	17.33	3.47	9.40		443.9	329.5	114.4
16	1.32	0.66	9.47	34.2	12.62	3.22	6.25		431.4	323.9	107.6
18	1.18	0.59	8.27	44.1	9.64	3.39	4.88		425.2	364.7	60.5
20	1.04	0.52	5.00	55.6	7.28	2.40	2.60		404.7	278.0	126.7
22	0.9	0.45	3.47	68.5	4.51	1.91	1.56		308.8	237.7	71.1
24	0.76	0.38	2.87	83.5	3.34	1.78	1.09		279.0	239.6	39.3
26				100.1	1.09				109.2		109.2
Total			151.47		151.47				3191.9	2363.9	828.0

[a] Assuming that trees in each diameter class are evenly distributed through the class and that each tree grows at the average rate.

Thus, the movement ratio for the 12-in. diameter class (Table 16-5) is

$$M = \frac{1.60}{2} = 0.80$$

The two digits to the right of the decimal point indicate the proportion of the trees in the class that will move one class more than indicated by the digit to the left of the decimal point. Therefore, for the 12-in. class, 0.80(17.33) = 13.86 trees move one class, and 0.20(17.33) = 3.47 trees move zero classes.

In Table 16-5 the movements for all classes are shown in columns 7, 8, and 9, and the future stand table in column 6. The arrows show how the trees are moved into the future stand. Columns 4 and 5 are the same as columns 5 and 6 in Table 16-4. Columns 10, 11, and 12 are determined as follows:

- Column 10 = column 6 × column 5
- Column 11 = column 4 × column 5
- Column 12 = column 10 − column 11

Note that the sum of column 12 in Table 16-5 equals the periodic gross growth, including ingrowth, and that ingrowth is 27.43 trees (0.42 + 27.01), or 342.9 cubic feet (27.43 × 12.5). This is a reasonable estimate of ingrowth.

3. *Recognize the actual position of trees in each diameter class and apply the diameter growth for individual trees in the class.* In this approach, movement percentages are calculated by applying actual individual increments to individual tree diameters. A graphic solution (Wahlenberg, 1941) may be used, but a simple tabular solution is equally satisfactory and lends itself to electronic data processing. For example, in Table 16-6 tree movement percentages are computed for the 8-in. diameter class from the data used to compute column 2 in Table 16-5. These percentages are applied to the present stand table to obtain the number of trees moving. Except for this calculation, the future stand table and the future stock table are predicted as in Table 16-5.

As indicated previously, if the method depicted in Table 16-5 is used to predict growth, reasonable estimates of *ingrowth* may be determined by including, in the initial stand table, several diameter classes below the merchantable limit. If the method depicted in Table 16-4 is used, inconsistent estimates of ingrowth may be obtained by this procedure. In any case, estimates of ingrowth are unreliable for long prediction periods or for rapidly growing stands.

Mortality, which was not considered in the preceding examples (Tables 16-4 and 16-5), may be accounted for in one of the following ways.

TABLE 16-6. Determination of Tree Movement Ratios from Raw Data from 8-in. dbh Class

	Raw Data					Summary		
Dbh Class (in.)	Present dbh (in.)	10-year dbh Increment (in.)	Future dbh (in.)	Classes Moved (number)		Classes Moved (number)	Trees Moving (number)	Trees Moving (%)
8	7.1	1.5	8.6	0		0	3	30
	7.3	1.6	8.9	0		1	5	50
	7.5	1.5	8.9	0		2	2	20
	7.7	1.8	9.3	1		Total	10	100
	7.9	2.5	10.4	1				
	8.1	1.6	9.7	1				
	8.3	1.8	10.1	1				
	8.5	2.6	11.1	2				
	8.7	1.7	10.4	1				
	8.9	2.2	11.1	2				

1. By deducting predicted number of trees dying from each diameter class of the present stand table prior to projecting the present stand table
2. By deducting predicted number of trees dying from each diameter class of the future stand table after projecting the present stand table, but before computing the future stock table

In thrifty middle-aged stands, or in stands under intensive management, mortality will not be large and can be predicted accurately. In young stands and in old stands, mortality will often be great and, because of its erratic nature, cannot be predicted accurately. In any case, allowances are made only for normal mortality resulting from old age, competition, insects, diseases, wind, and so on. No allowance is made for catastrophic mortality resulting from fire, epidemics, great storms, and so on.

Good information on mortality may be obtained from permanent sample plots. From such information for any given stand, one can determine functions relating mortality to age, diameter, stand density, and species and thus apply the mortality information to other stands. But often when we desire to make a prediction by stand-table projection, we lack suitable permanent sample plot data. Then, mortality estimates must be obtained from a stand inspection, which is normally made during the cruise. In the inspection, which is quite subjective, one estimates on plots or points the number of trees, by species and diameter classes, that died during some past period, say 10 years, or that will die during a future period. When the mortality information is summarized, it is expressed as percentages of the trees in each diameter class of the stand table.

A final word on stand-table projection: If accurate diameter growth information is used, any stand-table projection method will give an excellent estimate of gross growth of the initial basal area. Of course, basal area growth is an important component of volume growth. But so is height growth. Therefore, the determination of gross growth of the initial volume also depends on the stability, during the prediction period, of the height–diameter relationship for which the local volume table was constructed. It also assumes no change in form.

It has been demonstrated that the future height–diameter relationship will not necessarily be the same as the present height–diameter relationship (Chapman and Meyer, 1949). For large areas and for uneven-aged stands, this change may be slight, but for small areas and for even-aged stands, the change may be substantial, even for periods of 10 to 20 years. With the exception of abnormal conditions, form changes may be safely ignored for short periods.

Thus, stand-table projection will give good results for uneven-aged stands of immature timber that are understocked. Then mortality will be small and predictable. Ingrowth may be predicted accurately, and the height–diameter relationships will change only slightly. In even-aged stands, young dense stands, and overmature stands, stand-table projection will often give inaccurate results because of the change in the height–diameter relationships and because of the high and unpredictable mortality.

Although considerable emphasis is given to the prediction of diameter growth in stand-table projections, and although diameter growth predictions are usually quite accurate, height growth and mortality predictions are often crude. Therein lies the weak link of the method. Consequently, when height growth and mortality predictions are in question, it is a waste of time to give great attention to diameter growth. In this case, a simpler system (Section 16-2.2) would save time and would give just as good results.

16.2.4 Diameter Distribution Models

Diameter distribution models represent a hybrid between stand-level models and tree-level models. In these models, future stand-level parameters are predicted. Then, based on these predictions, the parameters of a distribution model such as the Weibull distribution (Section 8-3.3) are obtained.

There are two general approaches to diameter distribution models. In the first method, the future parameters of the distribution model are predicted directly from the current parameters and other information about the stand (density, basal area, volume, etc.). This approach is referred to as the *parameter prediction approach*. In the second approach, future values of the stand parameters are predicted directly, and the parameters of the diameter distribution model are recovered using estimates of the moments of the distribution derived from the stand parameters. This approach is referred to as the *parameter recovery approach*. The parameter recovery approach generally yields better results than the parameter prediction approach (Reynolds et al., 1988).

Hyink and Moser (1983) present a generalized framework for developing diameter distribution models. Reynolds et al. (1988) discuss various approaches to developing models and discuss model selection procedures.

16-2.5 Individual Tree Growth and Yield Models

Both distance-dependent and distance-independent models have been developed for a variety of species and stand conditions. Individual tree models have been developed for single-species even-aged stands (plantations and natural stands) as well as for mixed species stands (even-aged and uneven-aged).

Distance-dependent models require information about the spatial location (x–y coordinates) of individual trees as well as tree characteristics (e.g., species, dbh, height) as inputs. These models use measures of point density (Section 8-5.6) to estimate the level of competition for each tree and model growth as a function of tree size and competition. An example of a distance-dependent model is the model FOREST developed by Ek and Monserud (1974).

Distance-independent models only require information about tree characteristics as inputs. These models predict tree growth based on initial tree characteristics and general expressions of competition (e.g., stand density index, total basal area, basal area of larger trees, relative height). Distance-independent models are more common than distance-dependent models primarily because detailed information about tree locations is relatively unavailable.

Examples of distance-independent models include Prognosis (Stage, 1973; Wykoff et al., 1982), developed originally for mixed-species conifer stands in Idaho and Montana, ORGANON (Hester et al., 1989), developed originally for mixed-species conifer forests in southwestern Oregon; and TWIGS (Miner et al., 1988), developed for mixed-species stands in the central United States. The Prognosis model is now referred to as the Forest Vegetation Simulator (FVS), and a number of variants for many regions of the United States have been developed.*

Examples of other individual tree models and a detailed discussion of the process of building individual tree models can be found in Vanclay (1994).

16-2.6   Other Types of Models

The discussion of models above has been limited to those models that have been widely applied in forest management. There are numerous other approaches to modeling forest growth and development. For a thorough review of these, see Vanclay (1994).

Two modeling approaches that merit brief mention here are process models and forest succession models. *Process models* attempt to model growth using physiological processes such as light absorption, nutrient and water uptake, photosynthesis, and respiration (e.g., Mäkelä, 1992). *Forest succession models* attempt to model changes in species composition over long periods of time (e.g., Botkin, 1993). These models are useful for understanding growth and stand dynamics but have not been widely applied for predicting forest yields. These models have been widely applied to assess potential impacts of global climate change and increases in atmospheric carbon dioxide.

Process models have great potential in future forest management. Recent efforts have attempted to apply process models to forest management problems (e.g., Battaglia and Sands, 1998; Johnsen et al., 2001b). Other developments have included linking process models with empirical growth and yield models (e.g., Somers and Nepal, 1994; Baldwin et al., 2001) and collaborating process models with stand growth and yield data (e.g., Sievänen and Burk, 1994).

16-2.7   Stand and Landscape Visualization

Most forest growth and yield models are developed and applied at the stand level. If a forester wants to project several stands, each stand would have to be projected and summarized separately. Although this task is not onerous for a

---

*Current information on FVS variants and copies of the software can be obtained from the USDA Forest Service, Forest Management Service Center.

few stands, it can become quite time consuming if several hundred stands are involved. If several management alternatives are involved, the number of projections can become astronomical.

Traditionally, this problem has been dealt with by running large batch jobs on high-powered mainframe computers. A recent development, called the *landscape management system* LMS* (McCarter et al., 1998; McCarter, 2001), integrates individual tree growth and yield models with stand and landscape visualization tools (McGaughey, 1998). LMS provides a front end to the FVS and ORGANON growth and yield models. The system has the capability of interfacing with other models. Individual stands or entire forests can be simulated for one or more growth projection periods. Outputs are stored in separate directories for each projection period and the process can be set to any period, simplifying comparisons between management alternatives. The stand and landscape visualization tools enable foresters to assess different forest management scenarios visually and to build powerful demonstrations of forest management activities.

16-3. USING STAND GROWTH AND YIELD MODELS

The outputs from growth and yield models are used in a variety of forest management activities. Detailed forest management planning uses yield predictions to model the flows of timber and other resources. Models can be used to assess tree and stand responses to silviculture treatments and aid in the design and selection of appropriate treatments given management objectives. By linking growth and yield models to wildlife habitat suitability models (Section 10-3) changes in habitat quality can be assessed.

Forest inventories provide valuable information to the forest managers; however, these inventories represent the forest at a particular point in time. Forest inventories are expensive; therefore, inventories are generally conducted periodically, often at 10-year intervals. Growth and yield models can be used to predict changes in tree and stand values for periods between successive inventories.

16-3.1 Selecting Growth and Yield Models

The type of model selected will depend upon application and availability. The model selected should provide predictions that are sufficiently detailed and accurate for the use intended. Overly complicated models are not necessarily better than models utilizing a simpler approach.

---

*Current information on LMS and copies of the software are available from the Rural Technology Initiative, University of Washington, College of Forest Resources.

Vanclay (1994) sets out the following guidelines for selecting an appropriate model:

1. Does the approach make sense?
2. Will the model work for my application and input data?
3. What range of data was used to develop the model?
4. Do model assumptions and inferences apply in my situation?
5. What confidence can I place in model predictions?
6. Be skeptical and demand proof!

Buchman and Shifley (1983) provide a more detailed checklist.

16-4. ASSESSING STAND GROWTH AND YIELD IN FOREST INVENTORIES

In Section 13-9 we discussed the common approaches to repeated sampling in forest inventories. When assessing growth and yield, especially for model development, the approach utilizing the same sample at successive inventories (Section 13-9.2) generally yields the best results (Shiver and Borders, 1996). This approach has been the basis of the Continuous Forest Inventory (CFI) systems used throughout the United States.

CFI is a system of permanent plots located throughout the forest area of interest. CFI plots are generally fixed-area plots located systematically over the forest area. In the eastern United States, $\frac{1}{5}$-acre circular plots have been widely used. In a typical CFI system, plot centers are permanently located and individual trees are numbered and either marked with a tag or spray-painted with their assigned number. In some cases, the tree locations are mapped. Each plot is remeasured at a specified interval (usually, 5 or 10 years). At each measurement period, each tree is measured for a set of attributes which typically include dbh, total height, merchantable height, and a visual quality assessment. Trees that die or are cut are noted and new trees (ingrowth) are measured and assigned a number.

A CFI system is useful for tracking overall forest-level trends. Mortality, ingrowth, cut, and survivor growth can all be estimated from CFI data. Forest managers can assess how much volume is currently available and use growth rates to establish harvest levels.

The major drawback to most CFI systems is their cost. CFI systems are expensive to install and maintain and, as a result, the sample intensity is often very low (usually < 0.1%). As a result, CFI systems are generally not useful for identifying where timber is located, because many stands do not have a CFI plot present because of the low sample intensity. Another problem associated with CFI systems is uniformity of treatment. If the CFI system is to reflect the changes in the forest, the plots have to receive the same frequency and intensity of treatment as the rest of the forest.

Fixed-area plots are generally preferred over horizontal point samples in CFI systems for many reasons. The primary reason is that horizontal point samples yield incompatible growth estimates when the various components of growth (Section 16-1) are estimated. Several approaches to this problem have been addressed over the years, including those of Beers and Miller (1964), Flewelling (1981), and Roesch et al. (1989).

APPENDIX

TABLE A-1. Some Conversion Factors for Common Units of Measure

A. Length

	mm	cm	m	km	in.	ft	yd	link	rod	chain	mile
1 millimeter	1	0.1	0.001	10^{-6}	0.03937	0.0032808	0.001094	0.004971	0.0001988	4.971×10^{-5}	6.214×10^{-7}
1 centimeter	10	1	0.01	0.00001	0.3937	0.032808	0.01094	0.04971	0.001988	0.0004971	6.214×10^{-6}
1 meter	1000	100	1	0.001	39.37	3.28084	1.094	4.971	0.1988	0.04971	0.0006214
1 kilometer	10^6	10^5	1000	1	39,370	3,280.84	1,094	4,971	198.8	49.71	0.6214
1 inch	25.4	2.54	0.0254	2.54×10^{-5}	1	0.0833	0.02778	0.12626	0.005050	0.001263	1.578×10^{-5}
1 foot	304.8	30.48	0.3048	0.003048	12	1	0.3333	1.51515	0.06061	0.01515	0.0001894
1 yard	914.4	91.44	0.9144	0.009144	36	3	1	4.54545	0.18182	0.04545	0.0005682
1 link	201.168	20.1168	0.20117	0.0002012	7.92	0.66	0.22	1	0.04	0.01	0.000125
1 rod	5,029.2	502.92	5.0292	0.0050292	198	16.5	5.5	25	1	0.25	0.003125
1 chain	20,116.8	2,011.68	20.1168	0.0201168	792	66	22	100	4	1	0.0125
1 mile[a]	1,609,344	160,934.4	1,609.344	1.609344	63,360	5,280	1,760	8,000	320	80	1

[a] 1 International nautical mile = 1852 m.

B. Area[a]

	cm²	m²	ha	km²	in.²	ft²	yd²	chain²	acre	mile²
1 centimeter²	1	0.0001	10^{-8}	10^{-10}	0.155	0.001076	1.196×10^{-4}	2.471×10^{-7}	2.471×10^{-8}	3.86×10^{-11}
1 meter²	10^4	1	0.0001	10^{-6}	1,550	10.76	1.196	0.002471	2.471×10^{-4}	3.86×10^{-7}
1 hectare[b]	10^8	10^4	1	0.01	1.55×10^7	1.076×10^5	11,959.9	24.7105	2.47105	0.003861
1 kilometer²	10^{10}	10^6	100	1	1.55×10^9	1.076×10^7	1,195,990	2,471.05	247.105	0.3861
1 inch²	6.4516	6.452×10^{-4}	6.452×10^{-8}	6.452×10^{-10}	1	0.006944	7.716×10^{-4}	1.594×10^{-6}	1.594×10^{-7}	2.491×10^{-10}
1 foot²	929.0304	0.092903	9.2903×10^{-6}	9.2903×10^{-8}	144	1	0.1111	0.000230	2.296×10^{-5}	3.587×10^{-8}
1 yard²	8,361.2736	0.83613	8.36×10^{-5}	8.361×10^{-7}	1,296	9	1	0.00207	0.000207	3.228×10^{-7}
1 chain²[c]	4.0469×10^{-6}	404.69	0.04047	4.047×10^{-4}	627,264	4,356	484	1	0.1	1.5625×10^{-4}
1 acre[d]	4.0469×10^{-7}	4046.9	0.4047	0.004047	6,272,640	43,560	4,840	10	1	0.0015625
1 mile²	2.59×10^{10}	2,589,988.11	258.999	2.58999	4.014×10^9	27,878,400	3,097,600	6,400	640	1

[a]Basal area per unit land area conversion factors:

1 ft²/acre = 0.2296 m²/ha

1 m²/ha = 4.3560 ft²/acre

[b]1 hectare = 100 are.

[c]1 chain² = 10,000 link².

[d]640 acres = 1 section; 36 sections = 1 township (6 miles × 6 miles).

C. Volume[a]

	cm³	liter[b]	m³	in.³	ft³	yd³	oz[c]	pint[c]	qt[c]	gal[c]	qt[d]
1 centimeter³	1	9.9997×10^{-4}	10^{-6}	0.061024	3.531×10^{-5}	1.308×10^{-6}	0.03381	0.002113	0.001057	2.642×10^{-4}	9.0808×10^{-4}
1 liter	1,000.027	1	0.001	61.0254	0.03531	0.001308	33.81	2.113	1.0567	0.26417	0.9081
1 meter³	10^{6}	999.973	1	61,024	35.31	1.308	33,813	2,113.36	1,056.68	264.17	908.076
1 inch³	16.387	0.016387	1.6387×10^{-5}	1	0.000579	2.143×10^{-5}	0.5541	0.03463	0.01732	0.004329	0.01488
1 foot³	28,316.8	28.31608	0.028317	1,728	1	0.037037	957.5	59.84	29.922	7.4805	25.714
1 yard³	764,555	764.5342	0.764554	46,656	27	1	25,852.6	1,615.79	807.895	201.97	694.28
1 ounce[c]	29.5737	0.029573	2.9573×10^{-5}	1.8047	0.001044	3.868×10^{-5}	1	0.0625	0.03125	0.0078125	274.4997
1 pint[c]	473.179	0.473166	0.0004732	28.875	0.01671	0.00619	16	1	0.5	0.125	1.7187
1 quart[c]	946.359	0.946333	9.4635×10^{-4}	57.75	0.03342	0.001238	32	2	1	0.25	0.8594
1 gallon[c]	3,785.43	3.785328	0.0037854	231	0.13368	0.004951	128	8	4	1	3.4375
1 quart[d]	1,101.23	1.1012	0.001101	67.2	0.03889	0.00144	0.03636	0.5818	1.16365	0.2909125	1

[a]Volume per unit land area conversion factors:
1 ft³/acre = 0.06997 m³/ha
1 m³/ha = 14.29 ft³/acre
[b]Volume of 1 kg water at 4°C and 760 mm pressure.
[c]U.S. fluid measure. British imperial gallon = 277.24 in³ = 1.2009 U.S. gallons.
[d]U.S. dry measure. 32 quarts = 1 bushel.

D. Mass[a]

	grain[b]	ounce[b]	pound[b]	ton[b,c]	gram	kilogram	metric tonne
1 grain[b]	1	0.00228571	0.00014286	7.1428×10^{-8}	0.0647989	6.4799×10^{-5}	6.47989×10^{-8}
1 ounce[b]	437.5	1	0.0625	3.125×10^{-5}	28.3495201	0.0283495	2.83495×10^{-5}
1 pound[b]	7,000	16	1	0.0005	453.59232	0.4535923	0.00045359
1 ton[b,c]	1.4×10^7	32,000	2,000	1	907,184.6	907.18464	0.9071846
1 gram	15.43236	0.035274	0.0022046	1.10231×10^{-6}	1	0.001	10^{-6}
1 kilogram	15,432.36	35.273966	2.2046228	0.001102311	1000	1	0.001
1 metric tonne	1.543236×10^7	35,273.966	2,204.6228	1.102311	10^6	1000	1

[a]Mass per unit land conversion factors:

1 U.S. ton per acre = 2.2417 metric tonnes per hectare; 1 lb/acre = 1.120851 kg/ha

1 metric tonne per hectare = 0.44609 U.S. tons per acre; 1 kg/ha = 0.892179 lb/acre

[b]Avoirdupois system.

[c]U.S. ton; 1 imperial ton = 2240 pounds.

TABLE A-2. Areas of Some Plane Figures

Figure	Diagram	Formula
Rectangle		$A = lw$
Parallelogram		$A = bh$
Triangle		$A = \dfrac{bh}{2}$ or $A = \sqrt{S(S-a)(S-b)(S-c)}$ where $S = \frac{1}{2}(a+b+c)$
Trapezoid		$A = \frac{1}{2}(a+c)h$
Circle		$A = \pi r^2$ or $A = \dfrac{\pi D^2}{4}$ where $r = \dfrac{D}{2}$ Circumference $= 2\pi r = \pi D$
Circular sector		$A = \dfrac{\theta r^2}{2}$ where θ is in radians $A = \dfrac{\theta \pi r^2}{360}$ where θ is in degrees
Circular segment		$A = \frac{1}{2}r^2(\theta - \sin\theta)$ where θ is in radians
Ellipse		$A = \pi ab$ Perimeter $= 2\pi\sqrt{\dfrac{a^2+b^2}{2}}$ (approximately)
Parabola		$A = \frac{2}{3}ld$ Length of arc $= l\left[1 + \dfrac{2}{3}\left(\dfrac{2d}{l}\right)^2 - \dfrac{2}{5}\left(\dfrac{2d}{l}\right)^4 + \cdots\right]$

TABLE A-3. Volume and Surface Areas of Some Solids[a]

Solid	Diagram	Formula
Prismoid		$V = \dfrac{h}{6}(A_b + 4A_m + A_u)$ $S_l = \dfrac{L}{2}(P_b + P_u)$ $S_t = S_l + A_b + A_u$
Prism or cylinder		$V = A_b h$ $S_l = P_r L$ $S_t = S_l + 2A_b$
Pyramid or cone		$V = \dfrac{h}{3}A_b$ $S_l = \dfrac{L}{2}P_b$ $S_t = S_l + A_b$
Frustum of cone or pyramid		(treat as prismoid or) $V = \dfrac{h}{3}\left(A_b + \sqrt{A_b \cdot A_u} + A_u\right)$ $S_l = \dfrac{L}{2}(P_b + P_u)$ $S_t = S_l + A_b + A_u$
Sphere		$V = \frac{4}{3}\pi r^3$ $S_t = 4\pi r^2$
Paraboloid		$V = \dfrac{h}{2}A_b$ $S_l = \dfrac{2\pi r}{12h^2}\left[(r^2 + 4h^2)^{3/2} - r^3\right]$ $S_t = S_l + A_b$
Frustum of paraboloid		$V = \dfrac{d}{2}(A_b + A_u)$ $S_l = S_{l(acb)} - S_{l(gck)}$ $S_t = S_l + A_b + A_u$

Neiloid

$$V = \frac{h}{4} A_b$$

$$S_l = 2\pi \int_0^h X^{(3/2)}\sqrt{1+9X/4}\,dX$$

$$S_t = S_l + A_b$$

Frustum of neiloid

$$V = \frac{d}{6}(A_b + 4A_m + A_u)$$

$$S_l = S_{l(\text{acb})} - S_{l(\text{gck})}$$

$$S_t = S_l + A_b + A_u$$

---

[a]The following symbols are used in the formulas: V, volume; A_b, area of base; A_m, area of midsection parallel to A_b and A_u; A_u, area of upper section; A_r, area of right section; d, distance from base to intermediate section; h, altitude or height; L, slant height; P_b, perimeter of lower base; P_u, perimeter of upper section; P_r, perimeter of right section; S_l, lateral surface area; S_t, total surface area.

TABLE A-4. Critical Values of Student's t Distribution

Degrees of Freedom	Two-Tailed Probability of Obtaining a Larger Value									
	0.5	0.4	0.3	0.2	0.1	0.05	0.02	0.01	0.001
1	1.0000	1.3764	1.9626	3.0777	6.3137	12.7062	31.8210	63.6559	636.5776
2	0.8165	1.0607	1.3862	1.8856	2.9200	4.3027	6.9645	9.9250	31.5998
3	0.7649	0.9785	1.2498	1.6377	2.3534	3.1824	4.5407	5.8408	12.9244
4	0.7407	0.9410	1.1896	1.5332	2.1318	2.7765	3.7469	4.6041	8.6101
5	0.7267	0.9195	1.1558	1.4759	2.0150	2.5706	3.3649	4.0321	6.8685
6	0.7176	0.9057	1.1342	1.4398	1.9432	2.4469	3.1427	3.7074	5.9587
7	0.7111	0.8960	1.1192	1.4149	1.8946	2.3646	2.9979	3.4995	5.4081
8	0.7064	0.8889	1.1081	1.3968	1.8595	2.3060	2.8965	3.3554	5.0414
9	0.7027	0.8834	1.0997	1.3830	1.8331	2.2622	2.8214	3.2498	4.7809
10	0.6998	0.8791	1.0931	1.3722	1.8125	2.2281	2.7638	3.1693	4.5868
11	0.6974	0.8755	1.0877	1.3634	1.7959	2.2010	2.7181	3.1058	4.4369
12	0.6955	0.8726	1.0832	1.3562	1.7823	2.1788	2.6810	3.0545	4.3178
13	0.6938	0.8702	1.0795	1.3502	1.7709	2.1604	2.6503	3.0123	4.2209
14	0.6924	0.8681	1.0763	1.3450	1.7613	2.1448	2.6245	2.9768	4.1403
15	0.6912	0.8662	1.0735	1.3406	1.7531	2.1315	2.6025	2.9467	4.0728
16	0.6901	0.8647	1.0711	1.3368	1.7459	2.1199	2.5835	2.9208	4.0149
17	0.6892	0.8633	1.0690	1.3334	1.7396	2.1098	2.5669	2.8982	3.9651
18	0.6884	0.8620	1.0672	1.3304	1.7341	2.1009	2.5524	2.8784	3.9217
19	0.6876	0.8610	1.0655	1.3277	1.7291	2.0930	2.5395	2.8609	3.8833
20	0.6870	0.8600	1.0640	1.3253	1.7247	2.0860	2.5280	2.8453	3.8496
25	0.6844	0.8562	1.0584	1.3163	1.7081	2.0595	2.4851	2.7874	3.7251
30	0.6828	0.8538	1.0547	1.3104	1.6973	2.0423	2.4573	2.7500	3.6460
35	0.6816	0.8520	1.0520	1.3062	1.6896	2.0301	2.4377	2.7238	3.5911
40	0.6807	0.8507	1.0500	1.3031	1.6839	2.0211	2.4233	2.7045	3.5510
45	0.6800	0.8497	1.0485	1.3007	1.6794	2.0141	2.4121	2.6896	3.5203

50	0.6794	0.8489	1.0473	1.2987	1.6759	2.0086	2.4033	2.6778	3.4960
55	0.6790	0.8482	1.0463	1.2971	1.6730	2.0040	2.3961	2.6682	3.4765
60	0.6786	0.8477	1.0455	1.2958	1.6706	2.0003	2.3901	2.6603	3.4602
70	0.6780	0.8468	1.0442	1.2938	1.6669	1.9944	2.3808	2.6479	3.4350
80	0.6776	0.8461	1.0432	1.2922	1.6641	1.9901	2.3739	2.6387	3.4164
90	0.6772	0.8456	1.0424	1.2910	1.6620	1.9867	2.3685	2.6316	3.4019
100	0.6770	0.8452	1.0418	1.2901	1.6602	1.9840	2.3642	2.6259	3.3905
150	0.6761	0.8440	1.0400	1.2872	1.6551	1.9759	2.3515	2.6090	3.3565
200	0.6757	0.8434	1.0391	1.2858	1.6525	1.9719	2.3451	2.6006	3.3398
∞	0.6745	0.8416	1.0364	1.2816	1.6449	1.9600	2.3263	2.5758	3.2905

Source: Table was generated using the Splus Statistical Software Package (Insightful Corp., Seattle, WA).

REFERENCES

Arcos, A., E. Alvarado, and D. V. Sandberg. 1996. Volume estimation of large woody debris with a stereoscopic vision technique. Paper presented at the 13th Fire and Forest Meteorology Conference. Lorne, Australia.

Adams, E. L. 1971. *Effect of moisture on red oak sawlog weight.* Northeast. For. Exp. Sta. Res. Note NE-133. USDA Forest Service.

Adams, E. L. 1976. *The adjusting factor method for weight-scaling truckloads of mixed hardwood sawlogs.* Northeast. For. Exp. Sta. Res. Note NE-344. USDA Forest Service.

Alden, H. A. 1997. *Softwoods of North America.* For. Prod. Lab. Gen. Tech. Rep. FPL-102. USDA Forest Service.

Alemdag, I. S. 1978. *Evaluation of some competition indexes for the prediction of diameter increment in planted white spruce.* For. Manag. Inst. Inf. Rep. FMR-X-108. Canadian Forestry Service, Ottawa, Ontario, Canada.

Alexander, S. A., and J. A. Barnard. (1994). *Forest health monitoring: field methods guide*, Vol. 1. U.S. Environmental Protection Agency, Environmental Monitoring Systems Laboratory, Las Vegas, NV.

Aronoff, S. 1989. *Geographic information systems: a management perspective.* WDL Publications, Ottawa, Ontario, Canada.

Assmann, E. 1970. *The principles of forest yield study.* Pergamon Press, New York.

Avery, T. E., and H. E. Burkhart. 2002. *Forest measurements.* 5th ed. McGraw-Hill, New York.

Bailey, R. L., and T. R. Dell. 1973. Quantifying diameter distributions with the Weibull function. *For. Sci.* 19:97–104.

Baker, F. S. 1960. A simple formula for gross current annual investment. *J. For.* 58:488–489.

Baldwin, V. C., Jr., H. E. Burkhart, J. A. Westfall, and K. D. Peterson. 2001. Linking growth and yield and process models to estimate impact of environmental changes on growth of loblolly pine. *For. Sci.* 47:77–82.

Bartlett, M. S. 1948. Determination of plant densities. *Nature* 162:621.

Bartoo, R. A., and R. J. Hutnik. 1962. *Board foot volume tables for timber species in Pennsylvania.* Penn State Forest School Res. Pap. 30. Penn State University, University Park, PA.

Battaglia, M., and P. J. Sands. 1998. Process-based forest productivity models and their application in forest management. *For. Ecol. Manag.* 102:13–32.

Beers, T. W. 1962. Components of forest growth. *J. For.* 60:245–248.

Beers, T. W. 1964. *Cruising for pulpwood by the ton without concern for tree diameter: point sampling with diameter obviation.* Extension Mimeo F-49. Purdue University, West Lafayette, IN.

Beers, T. W. 1966. *The direct correction for boundary-line slopover in horizontal point sampling.* Agric. Exp. Sta. Res. Prog. Rep. 224, Purdue University, West Lafayette, IN.

Beers, T. W. 1969. Slope correction in horizontal point sampling. *J. For.* 67:188–192.

Beers, T. W. 1973. *Revised composite tree volume tables for Indiana hardwoods.* Agric. Exp. Sta. Res. Prog. Rep. 417, Purdue University, West Lafayette, IN.

Beers, T. W. 1974. *Optimum upper-log viewing distance.* Agric. Exp. Sta. Bull. 39, Purdue University, West Lafayette, IN.

Beers, T. W. 1977. Practical correction for boundary overlap. *South. J. Appl. For.* 1:16–18.

Beers, T. W., and C. I. Miller. 1964. *Point sampling: research results, theory, and applications.* Agric. Exp. Sta. Res. Bull. 786, Purdue University, West Lafayette, IN.

Beers, T. W., and C. I. Miller. 1973. *Manual of forest mensuration.* T&C Enterprises. West Lafayette, IN.

Beers, T. W., and C. I. Miller. 1976. *Line sampling for forest inventory.* Agric. Exp. Sta. Res. Bull. 934, Purdue University, West Lafayette, IN.

Beers, T. W., P. E. Dress, and L. C. Wensel. 1966. Aspect transformation in site productivity research. *J. For.* 64:691–692.

Behre, C. E. 1935. Factors involved in the application of form–class volume tables. *J. Agric. Res.* 51:669–713.

Bell, J. F., and J. R. Dilworth. 1993. *Log scaling and timber cruising.* O.S.U. Bookstore, Corvallis, OR.

Bender, L. C., G. J. Roloff, and J. B. Haufler. 1996. Evaluating confidence intervals for habitat suitability models. *Wildl. Soc. Bull.* 24:347–352.

Besley, L. 1967. Importance, variation and measurement of density and moisture. *Wood Measurement Conf. Proc.* Tech. Rep. 7. Faculty of Forestry, University of Toronto, Toronto, Ontario, Canada.

Bickford, C. A., F. S. Baker, and F. G. Wilson. 1957. Stocking, normality, and measurement of stand density. *J. For* 55:99–104.

Biging, G. S., and M. Dobbertin. 1995. Evaluation of competition indices in individual tree growth models. *For. Sci.* 41:360–377.

Birdsey, R. A., et al. 1995. Techniques for forest surveys when cluster plots straddle two or more conditions. *For. Sci. Monogr.* 31.

Bitterlich, W. 1947. Die Winkelzählmessung (Measurement of basal area per hectare by means of angle measurement). *Allg. Forst. Holzwirtsch. Ztg.* 59:4–5.

Bitterlich, W. 1959. Sektorkluppern aus Leichmetall (Calipering forks made of light alloys). *Wien. Holz-Kurier* 14:15–17.

Bonham, C. D. 1989. *Measurements for terrestrial vegetation.* Wiley, New York.

Botkin, D. B. 1993. *Forest dynamics: an ecological model.* Oxford University Press, Oxford.

Bower, D. R., and W. W. Blocker. 1966. Accuracy of bands and tape for measuring diameter increments. *J. For.* 64:21–22.

Braathe, O., and T. Okstad. 1967. Trade of pulpwood based on weighing and dry matter samples. *XIV IUFRO Congress*, Sec. 41, Vol. IX, pp. 236–242.

Brack, C. I. 1988. The RADHOP system. In *Modeling trees, stands and forests.* Bull. 5. School of Forestry, University of Melbourne, Melbourne, Australia, pp. 509–526.

Brender, E. V. 1973. *Silviculture of loblolly pine in the Georgia Piedmont.* Report 33. Georgia Forest Research Council, Macon, GA.

Brooks, R. P. 1997. Improving habitat suitability index models. *Wildl. Soc. Bull.* 25:163–167.

Brown, G. S. 1965. Point density in stems per acre. *N. Z. For. Res. Notes* 38.

Brown, J. K. 1974. *Handbook for inventorying downed woody material.* Intermtn. For. Range Exp. Sta. Gen. Tech. Rep. INT-16. USDA Forest Service.

Brown, J. K. 1976. Estimating shrub biomass from basal stem diameters. *Can. J. For. Res.* 6:153–158.

Brown, S. 1997. *Estimating biomass and biomass change of tropical forests.* FAO For. Pap. 134. FAO, Rome.

Brown, S. 1999. *Guidelines for inventorying and monitoring carbon offsets in forest-based projects.* Winrock International Institute for Agricultural Development, Arlington, VA.

Bruce, D. 1926. A method of preparing timber yield tables. *J. Agric. Res.* 32:543–557.

Bruce, D., and F. X. Schumacher. 1950. *Forest mensuration*, 3rd ed. McGraw-Hill, New York.

Buchman, R. G., and S. R. Shifley. 1983. Guide to evaluating forest growth projection systems. *J. For.* 81:232–234.

Buckland, S. T., D. R. Anderson, K. P. Burnham, J. L Laake, D. L. Borchers, and L. Thomas. 2001. *Introduction to distance sampling: estimating abundance of biological populations.* Oxford University Press, New York.

Buckman, R. E. 1962. *Growth and yield of red pine in Minnesota.* USDA Tech. Bull. 1272. U.S. Department of Agriculture, Washington, DC.

Bullock, J. 1996. Plants. In W. J. Sutherland (ed.), *Ecological census techniques: a handbook.* Cambridge University Press, New York, pp. 111–138.

Burk, T. E., and J. D. Newberry. 1984. A simple algorithm for moment-based recovery of Weibull distribution parameters. *For. Sci.* 30:329–332.

Burkhart, H. E. 1977. Cubic-foot volume of loblolly pine to any merchantable top limit. *South. J. Appl. For.* 1:7–9.

Büsgen, M., and E. Munch. 1929. (T. Thomson, trans.). *The structure and life of forest trees.* Chapman & Hall, New York.

Cailliez, F. 1980. *Forest volume estimation and yield prediction.* Vol. 1. *Volume estimation.* FAO For. Pap. 22/1. FAO, Rome.

Cain, S. A., and G. M. de Oliveira Castro. 1959. *Manual of vegetation analysis.* Harper & Row, New York.

Cairns, M. A., S. Brown, E. H. Helmer, and G. A. Baumgardner. 1997. Root biomass allocation in the world's upland forests. *Oecologia* 111:1–11.

Calkins, H. A., and J. B. Yule. 1935. *The Abney Level Handbook.* USDA Forest Service, Washington, DC.

Campbell, G. S. 1986. Extinction coefficients for radiation in plant canopies using ellipsoidal inclination angle distribution. *Agric. For. Meteorol.* 36:317–321.

Cao, Q. V., and W. D. Pepper. 1986. Predicting inside bark diameter for shortleaf, loblolly, and longleaf pines. *South. J. Appl. For.* 25:318–327.

Carr, B. 1992. Using laser technology for forestry and engineering applications. *Complier* 10:5–16.

Chamberlain, E. B., and H. A. Meyer. 1950. Bark volume in cordwood. *Tappi* 33:554–555.

Chambers, J. Q., and S. E. Trumbore. 1999. An age old problem. *Trends Plant Sci.* 4:385–386.

Chapman, H. H., and W. H. Meyer. 1949. *Forest mensuration.* McGraw-Hill, New York.

Chehock, C. R., and R. C. Walker. 1975. *Sample weight scaling with 3-P sampling for multiproduct logging.* State Private For. S.E. Area. USDA Forest Service, Atlanta, GA.

Chen, J. M., P. M. Rich, T. S. Gower, J. M. Norman, and S. Plummer. 1997. Leaf area index of boreal forests: theory, techniques and measurements. *J. Geophys. Res.* 102:29,429–29,444.

Chisman, H. H., and F. X. Schumacher. 1940. On the tree–area ratio and certain of its applications. *J. For.* 38:311–317.

Chudnoff, M. 1984. *Tropical timbers of the world.* USDA Agric. Handb. 607. U.S. Department of Agriculture, Washington, DC.

Clark, A. 1979. Suggested procedures for measuring tree biomass and reporting tree prediction equations. In *Workshop Proc.: forest resource inventories*, Colorado State University, Fort Collins, CO, July 23–26, 1979, pp. 615–628.

Clark, A., and J. Schroeder. 1977. *Biomass of yellow poplar in natural stands in western North Carolina.* Southeast. For. Exp. Sta. Res. Pap. SE-165. USDA Forest Service.

Clark, J. F. 1906. Measurement of sawlogs. *For. Q.* 4:79–93.

Clark, N. A., R. H. Wayne, and D. L. Schmidt. 2000. A review of past research on dendrometers. *For. Sci.* 46:570–576.

Cleveland, W. S. 1994. *The elements of graphing data*, rev. ed. Chapman & Hall, New York.

Clutter, J. L. 1963. Compatible growth and yield models for loblolly pine. *For. Sci.* 9:354–371.

Clutter, J. L., J. C. Fortson, L. V. Pienaar, G. H. Brister, and R. L. Bailey. 1983. *Timber management: a quantitative approach.* Wiley, New York.

Cochran, W. G. 1977. *Sampling techniques,* 3rd ed. Wiley, New York.

Cody, J. B. 1976. *Merchantable weight tables for New York State red pine plantations.* Appl. For. Res. Inst. Res. Note 23. College of Environmental Science and Forestry, Syracuse, NY.

Cook, E. R., and L. A. Kairiukstis (eds.). 1990. *Methods of dendrochronology: applications in the environmental sciences.* Kluwer Academic Publishers, New York.

Courteau, J., and M.-H. Darche. 1997. A comparison of seven GPS units under forest conditions. Spec. Rep. SR-120. Forest Engineering Research Institute of Canada, Vancouver, British Columbia, Canada.

Cunia, T. 1965. Continuous forest inventory, partial replacement of samples and multiple regression. *For. Sci.* 11:480–502.

Curtis, J. T., and R. P. McIntosh. 1950. The interrelations of certain analytic and synthetic phytosociological characters. *Ecology* 31:434–455.

Curtis, R. O., and D. D. Marshall. 2000. Why quadratic mean diameter? *West. J. Appl. For.* 15:137–139.

Daniels, R. F. 1976. Simple competition indices and their correlation with annual loblolly pine tree growth. *For. Sci.* 22:454–456.

Daniels, R. F., H. E. Burkhart, and T. R. Clason. 1986. A comparison of competition measures for predicting growth of loblolly pine trees. *Can. J. For. Res.* 16:1230–1237.

Daubenmire, R. F. 1945. An improved type of precision dendrometer. *Ecology* 26:97–98.

Dawkins, H. C. 1957. Some results of stratified random sampling of tropical high forest. *Proc. 7th British Commonwealth Forestry Conf.,* item 7(iii).

Dean, T. J., and J. N. Long. 1986. Variation in sapwood area–leaf area relationships within two stands of lodgepole pine. *For. Sci.* 32:749–758.

Dean, T. J., J. N. Long, and F. W. Smith. 1988. Bias in leaf area–sapwood area ratios and its impact on growth analysis in *Pinus contorta*. *Trees* 2:104–109.

Deitschman, G. H., and A. W. Green. 1965. *Relations between western white pine site index and tree height of several associated species.* Intermtn. For. Range Exp. Sta. Res. Pap. INT-22. USDA Forest Service.

Dennis, B. 1984. Distance methods for evaluating forest regeneration. *Proc. 1983 Society of American Foresters National Convention,* Portland, OR, pp. 123–128.

Diller, O. D., and L. K. Kellog. 1940. *Local volume tables for yellow poplar.* Central States For. Exp. Sta. Tech. Note 1. USDA Forest Service.

Doebelin, E. O. 1966. *Measurement systems: applications and designs.* McGraw-Hill, New York.

Donnelly, D. M., and R. L. Barger. 1977. *Weight scaling for southwestern ponderosa pine.* Rocky Mtn. For. Range Exp. Sta. Res. Pap. RM-181. USDA Forest Service.

Doolittle, W. T., and J. P. Vimmerstedt. 1960. *Site curves for natural stands of white pine in southern Appalachians.* Southeast. For. Exp. Sta. Res. Note 141. USDA Forest Service.

Drew, T. J., and J. W. Flewelling. 1977. Some recent Japanese theories of yield density relationships and their application to Monterey pine plantations. *For. Sci.* 23:517–534.

Drew, T. J., and J. W. Flewelling. 1979. Stand density management: an alternative approach and its application to Douglas-fir plantations. *For. Sci.* 25:518–532.

Duff, G. H., and N. J. Nolan. 1953. Growth and morphogenesis in the Canadian forest species. I. The control of cambial and apical activity in *Pinus resinosa* Ait. *Can. J. Bot.* 31:471–513.

Duff, G. H., and N. J. Nolan. 1957. Growth and morphogenesis in the Canadian forest species. II. Specific increments and their relation to the quantity and activity of growth in *Pinus resinosa* Ait. *Can. J. Bot.* 35:527–572.

Duff, G. H., and N. J. Nolan. 1958. Growth and morphogenesis in the Canadian forest species. III. The time scale of morphogenesis at the stem apex of *Pinus resinosa* Ait. *Can. J. Bot.* 36:687–706.

Eddlemann, L. E., E. E. Remmenga, and R. T. Ward. 1964. An evaluation of plot methods for alpine vegetation. *Bull. Torrey Bot. Club* 91:439–450.

Eichenberger, J. K., G. R. Parker, and T. W. Beers. 1982. *A method for ecological forest sampling.* Agric. Exp. Sta. Res. Bull. 969. Purdue University, West Lafayette, IN.

Ek, A. R., and R. A. Monserud. 1974. *FOREST: a computer model for simulating the growth and reproduction of mixed species forest stands.* Res. Pap. R2635. University of Wisconsin, Madison, WI.

Ellis, B. 1966. *Basic concepts of measurement.* Cambridge University Press, New York.

Evans, F. C. 1952. The influences of size of quadrat on the distributional patterns of plant populations. *Contrib. Lab. Vertebr. Biol.* 54:1–15.

Ferree, M. J. 1946. The pole caliper. *J. For.* 44:594–595.

FIA. 2001. Phase 3 field guide: down woody debris and fuels. *Forest inventory and analysis.* USDA Forest Service, Washington, DC.

Flewelling, J. W. 1981. Compatible estimates of basal area and basal area growth from remeasured point samples. *For. Sci.* 27:191–203.

Flewelling, J. W., R. I. Ernst, and L. M. Raynes. 2000. Use of three-point taper systems in timber cruising. In *Integrated tools for natural resources inventories in the 21st century. Proc. IUFRO Conf.*, Boise, ID, Aug. 16–20, 1998, pp. 364–371. North Central For. Exp. Sta. Gen. Tech. Rep. NC-212. USDA Forest Service.

Fogelberg, S. E. 1953. *Volume charts based on absolute form class.* Louisiana Tech Forestry Club of Louisiana Polytech. Institute, Ruston, LA.

Forward, D. F., and N. J. Nolan. 1961. Growth and morphogenesis in the Canadian forest species. IV. Radial growth in branches and main axis of *Pinus resinosa* Ait. under conditions of open growth, suppression and release. *Can. J. Bot.* 39:385–409.

Foster, R. W. 1959. Relation between site indexes of eastern white pine and red maple. *For. Sci.* 5:279–291.

Francis, J. K. 1986. *The relationship of bole diameters and crown widths of seven bottomland hardwood species.* South. For. Exp. Sta. Res. Note SO-328. USDA Forest Service.

Frayer, W. E. 1966. Weighted regression in successive forest inventories. *For. Sci.* 12:464–472.

Freese, F. 1962. *Elementary forest sampling.* USDA Agric. Handb. 232. U.S. Department of Agriculture, Washington, DC.

Freese, F. 1973. *A collection of log rules.* For. Prod. Lab. Gen. Tech. Rep. FPL-1. USDA Forest Service.

Freese, F. 1974. *Elementary statistical methods for foresters.* USDA Agric. Hand. 317. U.S. Department of Agriculture, Washington, DC.

Fritts, H. C. 1976. *Tree rings and climate.* Academic Press, New York.

Fritts, H. C., and E. C. Fritts. 1955. A new dendrograph for recording radial changes of a tree. *For. Sci.* 1:271–276.

Gaiser, R. N., and R. W. Merz. 1951. Stand density as a factor in measuring white oak site index. *J. For.* 49:572–574.

Garay, L. 1961. *An introduction to tarif volume tables.* For. Biom. Res. Group Rev. Pap. 1. University of Washington, Seattle, WA.

Garland, H. 1968. Using a polaroid camera to measure trucked hardwood pulpwood. *Pulp Paper Mag. Canada* 68:86–87.

Gerrard, D. J. 1969. *Competition quotient: a new measure of the competition affecting individual forest trees.* Mich. Agric. Exp. Sta. Res. Bull. 20.

Gevorkiantz, S. R., and L. P. Olsen. 1955. *Composite volume tables for timber and their application in the Lake States.* USDA Tech. Bull. 1104. U.S. Department of Agriculture, Washington, DC.

Gillespie, A. J. R. 1999. Rationale for a National Annual Forest Inventory Program. *J. For.* 97:16–20.

Gingrich, S. F. 1964. Criteria for measuring stocking in forest stands. *Proc. Soc. Amer. For.* 198–201.

Gingrich, S. F. 1967. Measuring and evaluating stocking and stand density in upland hardwood forests in the central states. *For. Sci.* 13:38–53.

Girard, J. W. 1933. Volume tables for Mississippi bottomland hardwoods and southern pines. *J. For.* 31:34–41.

Glover, G. R., and J. N. Hool. 1979. A basal area ratio predictor of loblolly pine plantation mortality. *For. Sci.* 25:275-282.

Godman, R. M. 1949. The pole diameter tape. *J. For.* 47:585–589.

Gove, J. H., M. J. Ducey, G. Ståhl, and A. Ringvall. 2001. Point relascope sampling: A new way to assess downed coarse woody debris. *J. For.* 99:4–11.

Graves, H. S. 1906. *Forest mensuration.* Wiley, New York.

Greig-Smith, P. 1957. *Quantitative plant ecology.* Academic Press, New York.

Grosenbaugh, L. R. 1948. Improved cubic volume computation. *J. For.* 46:299–301.

Grosenbaugh, L. R. 1952. *Shortcuts for cruisers and scalers.* South. For. Exp. Sta. Occ. Pap. 126. USDA Forest Service.

Grosenbaugh, L. R. 1954. *New tree-measurement concepts: height accumulation, giant tree, taper and shape.* South. For. Exp. Sta. Occ. Pap. 134. USDA Forest Service.

Grosenbaugh, L. R. 1955. *Better diagnosis and prescription in southern forest management.* South. For. Exp. Sta. Occ. Pap. 145. USDA Forest Service.

Grosenbaugh, L. R. 1958. *Point-sampling and line-sampling: probability theory, geometric implications, synthesis.* South. For. Exp. Sta. Occ. Pap. 160. USDA Forest Service.

Grosenbaugh, L. R. 1963a. Optical dendrometers for out-of-reach diameters: a conspectus and some new theory. *For. Sci. Monogr.* 4.

Grosenbaugh, L. R. 1963b. Some suggestions for better sample-tree measurement. *Proc. Soc. Am. For.* 36–42.

Grosenbaugh, L. R 1964. *STX-FORTRAN 4 PROGRAM: for estimates of tree populations from 3P sample-tree measurements.* Pac. Southwest. For. Range Exp. Sta. Res. Pap. PSW-13. USDA Forest Service.

Grosenbaugh, L. R 1965. *Three-pee sampling theory and program: "THRP" for computer generation of selection criteria.* Pac. Southwest For. Range Exp. Sta. Res. Pap. PSW-21. USDA Forest Service.

Grosenbaugh, L. R 1967. The gains from sample-tree selection with unequal probabilities. *J. For.* 65:203–206.

Grosenbaugh, L. R 1979. *3P sampling theory, examples, and rationale.* Bureau of Land Management, Tech. Note 331. U.S. Department of the Interior, Washington, DC.

Guttenberg, S., D. Fassnacht, and W. C. Siegel. 1960. *Weight-scaling southern pine sawlogs.* South. For. Exp. Sta. Occ. Pap. 129. USDA Forest Service.

Hamilton, D. A. 1978. *Specifying precision in natural resource inventories.* Rocky Mtn. For. Range Exp. Sta. Gen. Tech. Rep. RM-55. USDA Forest Service.

Hamilton, G. D. 1975. *Forest mensuration handbook.* For. Comm. Bookl. 30. Her Majesty's Stationery Office, London.

Hann, D. W., and R. K. McKinney. 1975. *Stem surface area equations for four tree species of New Mexico and Arizona.* Intermtn. For. Range Exp. Sta. Res. Note INT-190. USDA Forest Service.

Hardy, S. S., and G. W. Weiland. 1964. *Weight as a basis for the purchase of pulpwood in Maine.* Agric. Exp. Sta. Tech. Bull. 14. University of Maine, Orono, ME.

Harmon, M. E. 2001. Carbon sequestration in forests. *J. For.* 99:24–29.

Harmon, M. E., and J. Sexton. 1996. *Guidelines for measurements of woody detritus in forest ecosystems.* US LTER Publ. 20. US LTER Network Office, University of Washington, Seattle, WA.

Hassan, H. A., C. Y. Mun, and N. Rahman (eds.). 1996. *Multiple resource inventory and monitoring of tropical forests.* ASEAN Institute of Forest Management, Kuala Lumpur, Malaysia.

Haygreen, J. G., and J. L. Bowyer. 1996. *Forest products and wood science*, 3rd ed. Iowa State University Press, Ames, IA.

Hegyi, F. 1974. A simulation model for managing jack-pine stands. In J. Fries (ed.), *Growth models for tree and stand simulation.* Royal College of Forestry, Stockholm, pp. 74–90.

Helms, J. A. (ed.). 1998. *The dictionary of forestry.* Society of American Foresters, Bethesda, MD.

Hendricksen, H. A. 1950. Hojde-diameter diagram med logaritmisk diameter (Height-diameter diagram with logarithmic diameter). *Dan. Skovforen. Tidsskr.* 35:193–202.

Herrick, A. M. 1940. A defense of the Doyle rule. *J. For.* 38:563–567.

Hester, A. S., D. W. Hann, and D. R. Larsen. 1989. *ORGANON: Southwest Oregon growth and yield model user manual,* Version 2.0. Forest Research Laboratory, Oregon State University, Corvallis, OR.

Hitchcock, H. C., and J. P. McDonnell. 1979. Biomass measurement: a synthesis of the literature. In *Workshop Proc.: forest resource inventories,* Colorado State University, Fort Collins, CO, July 23–26, 1979, pp. 544–595.

Honer, T. G., M. F. Ker, and I. S. Alemdag. 1983. *Metric timber tables for the commercial tree species of Central and Eastern Canada.* Info. Rep. M-X-140. Canadian Forestry Service, Maritimes Forest Research Center. Fredericton, New Brunswick, Canada.

Hool, J. N., and T. W. Beers. 1964. *Time-dependent correlation coefficients from remeasured forest plots.* Agric. Exp. Sta. Res. Prog. Rep. 156. Purdue University, West Lafayette, IN.

Hummel, F. C. 1953. *Uses of the "volume/basal area line" for determining standing crop volumes.* London For. Comm. Rep. 1951/52. Her Majesty's Stationery Office, London.

Hummel, F. C. 1955. *The volume/basal area line: a study in forest mensuration.* London For. Comm. Bull. 24. Her Majesty's Stationery Office, London.

Husch, B. 1947. A comparison between a ground and aerial-photogrammetric method of timber surveying. Master's thesis. New York State College of Forestry, Syracuse, NY.

Husch, B. 1956. Use of age at dbh as a variable in the site index concept. *J. For.* 54:340.

Husch, B. 1962. *Tree weight relationships for white pine in southeastern New Hampshire.* Agric. Exp. Sta. Tech. Bull. 106. University of New Hampshire, Durham, NH.

Husch, B. 1963. *Forest mensuration and statistics.* Ronald Press, New York.

Husch, B. 1971. *Planning a forest inventory.* For. Prod. Stud. 17. FAO, Rome.

Husch, B. 1980. How to determine what you can afford to spend on inventories. Paper presented at the IUFRO Workshop on Arid Land Resource Inventories, La Paz, Mexico.

Husch, B., and W. H. Lyford. 1956. *White pine growth and soil relationship in southeastern New Hampshire.* Agric. Exp. Sta. Tech. Bull. 95. University of New Hampshire, Durham, NH.

Husch, B., C. I. Miller, and T. W. Beers. 1982. *Forest mensuration.* 3rd ed. Wiley, New York.

Hyder, D. N., R. E. Bement, E. E. Remmenga, and C. Terwilliger, Jr. 1965. Frequency sampling of blue gamma range. *J. Range Manag.* 18:90–94.

Hyink, D. M., and J. W. Moser, Jr. 1983. A generalized framework for projecting forest yield and stand structure using diameter distributions. *For. Sci.* 29:85–95.

Imprens, I. I., and J. M. Schalck. 1965. A very sensitive electric dendrograph for recording radial changes of a tree. *Ecology* 46:183–184.

IPPC. 1999. Greenhouse gas inventory reporting. *Instructions IPPC guidelines for national greenhouse gas inventories,* Vol. I. Bonn conf. Bonn, Germany.

IUFRO. 1959. *The standardization of symbols in forest mensuration.* International Union of Forest Research Organizations, Vienna, Austria.

Johnsen, K. H., D. Wear, R. Oren, R. O. Teskey, F. Sanchez, R. Will, J. Butnor, D. Markewitz, D. Richter, T. Rials, H. L. Allen, J. Seiler, D. Ellsworth, C. Maier, G. Katul, and P. M. Dougherty. 2001a. Carbon sequestration and southern pine forests. *J. For.* 99:14–20.

Johnsen, K., L. Samuelson, R. Teskey, S. McNulty, and T. Fox. 2001b. Process models as tools in forestry research and management. *For. Sci.* 47:2-8.

Johnson, E. W. 1972. *Basic 3-P sampling.* Agric. Exp. Sta. For. Dept. Ser. 5. Auburn University, Auburn, AL.

Johnson, E. W. 1973. *Relationship between point density measurements and the subsequent growth of southern pines.* Agric. Exp. Sta. Bull. 447. Auburn University, Auburn, AL.

Johnson, E. W. 2001. *Forest sampling desk reference.* CRC Press, Boca Raton, FL.

Johnson, F. A., J. B. Lowrie, and M. Gohlke. 1971. *3P sample log scaling.* Pac. Northwest. For. Range Exp. Sta. Res. Note PNW-162. USDA Forest Service.

Jonson, T. 1912. Taxatoriska undersökningar öfer skogsträdens form. III. Form-bestämninga stående träd (Forest mensurational investigations concerning forest tree form. III. Form determination of standing trees). *Sven. Skogsvardsforen. Tidskr.* 10:235–275.

Jonsson, B., S. Holm, and H. Kallur. 1992. A forest inventory method based on density-adapted circular plot size. *Scand. J. For. Res.* 7:405–421.

Kendall, R. H., and L. Sayn-Wittgenstein. 1959. *An evaluation of the relaskop.* Tech. Note 77. Department of Northern Affairs and Natural Resources, Canadian Forest Research Division, Ottawa, Ontario, Canada.

Kershaw, J. A., Jr. In review. Assessment of stocking in regenerating stands: a reappraisal of the stocked quadrat method. *North. J. Appl. For.*

Kershaw, K. A., and J. H. H. Looney. 1985. *Quantitative and dynamic plant ecology,* 3rd ed. Edward Arnold, Baltimore.

Kinerson, R. S. 1973. A transducer for investigation of diameter growth. *For. Sci.* 18:230–232.

Koch, P. 1972. *Utilization of southern pine.* USDA Agric. Handb. 420. U.S. Department of Agriculture, Washington, DC.

Köpf, E. U. 1976. *Prediction of time consumption in logging.* IUFRO Publ. 7, Div. 3, Forest Operations and Techniques. Royal College of Forestry, Garpenburg, Sweden.

Kraft, G. 1884. *Zur Lehre von den Durch Forstungen* (What we have learned about thinning). Schlagstellungen und Lichtungshieben, Hanover, Germany.

Krajicek, J. E., K. A. Brinkman, and S. F. Gingrich. 1961. Crown competition: a measure of density. *For. Sci.* 7:36–42.

Krebs, C. J. 1989. *Ecological methodology.* Harper & Row, New York.

Lahiri, D. G. 1951. A method of sample selection providing unbiased ratio estimates. *Bull. Inst. Int. Stat.* 33:133–140.

Landres, P., D. R. Spildie, and L. P. Queen. 2001. GIS applications to wilderness management: potential uses and limitations. Rocky Mtn. Res. Sta. Gen. Tech. Rep. RMRS-GTR-80. USDA Forest Service.

Larsen, D. R., and J. A. Kershaw, Jr. 1990. The measurement of leaf area. In J. Lassoie, and T. Hinkley (eds.), *Techniques in forest tree ecophysiology*. CRC Press, Boca Raton, FL, pp. 465–475.

Larson, P. R. 1963. Stem form development of forest trees. *Forest Sci. Monogr.* 5. Society Amer. For. Washington, DC.

Leary, R. A. 1988. Some factors that will affect the next generation of forest growth models. In A. R. Ek, S. R. Shifley, and T. E. Burk (eds.), *Forest growth modelling and prediction. Proc. IUFRO Conf.* Minneapolis, MN, pp. 22–32. Aug. 22–28, 1987. North Central For. Exp. Sta. Gen. Tech. Rep. NC-120. USDA Forest Service.

Leary, R. A. 1991. Near-normal, empirical, and identity yield tables for estimating stand growth. *Can. J. For. Res.* 21:353–362.

Leick, A. 1995. *GPS satellite surveying*. Wiley, New York.

Lessard, V., D. D. Reed, and N. Monkevich. 1994. Comparing N-tree distance sampling with point and plot sampling in northern Michigan forest types. *North. J. Appl. For.* 11:12–16.

Lexen, B. 1943. Bole area as an expression of growing stock. *J. For.* 39:624–631.

Liming, F. G. 1957. Homemade dendrometers. *J. For.* 55:575–577.

Loetsch, F., and K. A. Haller. 1964. *Forest inventory*. Vol. I. BLV Verlagsgesellschaft, Munich.

Loetsch, F., F. Zöhrer, and K. A. Haller. 1973. *Forest inventory*. Vol. II. BLV Verlagsgesellschaft, Munich.

Loewenstein, E. F. 1996. An analysis of the size and age structure of an uneven-aged oak forest. Ph.D. dissertation. University of Missouri, Columbia, MO.

Loewenstein, E. F., P. S. Johnson, and H. E. Garrett. 2000. Age and diameter structure of an uneven-aged oak forest. *Can. J. For. Res.* 30:1060–1070.

Loguercio, G., and G. Defossé. 2001. Ecuaciones de biomasa aérea, factores de expansión y de reducción de la lenga, *Nothofagus pumilio* (Poepp. Et Endl) [Equations and monitoring of aerial biomass, expansion and reduction factors for lenga *Nothofagus pumilio* (Poepp. et Endl)]. Krasser, en el SO del Chubut, Argentina. *Simposio Medición y Monitoreo de la Captura de Carbono en Ecosistemas Forestales*, Valdivia, Chile, Oct. 2001.

Long, J. N., and F. W. Smith. 1988. Leaf area–sapwood area relations of lodgepole pine as influenced by stand density and site index. *Can. J. For. Res.* 18:247–250.

Longley, P. A. 1999. *Geographical information systems: principles, techniques, applications and management*, 2nd ed. Wiley, New York.

Longley, P. A., M. F. Goodchild, D. J. Maguire, and D. W. Rhind. 2001. *Geographic information systems and science*. Wiley, New York.

Lynch, T. B., and R. Rusydi. 1999. Distance sampling for forest inventory in Indonesian teak plantations. *For. Ecol. Manag.* 113:215–221.

Maass, A. 1939. Tallens formbedömd av diametern 2.3. meter fran mårken (Stem form of pine as determined by diameter 2.3 meters above ground). *Sven. Skogsvardsfören. Tidskr.* 37:120–140.

MacArthur, R. H., and H. S. Horn. 1969. Foliage profile by vertical measurements. *Ecology* 60:802–804.

MacDicken, K. G. 1997. *A guide to monitoring carbon storage in forestry and agro forestry projects.* Winrock International Institute for Agricultural Development, Arlington, VA.

MacKinney, A. L., and L. E. Chaiken. 1939. *Volume, yield and growth of loblolly pine in the mid-Atlantic region.* Appalachian For. Exp. Sta. Tech. Note 33. USDA Forest Service.

MacKinney, A. L., F. X. Schumacher, and L. E. Chaiken. 1937. Construction of yield tables for nonnormal loblolly pine stands. *J. Agric. Res.* 54:531–545.

Macleod, W. K., and A. W. Blyth. 1955. *Yield of even-aged, fully-stocked spruce–poplar stands in northern Alberta.* Tech Note 18. Department of Northern Affairs and Natural Resources, Canada, Ottawa, Ontario, Canada.

Maguire, D. A., and J. L. F. Batista. 1996. Sapwood taper models and implied sapwood volume and foliage properties for coastal Douglas-fir. *Can. J. For. Res.* 26:849–863.

Maguire, D. A., and D. W. Hann. 1990. Bark thickness and bark volume in southwestern Oregon Douglas-fir. *West. J. Appl. For.* 5:5–8.

Mäkelä, A. 1992. Process-oriented growth and yield models: recent advances and future prospects. In T. Preuhsler, (ed.), *Research on growth and yield with emphasis on mixed stands.* Proc. S4.01 Mensuration, Growth and Yield, IUFRO Centennial Meeting, Berlin, Aug. 31–Sept. 4, 1992. Bayerische Forsrliche Versuchsund Foreschungsanstalt, Freising, Germany, pp. 85–96.

Marden, R. M., D. C. Lothner, and E. Kallio. 1975. *Wood and bark percentage and moisture contents of Minnesota pulpwood species.* North Central For. Exp. Sta. Res. Pap. NC-114. USDA Forest Service.

Marquis, D. A., and T. W. Beers. 1969. A further definition of some forest growth components. *J. For.* 67:493.

Marshall, J. D., and R. H. Waring. 1986. Comparison of methods of estimating leaf-area index in old-growth Douglas fir. *Ecology.* 67:975–979.

Martin, G. L., and A. R. Ek. 1984. A comparison of competition measures and growth models for predicting plantation red pine diameter and height growth. *For. Sci.* 30:731–743.

Martínez-Ramos, M., and E. R. Alvarez-Buylla. 1999. How old are tropical forest trees? *Trends Plant Sci.* 3:400–405.

Matérn, B. 1990. *On the shape of the cross section of a tree stem: an empirical study of the geometry of mensurational methods.* Section of Forest Biometry, Swedish University of Agriculture, Umeå, Sweden.

Mattney, T. G., and A. P. Sullivan. 1982. Variable top volume and height predictors for slash pine trees. *For. Sci.* 28:274–282.

Mawson, J. C. 1982. Diameter growth on small forests. *J. For.* 80:217–219.

Max, T. A., H. T. Schreuder, J. W. Hazard, J. Teply, and J. Alegria. 1996. *The region 6 vegetation and monitoring system.* Pac. Northwest. For. Range Exp. Sta. Res. Pap. PNW-RP-493. USDA Forest Service.

McCarter, J. B. 2001. Landscape management system (LMS): background, methods, and computer tools for integrating forest inventory, GIS, growth and yield, visualization and analysis for sustaining multiple forest objectives. Ph.D. dissertation. University of Washington, Seattle, WA.

McCarter, J. B., and J. N. Long. 1986. A lodgepole pine density management diagram. *West. J. Appl. For.* 1:6–11.

McCarter, J. B., J. S. Wilson, P. J. Baker, J. L. Moffett, and C. D. Oliver. 1998. Landscape management through integration of existing tools and emerging technologies. *J. For.* 96:17–23.

McClintock, T. F., and C. A. Bickford. 1957. *A proposed site index for red spruce in the northeast.* Northeast. For. Exp. Sta. Res. Pap. NE-93. USDA Forest Service.

McCormac, J. C. 1999. *Surveying,* 4th ed. Wiley, New York.

McGaughey, R. J. 1998. Techniques for visualizing the appearance of forestry operations. *J. For.* 96:9–14.

Meersschaut, D. V. D., and K. Vandekerkhove. 2000. Development of a stand-scale forest biodiversity index based on the state forest inventory. In *Integrated tools for natural resources inventories in the 21st century. Proc. IUFRO Conf.,* Boise, ID, Aug. 16–20, 1998, pp. 340–347. North Central Res. Sta. Gen. Tech. Rep. NC-212. USDA Forest Service.

Mesavage, C. 1965. Three-P sampling and dendrometry for better timber estimating. *South. Lumberman* 211:107–109.

Mesavage, C. 1967. *Random integer dispenser.* South. For. Exp. Sta. Res. Note 49. USDA Forest Service.

Mesavage, C. 1971. *STX timber estimating with 3P sampling and dendrometry.* USDA Agric. Handb. 415, U.S. Department of Agriculture, Washington, DC.

Mesavage, C., and J. W. Girard. 1946. *Tables for estimating board foot volume of timber.* USDA Forest Service, Washington, DC.

Mesavage, C., and L. R. Grosenbaugh. 1956. Efficiency of several cruising designs on small tracts in north Arkansas. *J. For.* 54:569–576.

Meyer, H. A. 1942. *Methods of forest growth determination.* Agric. Exp. Sta. Bull. 435. School of Agriculture, Pennsylvania State College, State College, PA.

Meyer, H. A. 1953. *Forest mensuration.* Penn's Valley Publishers, State College, PA.

Meyer, W. H. 1934. Growth in selectively cut ponderosa pine forests of the Pacific Northwest. USDA. Tech. Bull. no. 407. U.S. Department of Agriculture, Washington, DC.

Miller, C. I. 1959. *Comparison of Newton's, Smalian's, and Huber's formulas.* Department of Forestry and Conservation, Purdue University, West Lafayette, IN (mimeographed).

Miller, C. I., and T. W. Beers. 1975. *Thin prisms as angle gauges in forest inventory.* Agric. Exp. Sta. Res. Bull. 929. Purdue University, West Lafayette, IN.

Miner, C. L., N. R. Walters, and M. L. Belli. 1988. *A guide to the TWIGS program for the north central United States.* North Central For. Exp. Sta. Gen. Tech. Rep. NC-125. USDA Forest Service.

Miyata, E. S., H. M. Steinhilb, and S. A. Winsauer. 1981. Using work sampling to analyze logging operations. North Central For. Exp. Stat. Res. Pap. NC-213. USDA Forest Service.

Moore, J. A., C. A. Budelsky, and R. C. Schlesinger. 1973. A new index representing individual tree competitive status. *Can. J. For. Res.* 3:495–500.

Moore, P. G. 1954. Spacing in plant populations. *Ecology* 35:222–227.

Morrison, M. L., B. G. Marcot, and R. W. Mannan. 1992. *Wildlife–habitat relationships: concepts and applications.* University of Wisconsin Press, Madison, WI.

Moser, J. W., Jr. 1976. Specification of density for the inverse J-shaped diameter distribution. *For. Sci.* 22:177–180.

Moser, J. W., Jr., and O. F. Hall. 1969. Derived growth and yield functions for uneven-aged forest stands. *For. Sci.* 15:183–188.

Muhairwe, C. K. 2000. Bark thickness equations for five commercial tree species in regrowth forests of northern New South Wales. *Austr. For.* 63:34–43.

Munro, D. D. 1974. Forest growth models: A prognosis. In *Growth models for tree and stand simulation.* For. Res. Notes 30. Royal College, Stockholm.

Nash, A. J. 1948. The Nash scale for measuring tree crown widths. *For. Chron.* 24:117–120.

Newberry, J. D., and L. V. Pienaar. 1978. *Dominant height growth models and site index curves for site-prepared slash pine plantations in the lower coastal plain of Georgia and north Florida.* Plantation Manag. Res. Coop. Res. Pap. 4. University of Georgia, Macon, GA.

Nievel, B. W. 1993. *Motion and time study,* 9th ed. McGraw-Hill, New York.

Noone, C. S., and J. F. Bell. 1980. *An evaluation of eight intertree competition indices.* For. Res. Lab. Res. Note 66. Oregon State University, Corvallis, OR.

Norman, E. L., and J. W. Curlin. 1968. *A linear programming model for forest production control at the AEC Oak Ridge Reservation.* Rep. ORNL-4349. Oak Ridge National Laboratory, Oak Ridge, TN.

Nylinder, P. 1958. *Variations in weight of barked spruce pulpwood.* Virkeslära K. Skogshögsk. 15. Uppsats Institution, Stockholm.

Nylinder, P. 1967. *Weight measurement of pulpwood.* Virkeslära K. Skogshögsk. R57. Rapp Institution, Stockholm.

O'Brien, R., and D. D. Van Hooser. 1983. *Understory vegetation inventory: an efficient procedure.* Intermtn. For. Range Exp. Sta. Res. Pap. INT-323. USDA Forest Service.

Oderwald, R. G. 1981a. Point and plot sampling: the relationship. *J. For.* 79:377–378.

Oderwald, R. G. 1981b. Comparison of point and plot sampling basal area estimators. *For. Sci.* 27:42–48.

Oderwald, R. G., and B. A. Boucher. 1997. *Where in the world and what? An introduction to global positioning systems.* Kendall/Hunt, Dubuque, IA.

O'Hara, K. L., and N. L. Vallappil. 1995. Sapwood–leaf area prediction equations for multi-aged ponderosa pine stands in western Montana and central Oregon. *Can. J. For. Res.* 25:1553–1557.

Oliver, C. D., and B. C. Larson. 1996. *Forest stand dynamics.* Wiley, New York.

Oliver, C. D., and E. P. Stephens. 1977. Reconstruction of a mixed-species forest in central New England. *Ecology* 58:562–572.

Ondok, J. P. 1984. Simulation of stand geometry in photosynthetic models based on hemispherical photographs. *Photosynthetica* 18:231–239.

Opie, J. E. 1968. Predictability of individual tree growth using various definitions of competing basal area. *For. Sci.* 14:314–323.

Ore, O. 1988. *Number theory and its history*. reprint ed. Dover Publications, New York.

O'Regan, W. G., and L. G. Arvanitis. 1966. Cost effectiveness in forest sampling. *For. Sci.* 12:406–414.

Osborne, J. G. 1942. Sampling errors of systematic and random surveys of cover type areas. *J. Amer. Stat. Assoc.* 37:256–264.

Osborne, J. G., and F. X. Schumacher. 1935. The construction of normal-yield and stand tables for even-aged timber stands. *J. Agric. Res.* 51:547–564.

Paine, D. P. 1981. *Aerial photography and image interpretation for resource management*. Wiley, New York.

Pardé, J. 1955. Un dendrometre Blume–Leiss (The Blume–Leiss hyspsometer). *Rev. For. Fr.* 7:207–210.

Parresol, B. R. 1999. Assessing tree and stand biomass: a review with examples and critical comparisons. *For. Sci.* 45:573–594.

Payandeh, B., and A. R. Ek. 1986. Distance methods and density estimators. *Can. J. For. Res.* 16:918–924.

Peet, F. G., D. J. Morrison, and K. W. Pellow. 1997. Using a hand-held electronic laser-based survey instrument for stem mapping. *Can. J. For. Res.* 27:2104–2108.

Peet, R. K. 1974. The measurement of species diversity. *Annual Rev. Ecol. Syst.* 5:285–307.

Peterson, D. L., M. A. Spanner, S. W. Running, and K. B. Teuber. 1987. Relationship of thematic mapper simulator data to leaf area index of temperate coniferous forests. *Remote Sensing Environ.* 22:323–341.

Petterson, H. 1955. Yield of coniferous forests. *Medd. Statens Skogsforsoksanst.* 45:1B.

Phipps, R. L., and G. E. Gilbert. 1960. An electric dendrograph. *Ecology* 41:389–390.

Pielou, E. C. 1966. The measurement of diversity in different types of biological collections. *J. Theor. Biol.* 13:131–144.

Pielou, E. C. 1977. *Mathematical ecology*. Wiley, New York.

Pierce, L. L., and S. W. Running. 1988. Rapid estimation of coniferous forest leaf area index using a portable integrating radiometer. *Ecology* 69:1762–1767.

Pitt, M. D., and F. E. Schwab. 1988. *Quantitative determination of shrub biomass and production: a problem analysis*. Land Manag. Rep. 54. British Columbia Ministry of Forests and Lands, Victoria, British Columbia, Canada.

Post, W. M., R. C. Izaurralde, L. K. Mann, and N. Bliss. 1999. Monitoring and verification of soil organic carbon sequestration. In *Symposium: carbon sequestration in soils science, monitoring and beyond*, Dec. 3–5, St. Michaels, MD.

Prodan, M. 1965. *Holzmesslehre*. J. D. Sauerlaender's Verlag, Frankfurt.

Prodan, M. 1968a. (S. H. Gardiner, trans.). *Forest biometrics*, Pergamon Press, New York.

Prodan, M. 1968b. Punktstichprobe für die Forsteinrichtung (Random point sampling for forest inventory). *Forst. Holzwirtsch.* 23:225–226.

Prodan, M., R. Peters, F. Cox, and P. Real. 1997. *Mensura forestal*. Deutsche Gesellschaft für Zusammenarbeit (GTZ) FmbH: Instituto Interamericano de Cooperación para la Agricultura (IICA), San José, Costa Rica.

Raspopov, I. M. 1955. K metodike izucenija proekcii kron derevjev (A method of studying the crown projection of trees). *Bot. Zh.* 40:825–827.

Raunkiaer, C. 1934. *The life forms of plants and statistical plant geography.* Oxford University Press, Oxford.

Reed, D. D., and G. D. Mroz. 1997. *Resource assessment in forested landscapes.* Wiley, New York.

Reineke, L. H. 1927. A modification of Bruce's method of preparing timber yield tables. *J. Agric. Res.* 35:843–856.

Reineke, L. H. 1932. A precision dendrometer. *J. For.* 30:692–697.

Reineke, L. H. 1933. Perfecting a stand density index for even-aged forests. *J. Agric. Res.* 46:627–638.

Relaskop-Technik. No date. *Dial Dendro: the new band-dendrometer for the very precise measurements of the growth of trees.* Vertriebsges m.b.H.. Salzburg, Austria.

Rennie, J. C., J. D. Clark, and J. M. Sweeny. 2000. Evaluation of habitat suitability index models for assessing biotic resources. In *Integrated tools for natural resources inventories in the 21st century. Proc. IUFRO Conf.*, Boise, ID, Aug. 16–20, 1988, pp. 321–325. North Central For. Exp. Sta. Gen. Tech. Rep. NC-212, USDA Forest Service.

Reynolds, M. R., T. E. Burk, and W. Huang. 1988. Goodness-of-fit tests and model selection procedures for diameter distribution models. *For. Sci.* 34:373–399.

Richards, F. L. 1959. A flexible growth function for empirical use. *J. Exp. Bot.* 10:290–300.

Ripley, T. H., and L. K. Halls. 1966. Measuring the forest wildlife resource. *Proc. 15th Annual Forestry Symp.* Louisiana State University School of Forestry, 163–184.

Roach, B. A. 1977. *A stocking guide for Allegheny hardwoods and its use in controling intermediate cuttings.* Northeast. For. Exp. Sta. Res. Pap. NE-373. USDA Forest Service.

Roach, B. A., and S. F. Gingrich. 1962. *Timber management guide for upland central hardwoods.* Central States For. Exp. Sta. USDA Forest Service.

Roach, B. A., and S. F. Gingrich 1968. *Even-aged silviculture for upland central hardwoods.* USDA Agric. Handb. 355. U.S. Department of Agriculture, Washington, DC.

Roesch, F., E. J. Green, and C. T. Scott. 1989. New compatible estimators for survivor growth and ingrowth from remeasured horizontal point samples. *For. Sci.* 35:281–293.

Roloff, G. J., and B. J. Kernohan. 1999. Evaluating reliability of habitat suitability index models. *Wildl. Soc. Bull.* 27:973–985.

Ross, J. W. 1981. *The radiation regime and architecture of plant stands.* Dr. W. Junk, The Hague, The Netherlands.

Row, C., and C. Fasick. 1966. Weight scaling tables by electronic computer. *For. Prod. J.* 16:41–45.

Row. C., and S. Guttenberg. 1966. Determining weight–volume relationships for saw-logs. *For. Prod. J.* 16:39–47.

Rudis, V. A. 1991. *Wildlife habitat, range, recreation, hydrology and related research using forest inventory and analysis surveys: a 12-year compendium.* South. For. Exp. Sta. Gen. Tech. Rep. SO-84. USDA Forest Service.

Running, S. W., D. L. Peteron, M. A. Spanner, and K. B. Teuber. 1986. Remote sensing of coniferous forest land area. *Ecology* 67:273–276.

Schamberger, M., A. H. Farmer, and J. W. Terrell. 1982. Habitat suitability index models: introduction. FWS/OBS-82/10 USDI Fish and Wildlife Service, Washington, DC.

Schiffel, A. 1899. Form und Inhalt der Fichte (Form and volume of spruce). *Mitt. Forstl. Versuchsanst. Osterreiche* 24.

Schmid-Haus, P. 1969. Stichproben am Waldrond (Sampling at the edge of the forest). *Mitt. Schweiz. Anst. For. Versuchwes.* 43:234–303.

Schnur, G. L. 1937. *Yield, stand and volume tables for even-aged upland oak forests.* USDA Agric. Tech. Bull. 560. U.S. Department of Agricuture, Washington, DC.

Schreuder, H. T., and P. H. Geissler. 1998. Plot design for ecological monitoring of forest and range. *Proc. North American Science Symp.* Toward a unified framework for inventorying and monitoring forest ecosystem resources. Rocky Mtn. For. Range Exp. Sta. Res. Sta. Proc. RMRS-P-12. USDA Forest Service.

Schreuder, H. T., T. G. Gregoire, and G. B. Wood. 1993. *Sampling methods for multi-resource forest inventory.* Wiley, New York.

Schreuder, P., S. Brown, J. Mo, R. Birdsey, and C. Cieszewski. 1997. Biomass estima-tion for temperate broadleaf forests of the United States using inventory data. *For. Sci.* 43:424–434.

Schroeder, R. L. 1983. *Habitat suitability models: black-capped chickadee.* FWS/OBS-82/10.37. USDI Fish and Wildlife Service, Washington, DC.

Schroeder, J. G., M. A. Taras, and A. Clark. 1975. *Stem and primary products weights for longleaf pine sawtimber trees.* Southeast. For. Exp. Sta. Res. Pap. SE-139. USDA Forest Service.

Schumacher, F. X. 1939. A new growth curve and its application to timber yield studies. *J. For.* 37:819–820.

Scott, C. T. 1979. Midcycle updating: some practical suggestions. *Proc. Forest Resource Inventories Workshop*, Fort Collins, CO, pp. 362–370.

Scott, C. T., and W. A. Bechtold. 1995. Techniques and computations for mapping plot clusters that straddle stand boundaries. *For. Sci. Monogr.* 31.

Sheng, Y., P. Gong, and G. S. Biging. 2001. Model based conifer crown surface area from high resolution aerial images. *Photog. Eng. & Rem. Sensing* 67(8):957–963.

Shepperd, W. D. 1973. *An instrument for measuring tree crown width.* Rocky Mtn. For. Range Exp. Sta. Res. Note RM-229. USDA Forest Service.

Shinozaki, K., K. Yoda, K. Hozumi, and T. Kira. 1964. A quantitative analysis of plant form: the pipe model theory. II. Further evidence of the theory and its application in forest ecology. *Jpn. J. Ecol.* 14:133–139.

Shiryayev, A. N. 1984. *Probability.* Springer-Verlag, New York.

Shiue, C. J. 1960. Systematic sampling with multiple random starts. *For. Sci.* 6:42–50.

Shiver, B. D., and B. E. Borders. 1996. *Sampling techniques for forest resource inventory.* Wiley, New York.

Sievänen, R., and T. E. Burk. 1994. Fitting process-based models with stand growth data: problems and experiences. *For. Ecol. Manag.* 69:145–156.

Skovsgaard, J. P., V. K. Johannsen, and J. K. Vanclay. 1998. Accuracy and precision of two laser dendrometers. *Forestry* 71:131–139.

Smith, J. H. G., and J. W. Ker. 1959. Empirical yield equations for young forest growth. *B.C. Lumberman*, Sept.

Smith, J. H. G., J. W. Ker, and J. Csizmazia. 1961. *Economics of reforestation of Douglas fir, western hemlock, and western red cedar in the Vancouver Forest District.* For. Bull. 3. University of British Columbia, Vancouver, British Columbia, Canada.

Smith, J. R. 1970. *Optical distance measurement.* Crosby Lockwood and Sons, London.

Smith, W. B., and G. J. Brand. 1983. *Allometric biomass equations for 98 species of herbs, shrubs, and small trees.* North Central For. Exp. Stat. Res. Note NC-299. USDA Forest Service.

Somers, G. L., and S. K. Nepal. 1994. Linking individual-tree and stand-level growth models. *For. Ecol. Manag.* 69:233–243.

Spurr, S. H. 1952. *Forest Inventory.* Ronald Press, New York.

Spurr, S. H. 1962. A measure of point density. *For. Sci.* 8:85–96.

Stage, A. R. 1962. *A field test of point-sample cruising.* Intermtn. For. Range Exp. Sta. Res. Pap. 67. USDA Forest Service.

Stage, A. R. 1973. *Prognosis model for stand development.* Intermtn. For. Range Exp. Sta. Res. Pap. INT-137. USDA Forest Service.

Stage, A.R. 1976. An expression of the effect of aspect, slope and habitat type on tree growth. *For. Sci.* 22:457–460.

Stage, A. R., and D. E. Ferguson. 1984. Linking regeneration surveys to future yields. *Proc. 1983 Society of American Foresters National Convention*, Portland, OR, pp. 133–137.

Stein, W. I. 1984a. Regeneration surveys: an overview. *Proc. 1983 Society of American Foresters National Convention*, Portland, OR, pp. 111–116.

Stein, W. I. 1984b. Fixed plot methods for evaluating forest regeneration. *Proc. 1983 Society of American Foresters National Convention*, Portland, OR, pp. 129–135.

Stevens, S. S. 1946. On the theory of scales of measurement. *Science* 103:677–680.

Stoffels, A., and J. Van Soest. 1953. Principiele vraagstukken bije proefperken. 3. Hoogteregressie (The main problem in sample plots. 3. Height regression). *Ned. Boschb. Tijdschr.* 66:834–837.

Strickler, G. S., and F. W. Stearns. 1962. Determination of plant density. In *Range research methods: a symposium.* Misc. Publ. 940, pp. 30–40. USDA Forest Service, Washington, DC.

Sullivan, A. D., and J. L. Clutter. 1972. A simultaneous growth and yield model for loblolly pine. *For. Sci.* 18:76–86.

Sutherland, W. J. (ed.). 1996. *Ecological census techniques: a handbook.* Cambridge University Press, New York.

Swan, D. A. 1959. *Weight scaling in the Northeast.* Tech. Release 59–R5. American Pulpwood Association.

Swank, W. T., and H. Schreuder. 1974. Comparison of three methods of estimating surface area and biomass for a forest of young eastern white pine. *For. Sci.* 20:91–100.

Tallent-Halsell, N. G. (ed.). 1994. *Forest health monitoring: 1994 field methods guide.* EPA/620/R-94/-027. U.S. Environmental Protection Agency, Washington, DC.

Taras, M. A. 1956. *Buying pulpwood by weight.* Southeast. For. Exp. Sta. Res. Pap. 74. USDA Forest Service.

Tardif, G. 1965. Some considerations concerning the establishment of optimum plot size in forest surveys. *For. Chron.* 41:93–102.

Timson, F. G. 1974. *Weight and volume variation in truckloads of logs hauled in the central Appalachians.* Northeast. For. Exp. Sta. Res. Pap. NE-300. USDA Forest Service.

Tomé, M., and H. E. Burkhart. 1989. Distance-dependent competition measures for predicting growth of individual trees. *For. Sci.* 35:816–831.

Trofymow, J. A., H. J. Barclay, and K. M. McCullogh. 1991. Annual rates and elemental concentrations of litter fall in thinned and fertilized Douglas-fir. *Can. J. For. Res.* 21:1601–1615.

Trorey, L. G. 1932. A mathematical expression for the construction of diameter height curves based on site. *For. Chron.* 18:3–14.

Tufte, E. R. 1990. *Envisioning information.* Graphics Press, Cheshire, CT.

Turnbull, K. J., and G. E. Hoyer. 1965. *Construction and analysis of comprehensive tree-volume tarif tables.* Washington Department of Natural Resources Management, Olympia, WA.

Turnbull, K. J., G. R. Little, and G. E. Hoyer. 1963. *Comprehensive tree-volume tarif tables.* Washington Department of Natural Resources Management, Olympia, WA.

Turner, D. P., S. A. Acker, J. Means, and S. Garman. 2000. Assessing alternative allometric algorithms for estimating leaf area of Douglas-fir trees and stands. *For. Ecol. Manag.* 126:61–76.

United Nations. 1992. *Framework convention for climate change.* Geneva, Switzerland.

USDA. 1991. *National forest cubic scaling handbook.* USDA Forest Service, Washington, DC.

USDA. 1992. *Forest service resource inventories: an overview.* Forest Inventory, Economics, and Recreation Research, USDA Forest Service, Washington, DC.

USDA. 1998. *Forest health monitoring: 1998 field methods guide.* National Forest Health Monitoring Program, USDA Forest Service, Research Triangle Park, NC.

U.S. Department of the Interior. 1973. *Manual of instructions for the survey of public lands in the United States.* U.S. Government Printing Office, Washington, DC.

USMA. 1999. *Guide to the use of the metric system,* 14th ed. U.S. Metric Association, Northridge, CA.

Valentine, H. T., L. M. Tritton, and G. M. Furnival. 1984. Subsampling trees for biomass, volume, or mineral content. *For. Sci.* 30:673–681.

Vanclay, J. C. 1994. *Modelling forest growth and yield: applications to mixed tropical forests.* CAB International. Wallingford, Berkshire, England.

Van Dyne, G. M., W. G. Vogel, and H. G. Fisser. 1963. Influence of small plot size and shape on range herbage production estimates. *Ecology* 44:746–759.

Veiga, R. A. A., M. A. M. Brasil, and C. M. Carvalho. 2000. Aboveground biomass equations for 7-year-old *Acacia mangium* Willd. in Botucatu, Brasil. In *Integrated tools for natural resources inventories in the 21st century. Proc. IUFRO Conf.* Boise, ID, Aug. 16–20, 1998. North Central For. Exp. Sta. Gen. Tech. Rep. NC-212. USDA Forest Service.

Wahlenberg, W. G. 1941. *Methods of forecasting timber growth in irregular stands.* USDA Tech. Bull. 603. U.S. Department of Agriculture, Washington, DC.

Wang, Y. S., and D. R. Miller. 1987. Calibration of the hemispherical photographic technique to measure leaf area index distribution in hardwood forests. *For. Sci.* 33:210–216.

Ware, K. D. 1967. Sampling properties of three pee estimates. Paper presented at the 1967 Society of American Foresters–Canadian Institute of Forestry Meeting, Ottawa, Ontario, Canada.

Ware, K. D., and T. Cunia. 1962. Continuous forest inventory with partial replacement of samples. *For. Sci. Monogr.* 3.

Waring, R. H., P. E. Schroeder, and R. Oren. 1982. Application of the pipe model theory to predict canopy leaf area. *Can. J. For. Res.* 12:556–560.

Wenger, K. F. (Ed.) 1984. *Forestry handbook*, 2nd ed. Wiley, New York.

Wesley, R. 1956. Measuring the height of trees. *London Park Admin.* 21:80–84.

Westveld, M. 1954. *Use of plant indicators as an index to site quality.* Northeast. For. Exp. Sta. Pap. 69. USDA Forest Service.

Wharton, E. H., and D. M. Griffith. 1998. *Estimating total forest biomass in Maine, 1995.* Northeast. For. Res. Sta. Resource Bull. NE-142. USDA Forest Service.

Wilson, F. G. 1946. Numerical expression of stocking in terms of height. *J. For.* 44:756–761.

Wilson, F. G. 1979. Thinning as an orderly discipline: a graphic spacing schedule for red pine. *J. For.* 77:483–486.

Wilson, J. W. 1960. Inclined point quadrats. *New Phytol.* 58:92–101.

Wilson, J. W. 1965. Stand structure and light penetration. I. Analysis by point quadrats. *J. Appl. Ecol.* 2:383–390.

Wilson, R. L. 1989. *Elementary forest surveying and mapping.* O.S.U. Bookstore, Corvallis, OR.

Wykcoff, W. R., N. L. Crookston, and A. R. Stage. 1982. *User's guide to the Stand Prognosis Model.* Intermtn. For. Range Exp. Sta. Gen. Tech. Rep. INT-133. USDA Forest Service.

Yerkes, V. P. 1966. *Weight and cubic-foot relationships for Black Hills ponderosa pine sawlogs.* Rocky Mtn. For. Range Exp. Sta. Res. Note RM-78. USDA Forest Service.

Yocom, H. A. 1970. Vernier scales for diameter tapes. *J. For.* 68:725.

Young, H. E., L. Strand, and R. Altenberger. 1964. *Preliminary fresh and dry weight tables for seven tree species in Maine.* Agric. Exp. Sta. Tech. Bull. 12. University of Maine, Orono, ME.

Young, H. E., W. C. Robbins, and S. Wilson. 1967. *Errors in volume determination of primary forest products.* School of Forestry, University of Maine, Orono, ME (mimeographed).

Zanakis, S. H. 1979. A simulation study of some simple estimators for the three-parameter Weibull distribution. *J. Stat. Comput. Simul.* 9:101–116.

Zar, J. H. 1998. *Biostatistical analysis*, 4th ed. Prentice-Hall, Upper Saddle River, NJ.

Zarnock, S. J., and T. R. Dell. 1985. An evaluation of percentile and maximum likelihood estimators of Weibull parameters. *For. Sci.* 31:260-268.

Zeide, B. 1980. Plot size optimization. *For. Sci.* 26:251–257.

Zenger, A. 1964. Systematic sampling in forestry. *Biometrics* 22:553–565.

INDEX